THE FAREWELL OF THE WORD

THE FAREWELL OF
THE WORD

THE JOHANNINE CALL TO ABIDE

Fernando F. Segovia

FORTRESS PRESS   MINNEAPOLIS

A Elena

THE FAREWELL OF THE WORD

Scripture quotations, unless otherwise noted, are from the New Revised
Standard Version of the Bible, copyright © 1989 by the Division of
Christian Education of the National Council of the Churches of Christ
in the United States of America.

Interior design by Publishers' WorkGroup

The cover image is a reproduction of a Puerto Rican *santo* entitled "Cristo de los
Milagros" by Maestro Antonio Aviles of Orocovis (1990); cover design by Eric Lecy.

Library of Congress Cataloging-in-Publication Data

Segovia, Fernando F.
    The farewell of the word : the Johannine call to abide / Fernando
  F. Segovia
        p.   cm.
    Includes bibliographical references and index.
    ISBN 0-8006-2486-6 (alk. paper)
    1. Bible. N.T. John XIII, 31-XVI, 33—Criticism, interpretation,
etc. I. Title.
BS2615.2.S433 1991
226.5'066—dc20   91-28047
                                            CIP

The paper used in this publication meets the minimum requirements of
American National Standard for Information Sciences—Permanence of
Paper for Printed Library Materials, ANSI Z329.48-1984.

Manufactured in the U.S.A.   AF 1-2486
94   93   92   91   1   2   3   4   5   6   7   8   9   10

CONTENTS

PREFACE

THIS STUDY OF THE JOHANNINE FAREWELL has been in the making for some time, much longer than I originally anticipated. To any reader familiar with my earlier work in the Fourth Gospel, the reason will become readily apparent in the process of reading.

In my prior work I noted that hardly any recent interpreter of the Gospel looked upon the Johannine farewell speech as a literary unity. Such a literary position, of course, had important implications and consequences—for example, that the farewell speech is ultimately unintelligible in its present form; that its meaning is to be sought mostly outside the present text in any variety of ways, including the one I finally opted for (a redactional or excavative reading whereby different literary layers were exposed and the overall process of accretion and expansion explained with regard to purpose and sequence); and that a variety of authors was responsible for the various layers in question, not so much on the basis of differences in terminology and style but rather on the basis of theological thrust and social situation. Such a redactional theory—in effect, the dominant approach to the farewell in the latter half of the century—also had an important, but largely implicit, theological and ideological framework. The most important dimension of this framework involved the primacy of belief over praxis, if I may use such terms in separation from one another. The earlier literary layer—encompassing most of the original farewell discourse—was concerned with belief in Jesus as the Word of God, with an acceptance of Jesus' claims concerning his origins, mission, and destination. The later literary layers had to do, among other things, with matters of praxis, with issues of proper and correct behavior within the community of believers.

In the decade that has elapsed since that earlier dictum of mine, the nature and thrust of New Testament studies have changed radically. There has been an increasing awareness that such studies could no longer be conducted without a proper and informed theoretical foundation, whether in literary or social theory, and should no longer be carried out without a proper explanation of the social and ideological context of the reader and interpreter. The impact of such changes upon the discipline, though already profound, are still at a beginning stage, I believe. Such changes affect all students of the field, sooner or later, directly or indirectly.

Such changes also affected me, and the present work reflects their results. I now see the farewell speech as both an artistic and a strategic whole, with a unified literary structure and development, as well as unified strategic concerns and aims. To be sure, such a literary position has important implications and consequences as well. The speech is intelligible as it presently stands. There is no need to search for meaning outside the text, especially in terms of an excavative approach and by way of literary layers. There is no need to posit a variety of authors in the process of composition and addition of these layers. Such a literary position also has a very different theological and ideological framework: from its beginning the farewell is concerned with both belief in Jesus as the Word of God (the acceptance of Jesus' claims concerning his origins, mission, and destination) and matters of praxis (issues of proper and correct behavior within the community of believers).

At the same time, in this transition from a redactional perspective to what I would call an integrative perspective, I am not ready to deny that the Johannine farewell does contain salient literary difficulties. Indeed, no practitioner of an integrative approach has gone so far, though at the same time no one has properly addressed the presence of such difficulties from such a perspective. They are simply mentioned and then bypassed. In this study I attempt such an explanation as well. Although I see the present speech as indeed an artistic and strategic whole, I also see such a whole as the ultimate product of a process of accretion and expansion. However, I would argue that a theory concerning such a process of accretion and expansion sheds little light on the present meaning of the speech, even though it may illuminate its literary difficulties and the historical process of composition. Consequently, I advance a redactional theory at the end mostly by way of completion, especially given the fact that I too acknowledge such difficulties in the present speech. In other words, I find it impossible to accept such difficulties without attempting to account for their presence in the speech.

With this change from a redactional to an integrative perspective has come a further change from the idea of one sole and objective meaning in the text or in the author of that text—a general presupposition of the redactional approach—to the idea of meaning as a negotiation between text and reader. With such a change I would no longer claim to provide the definitive reading of this text against all those who posit a different reading. I seek to provide, instead, a reading that is comprehensive and persuasive, that reflects in some way my own social location and ideological stance as a reader and interpreter, and that is not presented as the only objective and definitive way to read this text. The reading proposed is one of several such readings, and I offer it as such to my own readers.

Finally, I deal briefly in this volume with the final stage of the interpretive process as I presently see it—the critical integration of the text into the world of the reader, both personal and social (the moment of intercultural dialogue and criticism). I hope to do more of this in the future. The call to abide and endure in a world of oppression, which I see as central to the Johannine farewell, is a call with immediate and direct relevance for a wide number of contemporary groups, including my own. What remains to be determined and negotiated is the extent to which the path traced for such a call in this text remains advisable for any group today. This is a crucial step in the struggle for freedom and liberation, and one that I must leave for a later time.

This study is unfinished. I have limited myself to what I consider to be a self-contained and coherent introduction or setting to the climactic farewell prayer of John 17, namely, to John 13:31–16:33. In a subsequent literary-rhetorical reading of John 17 I hope to engage the text at the level of intercultural criticism. I see the present study as the first of a projected trilogy on the Johannine corpus, a project that will entail a similar reading of both Gospel and Letters.

ACKNOWLEDGMENTS

As always, I find myself in debt to many individuals and institutions, directly and indirectly, for the completion of this volume, and I should like to express my profound gratitude hereby to all concerned. A few deserve special mention.

First and foremost, this volume is dedicated to my wife, Dr. Elena Olazagasti-Segovia, who has shared with me at every level a feeling not unlike that which I discern within the Johannine community itself—a sense of embattlement and oppression in a world that is ultimately not our own and a determination to resist with freedom and liberation in mind.

The initial research for this volume was carried out during an academic leave of absence from 1986 to 1987. I should like to thank the Divinity School at Vanderbilt University for the opportunity to engage in full-time research. Two generous grants also made such a leave of absence possible: a University Research Fellowship from the Graduate School at Vanderbilt University and a Research Fellowship from the Association of Theological Schools of the United States and Canada. I should especially like to thank in this regard Dr. Russell G. Hamilton, dean of the Graduate School and chair of the University Research Council, and Mr. William Baumgartner, associate director of the Association of Theological Schools.

I would also like to thank a man who encouraged and nourished this project from the very first and who was in every manner a gentleman: my good friend, the late Dr. John A. Hollar, former Editorial Director of Fortress Press; the editorial staff of Fortress Press, especially Dr. Marshall D. Johnson, its Editorial Director, who inherited the project and guided it wisely to its successful completion and publication; Dr. Charles B. Puskas, Jr., its Academic Editor, who supervised the editorial process with patience, wisdom, and kindness; and Ms. Mary Berry, who provided invaluable insight and assistance in matters of style and format.

I should like to thank as well the many graduate students in New Testament at Vanderbilt University who have been a source of challenge and inspiration over the years. I should also like to acknowledge my colleague Dr. Mary Ann Tolbert, a fellow fighter in the struggle for freedom and liberation.

Finally, I thank all my Hispanic American colleagues in the theological profession whose conversation and writings have helped me to define our very special and distinctive locus as readers, interpreters, and theologians within the North American scene.

—*Fernando F. Segovia*

ABBREVIATIONS

FREQUENTLY CITED WORKS

Barrett: C. K. Barrett. *The Gospel According to St. John.* 2d ed. Philadelphia: Westminster, 1978.

Becker: J. Becker. "Die Abschiedsreden im Johannesevangelium." *ZNW* 61 (1970) 215–46.

Behler: G. M. Behler. *Les paroles d'adieux du Seigneur (S. Jean 13–17).* LD 27. Paris: Les Éditions du Cerf, 1960.

Bernard: J. H. Bernard. *A Critical and Exegetical Commentary on the Gospel According to St. John.* 2 vols. ICC. Edinburgh: T. & T. Clark, 1928.

Bover: J. M. Bover. *Comentario al Sermón de la Cena.* 2d ed. BAC 68. Madrid: La editorial católica, 1955.

Brown: R. E. Brown. *The Gospel According to John.* 2 vols. AB 29, 29A. Garden City, N.Y.: Doubleday, 1966–70.

Bultmann: R. Bultmann. *The Gospel of John: A Commentary.* Translated by G. R. Beasley-Murray et al. Philadelphia: Westminster, 1971.

Dodd: C. H. Dodd. *The Interpretation of the Fourth Gospel.* Cambridge: Cambridge University Press, 1963.

Durand: A. Durand. "Le discours de la Cène (Saint Jean xiii,31–xvii,26)." *RSR* 1 (1910) 97–131, 513–39; *RSR* 2 (1911) 321–49, 521–45.

Haenchen: E. Haenchen. *John: A Commentary on the Gospel of John.* 2 vols. Edited by U. Busse. Translated by R. W. Funk. Hermeneia. Philadelphia: Fortress, 1984.

Hoskyns: E. C. Hoskyns. *The Fourth Gospel.* 2d ed., rev. and enl. Edited by F. N. Davey. London: Faber & Faber, 1956. (1st ed., 1940.)

Huby: J. P. Huby. *Le discours de Jésus après la Cène.* 2d ed., rev. VS. Paris: Beauchesne et ses Fils, 1942.

Kaefer: J. Ph. Kaefer. "Les discours d'adieu en Jn 13:31–17:26: Rédaction et Théologie." *NovT* 26 (1984) 253–82.

Lagrange: M.-J. Lagrange. *Évangile selon Saint Jean.* 3d ed., rev. Paris: J. Gabalda, 1927.

Lightfoot: R. H. Lightfoot. *St. John's Gospel: A Commentary.* Edited by C. F. Evans. Oxford: Oxford University Press, 1960. (1st pub., 1956.)

Lindars: B. Lindars. *The Gospel of John.* NCBC. Grand Rapids: Eerdmans, 1972.

Loisy: A. Loisy. *Le quatrième évangile et les épîtres dites de Jean.* 2d ed., rev. Paris: Émile Nourry, 1921.

Macgregor: G. H. C. Macgregor. *The Gospel of John.* MNTC. New York: Harper & Brothers, 1928.

Marsh: J. Marsh. *The Gospel of Saint John.* PNTC. Baltimore: Penguin, 1968.

Morris: L. Morris. *The Gospel According to John.* NICNT. Grand Rapids: Eerdmans, 1971.

Painter: J. Painter. "The Farewell Discourses and the History of Johannine Christianity." *NTS* 27 (1981) 525–43.

Schnackenburg: R. Schnackenburg. *The Gospel According to St. John.* 3 vols. Translated by K. Smyth et al. New York: Crossroad Publishing, 1982.

Schulz: S. Schulz. *Das Evangelium nach Johannes.* NTD 4. Göttingen: Vandenhoeck & Ruprecht, 1972.

Simoens: Y. Simoens. *La gloire d'aimer: Structures stylistiques et intérpretatives dans le Discours de la Cène (Jn 13–17).* AB 90. Rome: Biblical Institute Press, 1981.

Strathmann: H. Strathmann. *Das Evangelium nach Johannes.* NTD 4. Göttingen: Vandenhoeck & Ruprecht, 1951.

Swete: H. B. Swete. *The Last Discourse and Prayer of Our Lord: A Study of St. John xiv–xvii.* London: Macmillan & Co., 1913.

van den Bussche: H. van den Bussche. *Le discours d'adieu de Jésus: Commentaire des chapitres 13 à 17 de l'évangile selon Saint Jean.* Translated by C. Charlier and P. Goidts. BVC. Tournai: Éditions Castermann, 1959.

Wellhausen: J. Wellhausen. *Das Evangelium Johannis.* Berlin: G. Reimer, 1908.

Westcott: B. F. Westcott. *The Gospel According to St. John.* London: John Murray, 1903 (1st pub. 1880.)

Wikenhauser: A. Wikenhauser. *Das Evangelium nach Johannes.* 2d ed. RNT. Regensburg: Friedrich Pustet, 1957.

JOURNALS, SERIES, AND REFERENCE WORKS

AB   Anchor Bible.

ALGHJ   Arbeiten zur Literatur und Geschichte des hellenistischen Judentums.

AnBib   Analecta biblica.
ANRW   H. Temporini and W. Haase, eds. *Aufstieg und Niedergang*
               der römischen Welt. Berlin and New York: Walter de
               Gruyter, 1972–.
BAC   Biblioteca de Autores Cristianos.
BAGD   W. Bauer, W. F. Arndt, F. W. Gingrich, and F. W. Danker.
               Greek-English Lexicon of the New Testament and Other
               Early Christian Literature. 2d ed., rev. and enl. Chicago:
               Univ. of Chicago Press, 1979.
BDF   F. Blass, A. Debrunner, and R. W. Funk. *A Greek Grammar*
               of the New Testament and Other Early Christian Literature.
               Chicago: Univ. of Chicago Press, 1961.
BET   Beiträge zur evangelischen Theologie.
BETL   Bibliotheca ephemeridum theologicarum lovaniensium.
BibLeb   *Bibel und Leben.*
BVC   *Bible et vie chrétienne.*
CBQ   *Catholic Biblical Quarterly.*
ConBNT   Coniectanea biblica, New Testament.
EThL   *Ephemerides theologicae lovanienses.*
FRLANT   Forschungen zur Religion und Literatur des Alten und
               Neuen Testaments.
HNTC   Harper's New Testament Commentaries.
HTKNT   Herder's theologischer Kommentar zum Neuen Testament.
HUT   Hermeneutische Untersuchungen zur Theologie.
ICC   International Critical Commentary.
JBL   *Journal of Biblical Literature.*
JTS   *Journal of Theological Studies.*
LD   Lectio divina.
LS   H. G. Liddell, R. Scott, and H. S. Jones. *A Greek-English*
               Lexicon. 9th ed. Oxford: Clarendon, 1978.
LThK   *Lexikon für Theologie und Kirche.*
MNTC   Moffatt New Testament Commentary.
MTZ   *Münchener Theologische Zeitschrift.*
NCBC   New Century Bible Commentary.
NICNT   New International Commentary on the New Testament.
NovT   *Novum Testamentum.*
NovTSup   Novum Testamentum, Supplements.
NTD   Das Neue Testament Deutsch.
NTS   *New Testament Studies.*
PNTC   Pelican New Testament Commentaries.
RAC   *Reallexikon für Antike und Christentum.* Stuttgart:
               1950–72.

RB	*Revue biblique.*
RNT	Regensburger Neues Testament.
RSR	*Recherches de science religieuse.*
SANT	Studien zum Alten und Neuen Testament.
SBLDS	Society of Biblical Literature Dissertation Series.
SBLMS	Society of Biblical Literature Monograph Series.
Smyth	H. W. Smyth. *Greek Grammar.* Revised by G. M. Messing. Cambridge, Mass.: Harvard University Press, 1956.
SN	Studia Neotestamentica, Studia.
STANT	Studien zum Alten und Neuen Testament.
TDNT	G. Kittel and G. Friedrich, eds. *Theological Dictionary of the New Testament.* Grand Rapids: Eerdmans, 1964–76.
VS	Verbum salutis.
WMANT	Wissenschaftliche Monographien zum Alten und Neuen Testament.
ZNW	*Zeitschrift für das neutestamentliche Wissenschaft.*

1

INTRODUCTION

IN AN ANALYSIS OF the narrative principles at work in the Hebrew Bible, R. Alter points to the importance of recognizing the basic conventions of such narrative in order to be able to understand with greater accuracy not only the compositional artistry involved in the creation of biblical narrative but also the complex communication with an audience that such an artistic creation entails.[1] One of these essential conventions Alter describes is the frequent repetition in biblical narrative of more or less the same story with different characters or even with the same characters but in different sets of circumstances. Adopting traditional terminology from Homeric studies, Alter calls such a compositional pattern of repeated stories a "type-scene." Within biblical narrative a number of type-scenes, or recurrent episodes in the lives of the biblical heroes, can be identified, such as the annunciation of the hero's birth to his barren mother, the encounter with the future betrothed at a well, the epiphany in the field, the initiatory trial, the danger in the desert and the discovery of a well or other means of sustenance, and the testament or farewell of a dying hero. All of these type-scenes are dependent on the use of a fixed number of predetermined motifs.

Although significant in narrative research, the recognition of a type-scene and its constellation of constitutive motifs immediately involves another necessary phase as well. In effect, to become aware of the conventions in this regard is also to become aware of what happens in each application of the conventions, namely, to become aware of the variations in the use of these motifs within each type-scene. Only then, Alter continues, can the reader begin to understand the distinctive character of each example—for instance, what is included, what is excluded, the composition and arrangement of what is included, and the specific emphases in the presentation and development of what is included. In other words, all of the constitutive motifs of the recurrent narrative episodes need not be present in every example of the type-scene, in the same manner or order.

1. R. Alter, *The Art of Biblical Narrative* (New York: Basic Books, 1981) 47–62.

It is the given and deliberate manipulation of these predetermined motifs within the different examples of the same type-scene that ultimately accounts for the artistic individuality of each example. Indeed, it becomes clear from Alter's own analysis of one of these biblical type-scenes that the distinctive character of each example is also related in a direct and fundamental way to the character of the narrative within which the type-scene is located, thus involving a detailed focus on such matters as narrative development, characterization, literary structure and development, and overall thematic concerns. Only then, through this search for the artistic uniqueness of each example, can the reader come to understand with some degree of accuracy what the author was trying to communicate to the intended audience.

Alter's own analysis of the type-scene focuses on the repeated encounters of the biblical hero with his future betrothed at a well. However, it is the last type of recurrent narrative episode he identifies in biblical narrative—the testament or farewell of a dying hero—that is of particular interest for the study of John 13–17. These chapters of the Gospel constitute—as the unity of time, place, and characters readily shows—a large narrative section in which a Jesus who is aware of his impending death proceeds to bid farewell to his disciples in the context of a last meal with them.

JOHN 13–17 AS A NARRATIVE SECTION
AND FAREWELL TYPE-SCENE

In what follows I shall argue that these chapters constitute a narrative section and a farewell type-scene.

John 13–17 as a Narrative Section

With respect to time and place, the action in John 13–17 is located in an unspecified room in Jerusalem, where a meal involving Jesus and his disciples is taking place sometime prior to the feast of Passover (13:1–3; cf. 11:55–57; 12:1). As the reader learns, the meal happens on the day before the feast itself, which also occurs on a sabbath; thus, it is a day of preparation for both feast and sabbath (18:28, 39; 19:14, 31, 42). As such, the action can be distinguished from what precedes and what follows.

On the one hand, the preceding narrative unit (12:12–50), which forms part of a larger narrative section encompassing several visits of Jesus to Jerusalem (4:1–12:50), describes events surrounding the beginning of Jesus' final visit to the city: his entry and tumultuous reception by crowds from the city; the coming of some Greeks to see him, which gives rise to a very important declaration on his part concerning the arrival at last of his awaited "hour" (2:4; 7:30) and a preliminary explanation of its meaning and consequences; a conversation with unbelieving crowds; the narrator's negative summary of the preceding ministry; and Jesus' concluding brief discourse. On the other hand, the following narrative unit (18:1–27), which also forms part of a larger narrative section dealing with the final events of Jesus' life and ministry (18:1–21:25), recounts the first part of these events: the departure of the group from the room where the meal took place and from Jerusalem itself to a garden across the Kidron valley; the betrayal and arrest in the garden; and Jesus' separation from the disciples and appearance before Caiaphas in Jerusalem. All of John 13–17, therefore, focuses on this one meal in Jerusalem on the day before the feast of Passover—a meal that takes place at some point after the events surrounding Jesus' final entry into Jerusalem and immediately before his betrayal and arrest just outside the city.

With respect to the characters involved, only a minor and necessary change occurs during the meal itself. Throughout these chapters Jesus and an unidentified number of disciples are present in the room, although several are specifically mentioned: Judas Iscariot; Simon Peter, the disciple whom Jesus loved; Thomas; Philip; and the other Judas. The only change in characters takes place when one of these disciples, Judas Iscariot, is publicly exposed as the announced betrayer and is asked by Jesus to carry out his task of betrayal quickly, thus occasioning his departure from the room and the circle of the disciples (13:30). As such, the section can be distinguished from what precedes and what follows.

On the one hand, in 12:12–50, the disciples appear but briefly (12:16, 21–22), but many other groups are mentioned. These groups include the crowd that had come to the feast and that welcomes Jesus into the city; the crowd that had witnessed the raising of Lazarus at Bethany and whose own witness to this event in Jerusalem has led the previous group to welcome Jesus (although whether they form part of the welcoming crowd remains uncertain); the Pharisees; some Greeks who came to the feast; and a crowd standing by, whose relationship to either the welcoming crowd or the Greeks remains uncertain. Moreover, after the conversation with this latter group has ended and this crowd has rejected Jesus' proclamation, Jesus is said to withdraw from them (12:36d). A brief discourse or soliloquy is then recorded (12:44–50), with the narrator's summary of the preceding public ministry found between the notice of withdrawal and the brief speech. On the other hand, in 18:1–27, after Jesus and the disciples have moved to a garden outside the city (described as frequented by them in the past and thus well known to Judas Iscariot), Judas arrives at the head of a contingent of Roman soldiers and a band of guards sent by the rulers and Pharisees; this group takes Jesus back to the higher authorities in the city and thus away from the disciples. John 13–17, then, focuses on this one meal shared by Jesus and his disciples (with the presence of Judas Iscariot up to the moment of Jesus' own request that he proceed with his task without delay), a meal that follows his general reception by the crowds of Jerusalem and precedes his separation from the disciples by an arresting party led by one of his own disciples.

Within this large narrative section of the Gospel, three smaller units can be distinguished:

1. The washing of the disciples' feet by Jesus during the meal itself, followed by an explanation of what such washing means and entails (13:1–20).
2. An open announcement to the disciples, also during the meal, of a forthcoming betrayal—already alluded to twice in the course of the washing (13:10, with an explanation by the narrator in 13:11, 18)— by one of their own, with a subsequent identification of Judas Iscariot as the betrayer and an immediate request for him to undertake his mission (13:21–30).
3. A long speech to the remaining disciples in the face of the coming betrayal, now under way; arrest and separation from them; and ultimately death itself (13:31–17:26).

John 13–17 as a Farewell Type-Scene:
A Preliminary Sketch

From beginning to end, chapters 13–17 concretely and directly anticipate the approaching end of Jesus' life and ministry. The thought of Jesus' impending death permeates the entire section. For example, the introduction to the first unit reveals Jesus' awareness of what is about to take place—the forthcoming departure from this world to the Father (13:1–4). Similarly, in the second unit the act of betrayal, the first of the final series of events in Jesus' life and ministry, is described as imminent—so much so, in effect, that Jesus himself takes a decisive part in its launching and execution (13:27). Finally, the long speech to the remaining disciples begins and ends with references to the coming glorification of Jesus by and with the Father (13:31–33; 17:1–5, 24–26). As such, these chapters exemplify the testament or farewell type-scene, and the long speech pronounced at some point during the meal itself exemplifies a farewell discourse. Toward the beginning of his last visit to Jerusalem, after a rejection by the crowds of Jerusalem and prior to his arrest by the Jerusalem authorities, Jesus shares a final meal with his disciples; in the face of their forthcoming separation and his own impending death, he bids farewell to them in a speech that is quite extensive for the Gospel (13:31–17:26). John 13–17, therefore, is a good example of a recurrent episode in the lives of the biblical heroes—the testament or farewell of a hero who is about to die.

Although the main focus of this study is a close reading of the Johannine farewell speech (13:31–17:26), it will begin with a look at the farewell type-scene in general and its constellation of constitutive and recurrent motifs. In this way the individuality and uniqueness of this Johannine example will come to the fore with much greater clarity and precision.

FAREWELL TYPE-SCENES AND THEIR MOTIFS

The testament or farewell of a dying hero, a common feature of biblical narrative, is also present in both the extrabiblical Jewish literature and Greco-Roman literature. Several studies have been devoted to the analysis of such scenes in antiquity, both within and outside of the biblical tradition.[2] The present study will rely on the findings of such previous studies; however, given the varying identification of the constitutive components or motifs of such scenes in these studies, a critical overview of the main lines of approach and the results of this scholarly literature is in order.[3]

E. Stauffer (1950) provides an excellent point of departure. Beginning with the observation that the last words of great men represent a beloved theme in ancient literature,[4] Stauffer proceeds to trace the use and development of this literary tradition in four different bodies of material: the

2. See, e.g., E. Stauffer, "Abschiedsreden," *RAC* 1 (1950) 29–35; J. Munck, "Discours d'adieu dans le Nouveau Testament et dans la littérature biblique," in *Aux sources de la tradition chrétienne: Mélanges offerts à M. Maurice Goguel*, Bibliothèque théologique (Neuchâtel and Paris: Delachaux & Niestlé, 1950) 155–70; H.-J. Michel, *Die Abschiedsrede des Paulus an die Kirche Apg 20,17–38: Motivgeschichte und theologische Bedeutung*, SANT 35 (Munich: Kösel, 1973); E. Cortès, *Los discursos de adiós de Gn 49 a Jn 13–17: Pistas para la historia de un género literario en la antigua literatura judía*, Colectánea San Paciano 23 (Barcelona: Herder, 1976); W. S. Kurz, "Luke 22:14–38 and Greco-Roman and Biblical Farewell Addresses," *JBL* 104 (1985) 251–68. A number of dictionary and encyclopedia studies also deal with the topic, though usually very briefly; e.g., R. Schnackenburg, "Abschiedsreden Jesu," *LThK* 1 (1957) 68–69; K. Berger, "Hellenistische Gattungen im Neuen Testament," *ANRW* 25:2, ed. W. Haase (Berlin and New York: Walter de Gruyter, 1984) 1034–1452, esp. 1257–59 (*"Exitus illustrium virorum und ultima verba"*); J. Beutler, "Literarische Gattungen im Johannesevangelium: Ein Forschungsbericht 1919–1980," *ANRW* 25:3, ed. W. Haase (Berlin and New York: Walter de Gruyter, 1985) 2508–68, esp. 2550–52 ("Reden").

3. The terminology employed in this literature not only differs for the most part from that of Alter but is also in and of itself varied and fluid. Rather than adopt a common nomenclature by forcing Alter's own terminology on others, I have opted for a synonymous or coterminous use of the expressions in question.

4. Given the total absence, as well as can be determined, of farewell scenes involving women, this section uses the masculine gender. Thus, Stauffer's statement that the last words of "great men" represent a much beloved theme in ancient narrative is to be taken quite literally.

Greco-Roman literature, the Hebrew Bible and the extrabiblical Jewish material, the New Testament, and the later Christian literature.[5]

First, in the Greco-Roman literature three kinds of farewells may be distinguished by the different kinds of speakers in question: (1) famous men at the end of their lives, (2) divine men before their transfiguration and ascent, and (3) gods in human disguise prior to their homeward departure. In the last two types the formal elements of the first, described as set and recurrent,[6] are preserved but mythologically transformed.[7]

Second, in the Jewish literature, where the farewell is said to reach its most developed form, two (rather than three) different types are distinguished, again by the different speakers in question. The first Jewish type replaces the first two identified in the Greco-Roman literature: the one bidding farewell is no longer a famous man or a divine man, but rather a man of God, a mediator between God and human beings, appointed by God and pointing to God. The second type remains that of the divine epiphany.[8]

Third, in the New Testament, the use of the farewell with regard to Jesus becomes prominent; such usage also stands within the tradition of

5. Stauffer ("Abschiedsreden," 29) makes an important distinction within this literary tradition of last words: "a final cry or brief saying on the part of the dying hero containing a final summation of his life; longer speeches or conversations before death." For the former, see W. Schmidt, *De ultimis morientium verbis* (Marburg: Chr. Schaaf, 1914).

6. The example of Socrates in Plato's *Phaedo* becomes paradigmatic for the later development of the farewell of famous men in Greco-Roman literature; as a result, its own constitutive components eventually become the formal elements for all later farewell scenes. Such elements encompass both context and speech. First, there is a conversation between the dying man and his confidants in his last hours. Second, within such a conversation are a number of fixed and recurring elements: forebodings or prophecies of death, final instructions regarding the care of those left behind, the appointment of a successor, a prayer of thanksgiving to the gods, words of farewell and consolation for the intimate circle, an account of past activities, teachings and exhortations for the wider gathering, and political and philosophical testaments.

7. Such a transformation is described as follows. In the case of the divine man before his ascent, there are (a) omens pointing to the coming death; (b) prophecies of his fate, his ascent, or the course of events after his death; (c) an initiation of his disciples into anthropological and cosmological secrets by means of mysterious revelatory discourses; and (d) a greeting of the light from the world beyond in terms of a hymnic swan song. Frequently, the divine man appears after death to assure his followers of his continued divine existence, and a cult of worship in his honor is initiated. In such appearances, a further farewell is frequently found in which all the formal elements of the farewell before death are simply transplanted. Divine epiphanies involve a disclosure of divine origins, announcements of punishments for those who did not believe, and announcements of parting gifts or promises for those who did.

8. The constitutive components of the first type are identified as follows. The man of God (a) receives and discloses the revelation of his forthcoming death; (b) gives his last instructions; (c) announces a successor; and (d) turns to the assembled group with (1) accounts of his activities and words of consolation, (2) woes and attacks upon his enemies, (3) words of consolation and promises, (4) historical-theological overviews of the past and apocalyptic expectations for the future, (5) prayers on the behalf of the assembled group, and (6) blessings. Appearances with farewells after death are rare; however, revelatory discourses of visions received after a journey to heaven and before a final ascent are common. With regard to the second type, Stauffer observes that divine epiphanies of both God and angels can be found and that usually the identity of neither God nor angel is revealed.

the Jewish farewell.[9] However, the speaker, instead of being a man of God or an angel of God, now becomes the Son of man who has come down from heaven, gives his life for human beings, and ascends to his heavenly throne. Thus, Stauffer sees the formal components of Jewish farewells as preserved but also christologically intensified in the New Testament.

Finally, in the later Christian tradition the use of the farewell continues to be commonly applied not only to the figure of Jesus but also to the apostles and saints; at this point, however, the influence of the Greco-Roman farewell increasingly displaces that of the Jewish farewell.

In an appendix to a larger work, written at approximately the same time as this study of last words in antiquity, Stauffer summarizes his findings in a listing of twenty-six characteristics of such speeches and their contexts.[10] Although in this enumeration he does not differentiate between context and speech proper, doing so explicitly is more helpful for analysis and interpretation.[11] Concerning the farewell context, fourteen characteristics are identified:

1. Heaven reveals the approach of death.
2. The one about to die calls together those who are left behind.
3. He takes a last meal with his disciples.

---

9. With regard to Jesus, the constitutive components of the farewell are said to be distributed throughout the long narrative section encompassing the passion: forebodings and prophecies of death, historical-theological overviews of the past and anticipations of the future, "I" sayings, words of warning, woes and attacks, promises, words of consolation, intercessions, and final instructions concerning a successor. In addition, appearances after death with farewells become very important. Stauffer further points out that the farewell is used in Acts with regard to Stephen and Paul.

10. E. Stauffer, *Die Theologie des Neuen Testaments*, 4th ed. (Stuttgart: W. Kohlhammer, 1948) 327–30 (Beilage VI: "Abschiedsreden und Abschiedszenen"); for an English translation, see E. Stauffer, *New Testament Theology*, trans. J. Marsh (New York: Macmillan, 1955) 344–47 (App. 6: "Valedictions and Farewell Speeches").

11. Stauffer's listing, on the one hand, goes beyond—especially with regard to the farewell context—the formal elements outlined for the bodies of literature examined in the study. As such, it is not clear how the list relates to the study—that is, how the characteristics of the former relate to those of the latter. On the other hand, though the study deals with the farewell in four different bodies of literature, the listing omits all reference to the Greco-Roman literature and the later Christian literature. The reason for this omission is obvious: given the full placement of Jesus' farewells within the Jewish tradition, supporting texts from the Greco-Roman tradition are simply excluded from consideration. However, a comparison of the formal elements outlined for the Jewish farewell with those outlined for the Greco-Roman farewell reveals a great deal of similarity, though the actual content of the two farewell traditions may vary. Thus, most elements remain pretty much the same: announcement of forthcoming death; last instructions (e.g., care of those left behind); question of succession; thanksgiving to the gods/prayers; words of consolation; account of past activities; teachings and exhortations/woes and promises; and political and philosophical testaments/theological views of history and apocalyptic readings of the future. In fact, only the element of blessings in the Jewish tradition has no counterpart in the Greco-Roman tradition; similarly, only the element of the hymnic swan song in the Greco-Roman tradition has no equivalent in the Jewish tradition. In the end, therefore, both the narrower scope of the listing and its underlying theological presuppositions appear ironic.

4. He blesses those remaining behind.
5. Those remaining fall down and worship.
6. He is transfigured before them.
7. He rejects earthly food.
8. He parts from those remaining.
9. He utters his last words.
10. He climbs a solitary hill.
11. He enters heaven by ascension of body and soul.
12. The soul is redeemed.
13. Those remaining bewail their loss.
14. Those remaining rejoice in his ascension.

With regard to the farewell speech proper, twelve characteristics are given:

1. The one about to die announces his forthcoming ascension.
2. He explains to those remaining that he will then be beyond their vision and company and that such a situation will actually be of benefit to them.
3. He says farewell to friends or foes, with
   a. A theological review of history.
   b. Revelations about the future.
   c. Warnings and final injunctions.
   d. Exhortations to keep his words and instructions.
   e. Commandments to love.
   f. Woes and controversies.
   g. Words of consolation and promises.
   h. Problems of intercession.
   i. A prayer for those left behind.
   j. An appointment of a successor.

Whereas the entire listing provides what Alter refers to as the predetermined motifs of the farewell or testament type-scene, the latter grouping provides the set constellation of motifs for the farewell speech or discourse.

Although broad and comprehensive, Stauffer's proposal is problematic in some respects. For example, one can detect a theological concern in his insistence to locate Jesus' own farewells within the Jewish tradition, as if the canonical text were saved thereby from any sullying contact with the pagan tradition. Similarly, Stauffer's distinction between the farewell in the Greco-Roman tradition and the farewell in the Jewish tradition is too sharp and even unjustified given the similarity in the respective formal elements of each tradition outlined. Finally, not only is the listing of formal characteristics too long and disjointed but also the formal elements enumerated reveal too wide a variation in frequency, with some elements appearing often but others only once or twice. Nevertheless, both study and listing prove useful in a search for the basic set of conventions of the farewell type-scene.

In 1950, the same year that Stauffer's study appeared, J. Munck published a similar work. Although familiar with Stauffer's listing of the formal elements of the farewell, Munck does not mention the more detailed study on the farewell tradition in antiquity. Both the point of departure and the plan of development are different here.

Munck's main purpose is to analyze the farewell speeches of the New Testament in the light of the farewell tradition in ancient Jewish literature, both biblical and extrabiblical.[12] Munck therefore begins by tracing the use and development of the farewell speech in the Jewish tradition, which consists of: the Hebrew Bible, the late Jewish literature, and works within this latter category that reprise the subject matter of the Pentateuch.[13] Once the characteristics of the farewell speech in Jewish literature have been secured, Munck analyzes the New Testament examples in the light of these characteristics.

Munck mentions three different sets of formal components in the process. The first, which is very brief, applies only to the Hebrew Bible: before death or ascent to the heavens, the "faithful of the old covenant" address their kin or the people at large with words of farewell and predictions of what will take place after their death. The second set covers all of the extrabiblical Jewish literature (namely, the second and third bodies of material) and consists of four formal elements: before death or ascent into the heavens, a character taken from the Hebrew Bible gathers around him, his family, or all the people in order to give (1) a supreme and definitive teaching;

12. Three points of comparison are helpful. First, like Stauffer, Munck ("Discours," 156) also makes an important distinction between brief last words and longer farewell speeches, though he devotes no attention whatsoever to the former. Second, again like Stauffer, Munck (p. 165) also distinguishes between farewells before death and farewells in appearances after death and before a final ascent, though only with respect to Jesus. Third, in contrast to Stauffer, who only mentions the use of the farewell with regard to Jesus in the Gospels and Stephen and Paul in Acts, Munck (pp. 162–65) amplifies this list by including three letters (2 Peter, 1 Timothy, and 2 Timothy) as examples of this genre.

13. Aside from briefly listing its major examples, therefore, Munck devotes no time to the Greco-Roman literature. The use of the farewell in the Jewish tradition can be summarized as follows. There are only a few examples in the Hebrew Bible, of which Deuteronomy is the longest and most important. The farewell is common in the late Jewish literature, including that body of material within it characterized as developing further the subject matter of the Pentateuch, a group in which Munck includes the *Assumption of Moses*, the *Book of Jubilees*, and the *Testaments of the Twelve Patriarchs*. The reason for the distinction between the last two bodies of material lies, I believe, in Munck's comment that the latter texts resemble much more closely the farewell speeches in the New Testament ("Discours," 157).

(2) (quite frequently) words of exhortation to those left behind or predictions of what will happen if they follow his exhortations and obey the
Law or if they disobey; (3) (less frequently) an account of his life, from
which moral exhortations are drawn, so that his life serves as a model or
exemplar for those left behind to follow; or (4) (again, less frequently)
words of prophecy regarding the future of the people in the last times.[14]

Munck provides a third set of formal elements, now described as general
characteristics of the genre. Two of these, one having to do with the speech
itself and the other with the context, are presented as less essential:
(1) instructions regarding burial and (2) location within the context of a
meal. Two others, both having to do with the speech itself, are more central: (1) the one bidding farewell recalls the events of the past (2) with
accompanying exhortations. Although such retrospection may be used to
repeat what is commonly known, it may also insist on something decisive
and necessary. A comparison of this final set with the previous one shows
the addition of two new elements (those described as less essential),
whereas the other two elements more or less encompass the other four
formal elements of the previous listing.

In comparison with Stauffer's proposal, that of Munck has both advantages and disadvantages. To begin with, Munck devotes far more time to
farewell speeches in the Jewish tradition, but almost completely bypasses
the Greco-Roman tradition. Such a modus operandi reflects the same theological concern already detected in Stauffer, indeed with an even more
pronounced distancing of the New Testament farewell from any sullying
contact with the pagan tradition. As a result, Munck, like Stauffer, posits
too sharp and unwarranted a distinction between the farewell in the Greco-
Roman tradition and the farewell in the Jewish tradition. Finally, whereas
Stauffer's listing is extensive and includes elements widely varying in frequency, Munck's listing is brief and general, especially concerning the formal elements of the definitive teaching and exhortations in question. In the
end, given its broader basis and more comprehensive scope, Stauffer's work
is more useful in the search for the conventions of the farewell type-scene.

In a monograph devoted to a study of Paul's farewell speech at Miletus
in Acts, H.-J. Michel (1973) devotes considerable attention to the formal

---

14. The last two characteristics are described as less frequent because they appear for the
most part only in the third body of material. In fact, it is because of the very presence of these
two characteristics that such texts are said to provide the closest parallels to the farewells
found in the New Testament, where the one about to die also insists on the importance of his
own person and predicts difficult times after his death. Consequently, it is precisely because of
these two characteristics, given their relative absence from other texts of the late Jewish
literature and their prominence in the New Testament, that a formal division is introduced
within the nonbiblical Jewish literature.

components of farewell scenes. Michel explicitly defines his own goals in this regard by reference to the earlier studies by Stauffer and Munck. He sharpens and modifies the delineation of the various formal elements of the farewell already identified in these earlier studies, as well as addresses and pursues for the first time the question of the *Sitz im Leben*, the socio-historical matrix, for the genre. A third goal is closely related to that of the search for the sociohistorical matrix insofar as it raises for the first time the question of the basic functions of the farewell in ancient narrative. Michel's approach is similar to Munck's, but more extensive and detailed: an analysis of farewell scenes in the Hebrew Bible and the late Jewish literature that leads to an enumeration of the constitutive motifs of the genre, a sketch of its basic functions, and a sketch of its sociohistorical matrix; and a subsequent examination of farewell scenes in the New Testament that leads to a direct evaluation of such examples in the light of the preceding evidence from the Jewish tradition.[15]

Michel proposes thirteen groupings or categories of constitutive motifs, most of which have a set number of different and recurrent variations. Although most of these groupings concern the speech itself, some have to do with the farewell context. Once again, it is helpful to separate the former from the latter. Four of these groupings concern context:

1. The presence of a circle of confidants as the hero's addressees (usually consisting of sons or close relatives, the elders of the people, other office-bearers, or the people as a whole).
2. A blessing upon those gathered together as a gesture of farewell.
3. Other farewell gestures (for example, a kiss, an embrace, weeping and laments, a meal, or a common posture).
4. The arrival of death, which need not be portrayed immediately after the speech itself or before the assembled gathering.[16]

---

15. These farewell scenes are divided into four categories: (*a*) last words after the resurrection or farewells in appearances after death; (*b*) words of farewell prior to death and resurrection; (*c*) farewells in epistolary form; and (*d*) Paul's farewell at Miletus, the focus of Michel's own study.

16. A comparison of these four groupings with Stauffer's corresponding list of fourteen characteristics shows (*a*) the preservation of two elements (the calling together and the blessing), (*b*) the gathering together of a number of elements under the wider category of farewell gestures (e.g., a last meal, falling down and worshiping, rejection of earthly food, and bewailing of loss), (*c*) the omission of a number of elements that actually follow upon the farewell scene as such (e.g., transfiguration, parting from those remaining, last words, climbing of a hill, entering into heaven, redemption of the soul, and rejoicing of the audience in the ascension), and (*d*) the similar omission of an element that actually precedes the farewell scene as such (the revelation from above of the coming death).

The other nine groupings concern the speech itself:

1. The announcement of approaching death, either by means of the narration or by the speaker himself (usually then as the very opening of the speech).
2. Parenetic sayings or exhortations (for Michel this component represents the primary thrust of the farewell speech).[17]
3. Prophecies or predictions.[18]
4. Retrospective accounts of the individual's life.[19]
5. The determination of a successor.[20]
6. A prayer, which may take the form of thanksgiving, praise, request, or any combination.
7. Final instructions.
8. Further instructions concerning burial.
9. Promises and vows demanded of the gathering whereby the observance of the preceding exhortations and commands is secured and guaranteed.[21]

In the end, Michel proposes a pattern for a farewell scene consisting of four components: the presentation of the speaker; the gathering of the confidants; exhortations and prophecies; and the conclusion, with gestures of

17. Five more concrete motifs are identified within such exhortations: (a) theological overviews of history—recalling God's deeds among the people, their frequent disobedience and unfaithfulness, and their resulting punishment—often used for illustration and linkage at the beginning; (b) the use of figures from the past as models for imitation or examples to be avoided; (c) moral exhortations and calls to obey the covenant, the law, the commandments, or the cultic regulations; (d) words of encouragement and consolation; and (e) promises for those who obey and woes for those who do not.

18. Two different types of predictions can be distinguished: (a) predictions of a noneschatological nature concerning the near or immediate future and (b) predictions concerning the final events, with the presence of motifs well known from the apocalyptic literature. Both types are usually pessimistic.

19. Such accounts may take two different forms: (a) a justification or vindication of the individual either through an unfolding of his exemplary and irreproachable life or a self-accusation and admission of faults or (b) the present fulfillment by the individual of his task as admonisher of those left behind.

20. A successor can be determined in various ways: an actual naming or appointment, a formal installation, words of consolation to the successor, or a call to obedience on the part of all others.

21. A comparison of these nine groupings with Stauffer's corresponding list of twelve characteristics shows (a) the preservation of several elements (the announcement of death, the theological review of history, the revelations of the future, warnings and injunctions, moral exhortations, woes, words of consolation and promises, prayer, and the question of a successor), (b) the omission of two elements (death as better for those left behind and the question of intercession), and (c) the addition of several elements (final instructions, instructions concerning burial, and promises and vows from those in attendance).

farewell and a description of death.[22] Clearly, therefore, within this overall pattern the first two and the last components have to do with context, whereas the third (exhortations and prophecies) concerns the speech.

Michel shows that the use of farewell scenes with respect to great figures of antiquity has several important functions. First, such scenes confer tremendous authority on the work in question and its message. Second, given the focus of the scenes in the past and in an interpretation of that past from the point of view of the present in the light of intervening events, such scenes help those in the present to gain self-understanding. Third, through their pessimistic portrayals of the future, these scenes describe concrete experiences of the past as direct results of the failure to heed the exhortations, warnings, and good examples of the ancestors; thus, the present audience is warned as well. Therefore, the farewell can be said to possess a historiographic, didactic, and parenetic function.

Finally, Michel sees such functions as pointing directly to a sociohistorical matrix in the post-Exilic period and, more specifically, to a Deuteronomistic conception of history, according to which the faithful are rewarded and the unfaithful punished. In later times the farewell remains constant in both form and function. Consequently, for Michel the farewell always remains at the service of a parenesis whose fundamental aim is to show the strong connections between the past, the present, and the future on the basis of an ethical conception of history. The crucial moment of death, of a change of generations, becomes an ideal moment in which to bring out and emphasize such connections.

In the New Testament, then, farewells are said to occur at two decisive points of transition, namely, at the time of Jesus' departure and at the end of the so-called apostolic period, thus pointing again to a similar view of history. Therefore, the use of the farewell in the New Testament presupposes a sense of separation from the event of Jesus, of a history of the Christian movement, of an understanding of the present as in some way tied to the past. Although such farewells preserve both the formal elements and the basic functions of the Jewish farewell, their contents undergo a drastic change in the light of the Christian kerygma.

---

22. Michel also comments on both the frequency and location of these thirteen groupings of motifs. He divides their frequency into three categories: (a) most common (announcement of coming death, the circle of confidants, parenetic sayings, and the arrival of death), (b) quite common (prophetic sayings, accounts of the individual's life, a blessing, instructions for burial, and other gestures of farewell), and (c) common (appointment of a successor, a prayer, and final instructions). With regard to location, Michel proposes the following division: (a) the announcement of coming death and the reference to the circle of confidants are usually found at the beginning; (b) parenetic sayings, prophetic sayings, and accounts of the individual's life occur in the middle; and (c) the rest tend to appear in the conclusion.

Michel represents a step forward in some important respects. Using a wider number of constitutive motifs, he manages to preserve a strong sense of order through a useful grouping of the various motifs. Furthermore, he raises for the first time the important question of function and begins to provide some concrete directions in this regard. At the same time, his study has problematic aspects. Like Munck, he completely bypasses the Greco-Roman literature, perhaps for the same underlying theological reasons. Similarly, the functions Michel attributes to the farewell remain far too general and divorced from the farewell motifs listed. Finally, the proposed origins of the farewell in the Deuteronomistic tradition and its conception of history have in the end limited effects for the interpretation of any one example of the genre.

A few years later (1976), E. Cortès published what remains the most exhaustive study of the farewell in the Jewish literary tradition and the New Testament. His work is directly or indirectly set in the context of all these previous studies. First, Cortès faults Stauffer's list of twenty-six characteristics on three counts: given such a long listing of formal elements, a precise definition of what constitutes a farewell becomes impossible; some of the motifs are represented by only one or two texts; and frequently the texts given as examples of a particular motif are simply too dissimilar or divergent.[23] Second, Cortès states that all detailed monographs of individual farewells—such as Michel's work, which is not cited—are of minimal help in coming to terms with the genre.[24] In the end, Cortès sees only Munck's study as valuable in this regard. Cortès conceives and presents his own work as a further development of Munck's. It is a more precise determination of the form and content of the farewell genre in order to gain a better understanding of its use in the New Testament. This development is threefold and—once again—based solely on the use of the farewell in the Jewish tradition.[25]

Departing from Munck's second set of formal elements outlined above, Cortès proposes three instead of four motifs, all having to do with the speech:

1. The calling together of his own by the one about to die for a final address.

---

23. Cortès, *Discursos*, 49.

24. This is far too sweeping, as Michel's own detailed study of the formal components of the genre readily shows. See also in this regard the work of J. Randall (*The Theme of Unity in John 17:20–23* [Gembloux and Louvain: Louvain University Press, 1962] 42–98; "The Theme of Unity in John 17:20–23," *EThL* 41 [1965] 373–94).

25. This tradition is examined in terms of four different bodies of material: the Hebrew Bible; the apocryphal literature; the testamentary literature (*The Testaments of the Twelve Patriarchs*); and the targumic literature, especially *Tg. Onq.* Gen. 49:1–2 and parallels.

2. Exhortations to those assembled, consisting for the most part of calls to works of mercy, charitable deeds, love, or fraternal union.
3. Concluding remarks concerning the future of the people or the end times.

This order, however, is not fixed: the second and third elements may be found in reverse order or mixed. In addition, Cortès argues that recurring stylistic formulas can be readily discerned within the farewell tradition, and he identifies three: the one about to die (1) "calls" his confidants, (2) exhorts by giving "commands" of a moral sort, and (3) refers to those assembled as his "children."[26]

Finally, Cortès addresses the basic functions of the farewell, though not from the point of view of its socio-historical matrix, as in the case of Michel, but rather from the point of view of what he calls its *Sitz im Literatur*, or socioliterary matrix. Like apocalyptic literature, first of all, the farewell, in disclosing the future, offers consolation in the face of pessimistic circumstances by pointing to the more or less proximate fulfillment of the ancient promises and grounding such hopes—through the literary device of pseudonymity—in the past fulfillment of promises already known to the audience. Similarly, like historical literature, the farewell, in resorting to a historical frame or setting, also seeks to reinterpret the tradition in a new direction. Then, like sapiential literature, by offering advice the farewell also advances a definite way of life and behavior. In other words, the farewell possesses a consolatory, didactic, and parenetic function.[27]

Cortès reaches a general conclusion affirming the relative independence of the farewell in the New Testament vis-à-vis the formal characteristics of the genre. Thus, in direct contrast to the apocryphal literature, the New Testament is described as freely using all such characteristics. This relative independence is attributed either to the creative power of the author in question (Luke-Acts) or to a shift away from future events to events of a not-too-distant past (John).

In the end, though thorough and exhaustive, Cortès's work suffers from the same shortcomings as that of Munck: an unexplained bypassing of the entire Greco-Roman tradition (especially given Cortès's desire to understand the New Testament in the light of the genre as a whole), as well as a far too brief and general listing of the constitutive motifs of the farewell

26. Cortès also mentions a fourth motif as being common and identifies a further stylistic formula in connection with it: instructions for burial, with a reference to dying, sleeping, or being buried "with his fathers."
27. A comparison of these three functions with those previously advanced by Michel shows considerable similarity: both the second and third functions, the didactic and parenetic functions, are largely parallel. Only the first functions differ: Michel omits all mention of consolation, and Cortès does not refer at all to the granting of authority.

type-scene. In addition, the overall comparison of the New Testament with the preceding tradition of the farewell in the Jewish literature is too vague to be helpful. At the same time, Cortès's analysis of the farewell's basic functions is a step forward, along the earlier lines of Michel, though quite independently of him. In fact, Cortès's analysis shows a much closer correlation between the formal characteristics and the essential functions of the farewell than does Michel's analysis.

Finally, W. S. Kurz's study (1985) of Luke 22 from a farewell perspective is important, given its explicit concern for both the Greco-Roman and Jewish (mostly biblical) literary traditions of farewells. Although the focus remains throughout on Luke 22:14–38, Kurz does raise the question of the constitutive motifs of the genre as well as that of its essential functions.

Kurz studies farewells in both the Greco-Roman and the Jewish traditions, along with the two examples in Luke-Acts, according to a list of twenty formal characteristics adapted from both Stauffer and Michel.[28] Again, a division between context and speech proper, though not employed by Kurz, is useful. Of these twenty characteristics, four concern the fare-well context or scene: (1) the summoning of successors, (2) the blessing, (3) farewell gestures, and (4) the bewailing of the loss by the rest.[29] The other sixteen characteristics concern the speech as such: (1) the speaker's own mission as example, (2) his innocence and the doing of a job (an account of the speaker's own life), (3) the announcement of impending death, (4) exhortations, (5) warnings and final injunctions, (6) tasks for successors, (7) a theological review of history, (8) revelations of the future, (9) promises, (10) the question of successors, (11) future degeneration, (12) the renewal of a covenant, (13) care of those left behind, (14) consolation of the inner circle, (15) didactic speech, and (16) "ars moriendi."[30]

28. Kurz, "Luke 22:14–38," 262–63. Kurz also distinguishes between extended farewells and brief last words immediately before death.

29. Kurz has followed the four groupings regarding the context proposed by Michel rather than the fourteen characteristics in Stauffer. The only exception is that of the fourth motif identified, namely, the bewailing of the loss by the rest. For Michel the bewailing of the loss represents an example of a farewell gesture; Kurz has made such an example into a separate motif—following the terminology of Stauffer—and omitted the description of the arrival of death itself. The latter omission is understandable, since in the Gospel tradition the arrival of death is formally separated from the farewell proper.

30. For the most part, this list gathers together in a different and disjointed fashion the formal elements outlined by both Stauffer and Michel for the speech proper: whereas some are separated, others are brought together. In terms of omissions, the following should be noted: the prayer (Stauffer and Michel); death as beneficial for those left behind, as well as intercession (Stauffer); and final instructions, including instructions for burial (Michel). In terms of additions, note care of those left behind (though this would certainly qualify under final instructions for Michel), didactic speech, and an introduction to the "ars moriendi." These three latter elements, however, can be traced to the formal characteristics of the Greco-Roman farewell outlined by Stauffer but not found in the companion list of twenty-six.

The study gives rise to three conclusions. First, in the Greco-Roman tradition farewell speeches mostly concern statesmen or philosophers and focus on the meaning of death, questions about a noble death, and the further question of life after death. Second, the Jewish tradition focuses on God's plan, people, and covenant; on theodicy; and on theological interpretations of history. Third, the farewells in Luke-Acts, though having many elements in common with the Greco-Roman tradition, show a closer affinity to the Jewish tradition.[31]

Concerning the functions of the farewell, then, Kurz makes a formal distinction between parenetic and historiographic functions.[32] On the one hand, the *Sitz im Leben,* or sociohistorical matrix, of the farewell is traced to ancient wisdom, namely, the preservation and handing on of the lessons of the past to the next generation at the solemn moment of death. As such, a parenetic thrust and function are intrinsic to the farewell.[33] On the other hand, given their presence in larger narrative works, a historiographic thrust and function are essential as well: the legitimation of successors, showing continuity from the beginning to the present; the apologetic distancing of the founder from later deviations of the message; and the justification and illustration of the divine plan of history, of developments after the founder's death, and of the soundness of the foundation laid.[34]

Kurz's work again represents a step forward. He is the first since Stauffer to be aware of the need to study the use of the farewell in the New Testament in the light of both its Greco-Roman and Jewish examples, and he does so by combining the recurrent motifs observed by both Stauffer and

31. Kurz's position shows both similarities and differences in comparison to that of Stauffer. First, with regard to the relationship between the Greco-Roman and Jewish traditions, the explicit difference in speaker pointed out by Stauffer is preserved, and the implicit difference in content becomes explicit. Second, the affinity of the New Testament farewell with the Jewish tradition vis-à-vis the Greco-Roman tradition laid down by Stauffer, although clearly acknowledged and affirmed by Kurz, is not as sharply presented or defined. Finally, such an affinity is not as nuanced in Kurz as in Stauffer; the element of christological intensification—or basic difference in speaker—finds no counterpart whatsoever.

32. The distinction is borrowed from the work of E. von Nordheim on the testament genre (*Die Lehre der Alten: 1. Das Testament als Literaturgattung im Judentum der Hellenistisch-Römischen Zeit,* ALGHJ 13 [Leiden: E. J. Brill, 1980] 229–42).

33. Kurz points out that the most common elements of the farewell have to do either with the very situation of death (announcement of impending death, bewailing of the loss by the rest, care of those left behind, and consolation of an inner circle) or with this parenetic dimension (the summoning of successors, the speaker's mission as example, exhortations, warnings and final injunctions, promises, the question of a successor, and future degeneration).

34. Kurz singles out the following characteristics as particularly relevant with regard to each of these three historiographic functions: (*a*) legitimation of successors: the giving of promises, the question of a successor, and the renewal of the covenant through promises and vows; (*b*) attack on deviations: revelations of the future, whether by means of the issuing of warnings and final injunctions or the disclosure of future degeneration; and (*c*) justification of the divine plan: the speaker's innocence and doing of his job, the tasks assigned to the successors, the theological review of history, and the revelations of the future.

Michel. Kurz also opts for what could be called the Stauffer-Michel tradition in pointing to a larger field of such motifs, thus avoiding the more
sketchy approach adopted by the Munck-Cortès tradition. Finally, he takes
the question of function seriously, providing in the process an overall classification of such functions (parenetic and historiographic) and a closer
correlation than that of Cortès between these functions and the formal
characteristics of the farewell.[35]

Two final comments on Kurz are in order. The difference noted between
the Greco-Roman and the Jewish farewell traditions is unexpectedly, given
the course of the study, one of content rather than form or motifs. In addition, the list of characteristics proposed lacks organization. Nevertheless,
Kurz's brief study points in the right direction for all further inquiries of
individual farewells.

The preceding overview of recent scholarly research regarding farewell
scenes in antiquity provides a proper framework for the present study
of the Johannine farewell speech. However, given the differences in approaches and results observed within the literature, some decisions with
regard to an overall orientation and approach are necessary.

First, two basic approaches to the question of recurrent and constitutive
motifs in the farewell type-scene can be discerned. On the one hand is
a minimalist approach, adopted by Munck and continued by Cortès, with
a decision to limit drastically the number of such motifs by means of deliberately wide categories. Both adopted this approach in reaction to the
earlier work of Stauffer. On the other hand, a maximalist approach, first
encountered in Stauffer and later followed by both Michel and Kurz, opts
for a far larger number of recurrent motifs. For purposes of analysis and
interpretation, the latter, maximalist approach proves more helpful in coming to terms with the individuality of any one example. Indeed, the position
that such motifs need not appear in every speech, be used in the same
order, to the same extent, or with the same emphasis renders unnecessary
the excessive caution shown by both Munck and Cortès.

Second, such a maximalist approach should be marked both by a formal
distinction between farewell context and farewell speech and a proper
ordering of the different farewell motifs. On the one hand, a formal distinction between the recurrent motifs of context and speech within the
farewell scene is helpful in interpretation; the speech represents the major

35. Kurz's twofold division covers in effect all functions mentioned by Michel and
Cortès. Within the parenetic division, one would include the third function of both, plus the
first function of Cortès—the consolation of the disciples. Within the historiographic division, one would locate the second function of both, plus the first function of Michel—the
granting of authority to the work and its message.

component in such scenes and can be examined independently of the context. Two further distinctions should also be observed in this regard. The common tradition of brief last words immediately before death itself should be formally separated, whenever appropriate, from that of the farewell scene. Similarly, other motifs closely associated with the moment of death itself and its consequences for the hero should also be formally separated, whenever appropriate, from the farewell scene proper.

On the other hand, the identification of the recurrent motifs, whether of the farewell context or speech, should exhibit a definite sense of order, a helpful pattern of arrangement, in order to avoid too extensive or disjointed a listing. In this regard the concept of farewell grouping or category adopted by Michel is helpful: while preserving the rich variety of the motifs, it also conveys such richness in an orderly fashion.

Third, such a maximalist approach should not be limited to the presence and use of the farewell in the Jewish literary tradition. The wider Greco-Roman scene and its literature, of which the Jews represented a distinctive subculture, must be taken into account. Jewish cultural tradition was by no means isolated from the surrounding and pervasive Hellenistic culture. The association with Greco-Roman culture on the part of the New Testament writers is only to be expected and does not represent a sullying of the canonical text and the Word of God. In this regard it is Kurz who points in the right direction by opting for a combination of the farewell motifs provided by Stauffer and Cortès. As we have seen, a formal difference or a difference in the set of predetermined and recurrent motifs is minimal.[36]

Finally, a maximalist approach must also pay close attention to the functions that underlie the presence and use of the motifs in a farewell type-scene. It is not sufficient simply to identify the set of predetermined motifs present in such scenes; one must also identify the goals inherent in the common use of such motifs and scenes in ancient narrative. Five such functions will be used in this regard: didactic, consolatory, exhortative, admonitory, and polemical. Moreover, the close correlation between motifs and functions adopted by both Cortès and Kurz points in the right direction for the analysis of any one example of a farewell scene. Given the general functions inherent in such type-scenes, their immediate and concrete manifestations in all examples can be more readily secured and classified.

36. In fact, the difference in speaker (highly emphasized by Stauffer and to some extent preserved by Kurz) is not as evident as it would at first appear, at least not in the Gospel of John. Can one really say that the Jesus of the Fourth Gospel, the Word of God who was with God and is God from the very beginning and who became flesh in the world, comes closer to the "man of God" of Jewish literature than—using Stauffer's category simply for purposes of comparison—to the "divine man" or the "god in human disguise" of the Greco-Roman tradition?

This study of the Johannine farewell is guided by the following methodological considerations. First, it takes a maximalist approach to the
question of the constitutive motifs of the farewell type-scene and follows
Michel's fine proposal concerning the grouping of such motifs. Second, it
has a specific delimitation. In the light of the distinction between farewell
scenes and death scenes, this study bypasses the large number of important farewell motifs to be found in the next narrative section of the Gospel
(18:1–21:25). In the light of the further distinction between context and
speech within farewell scenes, this study focuses on the farewell speech.
Third, the study expands Michel's overall proposal by including farewell
motifs from the Greco-Roman literary tradition—in particular, those motifs mentioned by Stauffer in his own groupings or categories. Finally, the
study also explicitly pursues the question of function, showing, as both
Cortès and Kurz have done, the specific correlation between motifs and
functions.

   This study of the Johannine farewell speech nonetheless centers on a close
reading of the text. An analysis of the speech from the comparative perspective of the farewell genre is deferred to the final chapter. Because of the
disproportionate length of the speech in the Gospel and the problematic
nature of its present sequence and overall arrangement, the study begins
with a detailed literary-rhetorical analysis of the speech in terms of its major
units of discourse. Such an analysis ultimately brings to light the literary
structure and development, the overall strategic concerns and aims, and the
underlying rhetorical situation of the Johannine farewell as a whole. Only
upon the completion of this literary-rhetorical analysis, therefore, is the
speech examined from the comparative perspective of the farewell genre
and its uniqueness as a good example of a farewell speech brought forward.
In the end both the literary-rhetorical analysis and the comparative generic
analysis are helpful in coming to terms with the highly problematic issues of
disproportionate length and compositional difficulties.

COMPOSITIONAL DIFFICULTIES AND
TRADITIONAL RESOLUTIONS

As already noted, John 13–17 is a coherent and self-contained narrative
section of the Gospel as well as a clear example of a farewell type-scene, in
which three smaller narrative units can be distinguished: 13:1–20;
13:21–30; and 13:31–17:26. The first two units provide the farewell
context, and the third contains the farewell speech proper. Given the
focus of this study on the third unit, it is useful, by way of introduction, to
briefly consider the first two units of the section, 13:1–20 and 13:21–30,
from a farewell perspective.

The Farewell Context of John 13:1–20, 21–30

In the two narrative units of 13:1–20 and 13:21–30, are evident four important farewell motifs. The first concerns the deliberate gathering of an intimate circle by the hero who is about to die. Jesus gathers an unidentified number of his disciples in a room in Jerusalem, where they are to receive a necessary and symbolic washing, as well as final words of farewell in direct anticipation of Jesus' forthcoming death. This gathering of the disciples is sharpened by two concrete and related developments: (1) the presence and eventual departure from the scene of a disciple (Judas) who no longer qualifies as a disciple and a member of the intimate circle and (2) the first mention and presentation of "the disciple whom Jesus loved" with a privileged location and role within the scene. Whereas the former development points to the fact that not all within the intimate circle are proper and faithful disciples of Jesus, the latter introduces a distinction of rank within the intimate circle. The two developments are related. As the prototypical betrayer is exposed, the prototypical follower is revealed. With the gathering itself, then, the question of the succession, a second farewell motif, begins to be addressed as well.

The third farewell motif is that of the final meal between the hero and his intimate circle, in this case the last meal of Jesus with his disciples in an unidentified room in Jerusalem on the eve of both Sabbath and Passover. These first two units concern different aspects of this meal. John 13:1–20 focuses on a common practice of meals in antiquity, namely, the washing of the guests' feet. However, two unexpected elements of this washing particularly stand out: it is Jesus himself who undertakes such a washing—as the astonishment and objection of one of the disciples, Simon Peter, readily confirms—and the washing appears to take place during the course of the meal rather than prior to it. John 13:21–30 focuses on the taking of food by members of the assembled group, though again another unexpected element of such a meal stands out, namely, that only Jesus' dipping and giving of bread to a specific disciple is mentioned.

A fourth farewell motif, the conversation of the hero with the assembled gathering, is evident as well, in this case with a considerable amount of dialogue between Jesus and his disciples during the entire meal. Within this dialogue several other farewell motifs are detected. First, in 13:1–20 one finds the following:

- The explicit presentation of Jesus' action, the symbolic washing of the feet, not only as a proper way of behavior for Jesus himself but also as a model for the disciples to imitate.
- Definitive teaching about both the need to receive such washing and the need to reproduce it among themselves.

- A call to the disciples to act accordingly and wash one another's feet as Jesus had washed theirs.
- The juxtaposition of woes and promises connected with the washing (one has no part of Jesus if this symbolic washing is refused and not performed; the disciples are blessed if they comply with the exhortation and practice it among themselves).
- Prophecies and predictions of the future (two prophetic allusions to the coming betrayal by one of those present at the gathering, whereby not all who receive the washing are said to belong to the intimate circle).

Second, in 13:21–30 one finds (1) further prophecies and predictions of the future (an explicit disclosure of the coming betrayal by a member of the group and the subsequent identification of Judas Iscariot as its perpetrator) and (2) the question of the succession once again. The latter emphasizes the two explicit distinctions to be noted within the intimate circle itself. On the one hand, a request to the identified betrayer to leave the gathering of the intimate circle effectively marks his total separation from the group. On the other hand, an immediate response to the request by the "beloved disciple" discloses the specific (and dramatically effective) technique employed in revealing the identity of the announced betrayer. Thus, the dialogue within this second unit strongly reaffirms what the narration itself depicts: not all the disciples who accompanied Jesus in his ministry will function as his successors, and moreover, among those who will become his faithful successors, one will enjoy a place of distinction, appropriately conveyed by the designation "the one whom Jesus loved" throughout the narrative.

In both of these narrative units, therefore, the farewell motif of the meal is variously subordinated to: Jesus' action of washing the feet of the disciples, the identification of the betrayer through the giving of the bread, and the issues raised in the course of the ongoing dialogue. The meal simply serves as the occasion and setting for both the extended conversation and the specific actions in question. Thus, while Jesus' washing of the feet in 13:1–20 provides the grounds for the teaching, the exhortation, the woes and promises, and the prophecies conveyed to the disciples, the reference to the meal in 13:21–30 supplies the concrete means by which the preceding predictions are clarified for the disciples and the question of the succession further pursued. Such a subordinate role for the meal helps to explain the unusual features of both washing and food pointed out above (the performance of the washing by Jesus himself, thus providing the model or example to be followed; its occurrence within the course of the meal itself rather than before it, thus highlighting its central position and role within the context of farewell; and the giving of bread by Jesus to one of the disciples, thus focusing on the uncovering of the presence of a betrayer within the intimate circle).

Two observations are in order concerning the formal characteristics of the farewell context outlined by Michel. First, of the four farewell motifs encountered in this narrative context, three may be classified within two of these formal groupings: (1) the summoning of the circle of confidants, which here takes the form of the gathering of the disciples, and (2) the presence of farewell gestures, which here include both the last meal as the setting for the entire narrative section and the dialogue that takes place during the course of this meal.[37] All three of these features are recurring motifs in farewell scenes of both the Greco-Roman and Jewish traditions; whereas the former motif is understandably universal, the latter two motifs are less frequent.[38] The fourth motif, that of the succession, represents a formal characteristic of the farewell speech proper. Its dramatic portrayal here within the farewell context can only point to the great importance attached to this issue in the narrative as a whole, while at the same time setting the stage for further treatment in the speech that follows. Second, the various farewell motifs encountered in the ongoing dialogue—including that of the succession—also represent formal characteristics of the farewell speech; their presentation at this point, within the context itself, directly sets the stage for the speech that follows.

These first two narrative units, 13:1–20 and 13:21–30, thus begin to point the way to the final events of Jesus' life and ministry, anticipating their proximate occurrence, describing the early course of such events and its eventual denouement, and providing an initial and veiled explanation of the fundamental meaning and consequences of these events. Within this unmistakable context of a farewell gathering with his disciples at a meal, Jesus is portrayed as launching into a farewell speech to his remaining and faithful disciples in the face of the impending betrayal by one of their own, his approaching separation from all of them, and his inevitable and forthcoming death, thus giving rise to the third and final unit of the section. In

37. Neither Michel nor Kurz mentions the motif of conversation as such; for Stauffer, see n. 6 above. I believe that this motif can be readily placed under the rubric of farewell gestures, whether such a conversation forms part of a meal or not.

38. The third formal characteristic associated with the farewell context proposed by Michel, the blessing, may have been replaced in this scene by the washing of the feet. Although the washing clearly functions here as a further gesture of farewell, it is not used as such anywhere else; consequently, its present role here perhaps should be seen along the lines of a blessing—conferring a special status upon the disciples by means of a highly symbolic foot washing that anticipates their final washing of purification yet to come and their definitive union with Jesus (cf. 13:17). Michel's fourth formal grouping for the farewell context is not applicable to farewell scenes in the Gospels—namely, the description of death—since it forms part of a different narrative section altogether.

this speech the various farewell motifs introduced in the conversations of
13:1–20 and 13:21–30 receive further expansion and development.

Jesus' Farewell Speech of John 13:31–17:26: Compositional Difficulties

The expansion in the farewell speech of motifs from 13:1–20 and 13:21–
30 is considerable; the farewell speech proper encompasses all of
13:31–17:26. This discourse is by far the longest of Jesus' speeches in
the entire Gospel narrative. In fact, the entire farewell scene constitutes
the longest narrative scene in the entire Gospel narrative. The speech
also contains a number of compositional difficulties that the scholarly
literature has consistently pointed out and attempted to resolve in different ways. Such difficulties concern sequence, arrangement, and content. The following discussion of the most substantial and important
difficulties serves as an introduction to the different types of resolution
proposed in the scholarly literature.

The most obvious and significant of these difficulties is the twofold
command of Jesus to his disciples in 14:31d, toward the beginning of the
discourse: "Arise! Let us depart from here!" Such a command at this point
not only conveys a definite sense of finality and conclusion but also can be
interpreted (see my chapter 2) as part of the proper ending to the preceding block of speech material of 13:31–14:31. In other words, this twofold
command functions as the final element in the concluding section of a
coherent and self-contained unit of discourse.

If one regards this command as a proper ending to a unit of discourse,
however, one is faced with the fact that the command occurs approximately within the first third of the present speech and is ignored in the
narrative until the beginning of the following narrative section of the
Gospel (18:1–21:25), where the narrator describes the movement of Jesus
and his disciples away from the supper room in Jerusalem toward a common gathering place of theirs in a garden located across the Kidron valley
(18:1–27, especially 18:1–2). Moreover, the command to arise and leave
the room where the meal took place can be smoothly followed by this
beginning introduction of chapter 18: "Arise! Let us depart from here!"
. . . . "After these words, Jesus went out with his disciples across the
Kidron valley, where there was a garden, which he and his disciples pro-
ceeded to enter." In effect, the omission of the intervening speech material would not be missed in the resulting narrative sequence.

However, a large amount of material intervenes between the twofold
command and the description of withdrawal from both the room and Jerusalem. In fact, the block of speech material that lies between these two
points in the narrative amounts to twice as much as that which follows the
departure of Judas and precedes the twofold command. Without it, the

farewell speech would still be long, but consistent with other examples in the Gospel; with it, the farewell speech becomes disproportionately long.

In addition, whereas the speech material prior to the twofold command of 14:31d does reveal a smooth development from beginning to end, as my chapter 2 will demonstrate, the material that follows presents two different sorts of difficulties.

On the one hand, the resulting two blocks of material are not at first sight entirely complementary. For example, the second block contains a great deal of repetition of material from the first block, especially toward its central part, in the greater part of chapter 16. Similarly, and what is quite jarring, the same context contains a direct reproach of the disciples by Jesus for not pursuing the question regarding the destination of his forthcoming departure (16:4b–6), when in fact this is the initial question addressed to Jesus by a disciple, Simon Peter, in the first block of material (13:36–38). Again, in that same context is an ironic prediction of the disciples' forthcoming dispersal and abandonment of Jesus (16:31–32), a prediction that is not entirely in accord with Jesus' own later dismissal of his disciples at the time of his arrest in the garden (18:8–9).

On the other hand, in contrast to the first block of material, the second block does not in itself yield an overall principle of arrangement and organization but instead gives the impression of containing a wide combination of disparate and unrelated material. The second block begins abruptly with the development of the sustained metaphor of Jesus as the vine (first part of chapter 15), which in turn gives rise to a large number of exhortations and admonitions (last part of chapter 15 and some of chapter 16), before the large duplication of material from the first block begins (most of chapter 16). It concludes with a long prayer of Jesus to the Father on behalf of his disciples (chapter 17). From both an internal and a comparative point of view, therefore, the presence of these three chapters of material after the command of 14:31d remains problematic.

Difficulties in matters of content, especially of a theological nature, have often been pointed out as well, so that these two large blocks of material have been seen as presenting varying or even conflicting theological positions, for example, with regard to the figure and role of the Paraclete or the teaching concerning the parousia. None of these proposed clashes in theological content, however, are as weighty as the difficulties of length, development, and arrangement.

Jesus' Farewell Speech of John 13:31–17:26: Traditional Resolutions

The presence of the difficulties of length, development, and arrangement within Jesus' important farewell speech to his disciples has both remained a *crux interpretum* in the study of the Fourth Gospel and given rise to an ongoing discussion among this Gospel's many interpreters. This discussion is too complex to reproduce here;[39] however, recurring lines of resolution—ways of reading and approaching the present text in the face of all its difficulties—can be discerned in the literature. The emergence and application of these lines of resolution show a progression that reflects a corresponding methodological development within Johannine studies. This development in turn reflects the wider course of New Testament studies and interpretation. There are six basic approaches to the present text of the farewell speech: the historicizing, transpositional, redactional, symbolic, unfinished, and compositional approaches.

The historicizing approach regards the text as both mimetic and untouchable. It sees the present text of the Gospel as accurately recounting the life and ministry of the historical Jesus of Nazareth; as such, it approaches the difficulties of the farewell speech from a strictly historical point of view. These difficulties are addressed in terms of the present position of Jesus' twofold command of 14:31d within the speech and resolved by regarding such a command as pointing to a change in location during the actual delivery of the speech. Thus, the first block of material through the command itself is pronounced in one location, and the rest is continued from a different location. This change in location has received three recurring explanations: (1) the whole group's movement away from the table, with Jesus' continued delivery of the speech while standing in the room itself or in an adjacent courtyard or terrace;[40] (2) Jesus' departure from the room and his pronouncement of the second block of material while walking through the streets of Jerusalem on the way to the garden;[41] and (3) again, Jesus' departure from the room but with a stop at the temple precinct, where he delivers the rest of the speech.[42] All three cases, therefore, see the command of 14:31d as marking an end to the gathering of the group at the table—either by way of relocation elsewhere in the same

---

39. Monographic and comprehensive studies on the farewell discourse alone are numerous, e.g., Durand; Swete; P. W. von Keppler, *Unseres Herrn Trost*, 2d and 3d ed. (Freiburg: Herder, 1914); Huby; C. Hauret, *Les adieux du Seigneur: S. Jean XIII–XVII* (Paris: J. Gabalda, 1951); Bover; J. Könn, *Sein letztes Wort: Bibellesungen über die Abschiedsreden des Herrn* (Einsiedeln and Cologne: Benzinger Verlag, 1955); van den Bussche; Behler. For others, see Bover, 325–26.

40. This is by far the most common explanation; see, e.g., J. Knabenbauer, *Comentarius in Quatuor S. Evangelia Domini Nostri Iesu Christu, Pars IV: Evangelium secundum Ioannem* (Paris: P. Lethielleux, 1898); J. E. Belser, *Das Evangelium des heiligen Johannes* (Freiburg: Herder, 1905); Th. Zahn, *Das Evangelium des Johannes*, 5th and 6th ed., rev. and enl., Kommentar zum Neuen Testament 4 (Leipzig: A. Deichert, 1908); F. Tillmann, *Das Johannesevangelium*, 4th ed., Die heilige Schrift des Neuen Testaments 3 (Bonn: Hanstein, 1931).

41. See, e.g., F. Godet, *Commentaire sur l'Evangile de Saint Jean*, 3d ed., rev. and enl., Bibliothèque théologique, 3 vols. (Neuchâtel: J. Attinger, 1885); J. Corluy, *Comentarius in Evangelium S. Joannis in Usum Praelectionum*, 3d ed. (Gandavi: C. Poelman, 1889).

42. See, e.g., Westcott; Swete.

locale or by departure from this locale but not from Jerusalem itself—
and the beginning observation of 18:1 as indicating an actual departure
from the city proper.

This line of resolution, given its total respect for the Gospel text in its
present form as an accurate account of the life of Jesus of Nazareth, constitutes the traditional approach, which reigned supreme through the turn of
the century into the first decade or so of the present century. This interpretation continues to appear from time to time, especially among the more
conservative interpreters of the biblical text, although it is now usually formulated more cautiously than before.[43] Furthermore, the methodological
developments that the discipline has undergone in this century have rendered such an approach increasingly less viable. Above all, the gradual but
inexorable switch from interpreting the text as mimetic re-creation to interpreting it as artistic creation completely redirected the search for a satisfactory resolution. In addition, by focusing exclusively on the twofold command
of 14:31d, the historicizing approach never seriously addressed the other
difficulties of the present farewell discourse. Eventually, therefore, it was
completely dislodged as the dominant line of resolution and replaced by two
other approaches to the text, the transpositional and the redactional.

The transpositional or rearrangement approach considers the text neither untouchable nor (for the most part) mimetic. Rather, the text reflects
the design and intentions of its author; however, something happened
early in the process of transmission that gave rise to its present difficulties.
As a result, this approach pursues the solution to the problem from a
literary point of view, although with a clear historical explanation provided for the text's present state of displacement and confusion. It becomes
the interpreter's task to recover the original intentions of the author, a task
pursued through a transposition or rearrangement of various sections of
the present text to yield a smoother and more logical progression in sequence and development. Such a rearrangement can range from minimal
to extensive; at the same time, the underlying cause for the present displacement of the text can range from a complete accident (for example, a
transposition of sheets or the misplacement of a paragraph) to bad judgment on the part of an editor (for example, an infelicitous ordering of an
unfinished or disrupted text).

The proposed transpositions, whether minimal or extensive, reveal recurring similarities. First, the transposition can be limited to the problematic command itself; this command and its immediate context (14:25–31)

---

43. See, e.g., L. Bouyer, *The Fourth Gospel*, trans. P. Byrne (Westminster, Md.: Newman
Press, 1964); D. A. Carson, *The Farewell Discourse and Final Prayer of Jesus* (Grand Rapids:
Baker, 1980).

can be moved between chapters 16 and 17 so that the latter follows immediately upon the command itself and the present sequence of the three intervening chapters is largely preserved.[44] Second, the transposition can involve only chapters 15–16, which are placed elsewhere, always in the same order, in a number of different locations: after 12:50; 13:20; 13:31a; 13:32; or 13:35.[45] In the first two options the chapters precede the entire first block of speech material, whereas in the last three options these chapters are placed within this block itself, at different points within its introductory section of 13:31–38. In both cases, the prayer of chapter 17 again follows, as in the preceding position, directly upon the command of 14:31d. Finally, the transposition can be extended to all of chapters 15–17, which are then placed elsewhere in the same order, in reverse order (with chapter 17 before chapters 15–16), or separately (with chapters 15–16 and 17 in different locations altogether).[46] In all three options, therefore, the command of 14:31d is followed immediately by the statement of 18:1, while the three presently intervening chapters are located, once again, either immediately prior to the first block of material or within it, at its very beginning.

As already indicated, this line of resolution, which addresses the various difficulties of the present farewell and not just that of the present location of the command of 14:31d, was one of the two that gradually displaced the dominant historicizing approach in the very early decades of this century. The transpositional approach's emphasis on the intentions of the author of the text, its sharp criticism of the present shape of the text, its freedom to disassemble and reassemble the text, and its bold proposal for a clearer and more logical progression of thought than that exhibited by the text itself all point to the emergence of both tradition and source-critical methodologies in New Testament studies.

44. This is the least common position. See, e.g., B. H. Streeter, *The Four Gospels: A Study of Origins* (London: Macmillan & Co., 1924); F. B. Clogg, *An Introduction to the New Testament* (London: University of London Press, 1937).

45. This is the most common position. See, e.g., for after 12:50, B. Brinkmann, "Zur Frage der ursprünglich Ordnung im Johannesevangelium," *Gregorianum* 20 (1939) 55–82; idem, "Qualis fuerit ordo originarius in quarto Evangelium," ibid.: 563–69. See, e.g., for after 13:20, B. W. Bacon, "The Displacement of John xiv," *JBL* 13 (1894) 64–76; idem, *The Fourth Gospel in Research and Debate* (New Haven: Yale University Press, 1918). See, e.g., for after 13:31a, J. Moffat, *The Historical New Testament*, 2d ed. (Edinburgh: T. & T. Clark, 1901); Bernard. See, e.g., for after 13:32, F. W. Lewis, *Disarrangements in the Fourth Gospel* (Cambridge: Cambridge University Press, 1910). See, e.g., for after 13:35, H. H. Wendt, *Das Johannesevangelium* (Göttingen: Vandenhoeck & Ruprecht, 1900); Macgregor.

46. See, e.g., for the same order, F. Spitta, *Das Johannesevangelium als Quelle der Geschichte Jesu* (Göttingen: Vandenhoeck & Ruprecht, 1910); M. Lattke, *Einheit im Wort: Die spezifische Bedeutung von 'agapê/agapan' und 'philein' im Johannesevangelium*, SANT 41 (Munich: Kösel Verlag, 1975). See, e.g., for reverse order, Schulz. See, e.g., for separately, Bultmann; H. Becker, *Die Reden des Johannesevangelium und der Stil der gnostischen Offenbarungsrede*, FRLANT 68 (Göttingen: Vandenhoeck & Ruprecht, 1956); J. Heise, *Bleiben: Menein in den johanneischen Schriften*, HUT (Tübingen: J. C. B. Mohr, 1967).

The appeal of the transpositional approach remained strong through the 1940s; however, aside from a few adherents in more recent times, this approach had little support past the midcentury mark. Methodological developments in the discipline—especially the rise of form and redaction criticisms—eventually turned the tide completely against all such transpositions on the part of the interpreter. In fact, such rearrangements were increasingly regarded as unnecessary and even destructive, as abuses rather than proper or helpful interpretations of the text. This approach also failed to resolve its own inherent difficulties. For example, it entirely bypassed the question of the disproportionate length of the present discourse. Similarly, the resulting rearrangements not only failed to resolve many of the difficulties in question but without exception also introduced many others; the relocation of such large chunks of material elsewhere in the narrative could not but raise new and sometimes more severe difficulties. In addition, the reasons advanced for the present state of the text—at times complicated and almost whimsical—proved largely unconvincing. In the end the transpositional approach failed to be as attractive as the redactional approach, more or less its contemporary in the scholarly discussion.[47]

In the redactional approach the text is again neither untouchable nor (for the most part) mimetic. However, the text is no longer seen as confused and displaced but rather as reflecting a process of composition whereby an original farewell speech underwent a process of growth that ultimately resulted in the present shape of the farewell discourse of the Gospel. The overall conception of this process of composition is the same: the first block of speech material (minus perhaps some small sections also considered as later insertions and thus assigned to the expansion) is identified as the original farewell, whereas the second block is said to constitute its later expansion.

As in the transpositional approach, the redactional approach directly addresses the difficulties of the present farewell, though with considerably more success. The disproportionate length of the farewell no longer poses any problems, since the original farewell speech concluded with the two-fold command of 14:31d. The command itself was immediately followed at first by a narration of the group's departure from the supper room and thus a change of scene in chapter 18. All other difficulties arise directly from the subsequent expansion of the original speech. Consequently, the task of the interpreter is to examine the nature of the redaction in the light of the original farewell and to consider the fundamental reasons for its addition to it. As such, the solution to the present difficulties of the speech reveals a

47. Combinations of these two approaches can also be found; see, e.g., W. P. J. Boyd, "The Ascension According to St. John: Chapters 14–17, Not Pre-passion but Post-resurrection," *Theology* 70 (1967) 207–11.

literary character, though again with a clear historical grounding in terms of the addition as a direct response to both a changing historical situation and a changing theological climate in the Johannine community.

The basic variations within this approach, which again exhibit striking recurring similarities, arise as a result of the more concrete explanations offered for the addition of the redaction, and hence for the very process of composition of the present farewell. Two major positions present similar basic options. One position regards the second block of material as a single speech that was (1) written and added by the evangelist,[48] (2) written by the evangelist but added by someone else,[49] or (3) written and added by someone other than the evangelist.[50] The other position sees this second block of material as consisting of various speeches that were (1) written and added by the evangelist;[51] (2) written by the evangelist but added by someone else;[52] (3) written by the evangelist, other Johannine writers (prior to the composition of the Gospel), or both and added by someone else;[53] or (4) written and added by a variety of different authors.[54]

As already mentioned, the redactional and transpositional approaches were responsible for the gradual demise of the dominant historicizing approach in the early decades of the century and shared the limelight

48. See, e.g., A. Loisy, *Le quatrième évangile* (Paris: A. Picard et fils, 1903); M. Lepin, *La valeur historique du quatrième évangile*, 2 vols. (Paris: Letouzey et Ané, 1910); P. Gächter, "Der formale Aufbau der Abschiedsreden Jesu," *ZNW* 58 (1934) 155–207; A. Durand, "Discours" (both articles); idem *Evangile selon Saint Jean*, 2d ed., rev. J. Huby, VS 4 (Paris: Gabriel Beauchesne, 1938); D. Mollat, *L'évangile et les épîtres de Saint Jean*, La Sainte Bible traduite en français (Paris: Les Editions du Cerf, 1953); Bover; Behler.

49. See, e.g., Loisy; Strathmann; R. Borig, *Der wahre Weinstock: Untersuchungen zu Jo 15,1–10*, STANT 16 (Munich: Kösel Verlag, 1967).

50. J. Wellhausen, *Erweiterungen und Änderungen im vierten Evangelium* (Berlin: G. Reimer, 1907); idem, *Das Evangelium Johannis*; G. Richter, "Die Fusswaschung Joh 13:1–20," *MTZ* 16 (1965) 13–26; idem, "Die Deutung des Kreuzestodes Jesu in der Leidensgeschichte des Johannesevangeliums (Jo 13–19)," *BibLeb* 9 (1968) 21–36; the two latter reprinted in *Studien zum Johannesevangelium* (Regensburg: Pustet, 1977) 42–57 and 58–73, respectively; H. Thyen, "Joh. 13 und die 'kirchliche Redaktion' des vierten Evangeliums," in G. Jeremias, H.-W. Kuhn, H. Stegemann, eds., *Tradition und Glaube: Das frühe Christentum in seiner Umwelt, Festgabe für K. G. Kuhn* (Göttingen: Vandenhoeck & Ruprecht, 1971) 343–56.

51. Lagrange; A. George, "'L'heure' de Jean xvii," *RB* 61 (1954) 392–97; W. Wilkens, *Die Entstehungsgeschichte des vierten Evangeliums* (Biel: Evangelischer Verlag A.G., Zollikon, 1958); Lindars.

52. R. Schnackenburg, *Das Johannesevangelium, I Teil: Einleitung und Kommentar zu Kap. 1–4*, 2d ed., rev., HTKNT 4:1 (Basel, Vienna, and Freiburg: Herder, 1967; Eng. transl.: *The Gospel According to St. John*, 1982); Cortès.

53. Brown.

54. Becker; R. Schnackenburg, *Das Johannesevangelium, III Teil: Kommentar zu Kap. 13–21*, HTKNT 4:3 (Basel, Vienna, and Freiburg: Herder, 1975). I have followed this position in preliminary studies, e.g., "The Theology and Provenance of John 15:1–17," *JBL* 101 (1982) 115–28; "John 15:18–16:4a, A First Addition to the Original Farewell Discourse?" *CBQ* 45 (1983) 210–30.

through the 1940s. Already by midcentury, however, the redactional approach was proving much more viable than its counterpart. As the appeal of the transpositional solution gradually declined, that of the redactional solution steadily increased. It is the dominant approach of the latter half of the century.

Two developments within this redactional solution—that parallel its vibrant growth and consolidation—should be noted. First, whereas in its beginnings the first major position (chapters 15–17 as one integral discourse) predominated, eventually the second major position (chapters 15–17 as a collection of different discourses) came to the fore. Second, whereas the first option within both major positions (an emphasis on the role of the evangelist) prevailed at the beginning, it gradually gave way to the other two options (an emphasis on the role of persons other than the evangelist), with the third option (a sole emphasis on the role of others) first appearing in the 1960s but then becoming frequent up to the present.

On the one hand, therefore, the redactional solution's beginnings again point to the rise of tradition and source criticisms in New Testament studies, as its emphasis on the intentions and design of the author of the text, its criticism of the present shape of the text, and its proposal to see the text as the final result of a gradual process of composition readily indicate. On the other hand, its own later developments begin to reflect the rise of redaction criticism, given the emphasis on theological disagreements and clashes among the various sections of the present speech, the multiplicity of discourses, the presence of a hand or hands other than that of the evangelist, and the varying historical circumstances underlying the various speeches. Of the two successors to the traditional historicizing approach, the redactional line of resolution was in the end able to offer the simplest and most persuasive solution to all the present difficulties of the text. All such difficulties only emerged as a result of a later expansion or series of expansions effected on the original farewell discourse for very specific reasons and not at all haphazardly. The major liability of the redactional approach has always been the fact that, in immediately seeking a solution away from the present text by means of a theoretical reconstruction of its process of composition, this approach basically ignores the final arrangement and disposition of the present text.

The three remaining lines of resolution—the symbolic, the unfinished, and the compositional—arose out of a dissatisfaction with, and in direct reaction to, both the transpositional and redactional approaches. Each alternative insisted on the integrity of the text, but none ever achieved the appeal of either successor to the traditional line of resolution.

With the symbolic or softening approach the text is not (for the most part) regarded as mimetic, though it remains untouchable. As in the historicizing approach, the present difficulties of the discourse are addressed in terms of the present position of the command of 14:31d. However, rather than being a marker indicating an actual change in location, such a command is now seen as symbolic—as signifying something other than what it at first appears—thus softening its seemingly intrusive character in the text. The interpreter, therefore, must supply this other symbolic meaning, which for the most part is taken to reflect the intentions and design of the author. Consequently, the present difficulties of the text lie not in the text but rather in the reader's inability to discern the specific meaning and message in question. The proposed solution for such difficulties is thus literary: this approach, by supplying the key to the symbolism taken from the narrative itself, makes all the difficulties disappear and reveals the full meaning of the text.

Recurring types of resolution again appear within this approach. For example, the command itself can be seen as possessing a metaphorical rather than a literal meaning, which meaning is then directly connected with the events beginning in chapter 18; thus, the command points not to an actual departure from the supper room at this point but rather to a spiritual journey to meet the ruler of the world, to an acceptance of the coming destiny that begins to unfold with the narration of chapter 18. As such, though distant from chapter 18, the command metaphorically anticipates these later developments.[55] Similarly, the command can also be seen as an example of a Johannine literary device, indicating perhaps the closure of a stage in the progressive instruction of the disciples; as an instance of misunderstanding, whereby a metaphorical declaration of Jesus is understood at a literal level by the audience, thus allowing for further teaching and instruction; or as a specific marker within a larger structural design for the Gospel as a whole.[56] Finally, the command can also be seen in terms of intertextuality as a deliberate reference to the Synoptic Gospels, either by way of providing a metaphorical version of Mark 14:42/Matt 26:46 or by way of an addition to the text, similarly based on this previous verse and meant to signal thereby the great similarity in content and context between the two Gospel traditions.[57]

55. See, e.g., Dodd; J. M. Reese, "Literary Structure of Jn. 13:31–14:31; 16:5–6, 16–33," CBQ 34 (1972) 321–31.
56. See, e.g., for the first opinion, Lightfoot; Morris. See, e.g., for the second opinion, H. Zimmermann, "Struktur und Aussageabsicht der johanneischen Abschiedsreden (Jo 13–17)," BibLeb 8 (1967) 279–90. See, e.g., for the third opinion, D. Deeks, "The Structure of the Fourth Gospel," NTS 15 (1968–69) 107–29.
57. See, e.g., for the first option, Hoskyns; Marsh. See, e.g., for the second option, P. Corssen, "Die Abschiedsreden Jesu in dem vierten Evangelium," ZNW 8 (1907) 125–42; Haenchen.

The appeal of the symbolic line of resolution was always limited. Most of its adherents were in the 1950s and 1960s, though its origins can be traced to the beginning of the century, and it continues to resurface occasionally. This line of resolution can be seen as a reaction to the handling of the text within the transpositional and redactional approaches, as indicated by its counterbalancing emphasis on the satisfactory shape of the present text, the need to search for a solution within the text itself, and the location of such a solution within the intent and design of the text's author. This approach's failure to develop a wider acceptance can be explained by its inherent weaknesses. First, it limited itself to an explanation of the command of 14:31d and ignored all other points of contention in the present speech. Similarly, its interpretations of the command were too focused to provide an adequate interpretation of the large segments of speech material involved. Finally, the proposals advanced proved to be too disparate, with different interpreters suggesting different symbolic keys for the proper interpretation of the command and farewell. This approach, however, did try to wrestle with the text as is, to offer a coherent interpretation of its present shape and composition, and to do so from the perspective of the Gospel narrative as a whole.

Far less common than the symbolic or softening approach is the unfinished line of resolution, for which again the text is not mimetic but does remain untouchable. This approach accepts the difficulties of the present text as real and inescapable, ruling out thereby any possibility of a resolution. It regards the present text as incomplete—as left in an unfinished state by its author—so it rules out in principle any type of resolution. Thus, in the present text one finds two alternative or complementary speeches corresponding to the two large blocks of material preceding and following the command of 14:31d, which were neither fully incorporated into the narrative itself nor satisfactorily connected with each other.[58] The unfinished line of resolution is therefore a strictly historical solution to the difficulties.

Like the symbolic approach, the unfinished line of resolution appeared mostly in the 1950s and 1960s, once again beginning in the early part of the century but with no known recent adherents. Its lack of appeal can be attributed perhaps to its attempt to make a virtue out of a vice. The difficulties of the present speech are not only real but were there from

---

58. See, e.g., A. Fauré, "Die alttestamentliche Zitate im 4. Evangelium und die Quellenscheidungshypothese," ZNW 21 (1922) 99–121; W. F. Howard, The Fourth Gospel in Recent Criticism and Interpretation, 4th ed., rev., ed. C. K. Barrett (London: Epworth Press, 1955); W. Grundmann, Zeugnis und Gestalt des Johannes-Evangelium, eine Studie zur denkerischen und gestalterischen Leistung des vierten Evangelisten, Arbeiten zur Theologie 7 (Stuttgart: Calwer Verlag, 1961); D. M. Smith, The Composition and Order of the Fourth Gospel: Bultmann's Literary Theory (New Haven: Yale University Press, 1967).

the beginning of the text and are thus beyond any type of resolution, so the existing document emerges as a truncated and defective message from an author to the intended audience. In the end, however, this virtue remains too much of a vice: the search for any satisfactory explanation of the present text is too readily abandoned and an admission of its present disorganized and incomplete state too readily accepted. With the rise of the redactional methodology, the unfinished approach lost whatever chance for survival it once had; this type of capitulation before the text readily yielded to an intensive search for its basic (theological) principles of composition and arrangement.

The final and least common type of resolution, the compositional approach, provides an interesting contrast to the unfinished approach. As in the two preceding lines of interpretation, in the compositional approach the text is not mimetic but remains untouchable. This approach argues that the difficulties in question are indeed real and unsolvable, but they should be seen as being the result of a conscious and deliberate decision of the author of the Gospel. Here, the vice is really not a vice but a virtue. Thus, the present text indeed contains two alternative versions of Jesus' farewell speech, as the many parallels between the two large blocks of speech material readily show, but the presence of these two versions side by side is now interpreted as follows: they reflect an oral tradition and were developed at the same time in the pre-Gospel stages of composition; they were subsequently included in the Gospel by its author; and thus they formed an integral part of the Gospel narrative from its beginnings. Consequently, the presence of these two versions by no means points to an unfinished or incomplete text, as the unfinished solution would have it. Quite the contrary, through the deliberate incorporation of these two alternative versions, the text of the Gospel was meant to be complete. The proposed solution to the present difficulties of the speech is clearly historical. Therefore, given the presence of the two versions (or two earlier forms thereof) in the Johannine tradition and, implicitly, the great force of that tradition upon its heirs, the author of the Gospel could not but have included both versions of Jesus' farewell side by side.

Although the compositional approach addresses the difficulties of the present speech, too many methodological and theoretical questions remain unanswered. For example,

- Despite the many and unquestionable parallels between these two large blocks of material, can they be accurately described as representing alternative versions of the same speech?
- Can the preexistence of these versions be justified? If so, what accounts for the presence of two such fixed versions of the same speech within the same pre-Gospel tradition?

- Is the force of the oral tradition so strong and dominant that both versions had to be included in the same work despite the many difficulties engendered—and acknowledged—as a result?
- Is the freedom of the author in the creation of the final work so limited as to be forced to include two alternative versions of the same speech side by side?

In the end, the failure of the compositional approach to address such issues explicitly, as well as its corresponding failure to provide a satisfactory literary rather than historical explanation for the present shape of the farewell, no doubt accounts for its sparse support in the literature.[59]

The overall direction of the scholarly discussion regarding the present shape and composition of the Johannine farewell speech of Jesus may be summarized as follows. A traditional, historicizing line of resolution was gradually displaced from its dominant position by two other approaches that appeared concurrently in the early decades of the century, the transpositional and the redactional. In the course of the century, especially around midcentury, several reactions to these now dominant lines of resolution began to emerge in the form of the symbolic and the unfinished approaches, with a still later emergence for the compositional approach. In the years immediately following midcentury, the redactional solution steadily dislodged the transpositional approach to become the sole dominant approach in the literature. This dominance has continued to the present, although with two important internal developments: (1) the increasing association of the second block of speech material—first by way of addition only, but then by way of composition as well—with a hand or hands other than that of the evangelist, thus leading to a multiplicity of authors, and (2) the growing identification of a multiplicity of speeches within this second block of material.

Jesus' Farewell Speech of John 13:31–17:26: Most Recent Resolutions

The preceding interpretive background aids in the evaluation of the most recent comprehensive analyses of Jesus' farewell speech in the Fourth Gospel. Four such works, all published in the 1980s, will be considered.

Two works appeared in 1981: a brief study by J. Painter and a monograph by Y. Simoens. The former represents a development within the scholarly discussion depicted above, whereas the latter proceeds in a new direction altogether—the integrative approach.

---

59. See, e.g., Barrett.

Painter's work remains solidly within the dominant redactional approach of the 1950s through the 1970s. However, while subscribing to one of the two major developments noted above within the redactional approach itself (the trend toward the acceptance of a multiplicity of discourses within the second block of speech material), Painter goes completely against the other such development (the trend toward the acceptance of a multiplicity of authors in the creation of the present discourse).[60]

On the one hand, Painter identifies three distinct units of discourse within the second block of material: 15:1–16:4a; 16:4b–33; and 17. He says that these three units have been added to the original farewell of 13:31–14:31 in precisely that sequence. Whereas the first two represent additional farewell speeches, the third has a different form and genre altogether and, as a result, does not figure prominently in the discussion.

This part of the proposal is grounded on two points. First, the proposed delineation of the different units of discourse is based on the recognition of three major *aporias,* or literary seams, within the present farewell speeches (14:31d; 16:4b; and 16:33), thus yielding the three large subdivisions within chapters 15–17 mentioned above. Second, the specific sequence of additions posited, which coincides with that of the units in the text, is based on the identification and comparison of different theological thrusts within these units. Such thrusts are largely determined through an analysis of the Paraclete sayings found within each unit (with the exception of chapter 17). These thrusts are also seen as addressing different critical situations in the Johannine community over its history, so the units themselves are said to preserve clear traces of this history. A further comparison of the different thrusts and underlying community situations in question shows that the teaching concerning the Paraclete undergoes several reformulations in keeping with the changing community situations. The comparison leads to the position that the present sequence of the units in the farewell reflects the historical development of the Johannine community, beginning with the original farewell of 13:31–14:31, continuing with the two additional farewells of 15:1–16:4a and 16:4b–33, and concluding with the prayer of chapter 17.

On the other hand, however, Painter opts for the earliest position within the redactional approach: the evangelist was entirely responsible for both the composition of all these units of discourse and their incorporation into the Gospel narrative; at the same time, the evangelist also relied on the original farewell discourse of 13:31–14:31 for the creation of the second and third farewells. This part of the proposal is grounded in a

60. Painter (p. 528) describes his own study as a further development of C. K. Barrett's proposal: in effect, rather than being alternative versions forced upon the author by the tradition, the present speech consists of several different versions developed by the same author.

synoptic comparison of all the farewell units in question. First, stylistic and "word-thematic" resemblances are so strong in these chapters that a single author is demanded. Second, such resemblances suggest that the later units of discourse, except for chapter 17, build directly upon the first and function as new versions of it.

Painter's proposal shares the advantages and disadvantages of the general redactional resolution. On the one hand, his proposal addresses the difficulties of the speech and gives them a simple, effective, and comprehensive resolution: the difficulties arise directly from a series of additions to an original farewell discourse. Indeed, Painter's proposal constitutes a sharp example of this approach, insofar as it accounts not only for the very presence of, and need for, such additions but also for the present shape of the discourse. He proposes that different crises in the Johannine community called forth different theological responses on the part of the author of the Gospel. These responses were formulated in the form of farewell speeches, were modeled to some extent on the first such speech, and were incorporated into the Gospel narrative accordingly. On the other hand, the explanation Painter provides for the present composition of the discourse is mostly historical, insofar as the additions took place in keeping with the historical development of the community, though with some literary dependence of the later units on the first. Consequently, Painter's explanation lacks an overall conception of the discourse's literary structure and development, so that the present discourse emerges as a convenient, though rather shapeless, repository for later, similar material.

The proposal itself has weaknesses. First, the formal delineation of the units of discourse is limited; the argumentation for the various seams or breaks needs a more secure and comprehensive grounding. Also, the synoptic comparison of the various units is restricted; a more thorough literary analysis is needed than the given enumeration of stylistic and word-thematic characteristics. Finally, the determination of the theological thrust of each unit remains too narrowly focused on one component, the Paraclete sayings; attention must be given to the composition of each unit as a whole.

Simoens's strikingly new direction of research goes beyond the six traditional lines of interpretation. He begins by pointing out that modern scholarly research has disregarded the literary structure and development of the present discourse. He proposes, therefore, to go directly against this interpretive consensus by suspending all talk of compositional difficulties, traditions, and redactions to examine how the present text coheres and functions as a whole.[61]

---

61. Simoens (pp. 2–3) uses the redactional approach as a point of departure for his own proposal.

Simoens proposes to accomplish this task by a structural analysis of the present discourse.[62] This first involves a search both for the stylistic structures of the discourse and the formal criteria of composition furnished by the text as a whole, with the most important criterion being that of inclusion or repetition at all levels of the text (major and minor, global and partial). The identification of these inclusions or patterns of repetition ultimately points to a process of composition grounded in two other compositional criteria, concentric symmetry and parallelism. In effect, throughout the speech, the more global structures are reproduced in the more partial structures, which thus appear as duplications of the former, though on a smaller scale. Such a structural analysis ultimately leads to the discovery of a highly complex and hierarchical organization for the entire discourse (13:1–17:26). Second, the task involves the use of these stylistic structures as interpretive structures. These structures not only allow for an understanding of the present text as a unified and coherent whole but also point to these chapters as an example of a covenant rather than a farewell, thus providing the present speech with its definitive form and arrangement.

This structural analysis ultimately yields a chiastic structure in the form of ABCDCBA for the speech as a whole, with the themes of love and glorification as its major axes:

1. The outermost components (A: 13:1–38; 17:1–26) introduce the themes of love and glorification. Whereas the former presents these themes in that order at the beginning and end, respectively, the latter inverts the order, with glorification at the beginning and love at the end.
2. The middle components (B: 14:1–31; 16:4–33) focus on the themes of Jesus' departure/hour (already introduced in 13:1 and 17:1 in direct association with love and glorification) and on the encouragement of the disciples in the face of this departure. Again, the order of presentation differs. Whereas chapter 16 presents these themes in that order at the beginning and at the end, respectively, chapter 14

62. Simoens (pp. 54–55) situates his own approach within both the larger field of literary criticism and the narrower field of biblical criticism. On the one hand, he associates the basic thrust and aims of his literary approach with the work of both P. Guiraud (*Essais de stylistique,* Initiation à la linguistique B:1 [Paris: Klincksieck, 1969]) and M. Riffaterre (*Essais de stylistique structurale,* Nouvelle bibliothèque scientifique [Paris: Flammarion, 1971]). On the other hand, Simoens points out a basic similarity between his approach to biblical criticism and the interpretive tradition of Roman Catholic scholars at the Pontifical Biblical Institute, e.g., A. Vanhoye ("La composition de Jn 5.19–30," in A. Descamps, A. de Halleux, eds. *Mélanges bibliques en hommage au R. P. Béda Rigaux* [Gembloux: Duculot 1970] 259–74; *La structure littéraire de l'Epître aux Hébreux,* 2d ed., SN 1 [Paris: Desclée de Brouwer, 1976]) and I. de la Potterie (*La verité dans saint Jean,* 2 vols., AB 73–74 [Rome: Pontifical Biblical Institute, 1977]).

inverts the order, with encouragement at the beginning and departure at the end.
3. The innermost components (C: 15:1–11; 15:18–16:3) focus on two contrasting pairs of themes, joy/hatred and abiding/persecution-exclusion, again with a difference in the order of presentation. Whereas 15:1–11 has abiding/joy, 15:18–16:3 has hatred/persecution-exclusion.
4. At the very center (D) lies 15:12–17, with its presentation of the command to love one another.[63]

Such a structural analysis also leads Simoens to characterize these chapters as an example of a covenant rather than a farewell speech, although he identifies the latter as a subgenre of the former. On the one hand, he questions its designation as a farewell on two counts: its contents go well beyond those of the farewell genre, and the formal characteristics of the genre identified within it are not sufficiently found in other farewell speeches. On the other hand, the discourse reveals a close correspondence with the formal characteristics of the covenant genre:[64] (1) a historical prologue (13:1–38), (2) the great command (14:1–31), (3) stipulations (15:1–16:3), (4) blessings and woes (16:4–33), and (5) a song (17:1–26).[65] The present discourse of chapters 13–17 constitutes, therefore, a distinctive reformulation of the ancient covenant in terms of the new command to love one another and the gift of the Spirit.

Simoens's call for a different approach points to a fundamental weakness of the redactional resolution, and indeed of all other lines of resolution. A view of the speech as a whole in literary rather than historical terms is simply not to be found; a concern for the diachronic dimension of the text has generally ruled out a corresponding concern for its synchronic dimension, for a view of the finished product as a coherent whole. Such a call, furthermore, only brackets all talk of difficulties, traditions, and redactions; the latter are by no means called into question or ruled out, though Simoens would insist on a thorough reformulation of the speech as a whole

---

63. For Simoens, the overall validity of this proposal is confirmed by his additional proposal to the effect that chap. 17, the second outermost component (A′), recapitulates within itself this chiastic structure of the discourse as a whole.
64. The formal characteristics are taken from J. L'Hour, *La morale de l'alliance*, Cahiers de la Revue Biblique 5 (Paris: J. Gabalda, 1966). Simoens also applies the formal characteristics used by K. Baltzer (*Das Bundesformular*, 2d ed., WMANT 4 [Neukirchen: Neukirchener Verlag, 1964]): dogmatic part (13:1–31), parenesis (14:1–31; 15:1–16:3), and eschatological part (16:4–33 and 17:1–26).
65. For Simoens, once again, the overall validity of this proposal is further confirmed by the fact that chap. 17, the final component within this example of a covenant, also recapitulates within itself the five formal characteristics of the genre.

along the stylistic and interpretive structures outlined. As such, there is no question that Simoens's study provides a much-needed corrective.

At the same time, the proposal is problematic. First, the overall chiastic structure is so complex that it obfuscates, or even renders impossible, the desired reading of these chapters as a unified and coherent whole. In fact, as the inclusions, concentric symmetry, and parallelisms grow more extensive and complicated, the project becomes less persuasive. Second, as a comparison of the texts in question readily shows, the relationship between the chiastic literary structure and the covenant interpretive structure lacks coherence and congruence; the seven divisions of the former do not compare well with the latter's five, and the very center of the former, 15:12–17, disappears into the third large section of the latter (the stipulations of 15:1–16:3). Third, the characterization of these chapters as an example of the covenant genre is not felicitous. Not only is the argumentation on behalf of such a choice in itself quite unconvincing but also the very position of these chapters in the narrative points to the presence of a farewell type-scene. Fourth, the conclusion of the structural and interpretive analysis leaves the impression of a marvelously constructed literary whole but gives little sense of its intended functions with regard to its intended audience, aside from that of providing a reformulation of the covenant tradition; in other words, the speech's character as a message from an author to an audience largely disappears. Finally, given the acceptance of the present difficulties of the speech as real and the further acceptance of a diachronic dimension for the present speech, one would have wished at the end for an integration of the extensive synchronic analysis and this other diachronic dimension.

The most recent phase of the discussion continues with two works from 1984: a brief study by J. Ph. Kaefer and a monograph by G. A. Kennedy. The former represents a development within the course of the traditional scholarly discussion, whereas the latter embarks, like Simoens, on a different direction of research altogether—the integrative approach.

Kaefer's work represents a further contribution to the dominant redactional resolution. The work also subscribes to the two major developments within this approach noted above. On the one hand, it forms part of the trend toward an acceptance of a multiplicity of authors in the creation of the present discourse. On the other hand, it provides a further development of the corresponding trend toward an acceptance of a multiplicity of discourses within the second block of speech material. In fact, Kaefer's work makes impossible all talk of large units of discourse.

Kaefer begins by delineating an overall redactional scenario for the composition of the Fourth Gospel that consists of three major stages, of which the last two are particularly important for the composition and development of the present farewell speech.[66] While the second stage, attributed to "the evangelist," consists of a fairly complete Gospel narrative with a focus on faith in the Son who came from above to give life, the third stage is described as a final redaction in which "the final redactor" confers upon the whole work a distinctive stamp with a twofold focus: (1) a self-presentation as the editor of the Gospel by means of the figure of the beloved disciple as a witness to the events reported and (2) the introduction of both a theology of incarnation and a theology of mutual love, which together witness to an antidocetic struggle in the community. Kaefer then defines his own purpose in this study as that of analyzing the present discourse in the light of this redactional scenario.

Such a redactional enterprise ultimately leads, however, to a much more detailed and complex picture of the third stage of composition. Although the final redaction is attributed to the work of one person (both by composition and addition to the narrative), the actual redactional process is described in terms of four different phases, reflecting four different theological developments and situations in the community. Furthermore, this fourfold redactional process no longer involves large units of discourse but rather much smaller and dispersed sections taken from the various chapters, including material from the first block itself. As such, while subscribing to the more guarded view of only one hand other than that of the evangelist in the composition and addition of chapters 15–17 (although extending its reach into the original discourse as well), Kaefer moves beyond an acceptance of a multiplicity of discourses to that of a multiplicity of redactions involving a wide number of different and dispersed sections from the present discourse. At the same time, Kaefer does argue that the redactional process has been carefully and artistically elaborated, ultimately yielding a coherent whole with a clear synchronic unity and structure; however, he does not pursue this dimension of the discourse.

Kaefer's redactional methodology can be characterized as largely conceptualist or intellectualist, though he employs some linguistic and stylistic considerations as well. The concern, therefore, is not so much to look for and establish units of speech, whether major or minor, that can in some way be described as self-contained or coherent but rather to undertake a thematic analysis of the discourse with a special focus on theological thrust and

66. This general scenario represents a critical adaptation of the redactional theories of G. Richter, "Fusswaschung" and "Deutung"; H. Thyen, "Joh. 13" and "Entwicklungen innerhalb der johanneischen Theologie und Kirche im Spiegel von Joh. 21 und der Lieblingsjüngertexte des Evangeliums," in *L'Evangile de Jean: Sources, rédaction, théologie,* ed. M. de Jonge, BETL 44 (Gembloux and Louvain: Louvain University Press, 1977) 259–99; W. Langbrandtner, *Weltferner Gott oder Gott der Liebe: Der Ketzerstreit in der johanneischen Kirche: Eine exegetisch-religionsgeschichtliche Untersuchung mit Berücksichtigung der koptisch-gnostischen Texte aus Nag-Hammadi,* BET 6 (Bern: Lang, 1976).

development. Therefore, verses with a similar theological thrust—whether one, several, or many—are gathered into larger collections that are said to represent redactional stages added to the Gospel as specific theological responses to changes in the situation of the community.

The proposed redactional process is described as follows. First, the original farewell discourse—in itself encompassing four different redactional stages—consisted of 13:31–33; 14:1–14, 16–19, 22–31; 17:1–2, 4–5. Its main purpose was to console a community deeply troubled by Jesus' departure by affirming his continued presence among the disciples, first explaining it from the point of view of his relationship to the Father and then describing it from the point of view of his relationship to the disciples. Second, the final redaction involved four phases, each arranged in terms of two groupings. In each grouping a beginning phase introduces or resumes a question or problem, which then receives a much more detailed and definitive solution in the subsequent phase. In each grouping, therefore, the first phase also precedes the second. Moreover, the first grouping also precedes the second.

The main lines of this final redaction can be summarized as follows. The first grouping (16:4b–11, 16–23a) is concerned with the consolation of the disciples in the face of Jesus' departure, and it has been motivated by a resurgence of the problem regarding Jesus' absence first confronted in the original farewell. Whereas in the first phase (R1: 16:4b–11) the redactor reinterprets the theological position of the original farewell, in the second phase (R2: 16:16–23a) a definitive solution to this problem is provided. The second grouping (15:1–17, 18–25, 26–27; 16:1–4a, 12–15, 23b–33; 17:3, 6–26) is concerned with the disciples' gradual process of coming to understand Jesus' revelation. Whereas in the third phase (R3: 15:18–25; 16:1–4a, 12–15, 23b–33) the disciples are portrayed as still not capable of understanding Jesus' revelation, in the fourth phase (R4: 15:1–17, 26–27; 17:3, 6–26) they are presented as fully capable of understanding this revelation and indeed of extending it to the whole world. The final redaction also extends to the original discourse. Whereas 13:34–35 and 14:21 belong to the first phase (R1), 13:36–38, 14:15, and 14:20 belong to the fourth phase (R4).

Kaefer's proposal shares the advantages and disadvantages of any redactional solution. To be sure, he addresses and resolves the difficulties of the discourse by means of a theory of additions to an original discourse. The proposal, however, is not as sharp as Painter's. Although Kaefer also explains the present shape of the discourse in terms of specific responses to specific developments in the Johannine community, he does not provide a satisfactory explanation for either the present dispersal of texts belonging to the same response or redactional phase or the nature of the community developments in question. He does not address the present arrangement of the various texts and phases in question, and he presents the developments that brought about such responses in either too monolithic or too general a fashion. At the same time, though an interpretation of the present discourse as a coherent and unified whole is granted explicitly, the final explanation of its present structure and development remains throughout at a strictly historical level. Again, Kaefer's proposal is not as sharp as Painter's. Aside from certain linguistic and stylistic considerations, Kaefer gives even less attention to the literary relationships of the different redactional phases to one another or to the original discourse.

Kaefer's proposal also presents some difficulties of its own. First, the texts assigned to the various phases of the redaction are not properly delineated or analyzed as self-contained and coherent literary units; consequently, their separation from their immediate contexts appears arbitrary throughout, and the resulting texts themselves look truncated. Second, the thematic analysis of these texts is ultimately too conceptual or intellectualist, so the entire discussion becomes too narrowly focused on the theological thrusts of the various units in question, the determination of which is also in turn too narrowly based on one major theological theme present within each text. In the end, the present discourse emerges once again as a convenient, though even more shapeless, repository for later, similar material.

Kennedy's work also represents a strikingly new direction of research, going completely beyond the six traditional types of resolution.[67] The emphasis is again exclusively on the present discourse as a unified and coherent whole rather than on its various compositional difficulties, traditions, and redactions. As a student of classical rhetorical theory, however, Kennedy reads the New Testament texts from a rhetorical perspective. Thus, he begins by describing the basic presuppositions, aims, and methodology of rhetorical criticism and then turns to an introductory rhetorical analysis of various texts from the New Testament, including the Johannine farewell.

With regard to its basic presuppositions and aims, rhetorical criticism has three main interests: (1) the text as it presently stands, whether that be the work of one author or the product of revision; (2) the author's or editor's overall intent to persuade an audience as revealed through the finished text; and (3) the perception of this text as a whole by an audience of near contemporaries—in this case an audience of inhabitants of a Greek-speaking world in which rhetoric not only was the core subject of formal education but also informed all cultural preconceptions about appropriate discourse. From the point of view of the Johannine farewell, such basic aims may be more specifically described as follows: (1) a focus on chapters 13–17 as a large

67. G. A. Kennedy, *New Testament Interpretation through Rhetorical Criticism* (Chapel Hill: University of North Carolina Press, 1984) 73–85.

but proper rhetorical unit, within which smaller rhetorical units (for example, chapters 14, 15–17) can also be distinguished and analyzed in their own right; and (2) an analysis of this large unit as a self-contained and coherent whole, which some speaker of Greek, at some time, arranged in what seemed an effective and appropriate sequence and which was perceived as such by the intended audience as well.

With regard to methodology, rhetorical criticism begins with an identification of the given unit's rhetorical situation, rhetorical problem, and dominant rhetorical species. From the point of view of the Johannine farewell, this procedure can be described as follows. First, chapter 13 provides the rhetorical situation: the last meal of Jesus with his disciples, during which the disciples display much confusion and distress, while Jesus shows a corresponding concern for their limited understanding of his identity and mission.[68] Second, the rhetorical problem within such a situation becomes precisely that of overcoming such distress and limited understanding on the part of the disciples through the farewell speech to follow.[69] Third, this farewell of Jesus to his confused and distressed disciples represents an example of epideictic rhetoric—an attempt by an author to persuade an audience to hold or reaffirm some point of view in the present as the basis for a general policy of action, with a basic argument involving a change of attitude or a deepening of values.[70]

68. Every rhetorical situation is characterized by an actual or potential exigence, namely, a specific set of circumstances under which an individual is called upon to make a response; this response is conditioned by the situation and has some possibility of affecting the situation or its consequences (Kennedy, *Interpretation*, 34–35).

69. The rhetorical problem is defined as that overriding problem that the speaker faces in a rhetorical situation. At this point, Kennedy (*Interpretation*, 78) introduces too sharp a distinction between the problem faced by Jesus as the speaker and that faced by the evangelist as author. Thus, whereas the former confronts distress and limited understanding among his disciples, the latter is faced with how to present the scene with both pathos and glory. This distinction in effect presents Jesus' problem from an essentially historical perspective (the problem of Jesus of Nazareth with regard to his first disciples) and the author's problem as primarily artistic (as a problem affecting the composition of a prosopopoeia—a rhetorical re-creation of what Jesus might have said under the circumstances, a form practiced in the rhetorical schools and later employed in literary works). However, these two rhetorical problems may be brought much closer together if the problem Jesus faced is seen from a literary perspective (the problem of the character Jesus in the developing plot of the narrative) and thus as reflecting a similar problem faced by the implied author with regard to the implied readers. As such, in and through the re-creation of this speech, the implied author would also be directly addressing the implied readers and the problem in question. For implied author and readers, see R. A. Culpepper, *Anatomy of the Fourth Gospel: A Study in Literary Design*, Foundations and Facets (Philadelphia: Fortress, 1983) 15–18, 203–28; J. L. Staley, *The Print's First Kiss: A Rhetorical Investigation of the Implied Reader in the Fourth Gospel*, SBLDS 82 (Atlanta: Scholars Press, 1988) 21–37.

70. See Kennedy, *Interpretation*, 19–25. In a single speech more than one species may be used, thus making the definition of the species as a whole difficult to determine at times. For the most part, however, one species is usually dominant and reflects the author's fundamental purpose in speaking or writing.

More specifically, given Jesus' concern for the disciples' attitudes, feelings, and beliefs at the time of his departure from this world, this farewell is further identified as an example of a paramythetic, or speech of consolation, usually incorporated into a funeral oration but also present in consolatory speeches by one about to die. Kennedy cautiously presents such a designation, however, as probable and not conclusive. Furthermore, Kennedy says that although the speech does contain other elements not belonging to the epideictic species (for example, the giving of a new commandment and the disclosure of the difficulties that the disciples will encounter in the future), such elements are subordinated throughout to the disciples' understanding of the present situation of Jesus' departure and their reaction to it.

After such initial identifications, the method proceeds with an analysis of the rhetorical arrangement of the unit in question. In this regard epideictic rhetoric is said to be marked by two further characteristics: (1) a tendency toward amplification, with a fondness for ornamentation and a tolerance of description and digression, and (2) a threefold arrangement consisting of a proem or exordium, a main body usually devoted to an orderly sequence of amplified topics, and an epilogue or peroration (though, as is the case here, a narration and proposition may also be included).[71] Both of these traits can be observed in the overall structure and development proposed for the Johannine farewell:

1. The proem (13:1) is built on five material topics that are constantly restated in different words, different order, and different form in the remainder of the unit: Jesus' relationship to the Father, Jesus' departure, the world, love, and Jesus' relationship to the disciples.
2. A narration (13:2-30) is included and is important for a presentation of the rhetorical situation, as well as for an understanding of the discourse to follow. Within the narration three of the previous topics can be found: Jesus' relationship to the father, Jesus' departure, and Jesus' relationship to the disciples.
3. A proposition (13:31-38) is also included; it repeats all five topics introduced in the proem in the same order.
4. The main body (14:1-16:28) undertakes the consolation of the disciples by means of an extended amplification of the five topics presented

71. *Rhetorical arrangement* concerns the subdivisions of the text, the persuasive effect of these parts, and how they work together to some unified purpose in a rhetorical situation. Thus, it deals with the conventional structure of oratory, of which epideictic, with its usual threefold division, represents the simplest form. *Amplification* refers to the development of the basic thesis by means of the topics the author has chosen to employ; *topics*, in turn, refers to the ideas or facts to be said about the subject. In the case of the Johannine farewell, the topics are material, namely, the various propositions or definitions offered by the author. See Kennedy, *Interpretation*, 20-24.

in the proem and recapitulated in the proposition. This amplification of all five topics occurs in both chapter 14 and chapters 15–16.

5. Two epilogues (16:29–33; 17) are found. The former provides a conclusion to the main body, and the latter provides a conclusion to the entire rhetorical unit. The latter also recapitulates all five topics and provides an emotional fulfillment for the entire passage.

Kennedy singles out the repetitiveness of the entire discourse as its most striking rhetorical feature; in effect, the present farewell is almost entirely constructed out of five topics that are constantly restated from beginning to end in a wide variety of ways, while following a definite and effective sequential arrangement (introduction in the proem, partial development in the narration, complete recapitulation in the proposition, complete and extensive amplification in the main body, and final and complete recapitulation in the second epilogue). At the end, Kennedy does acknowledge that this repetitiveness may be due, in part, to the presence of editorial activity, since the present discourse does contain undeniable literary difficulties, elements of an epilogue at 14:25–31, self-contained rhetorical units in both chapters 14 and 15–16, and development of all five topics in both of these smaller rhetorical units. In fact, he even suggests a rhetorical motive for this editorial activity: the addition of the second block of speech material to the original discourse was meant to provide a deeper understanding of the topics enunciated in chapter 13 and already amplified in chapter 14.

The proposal has much to commend itself. Again, Kennedy's call for a different approach reaffirms the fundamental weakness of the redactional approach, as well as of all other traditional types of resolution: the concern for the diachronic dimension of the text totally eclipses a similar concern for its synchronic dimension, with the result that a conception of the present farewell as a unified and coherent whole is largely bypassed in the literature. Moreover, the rhetorical approach clearly does not reject, but rather fully accepts, the presence of literary difficulties, traditions, and redactions in the present farewell; the latter, however, are methodologically bracketed in favor of a view of the whole. Finally, this approach strongly emphasizes the twofold character of the text as both an artistic product and a concrete form of communication between an author and an audience, with both elements informing one another at a fundamental level.

Kennedy's proposal also reveals difficulties, which in part arise out of the global nature of the rhetorical analysis undertaken. Thus, despite the explicit focus on the finished product, the open acknowledgment of a diachronic dimension in the text does call for some sort of explanation, some sort of integration into the overall synchronic interpretation of the present text; otherwise, although the present arrangement of the speech as a whole is adequately explained, its salient difficulties remain unattended. Similarly, the given conception of the present discourse in terms of a continued amplification of five central topics from beginning to end does not provide an adequate explanation of its present literary structure and arrangement. Although the centrality of these five topics is made clear thereby, too much remains unsaid—too much is assumed in the delineation of the various units of discourse outlined, whether with regard to their own unity and development or their relationships to one another within the whole. Finally, the proposed view of the discourse as an exercise in the consolation of the disciples in the face of their distress and confusion, while true in part, is much too general and leaves too much unsaid. In effect, a far more concrete picture of both the basic functions of the speech and its underlying rhetorical situation is needed if its overall aims and goals are to be understood.

The most recent discussion of the Johannine farewell discourse can be summarized in terms of two distinctive developments. On the one hand, the dominance of the redactional type of resolution, firmly in place since mid-century, clearly continues. While the earlier trend toward an acceptance of a multiplicity of discourses within chapters 15–17 is clearly followed as well, the corresponding trend toward an acceptance of a multiplicity of authors in the creation of the present discourse is either abandoned (Painter) or restricted (Kaefer). Within the former trend, furthermore, two other developments should be noted. First, a great deal of emphasis is placed on the various units of discourse in question as specific responses to critical theological developments in the community (Painter). Second, the multiplicity of large units of discourse yields to a multiplicity of redactions, each consisting of a number of brief and dispersed units of discourse (Kaefer). On the other hand, the redactional approach clearly has been severely criticized for its almost exclusive focus on the diachronic dimension of the text. Such criticism—reflecting the increasing influence of literary criticism within New Testament studies since the mid-1970s—grants the presence of editorial activity but calls instead for a radically changed focus on the shape of the discourse as it presently stands, on the synchronic dimension of the text, either by way of structural analysis (Simoens) or rhetorical criticism (Kennedy).[72] Such criticism gives rise, in effect, to a seventh general line of resolution—the integrative approach.

72. Whereas both proposals have much in common, they also differ in several important respects. First, both are concerned with the overall structure of the farewell scene: whereas Simoens emphasizes the role of inclusions in this regard, Kennedy stresses that of topics. Second, both are also concerned with the relationship between genre and structure: whereas Simoens sees it in terms of covenant, Kennedy opts for seeing it as a consolatory discourse of

AIMS AND METHODOLOGY

The preceding overview of the scholarly literature provides a proper context within which to describe the approach to the Johannine farewell
discourse used in the present study. First, of the six traditional lines of
resolution, only the redactional approach, the dominant approach of the
last forty years or so, remains at all viable within the present climate and
direction of New Testament studies. At the same time, as some of the most
recent developments have shown, the established dominance and continued viability of the redactional approach no longer stand as secure and
unassailable as they once did. Given this approach's failure to deal with
the present shape and arrangement of the farewell discourse from a literary rather than a historical perspective, it is now justifiably seen as much
too narrow and restrictive in vision and scope, as overly concerned with
the excavative dimensions of the text while unconcerned with its present
literary structure and development.

The present text of the farewell speech undoubtedly did represent to
someone, somewhere, at some time, not only a unified and coherent literary
whole but also a proper and meaningful form of communication with an
audience—an artistic and strategic whole. This is a fundamental aspect of
the farewell that the redactional resolution has largely disregarded. In fact,
this resolution has moved increasingly toward ever greater diffusion rather
than coherence, with a logical outcome in the work of Kaefer. There exists,
therefore, an unquestionable need for a radical change in basic orientation,
for a view of the present speech as an artistic and strategic whole—in short,
for a continued development of the integrative approach. At the same time,
such a change in orientation should come to terms with the many difficulties posed by the present discourse. As the very pointed remarks of both
Simoens and Kennedy show, such difficulties do not yield to any sort of
definitive resolution within a properly integrative approach to the speech
but rather continue.

From a methodological point of view, it is valid to bypass such difficulties in order to attain a sense of the whole, as both Simoens and
Kennedy have opted to do; this is especially true where such a sense of the
whole has been largely nonexistent and unattractive. The meaning of
the text as it presently stands is by no means directly dependent on an

---

one about to die. Third, both are further concerned with the basic functions of the present
discourse in the light of its structure and genre: whereas Simoens sees the discourse as
establishing a new covenant in terms of the new command of love for one another, Kennedy
sees it as an attempt to overcome a rhetorical situation marked by sharp confusion and
distress on the part of the disciples with regard to Jesus' departure. Perhaps the best way to
summarize this relationship is in terms of literary vis-à-vis rhetorical criticism: whereas
Simoens stresses the character of the text as a highly artistic product, Kennedy stresses above
all its character as a means of persuasion.

understanding of its process of growth and composition; such a historical vision would be of great help with regard to an understanding of the gradual formation of the text but not with regard to an understanding of its present shape and arrangement. In the end, however, given the nature and scope of the text's present difficulties, a critical analysis of these chapters would benefit immensely from an approach that would address both the synchronic and diachronic dimensions. It seems to me that the present farewell both constitutes a unified and coherent whole and points to a process of accretion and expansion. As the century comes to a close, therefore, the integrative approach must be pursued in any number of ways and the redactional question reexamined from within such integrative standpoints.

The present study aims, therefore, to be both synchronic and diachronic in its approach to the present text of the farewell. Although in keeping with the recent calls for an integrative perspective, this study's primary emphasis will be on the synchronic dimension of the speech, it will not abandon altogether the diachronic dimension. As such, it is fully within the integrative line of resolution, but with a subordinate redactional interest as well. As already mentioned, this approach will entail a close reading of the text, involving a thorough and detailed literary-rhetorical analysis of the speech in terms of its constitutive units and in the light of the ongoing scholarly discussion.

This approach will involve two stages. The first stage will encompass chapters 2 through 5 and will consist of four steps within each chapter: delineation of the units of discourse, literary structure and development of the units of discourse, literary-rhetorical analysis of the units of discourse, and strategic concerns and aims of the units of discourse. The second stage will be pursued in chapter 6 and will consist of two parts: the synchronic dimension of the farewell and the diachronic dimension of the farewell.

Delineation of the Units of Discourse

Given the length of the farewell discourse, it is necessary to begin with a determination of its major units before a sense of the whole—of the relationship of these units to one another—can emerge.[73] Thus, the first stage in this study will involve a division of the present discourse into its major constitutive units, that is, units of discourse that, though parts of the greater whole, can also be considered in and of themselves self-contained and coherent wholes. The formal delineation of these units will take place

---

73. This is also the first step undertaken by both Simoens (pp. 52–80) and Kennedy (*Interpretation*, 33–34, 77–78). Whereas Simoens depends largely on the use of inclusion, Kennedy stresses above all signs of opening and closure. The criteria employed in the present study include such concerns but go beyond them as well. In effect, the greater the number and variety of criteria at work, the more secure the delimitation becomes.

at the beginning of chapters 2 through 5 and will depend on a number of different, though interrelated, criteria.

The specifics of these criteria will be set forth within each chapter, but the criteria as such can be outlined as follows:

- A sense of finality or conclusion, as well as a sense of a new departure or beginning.
- The use of a recurring formula, "These things I have said to you," as a literary marker of conclusion throughout the speech (14:25; 15:11; 16:1, 4a, 6, 25, 33).
- The presence of different and exclusive thematic concerns in different sections of the speech, which will be referred to as the controlling and overarching themes within such sections.
- Variations in the mode of development or presentation, specifically with regard to the presence or absence of the motif of conversation or dialogue.
- Differences in the tone of Jesus' address to the disciples.
- Differences in the temporal standpoint of Jesus as speaker of the discourse.

It is thus through the artful combination of such different general criteria—of a rhetorical, stylistic, thematic, and structural character—that the formal delineation of the boundaries for the various units of discourse will take place. Such a formal delineation will find ultimate confirmation and reinforcement in the course of the various steps that follow in the first stage (chapters 2 through 5). Thus, the units of discourse outlined should emerge as unified and coherent in terms of a comprehensive literary structure and development, a basic overall strategy, and a plausible rhetorical situation reflected in and addressed by such an artistic and strategic response. In each case, these constitutive units of discourse will be determined in full dialogue with previous scholarly discussion.

Literary Structure and Development of the Units of Discourse

The formal delineation of each major unit of discourse will be followed by a determination of its overall literary structure and development, which in turn will provide an initial confirmation of the outermost boundaries outlined in the first step.[74] In other words, for each proposed unit of discourse

---

74. For Simoens this step is included within the first step of formal delineation (pp. 52–80; see esp. pp. 77–80); for Kennedy it becomes part of the final step, namely, the analysis of the rhetorical arrangement of the material (*Interpretation*, 37–38, 78–85). For Simoens the main criterion continues to be that of inclusion. For Kennedy two such criteria can be identified: the

to function as a unified and coherent artistic whole, there must be a system of organization affecting all of its contents, all that lies between the two outermost boundaries; in some definite and demonstrable way, therefore, this intervening material must constitute a fully integrated whole. Such a system of organization will of course exhibit a wide variety of compositional principles or patterns, ranging from the most general to the very local, so one can speak in terms of a macrostructure and a microstructure in each unit. This second methodological step will be concerned with the macrostructure of each unit, that is, with the overall compositional principles or patterns that govern the unit as a whole. In effect, given the presence within each unit of definite overarching and controlling themes, this second step will examine how these dominant and exclusive thematic concerns are arranged and developed in each unit.

Central to a determination of the principles or patterns of organization and development, whether in terms of macrostructure or microstructure, is the frequent use of repetition in ancient narrative. Although operative in all forms of narrative and at all times in its very long literary history—from the heroic epic of Homer to the continuing dominance of the novel at the close of the twentieth century—the use of repetition is particularly salient and important in ancient narrative, including both Greco-Roman and biblical narrative. Such prominence in ancient narrative is largely due to the oral dimension of these narratives, whether by way of origins (descent from oral tradition) or purpose (to be read out loud to an audience). This phenomenon of repetition consists of two basic dimensions that will be of immediate help in coming to terms with both the macrostructure and the microstructure of each unit of discourse; again, Alter's work on biblical narrative provides a succinct and insightful exposition of this twofold dimension of repetition in ancient narrative.[75]

On the one hand, biblical narrative is said to be marked by an elaborately integrated system of repetitions of great variety and complexity. Such a system of repetitions involves the actual recurrence of individual phonemes, words, and short phrases, as well as the similar recurrence of images, ideas, actions, scenes, and series of scenes that form part of the world of the narrative that the reader reconstructs, although they are not

linear construction of ancient speeches, here with a fivefold development, and the identification and amplification of topics. In this study the main criterion will be that of repetition in general, thus encompassing all of the preceding criteria within a much wider field of patterns of repetition.

75. Alter, Narrative, 88–113. See also R. Scholes and R. Kellogg, The Nature of Narrative (London: Oxford University Press, 1966) esp. 17–56; B. F. Kawin, Telling It Again and Again: Repetition in Film and Literature (Ithaca: Cornell University Press, 1972); J. Hillis Miller, Fiction and Repetition: Seven English Novels (Cambridge, Mass.: Harvard University Press, 1982) 1–21.

necessarily part of its verbal texture.[76] Both kinds of repetitions are often
used together to reinforce each other and produce a concerted whole. On
the other hand, such a system of repetitions is also said to involve a wide
use of variation that not only serves stylistic purposes but often carries as
well important strategic connotations. Again, both dimensions of repetition can be extremely helpful in coming to terms with the literary structure and development of the Johannine farewell speech and its various
major units. Indeed, one of the most distinctive characteristics of this
farewell speech—as well as of the Gospel as a whole—is its highly repetitive character: from beginning to end one finds a recurrence of the same
general terminology, key words, phrases, themes, and motifs. At the same
time, such repetition also involves a wide range of stylistic and strategic
variations; from beginning to end one also finds ever new and changing
combinations of the same general terminology, key words, phrases,
themes, and motifs. As in biblical and ancient narrative, therefore, the use
of repetition in the farewell speech is by no means exclusively verbatim
(though it can be) but rather fluid and creative from different perspectives, both verbal and conceptual.

Given Alter's own focus on phrasal repetition, he is not much concerned
with the use of repetition as an interpretive key to the structuration and
development of narrative scenes and narrative episodes. However, these
two highly interrelated dimensions of repetition can indeed serve as such a
key, especially in a writing like the Gospel of John and in a narrative unit
such as that of the farewell speech, where repetition is so evident. Indeed,
within New Testament studies in general the use of formal patterns of repetition with regard to literary structure and development recently has been
the focus of several integrative approaches to texts of varying length and
complexity.[77] The present study, therefore, will explore the use of repetition as a means of determining both the macrostructure and microstructure of each proposed unit of discourse within the present farewell—and

76. Alter, *Narrative*, 91–97. A helpful classification of such patterns of repetition is also
provided, ranging from the most unitary to the most composite: key words (including cognates,
phonetic relatives, synonymity, and antonymity), motifs, themes, phrases, sequence of actions,
and type-scenes.
77. One can point to three different examples of such an approach. The first is the architectural analysis of C. H. Talbert on the whole of Luke-Acts (*Literary Patterns, Theological
Themes, and the Genre of Luke-Acts*, SBLMS 20 [Atlanta: Scholars Press, 1974] esp. 1–14,
67–82). The second example is the literary-rhetorical analysis of J. Dewey on Mark 2:1–3:6
(*Markan Public Debate, Literary Technique, Concentric Structure, and Theology in Mark 2:1–
3:6*, SBLDS 48 [Atlanta: Scholars Press, 1980] esp. 5–39). The third example is the literary-
structural approach associated with the Pontifical Biblical Institute in Rome and applied to a
wide number of different texts; see n. 62 above. For a very recent reading of the entire Gospel
from this particular perspective, see G. Mlakuzhyil, *The Christocentric Literary Structure of
the Fourth Gospel*, AB 117 (Rome: Pontifical Biblical Institute, 1987), from whom I have
borrowed the term *literary-structural* to describe the approach as a whole.

ultimately as a way to determine the present structure and development of the farewell as a whole.[78]

This second step, therefore, will outline the overall principles or patterns of repetition present within each unit of discourse. It also will analyze how such patterns delineate the major structural sections of the unit and their relationship to one another. Such analysis again will be in dialogue with previous proposals in the scholarly literature concerning structuration and development. Chapters 2 through 5 will each include an outline of the structure proposed for each unit of discourse. This will clarify how each unit has been constructed and developed as an artistic whole.

Literary-Rhetorical Analysis of the Units of Discourse

The third step follows directly from the second and involves a number of interrelated concerns, all of which in the end provide additional confirmation concerning the formal delineation of the outermost boundaries for each unit of discourse posited within the first step above.

To begin with, the preceding concern for the macrostructure of each unit yields logically to a similar concern for the microstructure.[79] Just as each proposed unit of discourse must function as a unified and coherent artistic whole, so must each of its constitutive and interrelated major sections outlined in the delineation of its macrostructure. In other words, each major section of the unit must also demonstrably display a system of organization encompassing all of the material within its own boundaries in an integrated whole. Thus, what the second step sets out to do in bold and general strokes, this third step proceeds to fill in with fine lines and figures. Consequently, this third step will be directly concerned, in part, with the more local compositional patterns and principles that govern the basic subdivisions of each unit.[80] As already indicated in the previous section, the use of repetition in both of its fundamental dimensions will be essential in determining the literary structure and development of each major section and, hence, the microstructure of each unit.

78. Although the precise nomenclature varies, these formal structural patterns of repetition are well known. For a helpful classification of such patterns of repetition in New Testament texts, see, e.g., J. Dewey, *Debate*, 31–37; Mlakuzhyil, *Structure*, 87–121, esp. 93–97, 106–11.
79. The concern for microstructure is prominent in Simoens's work, following immediately upon the search for the macrostructure; the use of inclusion continues to be by far the main criterion used. The concern for microstructure is equally prominent in Kennedy's work, though allowance has to be made for the more limited nature of his project. Such a concern forms part of his last methodological step, the analysis of the rhetorical arrangement, and this concern is carried out at the same time as the delineation of the macrostructure. The main criterion employed is the use of rhetorical figures.
80. Such subdivisions will be characterized as follows, in descending order: main sections, subsections, and subunits.

A first purpose of this third step, therefore, is to outline the more local patterns or principles of repetition to be found within each major section and to examine how such patterns mark off the structure of each major section and direct its development from beginning to end. Again, the structural outline to each of the next four chapters will aid in an analysis of how each unit has been put together and developed as an artistic whole.

This first concern for literary structure and development will be accompanied by a further concern for the verbal texture of each unit, so the formal focus on structure and design is balanced by a corresponding focus on expression and coloring. Thus, the analysis of each unit of discourse will also focus, whenever appropriate and to the point, on such elements of composition as grammatical forms and syntactic constructions; the use of placement, tone, and emphasis; and the employment of literary devices and rhetorical figures. In effect, each unit of discourse can only emerge as a fully unified and coherent artistic whole if both its structural or architectural dimension and its stylistic or expressive dimension are seen as fundamentally interrelated and interdependent, as being in close unison with each other.[81]

A third, related concern addresses the question of intertextuality from the point of view of the linear character of the present farewell speech, the linear sequence and succession of its constitutive major units. Consequently, this study will pay particular attention to the verbal and conceptual relationships among the various units of discourse in the course of the ongoing speech; these relationships will of course increase in number and complexity as the units succeed one another. Although for purposes of analysis this work divides the speech into its constitutive units, the discussion will clarify the developing interrelationships within the speech itself—the relationships of the various units to one another.

A final concern is also directly related to the previous three and focuses on the question of intertextuality from the point of view of the Gospel as a whole. The present farewell speech forms part not only of a larger narrative scene of farewell but also of a much longer biographical narrative tracing the life of Jesus of Nazareth, the Word of God, from his preexistence in the world of the Father to his final farewell (resurrection appearances) before his triumphal ascent or return to the world of the Father. As such, this study will pay particular attention as well to the linguistic and conceptual relationships between the various units of the farewell speech and the remainder of the Gospel narrative. This will further emphasize the individual character of each unit of discourse.

---

81. For Simoens, such stylistic concerns are not as important as, and remain completely subordinated to, the structural analysis. For Kennedy, such concerns are important and do form part, once again, of the final step regarding the rhetorical arrangement of the unit; however, due to the limited nature of his inquiry, such concerns do not figure prominently in his own analysis of the speech.

Strategic Concerns and Aims of
the Units of Discourse

Whereas the second and third steps are primarily concerned with each unit of discourse as a coherent artistic whole, the fourth and final step will address the character of each unit as a coherent strategic whole. In other words, this study also regards each unit of discourse as a concrete form of communication between two parties, as conveying a message from one party to the other, so that the artistic character of each unit is immediately and intrinsically related thereby to its strategic character— with each artistic whole constituting a strategic whole.[82] As such, this fourth step will provide final confirmation for the formal delineation of the outermost boundaries of the various units undertaken in the first step.

This form of communication takes place on two distinct levels.[83] The first is the literary level of the narrative plot itself, with its own rhetorical exigence, the farewell address of the main character (Jesus) to a corporate character (the group of his true followers or disciples). In view of his forthcoming death and departure from this world, the present situation of the group at the time of the speech itself, and their envisioned situation as those left behind in the world, Jesus proceeds to address them with a wide variety of concerns and aims in this long speech, concerns and aims that differ considerably from unit to unit. The second level is the extraliterary level of author and intended audience—the purpose behind the specific reconstruction of such a historical scene involving Jesus and his earliest disciples in a work written for a much later group of disciples. This second level involves, of course, the thorny and complex issues of the relationship between literature and society: Is there a much wider message to the intended audience in and through the construction of such a scene, with such a specific message of farewell on the part of the departing Jesus? Are the readers, the listeners, or both being explicitly addressed in and through the character of the earliest disciples as present or potential disciples of Jesus? Does such a message reflect and address the situation of this much later group of Christian disciples so that their sociohistorical situation provides the fundamental exigence being addressed by this speech, which situation can be discerned by means of the very nature of the address itself?

---

82. This aspect is also important for both Simoens and Kennedy. For Simoens, this step represents the final step of the investigation, in which the form and purpose of the scene as a reformulation of the covenant play a major role (pp. 200–49). For Kennedy this step represents the second, third, and fourth steps of the investigation, in which the rhetorical situation, the rhetorical problem, and the rhetorical species are pursued (*Interpretation*, 35–37, 73–78).

83. See n. 69 above.

Given that this Gospel has an explicit persuasive dimension—most evident perhaps in the climactic saying of Jesus of 20:29, as well as in the explicit statement of purpose the narrator provides in 20:30–31—this study regards these two levels of communication as highly interrelated. In this speech of farewell, in and through the group character of the assembled disciples, a much wider and later circle of disciples is being addressed as well, so the sociohistorical situation of the latter is seen as in some way reflected in, and addressed by, this speech. To be sure, the reconstruction of such a situation and the proposed match between situation and address—without any external controls whatsoever—remains perforce very problematic. Nevertheless, despite the inherent difficulties involved, following this line of direction as well is both proper and fruitful. In so doing, however, it is more appropriate to speak of the implied author and the implied readers—the sum total of what can be inferred from the text itself about the author and the readers.

Thus, the end of the analysis of each unit will include its basic strategic functions, determined from questions such as the following: What are the main strategic concerns and aims present within each unit of discourse as Jesus bids farewell to his disciples? How are such aims and concerns introduced and elaborated in the unit? How are they related to one another? In sum, how does each unit function as a unified and coherent strategic whole? In each case these questions will be addressed in the light of the preceding second and third steps—each unit as a highly unified and coherent artistic whole. Finally, in the light of the specific strategic functions at work within each unit, the issue of the sociohistorical situation demanded by such functions will be pursued—the perceived or rhetorical situation of the audience reflected in, and addressed by, the composition and development of such a unit.

The Synchronic Dimension of the Farewell

Whereas the first stage (chapters 2 through 5) will analyze the major units of discourse that make up the farewell speech, the first step of the second stage (chapter 6) will turn to the relationship of these major units to one another and thus to the farewell speech as a unified and coherent whole from both a literary and a strategic point of view. This first step will be directly concerned, therefore, with the synchronic dimension of the farewell speech.

Thus, given the discourse's literary structure and development, as well as the strategic concerns and aims identified within each of its major constitutive units, chapter 6 will examine the specific placement and function of such units within the overall sequence of the discourse. Such an analysis will yield in turn the literary structure and development, as well as the strategic concerns and aims, of the farewell speech as an artistic and strategic whole. A discussion of farewell type-scenes will allow the farewell speech to be approached from the wider comparative perspective of other such speeches in antiquity. The earlier discussion of the specific farewell context provided by 13:1–20 and 13:21–30 will enable the entire farewell speech to be further described from the point of view of the various farewell motifs already introduced, by way of preparation and anticipation, within the wider context of the farewell scene.

The Diachronic Dimension of the Farewell

The second step of this stage (chapter 6) will return to a discussion of the compositional difficulties within this speech. This step will explore whether behind the present speech—with its clear structure, development, concerns, and functions—a process of accretion and expansion can also be discerned and outlined. As such, this second step will be directly concerned with the diachronic dimension of the farewell speech. The preceding determination of the strategic aims and functions of the various units, as well as of the rhetorical situation of the audience that such functions reflect and address, will enlighten the analysis. In other words, this step will explore whether the functions identified and the underlying situation outlined for the major units of discourse point to the same basic context or to a number of different contexts that can be distinguished from one another. In support of the latter situation, chapter 6 will advance an overall proposal for such a process of accretion and expansion.

With these two final steps, therefore, the ultimate goal of the present study will have been achieved, namely, the elaboration of a twofold approach to the farewell speech of Jesus in the Fourth Gospel, an approach that seeks to examine both the synchronic and the diachronic dimensions of this text. Two final observations remain to be made. The first is technical and programmatic. As already observed, the Johannine farewell speech extends from 13:31 through 17:26; this study, however, does not cover chapter 17. The above discussion of farewell type-scenes pointed out that one of the constitutive and recurrent motifs of such scenes is that of a prayer by the dying hero. John 17, the prayer of Jesus to the Father, is in effect an example of such a motif within the present farewell speech; however, this prayer of Jesus not only is far longer than any other such prayer found within farewell scenes but also occupies a climactic position within the scene itself—the very end of both speech and scene. Consequently, a detailed analysis of this prayer from a farewell context will be pursued in a separate volume to follow the present study.

The second observation is more theoretical and personal. In the close reading of the farewell that follows, I make no claims that this is the only

and proper way to interpret this text. Indeed, my critical interactions with
my predecessors in the study of this text represent not only a helpful way of
coming to terms with my personal reading and interpretation but also a
concrete way of paying due respect to their own readings and interpretations. My intent here is to provide a reading of the farewell that brings the
artistic and strategic dimensions of the farewell closely together, from both
a synchronic and a diachronic perspective. Other such readings are certainly possible; this is but one. However, the result of this reading has been
for me—and I would hope for the reader of this study as well—an apprecia-
tion for this farewell discourse as a truly impressive and powerful creation.

2

YET A LITTLE WHILE I AM WITH YOU!

John 13:31–14:31

STRUCTURAL OUTLINE

A. The meaning and consequences of Jesus' glorification: Announcement of the forthcoming departure and negative consequences of the departure for the disciples (13:31-38)
   1. The announcement of Jesus' glorification (13:31c-32)
      a) Jesus' glorification as an accomplished reality (13:31c-d)
      b) Jesus' glorification as an outstanding reality (13:32)
   2. The meaning and consequences of glorification (13:33-38)
      a) Meaning of glorification: Announcement of the forthcoming departure (13:33a-b)
      b) Consequences of glorification: Negative consequences of the departure for the disciples (13:33c-38)
         (1) Impossibility of following Jesus (13:33c-e)
         (2) Parting legacy to the disciples: The command to love one another (13:34-35)
            (a) Promulgation of a new command (13:34a)
            (b) Identification of the new command (13:34b-c)
            (c) Significance of the new command (13:35)
         (3) Impossibility of following Jesus (13:36-38)
            (a) Peter's first reaction regarding the announced departure and separation (13:36a-c)
            (b) Jesus' reaffirmation and revision regarding the impossibility of following (13:36d-f)
            (c) Peter's second reaction regarding the announced departure and separation (13:37-38)
B. A call to courage and faith: The meaning of the departure and positive consequences of the departure for the disciples (14:1-27)

1. A call to courage and faith: A preliminary proposition (14:1-3)
   a) A call to courage and faith (14:1)
   b) The meaning of the departure and positive consequences of the departure for the disciples: A preliminary proposition (14:2-3)
      (1) The meaning of the departure: Jesus and the Father (14:2)
      (2) Positive consequences of the departure for the disciples (14:3)
2. The meaning of the departure: Jesus and the Father (14:4-14)
   a) Jesus as the way to the Father (14:4-6)
      (1) Disciples' presumed knowledge of the way (14:4)
      (2) Reaction: Thomas's question concerning the way (14:5)
      (3) Jesus' teaching concerning the way (14:6)
   b) Knowing and seeing the Father in Jesus (14:7-9)
      (1) Disciples' presumed perception of the Father (14:7)
      (2) Reaction: Philip's request concerning the Father (14:8)
      (3) Jesus' teaching concerning perception of the Father (14:9)
   c) The mutual presence of Jesus and the Father in one another (14:10-14)
      (1) Disciples' presumed knowledge of the mutual presence (14:10)
      (2) Disciples' proper reaction: A call to faith (14:11)
      (3) Jesus' promises to the disciples (14:12-14)
         (a) Promises to the disciples (14:12a-c)
         (b) Rationale: Jesus' departure to the Father (14:12d)
         (c) Promises to the disciples (14:13-14)
3. Positive consequences of the departure for the disciples (14:15-27)
   a) Promises concerning the Spirit-Paraclete (14:15-17)
      (1) Love for Jesus as condition (14:15)
      (2) Positive consequences of the departure for the disciples: Promises concerning the Spirit-Paraclete (14:16-17a)
      (3) Contrast between the disciples and the world (14:17b-e)
   b) Promises concerning Jesus and the Father (14:18-21)
      (1) Contrast between the disciples and the world (14:18-20)
         (a) The disciples and Jesus (14:18)
         (b) Contrast between the disciples and the world (14:19)
         (c) The disciples and Jesus (14:20)
      (2) Love for Jesus as condition (14:21a)
      (3) Positive consequences of the departure for the disciples: Promises concerning Jesus and the Father (14:21b-c)
   c) Promises concerning Jesus and the Father (14:22-23)
      (1) Contrast between the disciples and the world (14:22)
      (2) Love for Jesus as condition (14:23a-b)
      (3) Positive consequences of the departure for the disciples: Promises concerning Jesus and the Father (14:23c-d)

YET A LITTLE WHILE I AM WITH YOU!

d) Promises concerning the Spirit-Paraclete (14:24-27)
   (1) Love for Jesus as condition (14:24)
   (2) Positive consequences of the departure for the disciples:
       Promises concerning the Spirit-Paraclete (14:25-26)
   (3) Contrast between the disciples and the world (14:27)

C. The purpose of the present disclosures to the disciples, the meaning of
   the specific mode of departure, and positive consequences of the
   departure for the disciples (14:28-31)
   1. The purpose of the present disclosures (14:28-29)
      a) Summary of disclosures (14:28a-b)
      b) Purpose: Rejoicing and faith of the disciples (14:28c-29)
   2. The meaning of the mode of departure and positive consequences of
      the departure for the disciples (14:30-31c)
      a) Departure as an encounter with ruler of the world (14:30a-b)
      b) Proper interpretation of the encounter (14:30c-31c)
         (1) Jesus' relationship to the ruler of the world (14:30c)
         (2) Jesus' relationship to the Father (14:31a-c)
   3. Concluding commands (14:31d)

THE PROPOSED CONCLUSION TO THE FIRST unit of discourse, 14:31d, is
firmly established in the literature. However, the determination of a proper
beginning proves more problematic. The literature contains two well-
represented positions: (1) 13:31–14:31 as the first major unit of discourse
within the farewell speech[1] and (2) a somewhat smaller unit, 14:1–31, as
the first major unit of discourse. The main point of contention, therefore,
involves the role of 13:31–38 within the farewell scene. In fact, the second
position reveals three variations, depending on the function assigned to
these verses: (1) 13:31–38 as the conclusion to 13:1–30 and hence as a
formal part of the farewell context,[2] (2) 13:31–38 as a self-contained unit of
discourse,[3] and (3) 13:31–38 as an introduction to the farewell speech as a
whole.[4]

1. See, e.g., Westcott, 196; Dodd, 403; Wikenhauser, 259–63; Becker, 219–21; Schulz,
176–77; Schnackenburg, 3:53–54.
2. See, e.g., Lagrange, 365–70; Behler, 71; Marsh, 481. In the more recent literature,
see Simoens, 100–104; J. Beutler, *Habt keine Angst: Die erste johanneische Abschiedsrede
(Joh 14)* (Stuttgart: Verlag Katholisches Bibelwerk GmbH, 1984) 9–11.
3. See, e.g., Loisy, 402; Huby, 32; Barrett, 449; cf. Brown, 2:608.
4. See, e.g., A. Durand, *Évangile selon Saint Jean*, 2d ed., rev., ed. J. Huby, VS 4 (Paris:
Gabriel Beauchesne, 1938) 374–77; Bover, 15–17, 23; J. Schneider, "Die Abschiedsreden
Jesu: Ein Beitrag zur Frage der Komposition von Johannes 13,31–17,26," in *Gott und die
Götter: Festschrift für E. Fascher* (Berlin: Evangelische Verlagsanstalt, 1958) 103–12.

JOHN 13:31–14:31 AS A FIRST UNIT
OF DISCOURSE

The designation of 13:31–14:31 as the first unit of discourse, the majority position in the literature, is preferred. The critical observations that follow argue against a formal separation of 13:31–38 from chapter 14.

First, 13:30 contains the only change of characters within the farewell scene of 13:1–17:26. Therefore, with the departure of the betrayer from the circle of disciples, a third and final narrative unit begins: Jesus proceeds to bid farewell to the remaining disciples, with full knowledge and in full anticipation of his impending betrayal, arrest, and death (13:31–17:26). This change in characters brings the farewell context to an end and sets the stage for the long farewell speech that follows and hence for the first unit of discourse within it.

Second, 13:31–38 introduces the controlling and overarching themes of the first unit of discourse: the meaning of Jesus' departure and the consequences of this departure for the disciples. In addition, these themes are introduced from a negative perspective, setting the stage for the positive development to follow in the remainder of the unit.

Third, 13:31–38 introduces a prominent motif of the first unit: the motif of dialogue between Jesus and his disciples. The exchange with Peter of 13:36–38 is followed by further exchanges involving Thomas, Philip, and Judas; in all four cases the disciples serve as interlocutors of Jesus by means of their reactions to the ongoing declarations of Jesus.

John 13:38 represents a break in the farewell scene; it is not a major break serving as a literary marker for a narrative unit within the scene, however, but rather a minor break pointing to a major section within the first unit of discourse. On the other hand, it is 13:31–32 (the beginning announcement of Jesus' glorification) rather than 13:31–38 that functions as an introduction not only to the first unit of discourse but also to the farewell speech as a whole. John 13:31–14:31 should be seen as the first unit of discourse within the farewell speech, as the critical observations that follow argue.

The summary of the overarching themes of the unit, the twofold exhortation to joy and belief, the prediction regarding the forthcoming encounter with the ruler of the world, and the twofold command to the disciples to arise and depart in 14:28–31, all give these verses a sense of finality. In addition, the introduction and sustained development of the figure of the vine in 15:1–8 provide a sense of a new departure or beginning.

R. Schnackenburg has correctly pointed out that the recurring formula "These things I have said to you" serves as a concluding literary marker throughout the farewell speech (14:25; 16:1, 4; 16:33).[5] However, though alluding to it, Schnackenburg fails to make an explicit or useful distinction between breaks by way of anticipation and immediate breaks in the use of this formula; in effect, the conclusion to the various units of discourse can be signaled by either use of the formula or by both uses. The first example of the formula occurs in 14:25 and clearly anticipates the conclusion of the unit.

The beginning of chapter 15 contains a shift in the controlling themes introduced in 13:31–38 and developed through the end of chapter 14. The focus on the fundamental meaning of Jesus' departure and its consequences for the disciples is now replaced by a focus on the internal affairs of the community, on the proper relationship of the disciples to Jesus and to one another, with an emphasis on the need for the disciples to abide as disciples of Jesus.

The motif of dialogue between Jesus and the disciples, introduced in 13:31–38 and continued through chapter 14, disappears altogether after 15:1 and is not employed again until chapter 16. Consequently, all of chapter 15, as well as the first part of chapter 16, consists of Jesus' uninterrupted address to the disciples.

A shift occurs in the tone of Jesus' address to his disciples beginning with chapter 15. First, the primary tone of teaching and consolation of 13:31–14:31 gives way to a primary tone of exhortation and admonition. Second, the pronounced contrast between the disciples and the world, introduced in 13:31–38 and sustained throughout chapter 14, disappears altogether from the first part of chapter 15. Third, the positive view of the disciples in 13:31–14:31 changes. In 13:31–14:31 they are those who, despite their present failure to do so, will eventually understand Jesus' mission and message and thus become the sole recipients of the farewell promises extended. After 15:1 one views the disciples not only as already fully believing and understanding but also as facing the possibility of faltering and being separated from the community.

A further shift in the standpoint of Jesus as speaker of the discourse can also be discerned after 15:1. Whereas 13:31–14:31 presents a Jesus who

5. Schnackenburg (3:92, 161) also includes within this list John 16:6, 25. The former example (Jn 16:6), although occurring at the beginning of a new unit of discourse (16:4b–5), is said to represent a parenthetical resumption of the previous unit and thus to reinforce the major break already signaled by 16:1, 4. The latter example (16:25) is said to be very similar to that of 14:25 insofar as it too points toward the conclusion of the unit in question. I would also add 15:11; see chapter 3, n. 5, in this work. The relevance of this formula for a structural analysis of the farewell speech is by no means new; see, e.g., E. Lohmeyer, "Über Aufbau und Gliederung des viertens Evangeliums," ZNW 27 (1928) 29; Schneider, "Abschiedsreden," 108.

is both about to undergo the climactic events of "the hour" and who has already done so, except for its final events—the bestowal of the Spirit-Paraclete (his successor to and among the disciples) and the final return to the Father—the first part of chapter 15 reveals a Jesus who speaks as if he were already glorified with the Father, already beyond the final ascent to the Father.

In conclusion, 13:31 constitutes a proper beginning to the first unit of discourse. Therefore 13:31–14:31 should be regarded as the first self-contained and coherent unit of discourse within the farewell speech as a whole.

LITERARY STRUCTURE AND DEVELOPMENT

The scholarly literature agrees that 13:31–38 functions as an introduction to chapter 14. It also profoundly disagrees on the literary structure and development of chapter 14 itself; in fact, the chapter has been divided at one time or another into two,[6] three,[7] four,[8] five,[9] six,[10] seven,[11] eight,[12] and nine[13] major sections. Furthermore, a comparative analysis

6. See, e.g., P. Gächter, "Der formale Aufbau der Abschiedsreden Jesu," ZNW 58 (1934) 176–79 (John 13:1–27d, 27e–31); Dodd, 403–6 (John 14:1–26, 27–31); Becker, 220–21 (John 14:1–26, 27–31); Schnackenburg, 3:58 (John 14:1–24, 25–31).

7. See, e.g., Westcott, 196 (John 14:1–11, 12–21, 22–31); Loisy, 403–4 (John 14:1–14, 15–24, 25–31); Lagrange, 370–71 (John 14:1–11, 12–26, 27–31); Wikenhauser, 263–68 (John 14:1–14, 15–24, 25–31); Behler, 71–72 (John 14:1–11, 12–24, 25–31); Brown, 2:622–23 (John 14:1–14, 15–24, 25–31); Reese, "Literary Structure," 323–27 (John 14:1–6, 7–11, 12–31); Beutler, Angst, 13–15 (John 14:1–14, 15–24, 25–31). Close agreement can be found in Loisy, Wikenhauser, Brown, and Beutler.

8. See, e.g., Durand, Saint Jean, 389–90 (John 14:1–12a, 12b–17, 18–24, 25–31); Bultmann, xi, 595–631 (John 13:36–14:4, 5–14, 15–24, 25–31); Marsh, 498–516 (John 14:1–3, 4–11, 12–24, 25–31); van den Bussche, 49–51 (John 13:34–14:14, 15, 16–24, 25–31).

9. See, e.g., Wellhausen, 62–68 (John 14:1–4, 5–15, 16–17, 18–25, 26–31); Strathmann, 196 (John 14:1–4, 5–14, 15–24, 25–26, 27–31); Morris, 636–62 (John 14:1–7, 8–14, 15–17, 18–24, 25–31); Lindars, 466 (John 14:1–11, 12–14, 15–17, 18–24, 25–31); D. B. Woll, Johannine Christianity in Conflict: Authority, Rank, and Succession in the First Farewell Discourse, SBLDS 60 (Chico, Ca: Scholars Press, 1981) 17–31 (John 13:31–14:3, 4–11, 12–24, 25–26, 27–31).

10. See, e.g., Hoskyns, 447–65 (John 14:1–3, 4–11, 12–14, 15–17, 18–24, 25–31); Schneider, "Abschiedsreden," 106–7 (John 14:1–6, 7–12, 13–14, 15–24, 25–27, 28–31); Schulz, 182–93 (John 14:1–4, 5–14, 15–17, 18–24, 25–26, 27–31); Haenchen, 2:124–28 (John 14:1–3, 4–10, 11–12, 13–14, 15–26, 27–31).

11. See, e.g., Bernard, 2:530–57 (John 14:1–4, 5–7, 8–14, 15–20, 21, 22–24, 25–31); Huby, 38 (John 14:1–4, 5–11, 12–15, 16–18, 19–24, 25–26, 27–31).

12. See, e.g., W. Heitmüller, "Das Johannes-Evangelium," Die Schriftendes Neuen Testaments, 2 vols.; ed. J. Weiss; 2d ed., rev. (Göttingen: Vandenhoeck & Ruprecht, 1908) 823–29 (John 14:1–3, 4–7, 8–14, 15–17, 18–20, 21–24, 25–26, 27–31); Swete, 1–68 (John 14:1–3, 4–6, 7–11, 12–14, 15–17, 18–21, 22–24, 25–31).

13. See, e.g., Bover, 15–16, 35–84 (John 14:1–4, 5–7, 8–11, 12–14, 15–17, 18–21, 22–24, 25–26, 27–31); Simoens, 127–29 (John 14:1–5, 6–10, 11–14, 15–18, 19–22,

of the various proposals shows little agreement—aside from a recurring identification of the concluding section as either 14:25–31 or 14:27–31—with regard to the demarcation of chapter 14's major sections not only within each position but also across all the different positions.

J. Becker has laid out a foundation for all such further research. Becker's principles of organization for his proposed structure of the unit of discourse rest on solid literary markers within the unit itself. Although these markers are fundamentally sound, a different interpretation of them is possible, leading to a different formulation altogether of the literary structure and development of the unit as a whole.[14]

For Becker the literary markers in question are to be found in 14:1–3, so these verses become the key to the literary structure and development of the unit as a whole. Becker's proposal can be summarized as follows:

1. A distinct inclusion (14:1, 27) marks off the central major section, or main body, of the unit (14:1–26).
2. This inclusion further marks off an introduction, or first major section (13:31–38), as well as a conclusion, or third major section (14:27–31), with a peace wish as a formal introduction (14:27). As such, Becker proposes a threefold division for the unit as a whole.
3. Two central themes, the departure of Jesus and the return of Jesus, control the structure and development of the unit. The former is introduced in 13:31–38. In 14:1–26 the latter theme is introduced, and then both central themes receive extensive development. John 14:28–31 summarizes both themes, as well as a number of other themes from 14:1–26, and prepares the way for the final events of Jesus' ministry.
4. Within the main body itself, the saying of 14:2–3 plays an important structural role. On the one hand, while resuming the central theme of the departure from the introduction, the saying also introduces the other central theme of the unit, that of Jesus' return. On the other hand, the saying also sets the stage for a subsequent, sequential development of these two themes in the remainder of the main body (14:4–17 and 14:18–26), yielding thereby a threefold subdivision of the main body (14:1–3, 14:4–17, and 14:18–26).

23–24, 25–27, 28–29, 30–31). For Simoens these nine sections reveal an overall chiastic arrangement.

14. For a very similar assessment, see Schnackenburg, 3:58; idem, "Das Anliegen der Abschiedsrede in Joh 14," in *Wort Gottes in der Zeit: Festschrift Karl Hermann Schelkle zum 65. Geburtstag*, ed. H. Feld and J. Nolte (Düsseldorf: Patmos, 1973) 95–110; Woll, *Christianity*, 226.

In conclusion, Becker argues for a threefold linear and progressive development of the central themes of the unit, the departure of Jesus and the return of Jesus.

The repetition of the exhortation of 14:1a ("Let not your hearts be troubled!") in 14:27d—with an expansion in the form of a second imperative now attached to it by way of reinforcement ("not let them be afraid")—forms a clear and effective inclusion that frames the central major section of the unit.[15] However, given the clamping nature of inclusions in general and the position of the exhortation at the end of 14:27, a central major section consisting of 14:1–27 rather than 14:1–26 is more appropriate here.

The presence of this inclusion points to a threefold division of the unit, with a long central section framed by an introductory and a concluding section. With 13:31–38 as the first major section of the unit, 14:28–31 should be seen as the third major section, given the inclusion formed by 14:1a and 14:27d and the corresponding delineation of 14:1–27 as the central section of the unit. On the one hand, 14:27a–b is not a peace "wish" as such but instead part of an ongoing contrast between the disciples and the world developed within the main body of the unit. On the other hand, although the concluding section does have a summarizing function, such a summary begins with 14:28 itself.[16]

Such a proposal goes against the common designation of either 14:25–31 or 14:27–31 as the conclusion to the unit.[17] Both of these positions are ultimately based on the presence of certain formulas that are taken to mark the formal beginning of the conclusion. Whereas the former option emphasizes the recurring concluding formula of the farewell, "These things I have said to you," the latter relies, as Becker himself argues, on the proposed peace wish of 14:27, a common concluding marker. Both the concluding recurring formula of the discourse and the reference to the peace of Jesus form part of a recurring structural pattern within the central major section itself: the formula of 14:25 introduces the final promise of the main body, and the reference to the peace of Jesus introduces the final contrast between the disciples and the world.

---

15. As Becker himself points out, this inclusion has been widely recognized in the literature (e.g., Bultmann, 599; Schneider, "Abschiedsreden," 106). To the best of my knowledge, however, aside from Dodd (p. 403)—whom Becker does not mention in this regard—this inclusion has not been used in the determination of the literary structure of the unit; Dodd himself ultimately argues as well for 14:1–26 as the central major section.

16. In fact, all the themes Becker identifies as summarized in the conclusion are found in 14:28: Jesus' departure and return (14:28a–b), love and belief (14:28c), and the relationship of Jesus to the Father (14:28d–e).

17. A listing of those who favor 14:25–31 would be as extensive as a listing of those who argue for 14:27–31. Other options can also be found: Wellhausen, 67 (John 14:26–31); Westcott, 209; Schneider, "Abschiedsreden," 107 (John 14:28–31).

Becker identifies a linear and progressive development within this first unit of discourse. However, the overarching themes of the unit, once again, are the fundamental meaning of Jesus' departure and the consequences of such a departure for the disciples—not, as Becker identifies them, the departure and return of Jesus. It is these themes that are introduced in 13:31–38, developed at length in 14:1–27, and brought to a close in 14:28–31. This development can be further described as follows: these themes are introduced from a negative and troubling perspective in 13:31–38, given a positive and reassuring development in 14:1–27, and brought to a positive climax in 14:28–31.

Becker assigns a pivotal role within the central major section itself to 14:2–3—a saying that he further characterizes as traditional, with a parousia christology and soteriology that are then explicitly refuted in the remainder of the main body.[18] He further subdivides this section into three subsections. First, however, 14:2–3 resumes the controlling themes of the unit—the meaning of the forthcoming departure and its consequences for the disciples—from the introduction and develops them further by providing, in keeping with the beginning exhortation of 14:1a, a positive reading of these themes. Second, there is a further, sequential development of these themes in the remainder of the central section, beginning with the meaning of the departure in a second subsection and concluding with the consequences of the departure for the disciples in a third subsection. Third, such a development is not by way of opposition and refutation but rather by way of further exposition and expansion. In effect, the positive reading of 14:1–3 is continued, reinforced, and greatly amplified in the remainder of the section. Finally, a different delineation of these two subsections is in order. Whereas the meaning of the departure is pursued systematically in 14:4–14, the consequences of the departure are developed in a similarly systematic fashion in 14:15–27. Regardless of its original provenance, therefore, the saying is well integrated into the overall development of the unit.

In conclusion, there is a threefold linear and progressive development of the overarching themes of the unit, not only within the unit as a whole but also within its second and central major section. This conclusion follows the

---

18. Becker, 221–23; idem, *Das Evangelium nach Johannes*, 2 vols., Ökumenischer Taschenbuchkommentar zum Neuen Testament 4 (Gütersloh: Gütersloher Verlaghaus Mohn; Würzburg: Echter, 1979–81) 2:458–61. As Becker himself points out, the identification of 14:2–3 (sometimes in conjunction with 14:1) as an originally independent and self-contained tradition is by no means new in the literature. See, e.g., C. Clemen, *Die Enstehung des Johannesevangelium* (Halle: M. Niemeyer, 1912) 249; S. Schulz, *Untersuchungen zur Menschensohnchristologie im Johannesevangelium* (Göttingen: Vandenhoeck & Ruprecht, 1957) 159–61; Bultmann, 601. For a similar position regarding an explicit refutation of this saying in the unit, see Dodd, 404; for the saying as gnostic in provenance, see Bultmann, 601.

consensus position that the first major section, 13:31–38, serves as an introduction to the unit; agrees with the first and not uncommon position that chapter 14 is to be divided into two major sections; and follows minority opinion in proposing 14:28–31 as the third major section of the unit.

LITERARY-RHETORICAL ANALYSIS

The proposed literary structure and development of this third unit can be adequately summarized in terms of the following structural outline, to be developed in greater detail in this section:

I. The meaning and consequences of Jesus' glorification: the announcement of the forthcoming departure and the negative consequences of the departure for the disciples (13:31–38)

II. A call to courage and faith: the fundamental meaning of the departure and the positive consequences of the departure for the disciples (14:1–27)

III. The purpose of the present disclosures to the disciples, the meaning of Jesus' specific mode of departure, and the departure's positive consequences for the disciples (14:28–31)

First Major Section (John 13:31–38)

The first major section of the first unit of discourse, 13:31–38, covers the meaning and consequences of Jesus' glorification: the announcement of the forthcoming departure and the negative consequences of the departure for the disciples. This section introduces the two controlling themes of the unit from a negative, troubling perspective. The literature contains two traditional and well-represented positions with regard to the literary structure of these verses: (1) a twofold division—consisting of 13:31–35 and 13:36–38—based on the characters involved (Jesus and Simon Peter);[19] and (2) a fourfold division—consisting of 13:31–32, 13:33, 13:34–35, and 13:36–38—following the overall thematic sequence of these verses (glorification, departure, new command, and prediction of denial).[20]

19. See, e.g., Westcott, Hoskyns, Strathmann, Morris, and Schulz. Among those who connect these verses to chapter 13, see, e.g., Lagrange, Marsh, and Lindars; among those who see them as a formal introduction to the whole speech, see, e.g., Durand and Bover.

20. See, e.g., Loisy, Wikenhauser, Huby, Brown, Becker, and Schnackenburg. Among those who connect these verses to chapter 13, see, e.g., Swete and Behler; among those who see them as a formal introduction to the whole speech, see, e.g., Schneider, "Abschiedsreden."

I would argue, however, for a twofold division consisting of 13:31–32 and 13:33–38.[21] This first section introduces the two controlling and overarching themes of the unit in 13:33–38 by way of commentary on the beginning announcement of 13:31–32. In other words, the introduction to this first unit of discourse opens with an announcement of Jesus' glorification and then continues with an immediate exposition of what such glorification means (the announcement of the forthcoming departure) and entails (the consequences of such a departure for the disciples):

1. The announcement of Jesus' glorification (13:31–32).
2. The meaning and consequences of glorification (13:33–38).

The beginning announcement of Jesus' glorification in 13:31–32 functions as an introduction in two other ways. First, the announcement introduces the first unit of discourse, so all that follows in this first unit constitutes further commentary on this beginning declaration of Jesus. However, given the absence of this theme from the remainder of the unit, aside from a brief reappearance in 14:13, the meaning of the departure and its consequences for the disciples can be designated as the overarching themes of the unit. Second, the announcement introduces the entire farewell discourse, so the remainder of the speech constitutes still further commentary on this beginning declaration of Jesus. Again, given the general absence of this theme in chapters 15–16 (aside from 15:8; 16:14), the meaning of the departure and its consequences for the disciples again can be designated as the overarching themes of the farewell speech as a whole. In the end, therefore, the farewell speech can be seen as a sustained and detailed exposition of this beginning announcement, of what Jesus' glorification implies and entails.

The Announcement of Jesus' Glorification
(John 13:31–32)

John 13:31–32 begins with a brief introduction by the narrator; a beginning temporal clause again sets forth the immediate context for the farewell speech (13:31a, "when he [Judas] had left"; cf. 13:30), and the speaker is further identified (13:31b, "Jesus said"). The section then announces Jesus' glorification (13:31c–32). This announcement reveals a careful literary construction, as well as a complex temporal standpoint for Jesus as speaker of the discourse.

21. See also D. B. Woll, "The Departure of 'the Way': The First Farewell Discourse in the Gospel of John," *JBL* 99 (1980) 229; Woll, *Christianity*, 37–38, though the first section is extended through John 14:3.

First, the announcement is in the form of a chiastic structure with an ABCCBA pattern:

1. Its outermost components specify the time of reference for the specific glorification in question ($13:31c_1$, $32c$).
2. Its central components address different aspects of Jesus' glorification as the Son of man ($13:31c_2$, $32b$).[22]
3. Its innermost components deal with the glorification of God by Jesus as Son of man ($13:31d$, $32a$).[23]

Second, the two framing time references immediately point to the complex temporal standpoint of the speaker. On the one hand, the beginning time reference of $13:31c_1$ precedes the first aspect of Jesus' glorification. This beginning reference is formulated in the aorist tense of the verb (ἐδοξάσθη), with the adverb "now," emphasizing thereby the character of this glorification as already completed or accomplished. On the other hand, the concluding time reference of 13:32c repeats the future tense of the verb (δοξάσει) from the second aspect of Jesus' glorification and prefaces it with the adverb "immediately," thus emphasizing the character of this glorification as still to be accomplished or completed. This beginning announcement presents, therefore, a distinctive temporal standpoint. Whereas its first part (13:31c–d) portrays Jesus' glorification as being an already accomplished reality (even though, from a narrative point of view, such a glorification lies in the future), the second part (13:32) describes Jesus' glorification as being in some way an outstanding reality (despite the preceding statement of 13:31c–d and its reprise at the beginning of 13:32 itself).

Jesus' Glorification as an Accomplished Reality
(John 13:31c–d)

The first part of the chiastic structure, 13:31c–d, consists of a brief compound sentence whose first member functions as a condition for the second: the glorification of the Son of man (13:31c) results in the glorification of

---

22. On Jesus as the Son of man, see particularly 9:35–38.
23. The second innermost component (13:32a) is omitted by the best textual tradition (p^{66} ℵ° B C° D L W X Π f^1 al), thus raising the possibility that the conditional clause in question may be a secondary intrusion into such witnesses as ℵ^c A C^2 K f^{13} al; see, e.g., Barrett, 450. I favor the latter reading: its omission can be readily explained either in terms of homoeoteleuton (ἐν αὐτῷ at the end of both the preceding clause and the clause in question) or a supposed redundancy in the context (simply repeating the thought of the previous clause). Abbreviations for textual apparatus are from: *Novum Testamentum Graece*, ed. E. Nestle, K. Aland, et al., 26th ed. (Stuttgart: Deutsche Bibelsiftung, 1979) 39–72.

God by him (13:31d).[24] Both glorifications are presented as already accomplished realities.

The first time reference (13:31c$_1$) provides an excellent entrée into the important question of the temporal standpoint of the speaker. The use of the adverb "now" at this point conveys important connotations:

1. The immediately preceding departure of the betrayer, Judas Iscariot, from the room (13:30a, 31a).
2. The highly symbolic description of the time for this departure (13:30b)—with the onset of "night," with the preparations for the betrayal and arrest now in full force, "the light" begins to draw to a definite close.[25]
3. "The hour" of Jesus, that period that encompasses the climactic conclusion to his mission and ministry, beginning with his last journey to Jerusalem (12:23) and concluding with his return or ascent to the Father, anticipated but not narrated in the Gospel.[26]

With this first time reference, therefore, Jesus' announcement of glorification is clearly situated within "the hour" itself. Its formal beginning is now past and, with Judas's departure from the room, its climactic events are ever closer in sight.

This beginning reference to "the hour" and its various components is immediately expanded by the subsequent introduction and development of the theme of glorification in 13:31c$_2$–d; in effect, Jesus' "hour" is the hour of his glorification.[27] However, the use of the aorist tense—a constative aorist—to describe his own glorification as well as the resulting glorification of God by him presents this "hour" as if it were already completed or accomplished.[28] Thus, the Jesus who is still immersed in the process of

24. I believe that the prepositional phrase functions as a dative of personal agency: God is glorified by Jesus. For a different opinion and an excellent delineation of the different grammatical possibilities, see G. B. Caird, "The Glory of God in the Fourth Gospel: An Exercise in Biblical Semantics," *NTS* 15 (1968–69) 265–77.

25. For a similar symbolic use of "night," see 9:4–5; 11:9–10; see also 12:35–36.

26. The entire narrative is oriented from the beginning toward the arrival of this "hour" (2:4; 4:21, 23; 5:25, 28; 7:30; 8:20). Its formal beginning is identified by Jesus himself with the coming of the Greeks to see him at the start of his final journey to Jerusalem (12:20–23); from then on, the formal arrival of "the hour" is presupposed and reaffirmed throughout (13:1; 19:27).

27. For "the hour" as being the time for Jesus' glorification, see 12:20–23; see also 7:37–39.

28. Both glorifications are mentioned elsewhere in the narrative. With regard to Jesus' glorification, the term "glory" refers to Jesus' status as the only-begotten Son of God (1:14; 5:44; 12:41–43); this "glory" of Jesus, furthermore, can be perceived by his disciples (1:14), especially in and through his works (2:11). As the one sent by God into the world, therefore,

"the hour" within the narrative itself appears to speak at this point as one who has already surpassed "the hour"; in other words, the Jesus who now begins to bid farewell as he is about to die appears to speak as if he were already glorified as well.

Jesus' Glorification as an Outstanding Reality (John 13:32)

The second part of the chiastic structure, 13:32, is formulated in terms of a first-class condition in past time. Its protasis (13:32a) immediately repeats verbatim the conclusion of 13:31d (the glorification of God by the Son of man that takes place as a result of the Son of man's own glorification) and thus serves as a point of departure for the further development of the theme of glorification. Once this condition is fulfilled—that is, once God has been glorified by the Son of man (a glorification that again is presented as already fulfilled)—the apodosis (13:32b–c) describes a further glorification of the Son of man by God that is yet to be accomplished, a glorification by God "in himself."[29] This posits a glorification of Jesus that still lies in the future and that, given the protasis, can only be seen as following upon or completing that already announced in 13:31c–d.[30] The concluding time reference in the apodosis (13:32c) repeats this reference to a future glorification of Jesus and emphasizes it further by means of the adverb "immediately."

The thrust of 13:32, then, coming immediately upon the statement of 13:31c–d, is unexpected. What the former has described as already accomplished, the latter now qualifies and presents as in some way (though not altogether so, given the protasis) still to be accomplished. Therefore, the Jesus who begins to speak as if already glorified, as if already having surpassed "the hour," now emerges more precisely as a Jesus who still speaks as

---

Jesus manifests his "glory" in and through his mission. At the same time, Jesus is said "to be glorified" in and through his works (11:4), above all with respect to the events of "the hour" (7:39; 12:16, 23). Jesus, therefore, both manifests his "glory" and "is glorified" in and through his works, especially in and through his "hour." With respect to the glorification of God "by him," Jesus is said not to seek his own "glory" (7:18; 8:50, 54) but rather the "glory" of the one who sent him (7:18). At the same time, not only are his works said to be for "the glory of God" (11:4, 40), but his "hour" is said to "glorify" God as well (12:28). As the one sent by God into the world, therefore, Jesus also "glorifies" God in and through his works, especially in and through his "hour."

29. The masculine gender will be used with respect to God throughout, as in this prepositional phrase, because of the sustained use of the metaphor "the Father" with regard to God throughout the whole speech. The description of God, furthermore, is gender related in this Gospel and should be exposed for what it is.

30. The glorification of Jesus by God has also been mentioned already in the narrative. Jesus' "glory" is said not to come from human beings (5:41) but from God (5:44; 8:50; see also 1:14); furthermore, the Father is said to "glorify" Jesus both with regard to his works and his "hour" (8:54; 12:28). Therefore, just as Jesus is "glorified" and the Father is "glorified" by him in and through his mission and "hour," so it is in effect the Father who "glorifies" Jesus in and through that same mission and "hour."

if in some way immersed within the process of "the hour" and awaiting a further and final glorification by God.

The key to the precise temporal standpoint introduced by this beginning announcement of 13:31c–32 lies in the prepositional phrase that follows the second reference to Jesus' glorification within the chiastic structure (13:32b)—God will glorify the Son of man "in himself."[31] If this is a local dative, as I believe it is, what remains outstanding with respect to Jesus' glorification are simply the final events of "the hour": the bestowal of the Spirit-Paraclete, promised in the central major section, and the final ascent or return to the Father. As such, this beginning announcement of glorification presents, through an effective use of its chiastic structure, the process of "the hour" as accomplished (13:31c–d) except for its final events (13:32). Consequently, this beginning announcement of 13:31c–32 also portrays the Jesus who speaks as a Jesus who has virtually surpassed "the hour" (13:31c–d) but who is still in the world and to that extent still immersed in the process of "the hour" (13:32).

The first unit as a whole, therefore, can be described as delivered by Jesus from within the process of "the hour" itself, prior to the climactic events of this "hour" in the narrative (arrest, appearance before the authorities, death, resurrection, bestowal of the Spirit-Paraclete as successor, and return to the Father), but also by Jesus looking upon those events as if they had already transpired, with the exception of the last two events. Consequently, the speaker who in this way begins to bid farewell can also be described as a Jesus who, from the point of view of the narrative, is at the beginning of "the hour" and is about to be arrested and die, but at the same time as a Jesus who, from the point of view of the speech itself, is at the conclusion of "the hour" and is about to leave the world and the disciples for good. The unit could therefore be characterized as containing the final words of both a Jesus who is about to die and a Jesus who is already risen and is about to ascend to the Father.

The Meaning and Consequences of Glorification
(John 13:33–38)

The first section continues with an exposition of the beginning announcement of Jesus' glorification (13:33–38). Two major components can be discerned within this subsection: (1) the meaning of the glorification is briefly

---

31. The personal pronoun is to be preferred to the reflexive pronoun in the prepositional phrase. The textual evidence is strongly in its favor (p^{66} $\aleph^{*,c}$ B 2148 al); furthermore, the addition of the reflexive can be readily explained as an attempt to introduce greater precision. For the use of the personal pronoun in its unaspirated form as a reflexive in Hellenistic Greek, see B. M. Metzger, *A Textual Commentary on the Greek New Testament* (London and New York: United Bible Societies, 1971) 242; BDF, 64.1; 282.2, 3.

addressed in 13:33a–b, and (2) its consequences for the disciples are more extensively pursued in 13:33c–38. This second subsection, therefore, introduces the two controlling and overarching themes of the unit from a negative perspective.

The Meaning of Glorification:
The Announcement of the Forthcoming Departure (13:33a–b)

The first element of the exposition, 13:33a–b, briefly describes the implications of the glorification. Jesus tells the assembled disciples, whom he now addresses as "little children,"[32] that he will be with them for "yet a little while" (that is, that his presence among them is now drawing to a close).[33] This announcement of his forthcoming departure and separation from the disciples, therefore, constitutes the first explanation of what glorification implies. The explanation itself, however, is stark and unsettling. The impending departure is simply announced, with no explanation or development of its nature—its destination, duration, or reason. Abruptly, therefore, the disciples are simply told that Jesus is about to leave them.

The Consequences of Glorification:
The Negative Consequences of the Departure for
the Disciples (John 13:33c–38)

The second element of the exposition, 13:33c–38, describes what the glorification entails; it is more extensive than the first element and is presented in the form of an inclusion. In effect, it explains glorification in terms of the consequences of the announced departure for the disciples. The outer components (13:33c–e, 36–38) affirm the impossibility of any following of Jesus by the disciples at the time of the departure and thus posit a sharp separation between Jesus and the disciples as a result of this departure. The central component (13:34–35) discloses what appears to be a sole parting instruction of Jesus for the coming time of separation— the new command to love one another (13:34–35).

---

32. This is the only such characterization of the disciples in the Gospel (cf. 1 John 2:1, 12, 28; 3:7, 18; 4:4; 5:21). The term "little children" not only introduces the imagery of the household of God, to be further developed in the course of the unit, but also identifies the disciples as belonging to God. For believers as "the children of God," see 1:12; 11:52.

33. This is the first of several formulas of departure to be found throughout the farewell speech (14:19, 25, 30–31c; 16:4b–5a, 12, 16, 22); two other examples have already appeared in the course of Jesus' public ministry, one prior to (7:33b) and the other after (12:35b) the arrival of "the hour." Whereas all these formulas point directly to the impending departure and address a specific situation or relationship in the light of the departure, they also exhibit different forms and serve a variety of purposes. With regard to form, the present example follows, as do both 7:33b and 12:35b, the most common pattern: the use of different variations of the expression "yet a little while." With regard to purpose, the present example is used with regard to the disciples for the first time: whereas 7:33b has to do with the Jews, 12:35b concerns an unidentified crowd in Jerusalem. The formula, therefore, introduces a fundamental similarity between the disciples and the Jews.

The overall tone of this first delineation of the departure's consequences is thus negative, especially given the concluding prophecy in 13:36–38 concerning Peter's forthcoming denial of Jesus. At the same time, however, a veiled glimmer of hope is extended to the disciples. In fact, the outer components of the inclusion show a clear progression from negative to positive. The first component describes the coming separation as definitive (13:33c–e), reinforcing the preceding announcement of the forthcoming departure itself. The second component then introduces a subtle note of hope: the promise of a later following of Jesus by the disciples after the announced departure and separation (13:36–38), thus providing a radical revision of the first description of 13:33c–e and a word of comfort in the midst of these distressing announcements. However, this word of comfort is not only veiled and subtle—indeed, found within a further affirmation of the impossibility of following Jesus at this point—but also followed by the prediction of the denial of Simon Peter. As a whole, therefore, the subsection is negative indeed.

The first component of the inclusion (13:33c–e) starkly presents a first consequence of the departure: the disciples "will not be able to go" with Jesus at the time of the announced departure. This first consequence is developed in two steps: (1) the behavior of the disciples after the departure is anticipated (13:33c) and (2) a specific instruction with regard to such behavior is given (13:33d–e).

Jesus first characterizes the behavior of the disciples after his departure as one of "seeking for or after" him (13:33c).[34] He immediately portrays such an attitude on their part as misguided and pointless, since they will not be able "to go" with him "where he is going" (13:33d–e).[35] This instruction is given in the form of an inclusion: the framing components specify the applicability or addressees of such an instruction (13:33d$_1$, 33e), and the central component provides the instruction proper (13:33d$_2$). A progression can be detected in the outer components of the inclusion: whereas the first addressees are identified as "the Jews," specifically recalling a previous scene in the narrative (13:33d$_1$; 8:21–22), the second addressees are identified as the disciples themselves (13:33e). This basic instruction concerning the coming separation and the impossibility of going with Jesus

---

34. Such "seeking" (ζητεῖν) for or after Jesus is frequently used in the narrative with regard to unbelieving or hostile crowds, both during the time of the public ministry (e.g., 5:18; 6:24, 26; 7:1, 11, 19, 20, 25, 30; 8:37, 40; 10:39; 11:8, 56; 18:4, 7, 8) and the time after the departure (7:34a; 8:21b). The use of the term with respect to the disciples at this point strongly reinforces, therefore, the similar status accorded to both Jews and disciples with regard to the departure.

35. Whereas the behavior of the disciples is described by means of the verb ἐλθεῖν, the departure of Jesus is conveyed by means of a local clause with the verb to go away (ὑπάγειν), introduced here as part of a citation from an earlier declaration of Jesus in the narrative. See also 7:33–36; 8:14, 21–22 (the source of the citation); cf. 13:3.

(13:33d₂)—in itself a direct citation of a declaration of Jesus from the earlier scene—is explicitly extended from the unbelieving and hostile Jews to the disciples themselves. In this way the disciples are placed on exactly the same level as Jesus' opponents with respect to the forthcoming departure.[36] As a result, this first consequence of the departure is negative, especially given the parallel drawn between the disciples and the Jews.

The central component of the inclusion (13:34–35) provides a second consequence of the departure: a final instruction to the disciples for the coming time of the announced departure and separation—a command to love one another as Jesus loved them. Three steps can be discerned: (1) the giving of a "new" command is announced (13:34a), (2) the command itself is identified (13:34b–c), and (3) the significance of this command is explained (13:35).

First, a "new" command announced to the disciples is clearly meant to serve as a guiding principle for the coming time of separation and, therefore, as Jesus' parting legacy to the disciples (13:34a).[37] Second, this new command is introduced by an inclusion. The outer components identify the command (13:34b, 34c₂), and the central component provides both a grounding and an exemplar for the fulfillment of such a command (13:34c₁). Finally, the fulfillment of this new command—now repeated a third time with some stylistic variations—is presented as the preeminent and distinguishing characteristic of the disciples for all outsiders during the time of separation, underscoring thereby its importance as Jesus' farewell legacy to the disciples (13:35).

The command itself concerns the relationship of the disciples to one another after the departure; in effect, the command specifies that the correct role of the disciples as disciples of Jesus during the time of departure and

36. In fact, this entire subsection has many elements in common with the early farewells of Jesus to his antagonists in Jerusalem (7:33–36; 8:21–22): (a) an announcement of the departure, (b) a description of the addressees' behavior after the departure as one of "seeking for or after" Jesus, and (c) a statement to the effect that the addressees will not be able to follow Jesus. An important difference should also be noted: whereas in the farewells to the Jews the finality of the separation is emphasized (7:34: they will not find Jesus; 8:21: they will die in their sins), in the present farewell the finality of the separation will be radically revised. Although the disciples' status is the same as that of the Jews to begin with, it will ultimately be quite different.

37. Much has been written on the reasons for the designation of the love command as a "new" command, given its widespread appearance elsewhere in antiquity, not only within the biblical texts themselves (e.g., Lev 19:18, 34) but also in the wider Jewish traditions (e.g., *P. Aboth* 1:12) and Greco-Roman traditions (Pythagoreans and Stoics). The reasons offered are invariably extratextual and theological, e.g., the command is "new" because it is of infinite intensity and its reach knows no limits (Lagrange, 367–68). I would argue for a much simpler, intratextual reason: the command is "new" precisely because it is presented as a farewell instruction. The term "command" (ἐντολή) is not used for any other single instruction or teaching of Jesus; thus far, it has been used only with reference to the mission entrusted to Jesus by the Father (10:18; 12:49–50).

separation must be one of love for one another. Although what such love implies or entails is not explicitly pursued in the unit, it is implicitly revealed insofar as such love is specifically grounded in, and patterned after, Jesus' own love for them. The disciples are to love one another as Jesus himself loved them, that is, by giving total service to the point of death.[38] Therefore, this new command conveys an implicit warning as well: the disciples' own love for one another demands not only total service but also, if need be, the laying down of their lives for one another.

Given its immediate context, this new command of Jesus is meant to serve as a replacement for Jesus' presence in the midst of the disciples, as a counterbalance to their anticipated behavior of "seeking" after him by redirecting their attention toward one another, and as the sign to all outside the group of their own status as disciples of Jesus in the world. The disclosure of this new command also intensifies the negative thrust of the entire subsection. It now appears as if the disciples are being left behind, but with this one legacy to go on after the departure itself. Moreover, the legacy itself conveys a warning: because Jesus' love for the disciples entails persecution and death at the hands of the world, their own love for one another may also lead to persecution and death.

The final component of the inclusion (13:36–38) reaffirms the first consequence of the departure outlined in the first component: the disciples will not be able to follow Jesus at the time of the departure. At the same time, this last component also provides a twofold expansion of the first consequence: a fundamental revision of this earlier instruction through the addition of a temporal qualification, as well as a third consequence of the departure.

This third component represents the first reaction of a disciple to the ongoing declarations of Jesus and therefore is constructed as a brief interchange between Jesus and Simon Peter. In this double exchange, the narrator introduces each individual address (13:36a, 36d, 37a, 38a). The interchange follows a pattern of inclusion: its outer components (Peter's first question, Peter's second question and Jesus' second response) deal with Peter's reactions to the instruction of 13:33c–e concerning the

---

38. Such love—given the use of the constative aorist (ἠγάπησα)—encompasses the whole of Jesus' mission, including the climactic events of "the hour" and, above all, his own death on behalf of the disciples. For the love of Jesus for the disciples, see 13:1. Here such love is also described by the narrator in terms of the whole mission: both in terms of Jesus' relationship to them up to that point (13:1b) and in terms of the foot washing as a symbol of his forthcoming death (13:1c), as the description of such love as being "to the end" makes clear. For the love of the disciples for one another, compare the explanation of the foot washing in 13:12–20: as Jesus washed their feet (loved them to the end), so the disciples must wash one another's feet (love one another as Jesus loved them). The giving of the new command at this point can be seen, therefore, as an explicit formulation of the more symbolic instruction of 13:12–20.

inability of the disciples to go with Jesus at this time (13:36a–c, 37–38), and its central component (Jesus' first response to Peter) provides the fundamental revision of this earlier instruction (13:36d–f). The second outer component (13:37–38) introduces the third consequence of the departure: the forthcoming denial of Jesus by Peter.

In the first component of the interchange between Jesus and Simon Peter (13:36a–c), Peter returns to Jesus' instruction of 13:33c–e. He asks the destination of the announced departure as formulated in the instruction itself, that is, by means of the verb ὑπάγειν (13:33d$_2$). In so doing, Peter bypasses the new command of Jesus issued in 13:34–35.

In the central component of the interchange (13:36d–f), Jesus bypasses in turn Peter's question regarding the destination of the departure and instead repeats, with a fundamental revision, the earlier instruction of 13:33c–e. Thus, in effect, the disciples—even though formulated in the second person singular with reference to Peter, the revision is meant to extend to the others as well, as the remainder of the unit makes clear—are now extended a promise: although they will not be able to follow Jesus "now" (reaffirming thereby the first consequence of the departure already disclosed), they will do so "later" (ὕστερον).[39] The introduction of this temporal qualification of the coming separation is significant. First, it considerably softens the finality and severity of the coming separation: separation is inevitable, but it will be temporary rather than permanent. Second, the disciples are no longer placed on the same footing as the Jews with regard to Jesus' departure. They, unlike the Jews, will be able to follow Jesus, though again at a later time. Finally, the cumulative blow of the preceding disclosures is now softened for the first time by the promise of an eventual reunion after the departure.

The final component of the interchange between Jesus and Peter describes Peter's second reaction to the instruction of 13:33c–e as reaffirmed in 13:36d–f (13:37–38). Whereas his first reaction raises the question of the destination, his second reaction raises the question of the reason (διὰ τί) for the separation itself. In so doing, Peter completely bypasses the radical revision of the initial instruction of 13:33c–e in 13:36d–f. Instead of focusing on the given promise of a future following and reunion, he pursues the reaffirmed impossibility for the disciples to follow Jesus at the time of the announced departure itself (13:37b–c), as if the temporal qualification of 13:36d–f had not been introduced at all. In this sense Peter's second

39. The verb to follow (ἀκολουθεῖν) is used at this point not as a technical term for discipleship (e.g., 1:37, 38, 40, 43; 8:12; 10:4, 5, 27; 12:26; 18:15; cf. 21:19, 20, 22) but rather in a neutral sense, with reference to the physical accompaniment of Jesus as such (e.g., 11:31; 20:6). Although the temporal contrast, "now/later," is unique in the Gospel, a similar dialectic can be observed in 13:7; see also 13:19; 14:29; 2:17, 22; 12:16.

question ultimately returns, like the first, to the initial instruction of
13:33c–e.

Peter follows his second question, however, with an alternative proposal.
Rather than have the departure and separation take place as explained,
Peter proposes to follow Jesus even if it should mean the laying down of his
own life for Jesus (13:37d).[40] Peter is thus not only completely bypassing
the revision of the earlier instruction but also questioning the specific plan
of departure, separation, and eventual reunion disclosed by Jesus.[41] It is this
alternative proposal, with its implicit opposition to Jesus' disclosures, that
brings about the third consequence of Jesus' glorification within this subsection. After an ironic rhetorical repetition of Peter's proposal (13:38b),
Jesus solemnly prophesies a threefold denial of him by Peter (13:38c–d).
This ironic conclusion to the interchange is ultimately subordinate, given
its personal application, to the main issue at hand, the revision of the first
consequence of the departure.[42] However, the conclusion to the interchange, given its position at the conclusion of the section itself, intensifies
the negative thrust of the subsection after the unexpected softening of
13:36d–f.

This concluding interchange, therefore, offers the only note of hope
within the subsection, as it thoroughly revises Jesus' initial instruction
concerning the nature of the coming separation. However, the interchange also intensifies the negative thrust of all the preceding disclosures,
as it closes the subsection with both a reaffirmation of the preceding
instruction of 13:33c–e and a solemn prediction outlining the impending
demise of Peter by way of a threefold denial of Jesus.

40. According to the figure of the shepherd in 10:1–21, it is the role of Jesus as the good
shepherd—a role entrusted to him by the Father, the fulfillment of which results in the
Father's love for him (10:17–18)—to lay down his life for the sheep (10:11, 15). With this
alternative proposal, therefore, Peter completely reverses the roles of shepherd and sheep
and proceeds in complete opposition to the plan of God and the mission entrusted to Jesus. At
the same time, this alternative proposal is not without merit, since Peter is in fact offering
thereby to lay down his life for Jesus to prevent the announced separation (see also 11:16; cf.
15:13). Thus, even though the proposal is misguided from the point of view of Jesus' mission
and will give way to an outright denial of Jesus by Peter, it is in its own right a commendable
offer and in keeping with the "new" command just promulgated.
41. Cf. the similar interchange between Jesus and Peter in the foot washing (13:6–11).
However, unlike this earlier interchange, the present dialogue ends with severe criticism,
thus intensifying the negative thrust of the subsection.
42. Indeed, the entire interchange can be described as ironic. First, one finds several
instances of a character (first Jesus, then Peter) bypassing, whether partially or entirely, the
preceding statement of his interlocutor. Second, given his failure to understand the true
meaning of Jesus' departure, Peter's questions and alternative proposal prove ironic as well.
Finally, there is also irony in Jesus' rhetorical repetition of Peter's proposal and the immediately following prediction affirming its opposite in a matter of hours (13:38). The combined
effect of such an ironic development sharply underlines the serious lack of understanding on
Peter's part—and by extension, on the part of the other disciples as well—regarding Jesus'
status and role, even at the time of "the hour" itself.

The first section of the first unit of discourse (13:31–38) introduces the two controlling and overarching themes of the unit—the fundamental meaning of Jesus' departure and the consequences of the departure for the disciples—from a negative perspective. Several troubling announcements and disclosures are made: the forthcoming departure of Jesus, the sharp separation to come between Jesus and the disciples, the new command of love for one another as the one farewell legacy left to the disciples, the implicit warning conveyed by this final instruction, and the predicted threefold denial of Simon Peter. One strong, though veiled, glimmer of hope is also extended: the revision of the description of the coming separation as temporary instead of permanent.

The first section also introduces from the very beginning, in the announcement of Jesus' glorification (13:31–32), a distinctive temporal standpoint for the speaker—the Jesus who speaks is both a Jesus who is about to die (about to undergo the climactic events of "the hour") and a Jesus who has already surpassed "the hour" except for its final events. Both dimensions of this temporal standpoint are found in the initial exposition of this announcement of glorification (13:33–38). The announcement of the departure itself can be read from both perspectives (forthcoming death or final ascent to the Father). The first and final consequences of the departure (the inability of the disciples to go with Jesus at this point and the threefold denial of Peter) can be read from the point of view of the Jesus about to die. The other consequence of the departure and the revision of the first consequence (the command to love one another as Jesus had loved them and the promise of a later following) can be read from the point of view of the risen Jesus about to return to the Father.

Second Major Section (John 14:1–27)

The second major section of the first unit of discourse, 14:1–27, describes a call to courage and faith: the fundamental meaning of the departure and the positive consequences of the departure for the disciples. It represents an extensive, systematic development of the controlling themes of the unit as introduced in 13:31–38. Furthermore, the negative, troubling tone of the first section now yields to a positive, reassuring tone. This section presents a threefold linear and progressive development of the themes. A preliminary and positive proposition regarding the meaning of the departure and its consequences for the disciples in 14:1–3 is followed by an extensive and sequential exposition of these two themes in the remainder of the section—the fundamental meaning of the departure in 14:4–14 in terms of the relationship between Jesus and the Father, and the positive consequences of the departure for the disciples in 14:15–27. As such, the section can be described as a sustained exercise in the teaching and consolation of the disciples. Its structure can be outlined as follows:

1. A call to courage and faith: a preliminary proposition (14:1–3).
2. The fundamental meaning of the departure: Jesus and the Father (14:4–14).
3. The positive consequences of the departure for the disciples (14:15–27).

A Call to Courage and Faith: A Preliminary Proposition (John 14:1–3)

The first subsection, 14:1–3, plays a pivotal role within the unit as a whole. On the one hand, the subsection not only advances but also anticipates the overall development of the overarching themes of the unit. On the other hand, the subsection also introduces a radical change in tone with regard to this development. Two major components can be discerned: (1) a twofold call to the disciples (14:1) and (2) a preliminary proposition concerning the meaning of the departure and its consequences for the disciples (14:2–3).

The Call to Courage and Faith (John 14:1)

The subsection 14:1–3 begins with a twofold call to the disciples: a call to courage (14:1a) and a call to faith (14:1b–c). First, the negative tone of the preceding announcements and disclosures yields to an exhortation (14:1a) calling for courage on the part of the disciples. Given its pointed repetition and expansion in 14:27d, it is clear that this call to courage of 14:1a is issued on the basis of the further announcements and disclosures to follow in this second major section.[43] Second, the call to belief of 14:1b–c is in itself a twofold call, involving a call to believe in God (14:1b) and a call to believe in Jesus (14:1c).[44] In the light of Peter's failure in 13:36–38 to understand the nature and consequences of Jesus' mission—a failure that, as the rest of the unit shows, is by no means limited to Peter alone—the two exhortations of 14:1b–c call for belief on the part of the disciples as well. At the same time, given its repetition in 14:11, this call to belief is also issued on the basis of the further announcements and disclosures to follow in this

---

43. The use of the verb ταράσσειν in this regard is effective. The underlying reaction of the disciples to the preceding disclosures is portrayed thereby in the same terms as Jesus' own reaction to various aspects of "the hour" (11:33; 12:27; 13:21); consequently, this beginning call to courage also reflects Jesus' own determination before "the hour" (12:27–29).

44. The two calls are interrelated: belief in God entails belief in Jesus as God's messenger, and belief in Jesus implies belief in God as the one who sent Jesus. See, e.g., 5:24, 38; 6:29; 12:44.

second major section. The first part of this section specifically addresses the issue of belief as such—with a delineation of the relationship between Jesus and the Father and an understanding of Jesus' departure in terms of this relationship.

Both of these beginning calls, therefore, are interrelated and interdependent. On the one hand, both are grounded in the negative tone of the first section and issued on the basis of a far more positive message to follow in this second section. On the other hand, both also point to and reinforce one another: courage comes from belief, and belief gives rise to courage. These initial calls of 14:1 begin to redirect, therefore, the thrust of the entire unit, anticipating and informing all that follows in the central major section. In effect, with these calls the extended process of teaching and consolation begins.

The Fundamental Meaning of the Departure and the
Positive Consequences of the Departure for the Disciples:
A Preliminary Proposition (John 14:2–3)

The subsection continues with a brief preliminary proposition concerning the fundamental meaning of the forthcoming departure and its consequences for the disciples (14:2–3). This proposition both advances and anticipates the development of the two controlling themes of the unit. The proposition explains the meaning of the announced departure (14:2) and gives further consequences of the departure for the disciples (14:3). In so doing, it drastically changes the thrust of the development.

In the first part of the proposition (14:2), the previous announcement of Jesus' departure in 13:33a–b is developed by an explanation concerning the destination of and reason for the departure. To begin with, Peter's first question of 13:36–38 concerning the destination of the departure is given a concrete, though indirect, response: it is to "the house" of the Father that Jesus now goes (14:2a).[45] Then the question of the reason for the departure, also raised by Peter with regard to the inability of the disciples to follow Jesus at this time, is answered from the point of view of the departure itself: Jesus goes to the Father's "house" to prepare "a place" for

45. The response is indirect insofar as the proposition begins with a metaphorical description of the world of God, following the imagery of a household: "the house" (οἰκία) of the Father consists of "many rooms or abiding places" (μοναὶ πολλαί). This household imagery further develops the earlier characterization of the disciples in 13:34a as "little children": it is for the "little children" that the "many rooms" in "the house" of the Father are meant. In other words, the true home of the disciples is not in this world but in the world above, where Jesus is going. The use of "house" in 2:16–17 is to the point here: the temple of Jerusalem as "the house" of the Father is completely replaced by Jesus at "the hour," so "the house" of the Father now is restricted, to begin with (cf. 14:23), to the world above and meant only for Jesus' disciples. For a good summary of the background of this imagery, see Schnackenburg, 3:60–61. For a similar metaphorical description, see John 8:31–38.

the disciples (14:2b–c).[46] Both of these answers to Peter's questions represent a radical shift in the development of the unit's first controlling theme. The explicit identification of both the destination of and reason for the departure points well beyond the blunt announcement of 13:33a–b: Jesus is indeed about to leave the disciples, but in so doing, he is going to the Father's house for the sake of the disciples themselves.

In the second part of the proposition (14:3), the preceding delineation of the consequences of Jesus' departure of 13:33c–38 is further developed by an additional listing of such consequences.[47] Three such consequences of Jesus' departure to "the house" of the Father are listed: (1) a subsequent return to the disciples (14:3b$_1$), (2) a gathering together of the disciples unto himself (14:3b$_2$), and (3) a permanent reunion of Jesus with the disciples (14:3c).[48] Once again, this further delineation of consequences represents a radical shift in the development of the unit's second overarching theme. These positive promises point beyond the distressing consequences outlined in the first section; in fact, these promises ultimately expand the earlier promise of a later following.

The preliminary proposition of 14:2–3, therefore, radically shifts the tone from a negative to a positive presentation of what Jesus' glorification implies and entails. Following the lead of the beginning calls of 14:1, the brief statement of 14:2–3 represents a positive, reassuring proposition regarding the fundamental meaning of Jesus' departure and its consequences

---

46. The destination of the departure is now directly identified: it is to the Father's house that Jesus goes (with the verb πορεύεσθαι as well; see 7:35 and cf. 10:4). In addition, given the description of this "house" as consisting of "many rooms," the reason for the departure is also formulated in terms of household imagery—as preparing a "place" (τόπος) for the disciples. The use of this term in 4:20 and 11:48 is to the point: whereas the "place" of the Jews is in Jerusalem, in the temple, that of the disciples is in the world above. The precise formulation of this response is problematic. First, I favor the reading with the particle ὅτι on the basis of superior attestation (ℵ A B C° D pm) and because its omission can be readily explained in terms of a scribal attempt at simplification—either the common removal of a perceived ὅτι recitative or the specific removal of a highly ambiguous particle in the statement. Second, the clause can be construed as introductory (Bernard, 2:533–34; Bultmann, 601, n. 4) or causal (Lindars, 471; Barrett, 457). In my opinion, an explicative use of ὅτι, especially with the apodosis as interrogative, provides the most satisfactory reading—"If it were not so, would I have told you that I go to prepare a place for you?" This is not the only declaration of Jesus that is not found in the preceding narrative (see, e.g., 11:40). Besides, there is nothing intrinsically defective about a character's referring to a previous declaration not recorded in the narrative itself; in fact, such a reference can serve as a summary, reformulation, or explication of earlier statements in the narrative (see, e.g., John 12:26).

47. This listing (14:3b–c) is preceded, within a conditional sentence, by a repetition of the reason for the departure from 14:2 (14:3a), emphasizing thereby the true meaning of such a departure.

48. The "return" is expressed by means of the verb ἔρχομαι, used later with respect to the resurrection appearances of Jesus (20:19, 24, 26). The "gathering together" (παραλαμβάνειν) follows the household imagery and is ironic as well: whereas "his own" did not "receive" him (1:11), except to put him to death (19:16), Jesus now "takes to himself" the disciples as his own.

for the disciples. With 14:2–3, therefore, the extended process of teaching and consolation has begun in earnest.

The Meaning of the Departure:
Jesus and the Father (John 14:4–14)

The second subsection (14:1–27) continues with a further development of the first controlling theme of the unit of discourse, the fundamental meaning of Jesus' departure, as formulated in 14:2. Therefore, it is a direct and positive expansion of the first part of the preliminary proposition of 14:2–3. This expansion deals primarily with the question of the destination of the departure; the relationship between Jesus and the Father is carefully developed and explained for most of the subsection, whereas the question of the reason for the departure is pursued only briefly at the end of the subsection. As such, the subsection provides further direction, by way of teaching, to the call to believe in both God and Jesus of 14:1b–c and thus ultimately to the call for courage of 14:1a as well.

This second subsection can be seen as consisting of three subunits. Each presents a similar threefold structure in the form of an inclusion, thus lending harmony and balance to the subsection as a whole. The three subunits deal with specific aspects of the relationship between Jesus and the Father. These teachings—consisting for the most part of variations on previous declarations of Jesus concerning his status and role vis-à-vis the Father—are developed in a systematic linear or progressive fashion that proceeds throughout the subsection from the more basic to the more complex christological formulations. Thus, the exposition of the relationship between Jesus and the Father begins with the question of approaching the Father through Jesus, continues with that of perceiving the Father in Jesus, and concludes with that of identifying the Father with Jesus. This structure can be readily outlined as follows: (1) Jesus as the way to the Father (14:4–6), (2) knowing and seeing the Father in Jesus (14:7–9), and (3) the mutual presence of Jesus and the Father as in one another (14:10–14). Whereas the first subunit is closely connected to the first subsection of 14:1–3, the third subunit paves the way directly for the third subsection of 14:15–27. All three subunits reveal a similar threefold structure in the form of an inclusion.

First, each subunit begins with a statement by Jesus to the effect that the disciples do understand a certain aspect of his relationship to the Father, the destination of his forthcoming departure. In each case, this beginning statement proves ironic, since in effect, as Peter has already shown in a concrete way within the first major section, the disciples have little knowledge at this point of what the announced departure implies or entails.

Second, each subunit continues with a delineation of a reaction on the part of the disciples to the beginning statement. In the first two subunits, this middle component portrays actual reactions by the assembled disciples;

in the third subunit, the middle component outlines the correct reaction of the disciples. On the one hand, the actual reactions are conveyed, as in 13:36–38, by the introduction of two brief dialogues between Jesus and individual disciples. Both consist of a simple exchange between Jesus and the disciple in question, again with an identification by the narrator of each individual address (14:5a, 6a, 8a, 9a). In both cases the reactions reveal, again as in 13:36–38, a thorough lack of understanding with regard to the nature and implications of Jesus' mission and ministry, thus confirming the ironic character of the beginning component. On the other hand, the proper reaction is outlined by Jesus himself, again confirming the ironic nature of the beginning component. In the end, this final delineation of the proper reaction functions as a deliberate counterpart to the first two and actual reactions of the disciples.

Finally, each subunit returns to the beginning component for further development of the specific aspect of Jesus' relationship to the Father in question. Thus, in effect, not only is there christological development from subunit to subunit, but also within each subunit. From beginning to end, therefore, this second subsection of 14:4–14 reveals a linear and progressive development of the first controlling theme of the unit, the fundamental meaning of Jesus' departure, in terms of the relationship between Jesus and the Father.

Jesus as the Way to the Father (John 14:4–6)

The first subunit (14:4–6) begins to develop the question of the departure's destination by focusing on how to get there, on "the way" (ἡ ὁδός) to the Father's house. In so doing, this subunit is closely tied to 14:1–3 insofar as it continues the imagery of journeying conveyed in the first subsection by means of such terms as "going away" and "returning." From the point of view of the relationship between Jesus and the Father, the first christological teaching of the subsection deals with the question of approaching the Father through Jesus—Jesus as "the way" to the Father. Given the pattern of inclusion proposed for each subunit, the structure of this first subunit can be outlined as follows: (1) the presumed knowledge of the disciples concerning "the way" (14:4), (2) Thomas's reaction and the actual ignorance of the disciples with respect to "the way" (14:5), and (3) Jesus' teaching regarding "the way" (14:6).

In the first component (14:4), Jesus continues the disclosures of 14:2–3 by telling the disciples, as if in conclusion, that they already know "the way" to the destination of his departure.[49]

---

49. I follow the shorter reading at this point, "Where I am going you know the way" (p⁶⁶ᶜ ℵ B Cᵒ L W X al). The longer reading, "You know where I am going and you know the way," receives wide, early support (p⁶⁶ᵉ A C³ D K pm) but can be readily explained as both

The central component (14:5) describes a reaction of one of the assembled disciples, Thomas, to this beginning declaration of Jesus, setting up thereby an interchange with Jesus in 14:5 similar to that of 13:36–38.[50] Thomas's reaction also reveals the ironic character of the beginning statement concerning the disciples' presumed knowledge of "the way." In effect, Thomas responds by way of a question: because the disciples do not know the destination of the announced departure (14:5b–c)—Thomas thus indirectly repeats Peter's first question of 13:36—how can they be expected to know "the way" there (14:5d)? It is clear, therefore, that despite the preceding disclosures of 14:1–3, the disciples are still at a loss concerning the meaning and consequences of Jesus' departure, even with respect to its already announced destination.

In the final component (14:6), Jesus expands the beginning declaration concerning "the way" through further instruction: an explicit identification of himself as "the way" (14:6b$_1$), a further self-identification as "truth" and "life" (14:6b$_{2-3}$), and a concluding characterization of himself as the exclusive way to the Father (14:6c).[51] This exclusivity sets the stage directly for the second subunit of 14:7–9.

Knowing and Seeing the Father in Jesus (John 14:7–9)

The second subunit, 14:7–9, leaves behind the imagery of journeying so far connected with the question of the destination and continues the question's development by focusing on the relationship between Jesus and the Father. The christological teaching of 14:4–6 to the effect that Jesus is "the way"—and the only way—to the Father is now pursued in terms of the fundamental reason for this given exclusivity. The second subunit begins to do so by dealing with the question of how the Father can be perceived in Jesus—to know and see Jesus is to know and see the Father. The structure of this second subunit can be outlined in terms of the proposed pattern of inclusion: (1) the presumed perception of the Father by the disciples (14:7), (2) the reaction of Philip and the actual ignorance of the Father by the disciples (14:8), and (3) Jesus' teaching concerning the proper perception of the Father (14:9).

---

an attempt to improve the syntax of the shorter reading and an assimilation to the following reaction of Thomas.

50. For a similar failure to understand on the part of Thomas, see 11:7–16; 20:24–29.

51. The self-identifications of 14:6b$_{2-3}$ explain, by means of central metaphors from the Gospel, how it is that Jesus is "the way" to the Father, namely, insofar as he is "truth" (see, e.g., 1:14, 17; 5:33; 8:32; 18:37) and "life" (see, e.g., 1:4; 10:11; 11:25). Consequently, the concluding instruction of 14:6c specifies that there is no other "way" to the Father except through Jesus, who is both "truth" and "life." On Jesus as the exclusive way to the Father, see, e.g., 3:13; 6:37, 44–46, 65.

The first component of the second subunit (14:7) involves two steps: (1) an initial reproach of the disciples because of their lack of understanding with respect to the Father as the destination of the departure, Jesus as "the way" to the Father, and the exclusive character of this relationship (14:7a–b); and (2) a subsequent statement to the effect, again as if in conclusion, that from this point on, the disciples can truly perceive the Father (14:7c).

The first step is transitional. On the one hand, this step continues the strong emphasis on "knowing" (14:4–5) from the first subunit, as well as the specific concern of its final affirmation (14:6c)—the exclusive character of Jesus as "the way" to the Father—by specifying, in terms of a direct reproach of the disciples,[52] that a proper knowledge of Jesus entails a knowledge of the Father as well (in other words, that it is only through Jesus that the Father can be known). On the other hand, the formulation of this initial reproach leads directly to a declaration on Jesus' part, much like that of 14:4, concerning the present knowledge and understanding of the disciples. In the second step, therefore, Jesus tells the disciples, again as if by way of conclusion, that "from now on" they not only "know" the Father but can also "see" him.[53]

The central component of the second subunit (14:8) describes another reaction by one of the assembled disciples, Philip, to the beginning declaration of Jesus. This sets up yet another interchange with Jesus like that of 13:36–38 (14:8).[54] Philip's reaction here, like that of Thomas, reveals the ironic character of the beginning statement concerning the disciples' presumed perception of the Father. Indeed, the irony is even sharper here, given the reproach of the disciples in the beginning statement. Philip's reaction differs from the two previous ones, however. He does not ask a question but instead makes a request of Jesus: given Jesus' declaration that the disciples can now "see" the Father, Philip asks Jesus "to show"

52. The precise formulation of this first step is problematic. Two different versions, both equally strong from a textual point of view, are possible: (a) a real condition, implying a promise, "If you have come to know me (ἐγνώκατέ με [or ἐμέ]; p⁶⁶ ℵ D° al), you will know my Father as well (γνώσεσθε; p⁶⁶ ℵ D° al)"; (b) a contrary-to-fact condition, implying a reproach, "If you had known me (ἐγνώκειτέ με; A [without με] B C al), you would have known my Father as well (ἂν ἤδειτε; B C° al; ἐγνώκειτε ἄν; A al)." I favor the latter as the more difficult reading; it is easier to explain the omission of a reproach than its addition. In this regard I also consider the reading of B C° al as the more difficult, given the presence of γινώσκειν in the protasis. See also, e.g., Loisy, 406; Bernard, 2:538–39; Brown, 2:621.

53. For the knowledge of the Father in and through Jesus, see, above all, 8:55; 10:14–15 (see also 7:17; 10:37–38); for the seeing of the Father in and through Jesus, see, above all, 5:37 (see also 1:18; 3:11, 32; 6:36–38, 46; 8:38).

54. For a similar failure to understand on the part of Philip, see 1:43–46; 6:1–15; 12:20–22.

them the Father (14:8b–c) so that they can be satisfied (14:8d).[55] Such a request clearly indicates that despite the explicit instructions of 14:4–6 and the more indirect instruction of 14:7a–b, the disciples remain at a complete loss with regard to the nature and implications of Jesus' mission.

The final component of the second subunit (14:9) expands by way of further instruction the beginning statement concerning the disciples' perception of the Father. Here the emphasis is on "seeing" rather than "knowing." The formulation of this final component follows a pattern of inclusion: the outer components contain individual reproaches of Philip (14:9b–c, 9e–f), and the central component expands the beginning statement (14:9d).

On the one hand, the twofold reproach of Philip reinforces the initial reproach of the disciples in the beginning statement (14:7a–b). In the first example, 14:9b–c, the reproach is delivered in terms of the disciples' failure "to know" Jesus despite his extended stay among them. In the second example, 14:9d–f, the reproach is made by a rhetorical repetition of Philip's request, a procedure similar to that of the earlier repetition of Peter's alternative proposal in 13:37. Both reproaches further sharpen the ironic character of the beginning statement. On the other hand, the expansion of the beginning statement reformulates that statement's concluding affirmation—the disciples' present ability "to see" the Father—along the lines of the beginning reproach, though now in terms of a positive declaration: whoever sees Jesus sees the Father. In other words, it is only through Jesus that the Father can be seen. This expansion paves the way directly for the third subunit, 14:10–14.

The Mutual Presence of Jesus and the Father in One Another (John 14:10–14)

The third subunit, 14:10–14, ends the development of the question of the destination of the departure by continuing to focus directly, as in 14:7–9, on the relationship between Jesus and the Father, even though the imagery of journeying does reappear in the final component. At the same time, the question of the reason for the departure, which was completely absent from the first two subunits, also reappears in the final component. The third subunit pursues the fundamental reasons for the given exclusivity of the first christological teaching of 14:4–6 (Jesus as the only way to the Father). In so doing, this subunit develops the christological teaching of the second subunit (to know and see Jesus is to know and see the Father) by dealing

---

55. Philip's request for Jesus to show them the Father (δεῖξον ὑμῖν) represents a request to see God, whom Jesus claims as his Father—that is, a request for a theophany. With such a request Philip comes close to the position of the unbelieving Jews (cf. 2:18; 10:32).

specifically with the question of identifying the Father with Jesus—the mutual presence of Jesus and the Father in one another. The third subunit's structure follows the proposed pattern of inclusion for all three subunits: (1) the presumed knowledge of the disciples concerning the mutual presence (14:10), (2) a delineation of the proper reaction of the disciples (a call for belief in the mutual presence, 14:11), and (3) further teaching concerning the mutual presence by means of promises to those who respond to the call to faith (14:12–14). However, as this outline shows, there are important variations in the second and third components of this subunit— variations that prepare the way directly for the third subsection, 14:15–27.

The first component (14:10) is developed in two steps: (1) a declaration that the disciples already believe in the mutual presence of Jesus and the Father in one another (14:10a) and (2) an immediate explanation of what such a mutual presence entails with regard to Jesus' words and works (14:10b–c). The first step develops the second christological teaching of 14:7–9, the perception of the Father in Jesus, by pursuing its fundamental reason and thus, ultimately, the fundamental reason for the first christological teaching of 14:4–6 as well: to know and see Jesus is to know and see the Father, because Jesus is in the Father, and the Father is in him. Instead of being a statement of affirmation as if by way of conclusion, like those of 14:4 and 14:7c, the present declaration is formulated in terms of a question. However, the question clearly expects a positive response and thus presupposes the disciples' present knowledge of the mutual presence as well. The second step outlines the consequences of the mutual presence for Jesus' mission: the words (ῥήματα) that he speaks (λέγω/λαλῶ) are not his own (14:10b), and the works (ἔργα) that he performs are not his but the Father's (14:10c).[56] In other words, given the mutual presence, to perceive Jesus' words and works is to perceive the Father's own words and works.

The central component (14:11) no longer consists, as in the previous subunits, of a reaction by one of the assembled disciples. It is an explicit call by Jesus to believe in the mutual presence as set forth in 14:10, a call that clearly reaffirms and reinforces the beginning calls to belief of 14:1b–c. Therefore, instead of a concrete and negative reaction on the part of the disciples to the beginning statement concerning their presumed knowledge of the mutual presence, there is a direct appeal by Jesus to the disciples to believe in that mutual presence. Ultimately, such a call

56. For the mutual presence of Jesus and the Father in one another, see 10:37–38. For Jesus' words as the Father's words, see, e.g., 3:34; 8:47; 12:47–49. For Jesus' works as the Father's works, see, e.g., 4:34; 5:19–20, 36; 9:4; 10:25, 32, 37–38. Whereas in 14:10a the mutual presence is formulated in terms of the verb *to be*, in 14:10c the presence of the Father in Jesus is further described in terms of the verb *to abide*—"abiding in me"—the only such time in the Gospel.

is just as ironic, if not more so, as a misguided reaction by one of the disciples, given the preceding assumption that the disciples already believe in this mutual presence. At the same time, the delineation of their proper reaction serves as a counterpart to the two earlier reactions. The call itself is issued on two grounds, both taken from the beginning statement (14:10b–c), and is presented in the form of an inclusion. The outer components provide the grounds for the call—belief on the basis of Jesus' words (14:11a$_1$) or works (14:11b–c). The central component outlines the object of such belief by repeating the earlier statement of the mutual presence.[57]

The final component (14:12–14) is the most extensive of the subsection. On the one hand, it extends a number of promises to those who believe, who respond to the call of 14:11, so that this call emerges as the essential condition for these promises to take place. Such promises not only provide a further development of 14:3—a further delineation of the positive consequences of the departure for the disciples—but also directly anticipate and prepare for its extensive development in 14:15–27. On the other hand, the final component also expands the beginning statement concerning the mutual presence by reintroducing within these promises both the question of the reason for the departure (undeveloped since 14:2) and the theme of glorification (untouched since 13:31–32). This final component is presented in the form of an inclusion: (1) a first promise to the disciples (14:12a–c), (2) the grounding for such promises (14:12d), and (3) a second promise to the disciples (14:13–14).

The first component of the inclusion (14:12a–c) begins by repeating the essential condition for these promises to take place—belief in Jesus (14:12a–b$_1$). It then outlines the first such promise: the disciples will be able to duplicate and indeed surpass Jesus' own works (14:12b$_2$–c).[58]

---

57. I believe that the dative of the personal pronoun that functions as the indirect object of the first imperative ("believe me"), and hence as the first grounds for the call to belief (14:11a$_1$), refers to Jesus' words or speaking of 14:10b. The second grounds for the call to belief (14:11b–c, "on account of the works themselves") refer directly to Jesus' works of 14:10c; in addition, the abbreviated protasis, "if not," indicates a choice of alternative grounds (either me or the works themselves) parallel to that of 14:10b–c (neither Jesus' words nor his works are his own but the Father's). I interpret the introduction of the dative of the personal pronoun as an indirect object after the second imperative, despite wide and early support (A B K X Δ Θ Π pm), as an assimilation to the preceding construction with the first imperative. For belief in Jesus on the basis of his words and works, see 10:25–26, 37–38; see also 11:40–42.

58. The formulation of the essential condition at this point—"the one who believes in me"—shows that the promises of this final subunit are predicated not just on belief in the mutual presence as called for in the preceding exhortation of 14:11 but instead on the whole teaching of the subsection concerning the relationship between Jesus and the Father, with the mutual presence as its climax.

In the central component of the inclusion (14:12d), the grounding for the promises is disclosed (14:12d)—the departure (πορεύομαι) of Jesus to the Father. As such, this central component reintroduces the imagery of journeying; returns to the original formulation of the destination in 14:2; and reproduces the pattern of presentation to be found within the preliminary proposition of 14:2–3, namely, a disclosure of the meaning of the departure (going to the Father) accompanied by a delineation of its positive consequences for the disciples (the framing promises of 14:12a–c and 14:13–14).

The final component of the inclusion (14:13–14) outlines a second promise by means of yet another pattern of inclusion. The outer components identify the promise in question (14:13a, 14), and the central component provides the purpose for such a promise (14:13b).

The promise itself, repeated in the framing components with minor stylistic variations,[59] assures the disciples that Jesus will do whatever they ask of him in his name.[60] As such, the promise reintroduces at this point the question of the reason for the departure: in going to the Father, Jesus will not only prepare a "place" for the disciples but also will hear and grant the requests of the disciples. The central component discloses the basic purpose for the present and preceding promises:[61] the glorification of the Father by the Son. In so doing, the statement of purpose reintroduces the theme of glorification from the beginning announcement of 13:31–32: the Father will be glorified by Jesus even after "the hour" itself, in and through the

59. The second formulation of the promise in 14:14 is omitted in some manuscripts (X 565 1009 1365 al); however, not only does its presence receive much superior attestation (p[66] p[75] ℵ A B D L W pm), but its omission can be easily explained as either accidental (a beginning ἐάν in both 14:14 and 14:15) or deliberate (regarded as redundant after 14:13a or as contradicting 16:23).

60. The second formulation of 14:14 includes the accusative of the personal pronoun as the personal object of the verb to ask (αἰτεῖν), thereby identifying Jesus as the addressee for all such requests; not only does this reading enjoy superior backing (p[66] ℵ B W Δ Θ al), but also its omission (A D K L pm) can be explained by assimilation to the first formulation of the promise. As such, in this first promise of the farewell concerning the granting of the disciples' requests, the full mechanism of the promise is set forth: Jesus is presented as both addressee and grantor, and the procedure for such asking is also explained with reference to Jesus by means of an instrumental of manner, "in my name."

61. Although the statement of purpose is linked directly to this second promise, I see it as encompassing the first promise as well. In fact, both promises are interrelated. The disciples will be able to duplicate and surpass Jesus' own works (14:12a–c)—and there is no reason to restrict such works only to the signs or miraculous works as such (e.g., 4:34; 5:19–20; 6:28–29)—because Jesus will grant whatever they ask in his name when he is with the Father (14:13–14). As such, it is not so much the disciples themselves who will be able to do and surpass Jesus' works but Jesus who is with the Father. In effect, just as Jesus, in the course of his own mission, did the work or works of the Father, so will the disciples, in the course of their own mission, do the work or works of Jesus himself.

disciples' own mission.[62] The expansion of the beginning statement concerning the mutual presence takes place, therefore, by way of promises. More specifically, the statement is expanded through the reintroduction of both the question of the reason for the departure and the theme of glorification within such promises, showing thereby the relationship between Jesus and the Father after "the hour."

The third subunit, 14:10–14, plays an important role within the central major section. In ending the sustained development of the relationship between Jesus and the Father in 14:4–14, the subunit returns to the preliminary proposition of 14:2–3 and anticipates the following subsection, 14:15–27. On the one hand, the subunit (14:12–14) repeats the pattern of presentation found in 14:2–3: the meaning of the departure as presented in 14:2 is recalled (14:12d) and accompanied, as in 14:3, by a further delineation of positive consequences of the departure for the disciples (14:12a–c, 13–14). On the other hand, the subunit (14:11/14:12–14) introduces a pattern of presentation that will govern and inform all of 14:15–27: a statement of the essential condition for such promises to be fulfilled followed by a delineation of the promises themselves. In fact, it is the presence of this pattern that accounts for the variations in the second and third components of this final subunit mentioned above. This final subunit specifically returns, therefore, to the preliminary proposition of 14:2–3 after the development of 14:2 is completed in order to prepare the way directly for the subsequent development of 14:3 in the third subsection that follows.

This third subunit (14:10–14) also returns to the beginning announcement of 13:31–32 via the theme of glorification: The Father will continue to be glorified by the Son after "the hour" in and through the disciples. In so doing, this final subunit returns to the beginning announcement of glorification after the exposition of the fundamental meaning of that glorification in 14:4–14 is completed in order to prepare the way concretely for the further exposition of its consequences for the disciples in 14:15–27.

The second subsection (14:4–14) of the second major section (14:1–27) of the first unit of discourse is primarily a further exposition of the first controlling theme of the unit, the fundamental meaning of Jesus' departure, in

62. The glorification of the Father that Jesus has accomplished by his full compliance with the mission entrusted to him by the Father (13:31–32) will be continued by Jesus after his return to the Father by means of his promised granting of the disciples' requests in his name. Furthermore, insofar as it is the requests of the disciples that will be carried out by him, Jesus' continued glorification of the Father after the completion of his mission can be said to be in and through the disciples themselves and their coming mission.

terms of the relationship between Jesus and the Father. The exposition begins in the first subunit with the teaching that Jesus is "the way"—indeed, the only "way"—to the Father, insofar as he is both "truth" and "life." The other two subunits continue this exposition by focusing on the element of exclusivity. The second subunit explains this exclusivity in terms of the direct perception of the Father in Jesus: to know Jesus is to know the Father; indeed, to see Jesus is to see the Father. The third subunit ends the exposition by further explaining such exclusivity in terms of the mutual presence of Jesus and the Father in one another: Jesus is in the Father, and the Father is in Jesus. At the conclusion of this development the subsection, in direct preparation for the third and final subsection (14:15–27), returns to both the preliminary proposition of 14:2–3 and the beginning announcement of glorification of 13:31–32. It also concretely anticipates the specific pattern of development governing this final subsection.

The Positive Consequences of the Departure for the Disciples (John 14:15–27)

The third subsection of the second major section (14:15–27) further develops the second controlling theme of the unit, the consequences of the departure for the disciples, as formulated in 14:3. Therefore, 14:15–27 directly expands the second part of the preliminary proposition of 14:2–3. This expansion consists of four subunits, each of which presents a similar threefold structure and thus contributes to the harmony and balance of the entire subsection. Each subunit outlines, by way of promises, further positive consequences of the departure for the disciples. In so doing, the subsection follows an overall chiastic arrangement in the form of an ABBA pattern. There is development within this chiastic arrangement, but such development is not as linear and progressive as that of the second subsection; in fact, the third subsection presents a more repetitive and cumulative development. The two framing subunits deal with consequences concerning the Spirit-Paraclete, and the two central subunits focus on consequences concerning Jesus and the Father. This structure can be outlined as follows: (1) promises concerning the Spirit-Paraclete (14:15–17), (2) promises concerning Jesus and the Father (14:18–21), (3) promises concerning Jesus and the Father (14:22–23), and (4) promises concerning the Spirit-Paraclete (14:24–27).

All four subunits also reveal a similar threefold structure in the form of a linear development, though not always in the same sequence. The basic pattern has already been anticipated in 14:10–14, facilitating once again the transition from the concluding development of 14:2 to the beginning development of 14:3 within the central major section.

Each subunit begins with a statement of the essential condition for the consequences of the departure to take place (cf. 14:11, repeated in 14:12b₁). A change in formulation, with a corresponding expansion in meaning, can be observed: whereas 14:10–14 describes the condition in terms of "belief in Jesus," all four subunits here describe it in terms of "love for Jesus." In each case, furthermore, this condition is specifically formulated in terms of a definition explaining what such "love for Jesus" entails, namely, obedience to his commands, word, or words.

Each subunit continues with a delineation of further positive consequences of the departure for the disciples (cf. 14:12–14). This middle component presents as many variations as there are consequences or promises.

This twofold pattern is then expanded by a third major component: a direct contrast between the disciples and the world with regard to the consequences of the departure in question. In so doing, the subsection returns for further development to the beginning contrast between Peter and the Jews of 13:33c–38. The location of this third component in the different subunits varies. The contrast follows the twofold pattern in the outer subunits (14:15–17, 24–27) and precedes the pattern in the central subunits (14:18–21, 22–23). As a result, the location of this third component within the threefold structure of each subunit follows the chiastic arrangement of the subsection as a whole.

In the end, the subsection provides further shape and direction, by way of consolation, to the call for courage of 14:1a and, thus, ultimately to the twofold call for faith of 14:1b–c as well. This is especially salient in the light of the essential condition of love for Jesus, which includes belief in Jesus.

Promises Concerning the Spirit-Paraclete
(John 14:15–17)

In keeping with the proposed threefold structure for all four subunits of the third subsection, the structure of the first outer subunit (14:15–17) can be outlined as follows: (1) the essential condition for the further positive consequences of the departure to take place (14:15), (2) the delineation of further positive consequences of the departure for the disciples (14:16–17a), and (3) the contrast between the disciples and the world with regard to these consequences (14:17b–e). This first subunit introduces the figure of a coming successor to Jesus, the Spirit-Paraclete, with regard to the positive consequences of the departure.

In the first component (14:15), the essential condition is formulated in terms of a future more vivid condition. The protasis conveys the condition proper, and the apodosis defines it: "If you love me, you will carry out or obey (τηρήσετε) my commands (ἐντολάς)." Consequently, love for

Jesus is immediately defined in terms of obedience to his commands.[63]
Such a definition includes a number of different, though interrelated,
elements:

1. The new "command" of love for one another issued in 13:34–35 as
   Jesus' parting legacy to the disciples, the only practical or ethical
   directive to be so designated in the Gospel.
2. Other practical or ethical directives of Jesus to the disciples disclosed
   in the course of the narrative (for example, 4:35–38; 13:12–16;
   20:21–23), though again only that of love for one another is explicitly
   characterized as a "command" and indeed as the distinguishing command of Jesus.
3. The whole of Jesus' teaching and revelation.[64]

In other words, the disciples should see love for Jesus as encompassing love
for one another, a proper fulfillment of Jesus' other specific directives, as
well as belief itself.

The second component (14:16–17a) outlines a further positive consequence of the departure for the disciples: a promise concerning the coming of "another Paraclete" to them. This, then, refers indirectly to Jesus as
a first or earlier "Paraclete" and points to a successor after his forthcoming
departure.[65] Two major components can be readily discerned: a description of the origins of this figure (14:16a–b) and a brief description of its
envisioned role among the disciples (14:16c–17a). In both regards the
figure of the Paraclete remains closely tied to that of Jesus himself.

The Paraclete is described as "given" (δώσει) by God at the request of
Jesus; his origins, therefore, are, like those of Jesus, with the Father in the

63. Two variant readings for the future tense of the apodosis can be found: an aorist imperative (τηρήσατε), with good widespread support (A D K W X pm), and an aorist subjunctive
(τηρήσετε), with limited, early support (p⁶⁶ ℵ al). I favor the future indicative (B L Ψ al):
whereas the added emphasis of the imperative can be explained as a later scribal addition, the
subjunctive seems difficult here, though the growing intermixture of the future indicative and
the aorist subjunctive at this time should be recalled (BDF, 163).

64. Thus, for example, such "commands" include the calls to belief within the unit itself,
the imperatives of 14:1b–c and 14:11, and thus comprehend the preceding delineation of
Jesus' relationship to the Father in 14:4–14. Similarly, given the use of "command" with
reference to the mission that Jesus received from the Father (10:18; 12:49–50; see n. 37
above), such "commands" should also be seen as pointing to the whole of Jesus' revelation
and teaching in the course of his mission and ministry. Finally, a failure to love Jesus (3:19;
8:43; 12:43) always implies a failure to believe in him; therefore, love for Jesus implies belief
in Jesus as well.

65. The literature on the provenance and connotations of the term "Paraclete" is vast. See,
most recently, E. Franck, *Revelation Taught: The Paraclete in the Gospel of John*, ConBNT 14
(Uppsala: CWK Gleerup, 1985); G. Burge, *The Anointed Community: The Holy Spirit in
the Johannine Tradition* (Grand Rapids: Eerdmans, 1987). I am interested here only in how the
term functions within the farewell itself.

world above.[66] The Paraclete is assigned a twofold role among the disciples at this point. First, its stay among the disciples, unlike that of Jesus, is described as permanent ("so that it may be with you forever"). Second, its specific characterization as "the Spirit of truth" involves the Paraclete directly, like Jesus himself, in the meaning, disclosure, and proclamation of truth.[67] As Jesus' successor among the disciples, therefore, the Spirit-Paraclete is portrayed as having the same provenance and role as Jesus, except that its stay among the disciples will not be temporary but permanent. At the same time, however, a definite subordination to Jesus should be noted: not only does Jesus ask the Father that the Spirit-Paraclete be given to the disciples, but also Jesus has already identified himself as "truth" within the unit (14:4).

The final component (14:17b–e) provides the first contrast between the disciples and the world by describing the very different relationships of the world (14:17b–c) and the disciples (14:17d–e) to the coming Spirit-Paraclete. Such a description is given in the form of a tight antithetical parallelism. To begin with, the basic position of each party with regard to the figure of the Spirit-Paraclete is outlined in opposite terms (14:17b/ 14:17d): whereas the world is described as unable "to receive" (λαβεῖν) the Spirit-Paraclete (14:17b), the disciples themselves are assured that they will "know" (γινώσκετε) it, a futuristic present (14:17d). Each position then is followed by a twofold grounding, again formulated in opposite terms and by means of futuristic presents (14:17c/14:17e): whereas the world cannot receive the Spirit-Paraclete because of its failure "to see" (θεωρεῖ) and "to know" (γινώσκει) it (14:17c), the disciples will know the Spirit-Paraclete on account of its own "abiding" (παρ᾽ ὑμῖν μένει) among, and "presence" in (ἐν ὑμῖν ἐστιν), them.[68] A sharp differentiation

66. This is the first use of the verb ἐρωτᾶν with respect to a request of Jesus from the Father (16:26; 17:9, 15, 20; cf. 11:22).

67. Such a characterization also connects the Paraclete with all other references to "the Spirit" in the Gospel. Such references encompass both the relationship between Jesus and the Spirit and the relationship between the Spirit and the disciples. With regard to the former, it is clear that Jesus and the Spirit are closely associated elsewhere in the narrative: the Spirit characterizes in a specific way the nature of Jesus' mission and ministry (1:32–33; 3:34; 6:63; see also 3:6; 4:24; 19:30; 20:22). With regard to the latter, the possession of the Spirit clearly allows the disciples (a) to be born from above and thus to see/enter the kingdom or world of God (3:5, 6, 8), (b) to worship the Father properly (4:23–24), (c) to have "life" (6:63), and (d) to be a source of "life" (7:39). For a parallel association between Spirit and truth, see 4:23–24. This first promise of 14:15–17 reflects well, therefore, both of these relationships concerning the Spirit: as the Spirit of truth, the presence of the Paraclete among the disciples defines and characterizes their status in the world as disciples of Jesus.

68. The present reading ἐστιν (p[66] B D° W al) is preferred to the future ἔσται (p[66c] p[75vid] A D[b] L pm). Although the future receives early and widespread support, it can be readily explained, especially given the formulation of the entire contrast in the present tense, as a scribal attempt to insure that the abiding of the Spirit be understood as a still future event at this point (cf. 14:16).

is posited thereby between the disciples and the world after Jesus' departure: only the former will be able to receive Jesus' announced successor,
the Spirit-Paraclete, and possess the "truth."[69]

Promises Concerning Jesus and the Father
(John 14:18-21)

In the first central subunit (14:18-21) the proposed threefold structure
undergoes a change in sequence. The final component of the preceding
subunit—the contrast between the disciples and the world—now becomes
the first. The structure of this second subunit can be outlined as follows:
(1) the contrast between the disciples and the world with regard to the
further positive consequences of the departure to be outlined (14:18-20),
(2) the essential condition for such consequences to take place (14:21a),
and (3) the delineation of further positive consequences of the departure
for the disciples (14:21b–c). The second subunit focuses on the figures of
Jesus and the Father with regard to the positive consequences of the
departure.

The first component (14:18-20) continues the contrast between the
disciples and the world of the preceding subunit (14:15-17), though now
with specific reference to the further consequences of the departure still
to be outlined within the subunit (14:21b–c). The development of this
component is far more extensive than that of the first contrast and indeed
than that of any other single component in all four subunits. This contrast
is carefully constructed in the form of an overall inclusion. Its outer components deal, by way of promises, with the relationship between Jesus and
the disciples after the departure and thus with the future situation of the
disciples as such (14:18, 20). The central component presents a basic
contrast between the world and the disciples with regard to Jesus in the
time after the departure (14:19).

In the opening component (14:18) of 14:18-20, a negative description of the future situation of the disciples is followed by an explanation
for such a situation: the disciples will not be abandoned like "orphans"

---

69. This delineation of contrasting relationships to the coming Paraclete parallels the earlier delineation of contrasting relationships to Jesus himself: (a) For the failure "to receive"
Jesus, see, e.g., 1:11–12; 3:11, 32–33; 5:43–44; 12:48; (b) for the disciples' "knowledge" of
Jesus, see, e.g., 6:69; 8:28; 10:14; (c) for the failure "to see" Jesus, see, e.g., 6:40; 12:44–45
(in the affirmative in both cases); (d) for the failure "to know" Jesus, see, e.g., 1:10; 8:43;
(e) for Jesus' "abiding" among, and "presence" in, the disciples, see 6:58 and the next two
subunits. The "Spirit of truth" will be received, therefore, as "truth" itself was received. For a
similar use of "abiding" and "presence," see the Father's relationship to Jesus of 14:10; it
should be noted here that there is no formula of a mutual presence with regard to the Paraclete
and the disciples.

(14:18a), because Jesus will return to them (14:18b).[70] In the concluding
component (14:20) this return of Jesus is associated with a fundamental
change in the disciples' understanding. At that time (14:20a) the disciples
will come to know (1) that Jesus is in the Father (14:20b), (2) that they are
in Jesus (14:20c), and (3) that Jesus is in them (14:20d). Both framing
components return, therefore, to earlier declarations of the central major
section. On the one hand, for example, the opening component repeats the
first promise of 14:3—the return of Jesus to the disciples. Similarly, on the
other hand, the concluding component returns to the third christological
teaching of 14:10–14, repeating the first part of the formula of the mutual
presence and expanding it in terms of a mutual presence of the disciples in
Jesus and Jesus in them.[71] As such, the future situation of the disciples
with respect to Jesus will be marked by his return to them, as well as by a
mutual presence in one another that will parallel that of Jesus and the
Father in one another.

The central component of 14:18–20 contains the contrast proper
(14:19). The contrast returns to one of the formulations of the first contrast
of 14:17b–e—the first reason given for the inability of the world to receive
the Spirit-Paraclete, namely, its failure "to see" the Spirit-Paraclete. This
formulation is further developed as the main distinguishing characteristic
between the world and the disciples with respect to Jesus' announced return: in a little while the world, as in the case of Jesus' successor, will not be
able "to see" Jesus (14:19a), but the disciples "will see" him (14:19b).[72] At
the end, the fundamental reason for such a contrast is provided, though only
from the point of view of the disciples themselves (14:19c)—the disciples
will see Jesus because they, like Jesus himself, "will live."[73] This reason

70. This first component resumes the prominent household terminology and imagery of
14:2–3: Jesus' departure can in no way be characterized as a "leaving behind or abandonment" of the disciples as "orphans" (ὀρφανούς); the proper characterization for the disciples
in the world after Jesus' departure is not that of "orphans" but "little children."
71. For a similar change in understanding on the part of the disciples, see, e.g., 2:17, 22;
12:16; 13:7. The change involves a full understanding of the mutual presence of Jesus and the
Father in one another as presented in 14:12–14, as well as a further perception of the mutual
presence of Jesus and the disciples in one another. This change is specifically connected, by
means of the beginning temporal reference of the second outer component (14:20a, "on that
day"), with Jesus' return as announced in the first component. This expansion of the mutual
presence, elaborated here for the first time in the narrative, is anticipated on two occasions
within this first unit: (a) in 14:3, where the disciples are promised that they will be with Jesus
"wherever he is," and (b) in the previous subunit of 14:15–17, where the Paraclete is promised
to the disciples forever, "abiding" among them and "being" in them.
72. This is the second example of a formula of departure in this unit (see n. 33 above). With
regard to form, the present example again follows the most common pattern, a variation of the
expression "yet a little while." With regard to purpose, the present example introduces, unlike
that of 13:33a–b, a fundamental contrast between the world and the disciples.
73. This reason is grounded in the previous characterization of Jesus as "life" in 14:6; as
such, the self-identifications of Jesus as "truth" and "life" of 14:6 are explicitly and respectively

defines even further the future situation of the disciples with regard to Jesus as specified in the outer components: Jesus' return to them and the mutual presence that will ensue as a consequence of such a return can be further characterized as the possession of "life."

Such a carefully crafted contrast widens even further the sharp differentiation between the world and the disciples after the departure of Jesus. Therefore, while its central component advances this contrast by continuing a theme from the first contrast and extending its applicability from the figure of the Spirit-Paraclete to that of Jesus himself (you will "see" me, but the world will not), the framing components effectively reinforce this widening contrast by extending certain declarations from the preceding subsections as promises: a return on Jesus' part to the disciples and a resulting understanding on their part with regard to not only the mutual presence of Jesus and the Father in one another but also the mutual presence of Jesus in them and they in Jesus. The introduction and further development of these earlier declarations as promises within the contrast, furthermore, anticipate the subsequent delineation of the additional promises to be outlined within the subunit.

The central component (14:21a) of 14:18–21 repeats the essential condition for the further consequences of the departure to take place: "love for Jesus" is again defined in terms of obedience to his commands. This component introduces some stylistic variations. One now finds participial phrases and the verb *to have* in conjunction with the verb *to obey:* "the one who loves me" is "the one who has my commands and obeys them."

The final component (14:21b–c) of 14:18–21 outlines further positive consequences of the departure for the disciples. After a beginning recapitulation of the essential condition from 14:21a (14:21b₁, "the one who loves me"), three such promises are extended (14:21b₂–c): the love of the Father (14:21b₂), the love of Jesus (14:21c₁), and the self-manifestation of Jesus to the disciples (14:21c₂). Whereas the first two promises continue the theme of love from the essential condition of 14:21a,[74] the last promise (the

---

developed in the first two subunits. In the Gospel the present participle of the verb *to live* is used to modify certain metaphors that refer directly to Jesus, e.g., "living water" (4:10, 11) and "living bread" (6:51). Whoever believes in Jesus, moreover, is said "to live" (5:24–25; 6:50–51; 11:25–26) and, indeed, to be a source of "life" as well (7:38). Upon Jesus' return, therefore, as the beginning time reference indicates ("yet a little while"; cf. 13:33b, where the same expression is used with regard to the departure), the disciples will "see" because they "live"; in other words, the disciples then will come to see fully the true nature and implications of Jesus' mission and ministry. In this regard, given the previous promise of the Spirit-Paraclete, the role of the Spirit as the giver of "life" is to the point (6:63). The fourth subunit brings these two dimensions of "life" closely together, insofar as full understanding is closely tied to the role of the Spirit-Paraclete among the disciples.

74. This is the first reference in the narrative to the love of the Father for the disciples. The contrast with 3:16 is pointed: by the time "the hour" has arrived in the ministry of Jesus,

self-manifestation of Jesus to the disciples) returns to the promises already outlined within the beginning contrast of 14:18–20.[75] In other words, with the self-manifestation of Jesus comes his return to them, their mutual presence in one another, and their own possession of "life."

Promises Concerning Jesus and the Father (John 14:22–23)

The second central subunit (14:22–23) preserves the same structure as the first: (1) the contrast between the disciples and the world with regard to the further positive consequences of the departure to be outlined (14:22), (2) the essential condition for such consequences to take place (14:23a–b), and (3) the delineation of further positive consequences of the departure for the disciples (14:23c–d). At the same time, a different format is now employed—namely, one more reaction on the part of an individual disciple, Judas[76]—setting up thereby a fourth and final interchange of the disciples with Jesus. Like the previous dialogue with Thomas and Philip in 14:4–14, the present interchange with Judas consists of a single exchange, with each individual address identified by the narrator (14:22a–b, 23a). Within this final interchange, the three components of the subunit are distributed as follows: Judas's reaction constitutes the first component, and Jesus' response encompasses the other two. This third subunit continues to focus on

---

the love of the Father is clearly limited to those who love Jesus, and the world is deliberately excluded from this love, as well as from all other promises. For the love of Jesus for the disciples, see the parting instruction of 13:34–35. However, that command presents the love of Jesus for the disciples in terms of the ministry as a whole and, above all, in terms of his death, whereas Jesus' love for the disciples specifically refers at this point to his return to the disciples.

75. Jesus' return to the disciples, formulated within the contrast in terms of the verb ἔρχεσθαι (14:18, as in the preliminary proposition of 14:3), is now phrased in terms of the verb ἐμφανίζειν with the reflexive (only here and in the following subunit, 14:21, 22), namely, a self-manifestation; such a return clearly refers at this point to Jesus' resurrection appearances to the disciples. As such, all of the consequences postulated within this second subunit should be seen in the light of such a return. Jesus' return via the resurrection appearances (a) will be a sign of his love for them; (b) will be a sign of the Father's own love for them as well; (c) will allow the disciples "to see" Jesus physically in a way that the world cannot "see" him; (d) will also allow the disciples "to see" him in terms of his mission and identity as the world cannot "see" him, by bringing about a direct and immediate change in their perception of his relationship to the Father as well as of their own relationship to him; (e) will allow them "to live" as Jesus "lives" and thus "to see" fully, both physically and conceptually.

76. Of the four disciples who react to Jesus' statements in the course of the farewell, Judas (whom the narrator differentiates from the betrayer) is the only one who does not appear elsewhere in the Gospel. The thrust of his reaction is similar to those of Peter, Thomas, and Philip. On the one hand, the reaction is ironic, following upon the promises already extended to the disciples and denied to the world. On the other hand, Judas's reaction shows once again how far the disciples are at this point from understanding the nature and implications of Jesus' mission; in fact, just as they fail to understand the nature of the announced departure, so too do they fail to understand the nature of the announced return.

the figures of Jesus and the Father with regard to the positive consequences of the departure.

The first component (14:22) is introduced by means of a question (as in the previous reactions of Peter and Thomas) on the part of an individual disciple, Judas, concerning the fundamental reason for Jesus' announced self-manifestation to the disciples (14:22). The question focuses on Jesus' promise of a return as formulated in the final component of the preceding subunit (14:21c₂). At the same time, the question also recasts this promise in terms of a basic contrast between the disciples and the world by seeking the fundamental reason for the exclusive nature of the promise (the reason for a self-manifestation to the disciples but not to the world). In so doing, this third contrast of the subsection not only looks back to the preceding delineation of promises within the second subunit (14:21b–c) but also looks forward to the following delineation of promises within the present subunit (14:23c–d). Like the two previous contrasts within the subsection, therefore, this third contrast is also specifically developed with reference to the given delineation of promises within its own subunit. Judas's question, furthermore, widens the differentiation between the world and the disciples.

The second component (14:23b), the first part of Jesus' response to Judas, repeats the essential condition for the promises to take place. Stylistic variations are introduced—for example, the return to a future more vivid condition, as in the first subunit, but now phrased in the third person singular: "if someone loves me." The definition itself now has a slightly different formulation: "love for Jesus" is defined in terms of obedience to his "word" (λόγος). Such a change, however, follows and confirms the previous use of "commands" in the preceding subunits. The use of the singular "word" again encompasses not only the specific directives of Jesus to the disciples in the Gospel (above all the distinguishing command of love for one another) but also the whole of Jesus' teaching and revelation.[77] As such, obedience to Jesus' word entails not only the proper fulfillment of the love command and all other such specific directives of Jesus in the Gospel but also belief in Jesus.

---

77. The term "word" possesses a wide meaning. First, it can refer to a specific declaration of Jesus (2:22; 4:50; 6:60; 7:36; cf. 18:19, 32), with the plural used for an extended declaration as well (7:40; 10:19). Second, "word" can refer, always in the singular, to the whole of Jesus' mission and message (4:41; 5:24; 8:31, 37, 43, 51–52; 12:48). Finally, "word" can be used as a metaphorical designation for Jesus himself (1:1, 14). The use of the singular form at this point includes, therefore, both the ongoing declarations of Jesus in this first unit of discourse—thus encompassing the specific directive of love for one another as well as the extended delineation of Jesus' relationship to the Father—and the whole of his teaching and revelation during the ministry. On obedience to Jesus' word, see 8:51–52; on acceptance or rejection of Jesus' word, see 4:41; 5:24, 31, 37; 8:43.

The third component (14:23c), the second part of Jesus' response to Judas, outlines further positive consequences of the departure for the disciples: the love of the Father, the coming of both Jesus and the Father to them, and the abiding of both Jesus and the Father in them. The first promise is repeated, with a change of voice, from the second subunit. The other two promises expand previous promises outlined in the second subunit: not only Jesus, but also the Father, will come to the disciples;[78] similarly, upon coming, they will make their "abiding place" among the disciples.[79] Given the specific role assigned to Jesus within the promises, the last two promises are clearly anticipated in the beginning contrast of 14:22. In other words, with the self-manifestation of Jesus comes his joint return to the disciples and his abiding among them with the Father.[80]

Promises Concerning the Spirit-Paraclete (John 14:24–27)

In the second outer subunit (14:24–27), the first component of the central subunits—the contrast between the disciples and the world—again becomes, as in the first subunit, the third component in the structural sequence: (1) the essential condition for the further positive consequences of the departure to take place (14:24), (2) the delineation of further positive consequences of the departure for the disciples (14:25–26), and (3) the contrast between the disciples and the world with regard to these consequences (14:27). This fourth subunit also continues the focus of the first subunit on the figure of the coming successor to Jesus, the Spirit-Paraclete, with regard to the positive consequences of the departure.

78. As in 14:3, 18, the verb ἔρχεσθαι is used here with reference to Jesus' return, now extended to a coming of the Father as well. Given the additional promise of an "abiding" at this point, such a return on the part of Jesus certainly comprehends the resurrection appearances (see n. 75 above) but points beyond them as well. This extended return is in keeping with the promise of both a mutual presence of Jesus and the disciples in one another (14:20) and a permanent reunion (14:3). To be sure, it is the coming of the Spirit-Paraclete that will make possible this coming of Jesus and the Father to the disciples in the world.

79. As in the cases of the Father in Jesus (14:10) and the Paraclete in the disciples (14:17), the presence of Jesus in the disciples is now further described in terms of "abiding" among them (cf. 14:20), though now using the expression "make our abiding place (μονή) in them" rather than the verb with the corresponding locative of space. At the same time, the disciples now become the "abiding place" of the Father as well. The use of this expression immediately points back to the preliminary proposition of 14:2–3: while the disciples do have their ultimate "abiding places" in the house of the Father, both Jesus and the Father will have their own "abiding place" among the disciples in the world. Thus, although the final goal of the disciples is to be with Jesus in the Father's house, in the meantime they will be able to be with both Jesus and the Father in this world, insofar as the latter will come to them and abide among them. As with their coming, what makes possible this "abiding" of Jesus and the Father in the disciples is the figure of the Spirit-Paraclete, who will be with them forever, being present in, and abiding among, them (14:17). The household imagery of the unit is further developed: the "little children" will not be "orphans," because they will be the "abiding place" of both Jesus and the Father in the world.

80. The inclusion of the figure of the Father in these promises explains the love of the Father mentioned in both central subunits: in coming to them and abiding among them, the Father, like Jesus, shows his love for the disciples.

The first component (14:24) reiterates the essential condition for the promises to take place. However, in contrast to the three previous sub-units, its formulation undergoes a limited expansion: the condition as such (14:24a) is now followed by a further description of the origins of Jesus' "word," the plural form of which is employed in the definition of the condition (14:24b).

Some stylistic variations occur. In a simple sentence, the condition itself is the subject by means of a participial phrase, and the definition encompasses both predicate and object: "The one who does not love me does not obey my words." In addition, the condition itself (14:24a) gets a different formulation: it is now phrased in the negative for the first time, and the plural "words" replaces the singular "word" of the preceding subunit. Consequently, a failure to love Jesus is now defined as a failure to obey his words. Both changes reinforce the thrust of the preceding definitions. On the one hand, the second change—the use of the plural "words"—follows and confirms the use of "commands" and "word" in the preceding subunits to encompass both the specific directives of Jesus to the disciples (above all the preeminent command of love for one another) and the whole of Jesus' teaching and revelation.[81] A failure to obey Jesus' words entails, therefore, a failure to carry out the practical directives of Jesus, to love one another, or to believe in Jesus. On the other hand, in closing the subsection with the opposite of love for Jesus, the first change further emphasizes the reason for the restriction of the promises to the disciples themselves and thus the ongoing contrast between the disciples and the world: the world does not love Jesus.

The condition itself (14:24a) is immediately followed by an explicit identification of the origins of Jesus' "word" (14:24b), thereby reverting to the singular form of the third subunit and confirming the interchangeable character of all these singular and plural forms in these four definitions—Jesus' "word" is not his own but the Father's.[82] As such, this additional identification of origins explains that obedience to Jesus' "word(s)" or "commands" implies obedience to the Father's own "word(s)" or "commands" and,

---

81. The plural form, "words," is used elsewhere in the Gospel with reference to extended declarations of Jesus (7:40; 10:19; see n. 77 above). As such, its use at this point certainly includes the ongoing declarations of Jesus in this first unit of discourse, thus encompassing both the command to love one another and the teaching concerning the relationship between Jesus and the Father. At the same time, there is no reason why the use of "words" here cannot also include the second denotation of the singular "word"—namely, a reference to the whole of Jesus' teaching and revelation in the course of his mission and ministry—especially given the use of the singular form again in the following declaration of 14:24b.

82. On the origins of Jesus' "word" with the Father, see, e.g., 5:24; 8:37–38; 12:48–49; cf. 5:38; 8:55. This description of origins also reiterates—though now using the term λόγος instead of ῥήματα—one of the consequences of the mutual presence of Jesus and the Father in one another from 14:10–14 (14:10b–c). Note the use of singular and plural forms, even of different terms.

consequently, that love for Jesus also implies love for the Father. This also accounts for the prominent role of the Father in the two central subunits.

The second component (14:25–26) outlines a further positive consequence of the departure for the disciples. Once again, in contrast to the three previous subunits, its formulation at this point also undergoes a limited expansion: a beginning statement recalling the fleeting character of Jesus' presence among the disciples (14:25) now precedes the delineation of the further consequence in question (14:26). With this expansion, furthermore, comes the first example of the recurring concluding formula of the discourse, "These things I have said to you," as an introduction to the beginning statement. This formula also signals, by way of anticipation, the approaching conclusion of this first unit of discourse.[83]

The beginning statement (14:25) describes the ongoing disclosures of the unit as the declarations of one who still "abides" among the disciples. Such disclosures represent the immediate reference of the beginning demonstrative pronoun "these things."[84] This beginning statement plays an important role within the subsection. In recalling the forthcoming departure, the statement begins to point the way toward the conclusion of not only the central section but also of the unit itself, especially given its use of the concluding formula of the discourse. By addressing the disciples directly after the negative formulation of the essential condition, the statement also allows for the subsequent formulation of the positive consequences in the affirmative, as addressed to the disciples, to those who love Jesus and obey his words. Finally, the statement prepares directly for the reintroduction of the figure of the Spirit-Paraclete; as Jesus' "abiding" among them comes to an end, the permanent "abiding" of the Spirit-Paraclete begins.

The delineation of a further positive consequence of the departure (14:26) expands the earlier promise of the Spirit-Paraclete as a successor to Jesus. The same two major components can again be readily discerned: (1) a description of the provenance of this figure (14:26a–b) and (2) a description of its envisioned role among the disciples (14:26c). As in the first subunit, the figure of the Spirit-Paraclete remains closely tied to that of Jesus in both regards.

83. The beginning statement combines the concluding formula of the discourse (see n. 5 above) and a formula of departure (see nn. 33 and 72 above). With regard to form, the present example follows a different pattern, namely, the use of an expression (a participial phrase) indicating or anticipating the coming break in the relationship with the disciples, "while abiding among you." In terms of purpose, the present example introduces for the first time a contrast between the present and future situation of the disciples themselves.

84. For a similar "abiding" of Jesus during the ministry, with an emphasis on the relationship as such, see 4:40; cf. 1:38–39. For an emphasis on the locale in question, see 2:12; 7:9; 10:40; 11:6, 54.

On the one hand, the origins of the Paraclete are again identified. Stylistic variations are introduced (the use of the verb "to send" rather than "to give"; the use of an instrumental of cause, "in my name," to describe Jesus' request of the Father). The Paraclete's origins are given as being with the Father in the world above, a provenance that is emphasized at this point by means of its specific characterization as "the holy Spirit" (τὸ ἅγιον). Thus, the Paraclete is described as "sent" (πέμψει) by the Father at the request of Jesus himself (14:26a–b).[85] On the other hand, the Spirit-Paraclete is again assigned a twofold role among the disciples (14:26c): "to teach" (διδάξει) the disciples "all things" (πάντα) and "to recall" (ὑπομνήσει) for them "all that [Jesus himself] said to them" during the ministry (πάντα ἃ εἶπον ὑμῖν).[86] These two functions of the Spirit-Paraclete explain in greater detail, therefore, the previous association of the Spirit-Paraclete with the meaning, disclosure, and proclamation of "truth" (14:17a). The subordination of the Spirit-Paraclete to Jesus is again clear: not only is the Spirit-Paraclete sent by the Father at the request of Jesus, but also its assigned role is directly connected to Jesus' own revelation and teaching.

The two functions envisioned are interdependent. The recalling of Jesus' mission and message for the disciples implies much more than a simple recollection of the events and teaching in question; such recalling involves further teaching as well, allowing the disciples to begin to understand at last the full implications of that mission and message. As Jesus' permanent successor among the disciples, therefore, it is the Spirit-Paraclete that brings the disciples to that change of perception promised within the unit itself (14:7b, 20), a change that in turn forms the basis for most of the other consequences or promises extended.[87] In other words, it is the promise of

85. As an instrumental of manner, the prepositional phrase ("in my name") also points to the role of the Paraclete as Jesus' successor among the disciples. Whereas the first characterization of the Paraclete as "Spirit" (of truth) emphasizes its assigned role among the disciples, its second characterization as "Spirit" (holy) at this point emphasizes its origins in the world above (cf. 1:33; 7:39; 20:22).

86. For Jesus' mission as "teaching," see, e.g., 6:59; 7:14, 28, 35; 8:20, 28; 9:34; 18:20. For concrete examples of such "recalling" and its results, see 2:17, 22; 12:16. It is clear from these examples that such recalling involves not just a simple recollection of what Jesus said but also a proper understanding of its meaning and implications.

87. In effect, the promise of the Spirit-Paraclete also functions as a condition. As one of many promises, the coming of the Spirit-Paraclete is dependent upon the love of the disciples for Jesus. At the same time, given the reactions of the disciples during this first unit and the specific description of the Spirit-Paraclete's role among them in this last promise, proper love for Jesus on the part of the disciples clearly cannot exist without the presence and assistance of the Spirit-Paraclete among them; as such, the promise can be said to function as a condition as well. In other words, only upon Jesus' return and the bestowal of the Paraclete, the Holy Spirit and the Spirit of truth, can the disciples come to know "truth" and can the other promises follow as announced. Two further points are in order. First, because full belief and understanding are impossible without the reception of the Spirit-Paraclete upon Jesus'

the Spirit-Paraclete that functions as the key to full belief and understanding and thus as the key to most of the other promises of Jesus for the time after "the hour."[88]

The final component (14:27) provides the last contrast between the world and the disciples. In contrast to the three preceding subunits, a difference in formulation should again be noted. First, this final contrast is not developed with reference to the statement of promises within its own subunit. Instead of dealing with the different relationships of the world and the disciples to the coming figure of the Spirit-Paraclete, the contrast introduces the theme of "peace" at this point. Second, the point of view of the contrast itself is now different as well. It is no longer the disciples and the world that are being contrasted directly but rather Jesus and the world with respect to the disciples.

The contrast opens, therefore, with a preliminary statement concerning Jesus' bestowal of "peace" on the disciples (14:27a–b).[89] The contrast

return, the disciples' present lack of understanding unquestionably is presented as inevitable but temporary. Second, because the presence and abiding of the Spirit-Paraclete (unlike that of Jesus) among the disciples is conceived as unending, its role among the disciples also should be seen as permanent and unending; in other words, the tasks of calling to mind and teaching should not be seen as instantaneous and total but rather as evolving and deepening. Consequently, the disciples' understanding of the full nature and implications of Jesus' message and mission, while undergoing a significant and qualitative transformation upon Jesus' return and the reception of the Spirit-Paraclete, also should be seen as an ongoing and open-ended task. This second point immediately connects the final delineation of promises with the earlier delineation of promises at the end of the second subsection (14:12–14). The disciples will continue, and even surpass, Jesus' own works not only because Jesus himself will do whatever they ask of him in his name but also because they will be given by the Father, at Jesus' own request, another Paraclete; it will be with them forever, further teaching and explaining to them the nature and implications of "truth." Thus, in effect, the Spirit-Paraclete will continue Jesus' own mission in the world in and through the disciples.

88. Only one promise within the subsection is presupposed by that of the Spirit-Paraclete, namely, Jesus' return within "the hour" (14:18–21). The bestowal of the Spirit-Paraclete ultimately follows and depends upon Jesus' self-manifestation (resurrection appearances) to the disciples as one of the final events of "the hour" (20:19–23). All the other promises within the subsection follow and depend upon this coming of the Spirit-Paraclete: (a) the disciples will begin to understand the full nature and implications of Jesus' mission and message and "live" (14:19–20); (b) beyond the resurrection appearances there will be a continued abiding of Jesus among the disciples, as well as a mutual presence of Jesus and the disciples in one another (14:20; 14:22–23), best understood as taking place in and through the figure of the Paraclete itself; and (c) with Jesus, in and through the Paraclete, the Father himself will come to the disciples and abide among them (14:22–23). Finally, all these promises, from that of a return via the resurrection to that of a continued abiding in and through the Paraclete, can be described in terms of Jesus' love for the disciples, as well as the Father's own love for them.

89. This bestowal of "peace" is strongly emphasized by two specific pronouncements within this preliminary statement, one employing the verb to leave behind and the other, the verb to give: "My peace I leave to you; my peace I give to you." Only the second verb is resumed and developed within the contrast proper that follows. Jesus' "peace" has a present as well as a future dimension. On the one hand, such peace should come about as a result of the promises that have been outlined throughout this entire central section and, above all, in the third subsection. On the other hand, such peace cannot actually come about until the promises themselves begin to be realized, especially those of Jesus' return and the bestowal of the Spirit-Paraclete. For this future dimension of Jesus' peace, see 20:19–23.

proper is then developed from the point of view of the bestowal itself—not as the world "gives" does Jesus "give" peace (14:27c). Although the term "peace," given its specific context, clearly comprehends the Spirit-Paraclete as a source of that "peace," it also refers to all the previous promises extended to those who love Jesus—who believe in him, love one another, and carry out all his other directives. In other words, the "peace" that Jesus bestows upon the disciples is a "peace" that results from all the preceding promises and their assured fulfillment. It is these promises and consequences of the departure, and hence this "peace," that only Jesus, and not the world, can "give."

On the one hand, the contrast is not developed in terms of the Spirit-Paraclete, as would have been expected, but rather in terms of Jesus' "peace." This deviation from the preceding patterns of contrast can be explained in terms of the wider reference of the term "peace" at this point. At the end of the subsection, therefore, the final contrast between the disciples and the world is deliberately expanded to include not only the given promise of its own subunit but also all the preceding promises of the subsection, as well as of the entire central major section of the unit.

On the other hand, the contrast is specifically developed in terms of Jesus and the world rather than the disciples and the world. This second deviation from the preceding pattern of contrast can also be explained as a means of presenting the world as a whole as a rival authority to Jesus himself. Once again, then, at the end of the subsection, the final contrast is deliberately expanded to portray the world not only as those excluded from the promises but also as those who have nothing of value to offer to the disciples. As a result, the world is ultimately depicted as opposed not only to the disciples of Jesus but also to Jesus himself. One could say, in effect, that it is precisely because the world, unlike the disciples, receives nothing that it, unlike Jesus, can give nothing. In fact, a subtle warning is conveyed thereby at this point: not only does the world have nothing of value to offer to the disciples, but what it does have to offer may be the very opposite. Therefore, if what the world considers "peace" is not to be the lot of the disciples in this world, as the contrast implies, then what the world does have to give to the disciples is ominous indeed. As such, the contrast looks back to the "new" command of 13:34–35—the exercise by the disciples of their preeminent command may entail death for one another at the hands of the world. The contrast also points forward to the final major section by means of a reference to the ultimate ruler of such a world.

Finally, the choice of the term "peace" at this point to encompass all of the promises previously extended to the disciples in the course of the unit is deliberate and effective. In contrast to the negative, troubling announcements of the first major section (13:31–38), the positive, reassuring disclosures of the central major section (14:1–27) console the assembled disciples. As the teaching and consolation come to an end, the term "peace" provides an appropriate summary of, and climax to, the entire process. Indeed, its use at the conclusion of 14:15–27 sets the stage for the repetition and expansion of the beginning exhortation of 14:1a in 14:27d, thus bringing the central major section to an end. It is peace, not fear or consternation, that Jesus' departure brings to those who understand the nature and implications of his mission and message and hence the meaning and consequences of such a departure.

The third subsection (14:15–27), then, is primarily a further exposition of the second controlling theme of the unit, the consequences of Jesus' departure for the disciples, by means of presenting a large number of promises or positive consequences of the departure to the disciples. Such promises are extended to the disciples as those who love Jesus, who believe in him and obey his commands—above all the command of love for one another.

The promises, which concern both the figure of the Spirit-Paraclete and the figures of Jesus and the Father, are interdependent. The promises also have a strong repetitive and cumulative effect as the subsection develops. The promises concerning the Father and Jesus (the return or self-manifestation of Jesus, the love of both Jesus and the Father, and the coming of both Jesus and the Father to abide in the disciples) show the continued, direct involvement of Jesus and the Father in the life of the disciples in the world. The promises concerning the Spirit-Paraclete (a permanent stay, the teaching of all things, and the recalling of all that Jesus himself said) involve a time beginning with the return or self-manifestation of Jesus to the disciples in and through the resurrection appearances. These promises not only introduce a successor to Jesus but also provide the specific channel for the fulfillment of the other promises concerning Jesus and the Father. In other words, it is the Spirit-Paraclete as Jesus' successor to and among the disciples that renders concrete and specific the continued involvement of both Jesus and the Father in the life of the disciples in the world. As a result, other promises are extended as well: a full understanding of the mutual presence of Jesus and the Father in one another, a full understanding of the mutual presence of Jesus and the disciples in one another, and the assurance of "living" as Jesus himself "lives."

Such promises are also systematically and radically denied to the world—to those who do not love Jesus, who do not obey his commands or word(s), and who function as a rival authority to Jesus himself. This series of contrasts between the disciples and the world also has a repetitive and cumulative effect as the subsection develops, showing thereby an ever-widening gulf between the disciples and the world. Although the disciples may have "peace" in Jesus, therefore, they also find themselves in the midst of an unloving and unbelieving world.

After the troubling disclosures of 13:31–38, the central major section of the unit represents a sustained exercise (aside from the veiled warning of 14:27) in the instruction and consolation of the disciples; the beginning and concluding calls to courage of 14:1a and 14:27d make this clear. This section, in its extensive development of the two controlling themes of the unit, leaves behind the negative tone of the first major section and develops instead the one element of hope within that section—the statement that the coming separation, though inevitable, will be but temporary. What follows now is a positive explanation of the departure's meaning in terms of the relationship between Jesus and the Father and a positive description of the consequences of the departure for the disciples.

The central major section further preserves the distinctive temporal standpoint of Jesus as speaker introduced in 13:31–38, namely, both the Jesus who is about to undergo the climactic events of "the hour" and the Jesus who has already surpassed "the hour" except for its final events. First, the teaching concerning the relationship between Jesus and the Father can be read from either standpoint and represents an excellent compendium of Johannine teaching. Second, the promises admit of various readings.

Some of the promises can be read from the standpoint of the Jesus about to die: the self-manifestation of Jesus to the disciples, Jesus' gathering together of the disciples unto himself, and the love of Jesus for the disciples. All these promises can be understood from the perspective of the resurrection appearances. Many of the promises can be interpreted from the standpoint of the risen Jesus about to return to the Father: the permanent reunion and association envisioned upon the return and the gathering together; the ability of the disciples to continue and surpass Jesus' works or mission in the world because Jesus himself will do whatever they ask of him in his name; the coming of another Paraclete as a successor to Jesus—the Holy Spirit and the Spirit of truth—who will be with them forever (abiding among, and being present in, them), teach them all things, and recall for them all that Jesus himself taught and revealed (bringing them to full understanding and belief); the love of both Jesus and the Father as expressed in their coming to the disciples to make their own "abiding place" in and among them; the mutual presence of Jesus and the disciples in one another; and the ability "to live" as he "lives." All these promises can be understood from the perspective of the conclusion of "the hour," immediately prior to the bestowal of the successor and Jesus' return to the Father. In fact, all these promises ultimately cohere around that of the successor.

In addition, the initial promises from the preliminary proposition of 14:2–3 admit of other readings from different perspectives. These promises can be read from the perspective of the death of the disciples after the return of Jesus to the Father: the return of Jesus, his gathering together of the disciples unto himself, and the disciples' permanent reunion and association with Jesus. Such promises can be read as well from an eschatological or parousia perspective. Such readings are by no means mutually exclusive but instead reflect the multidimensional nature of these promises. However, the emphasis remains throughout on the first general perspective above— the reading of the promises in the light of both the resurrection appearances and the figure of the successor.

Third Major Section (John 14:28–31)

The third major section of the first unit of discourse, 14:28–31, discusses the purpose of the present disclosures to the disciples, the fundamental meaning of Jesus' specific mode of departure, and the departure's positive consequences for the disciples. This section concludes the development of the overarching themes of the unit as presented in the central major section. In so doing, despite the introduction of a disturbing note, the section also continues the reassuring tone of the central major section. To begin with, this final section reveals the fundamental purpose for all the preceding announcements and disclosures of the unit concerning the forthcoming departure, its fundamental meaning, and its consequences. Second, the section addresses the specific mode of Jesus' departure to the Father, providing thereby a positive interpretation of its fundamental meaning and consequences for the disciples. Finally, the section clearly ends the entire unit of discourse. This structure can be outlined as follows:

1. The purpose of the present disclosures to the disciples (14:28–29).
2. The fundamental meaning of the specific mode of departure and its positive consequences for the disciples (14:30–31c).
3. Concluding commands (14:31d).

The Purpose of the Present Disclosures to the Disciples (John 14:28–29)

The first subsection (14:28–29) begins with 14:28a–b, a brief and explicit summary of the controlling themes of the unit as developed in 14:1–27, the central major section. In 14:28c–29 it sets forth the fundamental purpose behind all of Jesus' announcements and disclosures concerning the forthcoming departure.

The summary explicitly recalls previous disclosures from the central major section (14:28a–b): an introductory formula specifically pointing the disciples to the earlier declarations (14:28a) precedes the citation of the declarations in question (14:28b).[90] The summary repeats the controlling themes of the unit as presented in the preliminary proposition of 14:2–3: Jesus' forthcoming departure to the Father and his subsequent return to the disciples.[91] Immediately after the central major section ends, therefore, the concluding section explicitly recalls its first, positive subsection.

The fundamental purpose behind the preceding announcements and disclosures (14:28c–29) is then presented as twofold: rejoicing (14:28c–e) and belief (14:29) on the part of the disciples. As such, the statement of purpose returns to the beginning calls of the central section, the calls to courage and belief of 14:1, for further development. To begin with, the statement makes explicit what was only implicit in the calls themselves— the central section as a sustained exercise in the teaching and consolation of the disciples. The statement also characterizes the proper attitude of the disciples with regard to the forthcoming departure in terms of actual rejoicing—joy also comes from proper belief, therefore, and proper belief results in joy.[92] Finally, the statement begins to focus as well on the time of the departure itself—belief as the proper attitude of the disciples at the time of the departure.

This twofold purpose is disclosed by both a reproach of, and an exhortation to, the disciples. The reproach is used with respect to the desired attitude of rejoicing, and the exhortation is employed with regard to the desired response of belief. This juxtaposition of reproach and exhortation provides an effective contrast showing, first, how the disciples should react to the announcement of the forthcoming departure and, second, how

90. For a previous recollection of earlier declarations of Jesus to the disciples, see 14:2b–c. In both cases, the citation in question, whether from the public ministry or from within the unit itself, does not appear as given anywhere else in the Gospel but instead represents a variation on, or reformulation of, such earlier declarations.

91. The first part recalls the announced departure—without an explicit identification of its destination—as formulated in 13:31–38 and 14:4–6, namely, by means of the verb ὑπάγειν (13:33, 36, 38; 14:4, 5). The second part recalls the promised return as phrased in 14:1–3, 18–21, 22–24—namely, by means of the verb ἔρχεσθαι (14:3, 18, 23). Such a close juxtaposition of these themes is found only in 14:2–3.

92. "Rejoicing," like "peace," has both a present and a future dimension; see n. 89 above. Rejoicing should first come about as a result of all the preceding announcements and disclosures of the unit. At the same time, rejoicing cannot actually come about until a full understanding of all such disclosures and announcements begins to take place. Rejoicing, like peace, therefore, is closely connected with full faith and understanding and thus with Jesus' return and his bestowal of the Spirit-Paraclete. For this future dimension of rejoicing, see 20:19–23 (v. 20) again. In the remainder of the narrative, joy and rejoicing are often associated with the completion of an appointed task (3:29, the Baptist; 4:36, Jesus and the disciples; 8:56, Abraham; 11:15, Jesus with regard to the disciples). In this case the rejoicing of the disciples clearly can take place only when the full implications of Jesus' mission and message begin to be understood.

they are to react at the time of the departure itself. To be sure, the two desired reactions are interdependent.

The reproach is conveyed by a mixed contrary-to-fact condition (14:28c): if the disciples loved Jesus, they would have rejoiced. Thus, the protasis reiterates the essential condition for the promises extended in 14:15–27 (love for Jesus), and the apodosis outlines the proper attitude that all those who love Jesus should have at this point (rejoicing). Rejoicing is defined as the correct attitude with regard to the announced departure, and the actual response of fear and consternation on the part of the disciples is criticized.[93] Such a desired response is then further grounded by a return to, and further development of, the destination of the departure (14:28d–e). On the one hand, the Father is again identified as the destination of the departure (14:28d); on the other hand, the relationship of Jesus to the Father is further defined in terms of status and rank—the Father is greater than Jesus (14:28e).[94] In other words, those who know the fundamental meaning of Jesus' departure and thus fully understand the nature and implications of his mission and message are those who love Jesus and rejoice at the announcement of his departure. It is joy, not fear or consternation, that should prevail among the disciples at this point, especially in the light of the preceding disclosures and announcements on Jesus' part.

The exhortation (14:29) is conveyed by an explicit temporal contrast between the present announcement of the departure ("now, before it does happen") and its future realization ("when it does happen"). Thus, Jesus' preceding announcements and disclosures concerning the meaning and consequences of his impending departure (14:29a) are meant to elicit belief in him and in God on the part of the disciples at the time of the departure itself (14:29b). In other words, for those who fully understand the nature and implications of Jesus' mission and message, belief is the proper response at the time of the departure. This emphasis on the need for belief at the time of the departure begins to focus on the mode

93. For a previous reproach of the disciples, see 14:7–9. The present reproach can be seen as a climax to the repeated failures to understand on the part of the disciples—instead of a rejoicing grounded in love, consternation and fear rule. Again, this reproach must be seen in the wider context of the promises extended in the unit. Because full belief and understanding are impossible prior to Jesus' return and the bestowal of the Spirit-Paraclete, the disciples' failure to understand is inevitable at this point and hence temporary; consequently, neither the reproaches nor the irony in the disciples' responses throughout the unit, though decidedly sharp and pointed, can be considered ultimately destructive.

94. Such a distinction in rank and status can be understood in the light of the relationship between Jesus and the Father outlined in the second subsection (14:4–14). There is a definite sense that the one who is sent is subordinate to the sender; in fact, exactly the same subordination exists in the relationship between Jesus and the Spirit-Paraclete. Just as the "other Paraclete" to come is subordinate to Jesus, so is the first or earlier Paraclete (Jesus) subordinate to the Father and thus the Father greater than he (Jesus).

of the departure, paving the way for the second part of this concluding section. The desired responses—rejoicing at the announcement of the departure and belief at the time of the departure—are interrelated. The rejoicing that should characterize the present attitude of the disciples can only come about from a full understanding of the meaning and consequences of Jesus' departure. Similarly, the belief that should characterize the future attitude of the disciples at the time of the departure can only result in rejoicing for those who understand the fundamental meaning and consequences of that departure.

The Fundamental Meaning of the Specific Mode of Departure and Its Positive Consequences for the Disciples (John 14:30–31c)

The second subsection (14:30–31c) continues the focus of 14:29 on the time of Jesus' departure by turning to the specific mode of the departure—Jesus' death at the hands of the ruling authorities of the world. In so doing, this subsection prepares the way for the climactic events of "the hour" in and around Jerusalem. Two major components can be discerned: (1) a beginning characterization of the mode of departure as an encounter with "the ruler of the world" (14:30a–b) and (2) a proper interpretation of such an encounter in terms of its fundamental meaning and consequences for the disciples (14:30c–31c).

The beginning characterization of the specific mode of departure is introduced by another formula of departure (14:30a), thus explicitly recalling the rapidly approaching end of Jesus' presence among the disciples.[95] The characterization itself is then provided as the reason for such a recalling at this point (14:30b)—the approach of "the ruler of the world" (ὁ τοῦ κόσμου ἄρχων).[96] Consequently, Jesus' departure is ultimately presented as an

---

95. This is the fourth formula of departure in the unit (see n. 33 above). With regard to form, the present example follows a third pattern, namely, the use of a temporal adverb ("no longer") to signal the coming break in the relationship. With regard to purpose, the present example is used as an introduction to proper teaching. The occurrence of the majority of these formulas toward the latter half of the unit, especially in the case of the back-to-back examples of 14:25 and 14:30a, clearly signals that Jesus' speaking is rapidly drawing to a close.

96. The term "ruler(s)" has been used to describe the Jewish authorities (3:1; 7:26, 48; 12:42), as well as Satan (12:31). Both these figures have also been identified by household imagery: the devil as "the father" of the Jews, who are his "children" (8:44). This grounding refers to a coming encounter with the devil and its earthly "children." In the light of the farewell context (13:1–30), this grounding also refers to the process of betrayal already at work and the coming encounter with Satan through the figure of Judas (13:2, 27; see 6:70). For the encounter itself, see 18:1–11.

encounter between Jesus (the one sent by the Father from the world above) and Satan (the ruler of the world below), an encounter that will result in Jesus' departure from this world. Given the repeated and pointed contrasts of 14:15–27 between the disciples and the world and between Jesus and the world with respect to the disciples, this encounter clearly will be with the forces of hatred and unbelief—that is, with those who do not love or believe in Jesus, as well as with their leader, the ruler of this hostile and unbelieving world.

The tone of such a characterization is ominous, especially coming at the end of the unit. On the one hand, such a description goes against the extended process of teaching and consolation that began with the calls of 14:1, continued strongly through 14:27, and extended right into the first subsection of this concluding section (14:28–29). This description of the forthcoming departure deals a sudden blow to the "peace" and "rejoicing" intended by such a process (14:27, 28). On the other hand, the description returns to the negative, troubling tone that pervaded the first major section as a whole: Jesus' departure to the Father also entails an encounter with the demonic powers who rule the world. At the conclusion of the unit, therefore, as at its beginning, the disciples receive a sharp jolt.

A further description of this forthcoming encounter provides its correct interpretation and casts it in a reassuring light both from the point of view of the relationship between Jesus and "the ruler of the world" (14:30c) and the relationship between Jesus and the Father (14:31a–c). Although the coming encounter does result in Jesus' departure and would appear to represent an outright victory for "the ruler of the world," the given explanation of these two relationships makes it clear that the outcome is only an apparent defeat for Jesus at the hands of the ruling authorities and their own ruler.

"The ruler of the world" is curtly described as "having no power or hold" whatever over Jesus in this encounter (14:30c).[97] However, the purpose (14:31a₁) and nature (14:31a₂–c) of such an encounter are described from

---

97. The description itself is not without difficulties; the specific meaning of οὐδὲν ἔχειν with the preposition ἐν—literally, "he has nothing in me"—is hard to establish. First, the basic point of departure for its interpretation must be the contrast of 14:30b and 14:30c: whereas the former interpretation (the encounter with Satan) is completely incorrect, the latter (Satan has no power over Jesus) is the only correct one. Second, the expression comes close to that of 19:11, especially given the context of the trial before Pilate as a further stage in the encounter with "the ruler of the world" that began in 18:1–11: "You have no power (ἐξουσία) over me." See also 10:17–18: Jesus lays down his life of his own accord and in compliance with the Father's commands. Finally, such an interpretation does find support elsewhere in the literature (BAGD, 1.7; cf. Appian, *Bell. Civ.* 3.32.125). As such, it is better to interpret this expression along the lines of 19:11: despite all appearances to the contrary, the ruler of the world has no hold on Jesus, and the coming encounter in no way represents a defeat for Jesus.

the point of view of Jesus' relationship to the Father, thereby revealing its fundamental meaning and consequences for the disciples. With regard to the encounter's fundamental meaning, Jesus' role in it is specifically presented—following the repeated formulations of the essential condition for the promises to take place within 14:15–27—as "love for the Father" (14:31a$_2$)[98] and further defined in terms of obedience to what the Father "commands" (14:31b–c).[99] With regard to the encounter's purpose or consequences for the disciples, Jesus' role is further presented as a sign of love to the world, a way that the world can come to know his love for the Father in and through such an encounter.[100] The fundamental meaning and consequences of the encounter are explicitly described not as a defeat of Jesus by Satan, therefore, but as a deliberate act of obedient love for the Father on Jesus' part for the sake of the world, insofar as the encounter forms part—indeed, the climactic part—of his mission to the world as entrusted to him by the Father and continues to serve as a sign to the world after his departure by means of the disciples' own mission in and to the world.

As such, the process of teaching and consolation is resumed at the end, which softens the first, ominous description of the specific mode of departure. Although Jesus' mode of departure does constitute an encounter with Satan and can be perceived as a defeat for Jesus, the further description of this encounter reveals its correct interpretation, its fundamental meaning and consequences: not only does Satan have no power over Jesus but also Jesus acts solely out of obedient love for the Father for the sake of the world, so that the latter can come to know such love in and through the ongoing mission of the disciples.

The final section ends, therefore, on a reassuring note. The impending events are presented as the opposite of what will appear to be happening: what appears to be a victory for the forces of hatred and unbelief—for Satan and his "children"—is actually an ironic triumph for Jesus and the disciples as his "little children." This mollifies the preceding blow to the "peace" and

98. This is the only reference to Jesus' love for the Father in the Gospel; cf. 15:10. Such love is specifically described at this point in terms of Jesus' death. For the love of the Father for Jesus, see 3:35; 5:20; 10:17. The example of 10:17 is appropriate here, insofar as such love is again defined in terms of Jesus' death.

99. Such obedience is now expressed in terms of the verb ποιεῖν (so I do), with the commands of the Father expressed by the verb rather than the noun form, ἐντέλλεσθαι (as the Father commands me). For Jesus' obedience to the Father's commands or word(s), see, e.g., 8:54–55; 10:17–18; 12:49–50. Again, the Father's command at this point has to do with the specific mode of departure as such, namely, the death Jesus is about to undergo.

100. The meaning of the term "the world" has shifted at this point: the world not as the locus of hatred and unbelief but rather as a source for future believers in Jesus, for those who will come to see—in and through the mission of the disciples—the mode of Jesus' departure as an act of love for, and obedience to, the Father. For "the world" as neutral, see, e.g., 1:29; 3:16–17; 4:42; 8:12; 9:5; 12:46–47; 18:37.

"rejoicing" of the disciples. However, what is about to happen remains an encounter with the demonic power and its representatives in the world.

The concluding description of the mode of Jesus' departure can be directly related to the "new" command issued to the disciples in 13:34–35. On the one hand, Jesus' death at the hands of "the ruler of the world" is not only an act of obedient love for the Father but also an act of love for the disciples, which in turn serves as both a foundation and an exemplar for their own relationship of love for one another. Their love for one another is again indirectly tied to the possibility of death for one another at the hands of the world (cf. 14:27) and hence to the possibility of a similar encounter on their part with "the ruler of the world." On the other hand, just as Jesus' death is meant to serve as the sign to the world of his obedient love for the Father, so is the love of the disciples for one another (a love that may entail, if need be, death itself at the hands of the world and its ruler) meant to serve as a sign of their discipleship (of their love for, and belief in, Jesus) to all outsiders. To be sure, all these references to what the exercise of this "new" command of love in the world may entail for the disciples are indirect or implicit in this unit; they are veiled warnings of things to come.

Concluding Commands (John 14:31d)

A brief twofold command to the disciples to arise and depart (14:31d) brings the section and unit to a definite end. The command itself represents a multilayered signal on Jesus' part to leave the safety of the supper room, to begin the impending encounter with the ruler of the world, to undertake the announced departure, and to submit to the remaining and climactic events of "the hour."

The final section (14:28–31) ends the ongoing development of the controlling themes of the unit—the fundamental meaning of Jesus' departure and its consequences for the disciples—by explaining the fundamental purpose for all of the preceding announcements and disclosures of the unit and providing a correct interpretation of Jesus' specific mode of departure to the Father. The section presents rejoicing and belief at the time of the departure as the fundamental purpose behind such a development and therefore as the proper attitudes toward the forthcoming departure. The section also explains that the coming encounter with "the ruler of the world" is not a defeat for Jesus at the hands of the demonic powers but instead an act of love for the Father and of compliance with the Father's mission for the sake of the world.

The final section also preserves the distinctive temporal standpoint of Jesus as speaker introduced in 13:31–38 and continued in 14:1–27, though with an emphasis on the first dimension—on the Jesus about to undergo the climactic events of "the hour." All elements can be read from the perspective of the Jesus about to die: the promised return to the disciples as pointing to the resurrection appearances; the call for belief at the time of the departure itself; the call for rejoicing in the light of the fundamental meaning of the departure, the relationship between Jesus and the Father; the description of the departure in terms of an encounter with "the ruler of the world"; and the teaching concerning the proper and correct interpretation of such an encounter. At the same time, several of these elements can also be read from the perspective of the risen Jesus about to give the Spirit-Paraclete to the disciples and return to the Father: the return as ultimately pointing to the Spirit-Paraclete as well; the calls for belief and rejoicing as the proper attitude of the disciples; and the teaching in question, with regard to both the relationship between Jesus and the Father and the encounter itself. The emphasis on the first temporal dimension at the end points to, and again prepares the way for, the climactic events of "the hour" about to unfold.

STRATEGIC CONCERNS AND AIMS

The preceding literary-rhetorical analysis of John 13:31–14:31 shows that this proposed first unit of discourse can be seen as a coherent artistic whole that is highly unified and carefully developed from beginning to end. This first unit of discourse can also be seen as a coherent strategic whole with concerns and aims at work through the use of such a literary structure and development. First, this unit is concerned with the final events of Jesus' mission and ministry—the climactic events of "the hour"—and focuses on the proper interpretation of his forthcoming departure from the world from the point of view of both its fundamental meaning and its consequences for the disciples. Second, such concerns are guided by a number of interdependent aims, yielding a variety of strategic functions for the unit as a whole: didactic and consolatory functions are primary, while exhortative, admonitory, and polemical functions are secondary or subordinate.

The didactic function is present in all three major sections of the unit. It involves both Jesus and the disciples. With regard to Jesus, the didactic function reveals a clear structural dimension insofar as the unit represents an extended commentary on, or exposition of, the beginning announcement of Jesus' glorification of 13:31–32. Thus, a large part of this first unit of discourse is directly concerned with the fundamental meaning of such a glorification. Furthermore, a movement from an initial, stark announcement to a detailed, reassuring explication can also be observed.

The first section begins by briefly explaining the glorification of Jesus in terms of his forthcoming departure from the world. The second section pursues the meaning of this forthcoming departure at length, providing thereby an excellent compendium of Johannine teaching on Jesus. This section progressively explains the departure in terms of the relationship between Jesus and the Father. It proceeds throughout from the more basic to the more complex claims of Jesus vis-à-vis the Father made in the course of the public ministry: from Jesus as going to the house of the Father; to Jesus as the only "way" to the Father, insofar as he is "truth" and "life"; to the direct perception of the Father in Jesus, so that whoever sees and knows Jesus sees and knows the Father in him; to the close identification of Jesus and the Father, given their mutual presence in one another. Finally, the third section further pursues the meaning of the departure in terms of the relationship between Jesus and the Father. On the one hand, this relationship is now expressed in terms of rank—the Father as greater than Jesus. On the other hand, the mode of the departure itself, Jesus' death and encounter with the demonic powers, is depicted as an act of love for the Father in obedience to the command of the Father. As such, the forthcoming departure of Jesus is thoroughly and systematically explained in the course of the unit from both a general and a specific point of view.

The didactic function with regard to the disciples can be summarized as follows. In the first section the disciples are not only provided with a final instruction that is meant to serve as their preeminent and distinguishing command as disciples of Jesus in the world—to love one another as Jesus loved them—but also characterized thereby as the "little children" whom Jesus himself has loved. In the second section special emphasis is placed on the disciples' belief in Jesus and love for Jesus (love for one another, fulfillment of other practical directives, and belief in Jesus) as the essential condition for the reception of the farewell promises extended. Finally, both of these sections contain an ironic use of the disciples' reactions to the ongoing declarations of Jesus. Given the disciples' repeated failure to understand, such reactions allow Jesus to extend his teaching about the meaning and consequences of the departure. At the same time, such failure to understand—including Peter's anticipated demise—is presented throughout as inevitable and temporary, and assurances of future understanding are repeated. As a result, the privileged status and role of the disciples as disciples of Jesus is reinforced in the unit.

A consolatory function is also present in all three major sections of the unit and again reveals a clear structural dimension, given the design of the unit as an extended commentary on, or explication of, the beginning announcement of Jesus' glorification in 13:31–32: a large part of the unit is similarly concerned with the consequences of such a glorification for the disciples. Once again, the narrative moves from a few initial negative consequences to a wide number of positive consequences.

The first section, in the midst of a series of negative announcements, contains a first, though veiled, promise that the disciples will be able to follow Jesus at a later time. The second section extends a large number of positive promises to the disciples. These interdependent promises reveal a cumulative development throughout the section. Foremost among these promises are the following: (1) Jesus' return or self-manifestation to the disciples after the announced departure so that the disciples will be able to see him again and be gathered together by him, and (2) the coming of the Spirit-Paraclete, Jesus' successor to and among them, who will be with them forever to teach them all things and recall for them all that Jesus himself taught and revealed. Other promises follow directly from these: the disciples will be permanently reunited with Jesus; they will be able to perform and even surpass Jesus' own works in their own mission in and to the world; they will be granted whatever they ask for in Jesus' name; they will live, as Jesus lives; they will come to a proper understanding of the relationship between Jesus and the Father; they will be loved by both Jesus and the Father; they will serve as the abiding place of Jesus and the Father in the world; and they will ultimately be wherever Jesus is, whether in the world or in the house of the Father—the mutual presence of Jesus and the disciples in one another. Finally, the third section briefly recalls the promise of Jesus' return. After a disturbing beginning, therefore, many brief, undeveloped, and interrelated promises are extended to the disciples.

Exhortation, warning, and polemics also emerge as secondary functions of the unit. The exhortative function is present in all three sections of the unit. It is indirectly present in the first section insofar as the new command of love calls upon the disciples to love one another as Jesus loved them, especially since such love forms part of the essential condition for the farewell promises to take place. The exhortative function appears directly in the second section when the disciples are explicitly urged to have neither fear nor consternation and to believe in Jesus and God. In the third section the exhortative function is directly present when the fundamental purpose for such announcements and disclosures on Jesus' part is described in terms of both rejoicing with regard to the departure and belief at the time of the departure itself. Such exhortations are grounded in the extensive teaching and consolation provided by the unit as a whole: such knowledge and promises should give rise to courage, rejoicing, belief, and love.

The admonitory function is also present in all three sections of the unit, though it remains indirect or implicit. In the first section the comparative element of the new command—the disciples' love for one another as Jesus loved them—introduces the possibility of death in the exercise of such love. In the second section the sharp contrast between the peace of Jesus and the peace of the world points to the possibility of opposition from, and conflict with, the world. Finally, in the third section the description of Jesus' departure as both an act of love for the Father and an encounter with "the ruler of the world" again introduces the possibility of a similar encounter with the world and its ruler on the part of the disciples in the course of their own mission in and to the world. Such veiled warnings provide a counterbalance to both the didactic and consolatory functions of the unit. Despite the extensive teaching and consolation offered, the departure has an ominous dimension with regard to both Jesus and the disciples. However, this dimension remains subdued in the present unit.

Finally, the polemical function is operative in all three major sections as well: the disciples are explicitly and repeatedly differentiated from the world at large. While their own claims are affirmed and reinforced, the claims of the world are directly questioned and attacked.

The differentiation of the disciples from the world begins in the first section. After an initial description of the envisioned situation of the disciples after the departure in the same terms as that of "the Jews"—the disciples too will not be able to go with Jesus where he is going—a radical difference is posited: the disciples will follow Jesus later. The differentiation becomes sharp in the second section. First, all that is promised to the disciples is explicitly denied to "the world" as those who have no love for Jesus and do not obey his words. Second, the world itself is presented as a rival authority to Jesus with regard to the disciples—the peace that Jesus provides for them is not at all like the peace of the world. Finally, the differentiation comes to a climax in the third section when this unbelieving and unloving world is directly associated with Satan as "the ruler of the world." Unlike the "little children," therefore, who constitute the abiding place of the Father and the Son in the world, the world itself belongs to the demonic powers.

Consequently, the disciples stand out as disciples of Jesus in the midst of an unbelieving and unloving world, a world that is under the direct and explicit rule of the demonic powers. Furthermore, this world is specifically associated with the Jews as its preeminent representatives, as the children of Satan par excellence. Despite all the evidence to the contrary, therefore, this polemical function assures the disciples that it is they who represent the ways of God in the world.

The character of this unit as a strategic whole points to a twofold rhetorical situation or view of the implied readers by the implied author. On the one hand, the disciples are viewed in a positive light: Their status as disciples of Jesus—as the "little children" who believe in and love Jesus—is acknowledged and affirmed. Their repeated failure to understand is ultimately presented as temporary, as inevitable, and as ultimately yielding to a complete understanding. Their status and role in the world are sharply set off against an unbelieving, unloving, and demonic world. On the other hand, the disciples are also viewed as being in great need of teaching and consolation. Although their status and role as disciples of Jesus are affirmed, the disciples are also perceived to be under great duress and hence in need of sustained and extensive teaching and consolation. In the end, it was this twofold rhetorical situation, with its perceived socioreligious exigencies, that called forth the complex and effective response contained within this first unit of discourse.

3

ABIDE IN ME!
ABIDE IN MY LOVE!
John 15:1–17

STRUCTURAL OUTLINE

A. Abiding in Jesus, the vine (15:1-8)
  1. The vine, the vinedresser, and the branches: Jesus, the Father, and the disciples (15:1-2)
     a) The vine and the vinedresser: Introduction and identification (15:1)
     b) The role of the vinedresser vis-à-vis the vine: The vinedresser and the branches (15:2)
        (1) The vinedresser and the unfruitful branch: Removal (15:2a-b)
        (2) The vinedresser and the fruitful branch: Pruning (15:2c)
  2. A call to the disciples to abide in Jesus as branches in the vine: The bearing of fruit (15:3-7)
     a) The relationship between Jesus and the disciples: Reaffirmation and origins (15:3)
        (1) Present status of disciples as clean or pruned (15:3a)
        (2) Rationale: Acceptance of Jesus' word (15:3b)
     b) The call to the disciples to abide in Jesus (15:4-7)
        (1) The call to abide (15:4a-b)
        (2) Abiding in Jesus, the vine: Meaning and implications (15:4c-6)
           (a) Abiding as essential condition for the bearing of fruit (15:4c-d)
           (b) The vine and the branches: Identification (15:5a-b)
           (c) Abiding as essential condition for the bearing of fruit (15:5c-6)
        (3) A promise to the abiding disciples (15:7)
  3. The abiding or fruitful disciples and the Father (15:8)
     a) Disciples' role vis-à-vis the Father: Glorification (15:8a)
     b) Grounding (15:8b)

B. Abiding in the love of Jesus (15:9-17)
   1. The chain of love: The Father, Jesus, and the disciples (15:9a-b)
      a) Father's love for Jesus as grounding and exemplar (15:9a)
      b) Jesus' love for the disciples (15:9b)
   2. A call to the disciples to abide in the love of Jesus, in the chain of love:
      The carrying out of Jesus' commands (15:9c-11)
      a) The call to abide (15:9c)
      b) Abiding in the love of Jesus (15:10)
         (1) Obedience to Jesus' commands as condition for abiding in the
             love of Jesus (15:10a-b)
         (2) Jesus' relationship to the Father as grounding and exemplar
             (15:10c)
      c) Promise to the abiding disciples (15:11)
   3. The expansion of the chain of love: The disciples and the command of
      love for one another (15:12-17)
      a) Jesus' command to love one another (15:12-13)
         (1) Identification of Jesus' command (15:12)
         (2) Definition of Jesus' love for the disciples (15:13)
      b) Disciples' role as Jesus' friends (15:14)
         (1) Disciples' status as Jesus' friends (15:14a)
         (2) Condition: Obedience of Jesus' commands (15:14b)
      c) Disciples' status as Jesus' friends (15:15)
         (l) Disciples' former status as servants (15:15a-b)
         (2) Disciples' present status as friends (15:15c-d)
      d) Disciples' role as Jesus' friends (15:16)
         (1) Disciples' status as chosen (15:16a-b_1)
         (2) Disciples' role as chosen: Bearing fruit (15:16b_{2-3})
         (3) Promises (15:16c)
      e) Jesus' command to love one another (15:17)

THE BEGINNING FOR THE SECOND unit of discourse, 15:1, within the farewell speech is firmly established; the literature agrees that 14:31d ends the first unit of discourse. The preceding literary-rhetorical analysis of 13:31–14:31 confirms the scholarly consensus; the first unit of discourse can indeed be regarded as a self-contained artistic and strategic whole, with a clear literary structure and development involving a linear and progressive threefold development, as well as a clear combination of strategic concerns and aims.

JOHN 15:1-17 AS A SECOND UNIT
OF DISCOURSE

The determination of a conclusion for this second unit of discourse proves more problematic. The literature contains three traditional and well-represented positions. The most frequent position, the designation of 15:17 as a major break in these chapters and the corresponding identification of 15:1-17 as the first unit of discourse within John 15-16, is based on two critical observations. First, the figure of the vine, introduced and developed within 15:1-8, reappears in 15:16, which in turn forms part of the ongoing development of the theme of love in 15:9-17. Second, as opposed to the immediately following discourse material beginning with 15:18, 15:1-17 focuses on the internal affairs of the community, on the proper relationship of the disciples to Jesus and one another.[1]

A second, less common position is the placement of a major break prior to 15:17, usually at 15:8, with a further major break at 15:17, formally separating thereby the figure of the vine from the theme of love. Such a position rests on an overall division of chapters 15-16 into a large number of constitutive major units—usually five or six in all, though at times even more.[2] Another division prior to 15:17, with a break at 15:10 or 15:11, has occasionally been proposed in the literature on the following grounds: the further development of the command to abide in Jesus of 15:4 in 15:9-10(11) and the specific focus of 15:12-17 on the love of the disciples for one another.[3]

A third, more common position is the designation of a major break after 15:17, usually at 16:4a; this yields a larger unit encompassing 15:1-16:4a. This theory divides chapters 15-16 into a more limited number of constitutive major units—usually two, and rarely three, such units in all. This position argues that by way of contrast to what precedes and follows, 15:1-16:4a focuses on both the internal and external affairs of the community in the world.[4]

1. See, e.g., Heitmüller, "Johannes," 830; Loisy, 417; Macgregor, 286; Brown, 2:658; Bultmann, 523, 529; Lindars, 486; Barrett, 470; Haenchen, 2:129. In the more recent literature, see Heise, *Bleiben*, 80-81; Becker, 230-31; Kaefer, 278-79.
2. See, e.g., Hoskyns, 471-76; Strathmann, 208-11; van den Bussche, 101; Wikenhauser, 282-84; Schulz, 193-96. Cf. Bernard (2:477-85), who argues for three such units in all (15:1-8, 9-11, 12-17) with a further break at 15:11.
3. For a break at 15:10, see, e.g., Westcott, 216. For a break at 15:11, see, e.g., Durand, *Saint Jean*, 411-18. Within such a division, 15:11 is regarded as a transition verse easily included in either section. In the more recent exegetical literature, see Borig, *Weinstock*, 19.
4. See, e.g., Wellhausen, 68; Huby, 70; Bover, 15-16; Behler, 129-31; Schnackenburg, 3:91, 94. In the more recent literature, see Painter, 534; Simoens (with John 16:3 as conclusion), 130. Other divisions can also be found in the literature; e.g., John 15:1-27 (Marsh,

The first position, the majority position in the literature, is preferred: John 15:1–17 should be seen as the first unit of discourse within chapters 15–16. The critical observations that follow argue against either a further subdivision of 15:1–17 or its incorporation into a larger unit of discourse. The final reappearance of the figure of the vine in 15:16, not only within the wider development of the theme of love in 15:9–17 but also within the more specific development of the command to the disciples to love one another in 15:12–17, gives the latter verses a sense of conclusion. In fact, this reappearance constitutes an effective way of connecting, by way of conclusion, 15:9–17 to the earlier development of the figure in 15:1–8. At the same time, the warnings of 15:18–21 concerning the world's forthcoming severe opposition to the disciples convey a sense of a new beginning or point of departure.

A second example of the recurring concluding formula of the discourse, "These things I have said to you," appears in 15:11. In the light of the twofold use of this formula throughout the speech, I would argue, against R. Schnackenburg, that this example also signals the conclusion of a self-contained unit of discourse by way of anticipation. In fact, its distance from 15:17, the proposed conclusion for this second unit of discourse, is approximately the same as that of 14:25 from its respective end.[5]

The overarching and controlling theme of 15:1–17 shifts with the remainder of chapter 15. The primary focus of 15:1–17 on the internal affairs of the community (on the correct relationship of the disciples to Jesus and one another) is replaced in the latter half of chapter 15 by a similar focus on the external affairs of the community (on the proper relationship of the disciples to the world at large). With this shift in focus comes a shift in the controlling thematic concerns: the sustained emphasis of 15:1–17 on the need for the disciples to abide as disciples of Jesus is replaced by a similar emphasis on the opposition of the world to the disciples as disciples of Jesus.

The primary tone of exhortation and warning of 15:1–17 continues through chapter 15, but the tone of Jesus' address to the disciples shifts after 15:18:

1. A sharp contrast between the disciples and the world is now introduced.

---

516); John 15:1–16:15 (Dodd, 399–400, 409–10). Behler, Dodd, and Schnackenburg identify John 15:1–17 and 15:18–16:4a as major sections within this unit. The others argue for the following major sections within the unit: Huby, John 15:1–8, 9–17; Painter, John 15:1–10, 11–17; Marsh and Simoens, John 15:1–11, 12–17; Bover, John 15:1–8, 9–11, 12–17.

5. See chap. 2, n. 5. For Schnackenburg (3:92), John 15:11 represents a minor break within 15:1–16:4a, pointing to a subsection (15:1–11, 12–17) within 15:1–17, the first major section of this unit.

2. The disciples no longer appear to be in possession of full belief and understanding or already "clean" because of the word that Jesus has spoken. Instead, they appear about to receive the Spirit-Paraclete, who will witness to Jesus in and through them.
3. The possibility of the disciples' faltering and being separated from the community, so vividly described in 15:1–17 as an everyday reality, now appears remote.

Finally, the standpoint of Jesus as speaker of the discourse shifts as one proceeds from 15:1–17 to the rest of chapter 15. The Jesus who had spoken as if already glorified and with the Father is now a Jesus who speaks as if "the hour" were already behind him and all that remained were its final events (the bestowal of his successor, the Spirit-Paraclete, and his own final journey or return to the Father).

On the one hand, although 15:8 and 15:11 represent breaks in the farewell speech, neither should be seen as a major break pointing to a self-contained unit of discourse. Instead, both should be seen as minor breaks, with 15:1–8 as pointing to a major section and 15:11–17 to a subsection within the second unit of discourse. On the other hand, John 15:1–17 does not belong within a larger unit of discourse, because the similarity in question points not to one and the same unit of discourse but instead to the links that tie these two major units of discourse to one another within the ongoing farewell speech. In conclusion, 15:17 constitutes a proper ending to the first unit of discourse within chapters 15–16, and therefore, 15:1–17 should be regarded as the second self-contained unit of discourse within the farewell speech as a whole.

LITERARY STRUCTURE AND DEVELOPMENT

A review of the scholarly literature shows four recurring possibilities with regard to the overall organization of 15:1–17. One is a majority position and the other three, minority positions. A great deal of the discussion focuses on the perceived centrality of 15:8 within the unit.

The majority position argues for a twofold division of these verses with a break at 15:8, yielding two major sections consisting of 15:1–8 and 15:9–17.[6] The arguments for this position duplicate the arguments for another major division of the farewell at 15:8. Such a division is once more affirmed, therefore, though now only as a subdivision within 15:1–17 itself. Thus, the first major section of the unit develops the figure of the vine (15:1–8), and

6. See, e.g., Lagrange, 400–405; Bultmann, 529; Becker, 229. Among those who argue for a self-contained major section within a larger unit of discourse, see, e.g., Behler, 130; Dodd, 410–12.

the second major section focuses on the theme of love (15:9–15). The most thorough example of this position is that of R. Bultmann, for whom both major sections reveal a parallelism:[7]

1. Both 15:1 and 15:9 begin with a reference to the Father.
2. The imperative "Abide!" of 15:4 is repeated in 15:9.
3. The declaration of 15:3, "You are already clean," is paralleled by that of 15:14, "You are my friends."
4. The expression "nothing without me" of 15:5 is matched in 15:16 by the words "not you . . . but I," with the role of the disciples presented in terms of "bearing fruit."
5. In both sections the disciples are assured that the Father will hear and grant their requests (15:7, 16).

Bultmann summarizes this proposed parallelism by arguing that 15:9–17 provides a variation of the central theme of 15:1–8 insofar as the imperative of 15:4 ("Abide in me!") is now expounded as "Abide in my love!" beginning with 15:9.

The first minority position also argues for a twofold division of these verses, but with a break past 15:8, at 15:10 or 15:11, yielding thereby two major sections consisting of either 15:1–10 and 15:11–17 or 15:1–11 and 15:12–17. In this position 15:11 functions as a transitional verse, seen as either the climax to the first section or the beginning of the second, though the former stance usually is adopted.[8] Again, the arguments on behalf of this division are similar to the arguments for another major break in the farewell at 15:10(11); such a division is acknowledged, but only as a subdivision within 15:1–17 itself. The first major section (15:1–10[11]) is said to develop the theme of abiding, with respect to both the figure of the vine and the love of Jesus. The second major section (15:10[11]–17) focuses on the love of the disciples for one another, which is delineated by the inclusion of 15:12 and 15:17. Schnackenburg, who argues for 15:1–17 as a major section within 15:1–16:4a, represents the best example of this position: 15:11 not only represents a further example of the recurring concluding formula of the discourse, signaling a minor break at this point, but also

---

7. Such parallelism has been acknowledged by others as well; see, e.g., Wikenhauser, 285; Schulz, 196.

8. See, e.g., Marsh, 518, 523; Lindars, 488–93; Schnackenburg, 3:92–93, 95–96. See also Simoens (140–43, 146–50), who posits an overall pattern of inclusion within John 15:1–11: whereas the outer components (15:1–5a, 8–11) focus on the abiding of the disciples in Jesus as the vine or in the love of Jesus, the central component (15:5b–7) sharply outlines the two possibilities open to the disciples in this regard (abiding or failing to abide in Jesus).

contains the theme of joy, which is used elsewhere in the farewell as a concluding literary marker (16:24).

The second minority position argues as well for a twofold division of these verses, but with a break prior to 15:8, at either 15:6 or 15:7; thus, there are two major sections, 15:1–6 and 15:7–18 or 15:1–7 and 15:8–18. Within this position 15:7 functions as a transitional verse—either a conclusion to the first section or the introduction to the second.[9] The first major section develops the figure of the vine proper (15:1–6[7]), and the second major section provides a parenetic development of this figure (15:7[8]–17). The figure proper ends, therefore, with either the contrast between the fruitful and unfruitful branches of 15:5–6 or the delineation of the promise extended to the fruitful branches in 15:7. R. Brown provides the most thorough example of such a proposal.[10] First, according to Brown, such a division follows that of 10:1–21, where a first section (10:1–5) contains figurative sayings about the shepherd, and a second section (10:7–18) provides different developments of this figure. Second, inclusion occurs within 15:1–6 ("I am the vine" in 15:1, and 5) and 15:7–17 (bearing fruit in 15:8, 16; asking and receiving in 15:7, 16). Third, says Brown, the development of 15:7–17 follows a chiastic pattern.[11]

Finally, the third minority position opts for a threefold division, with a first break at either 15:6 or 15:8 and a second break at 15:11, ultimately yielding three major sections comprising either 15:1–6, 15:7–11, and 15:12–17 or 15:1–8, 15:9–11, and 15:12–17.[12] To begin with, the first major section focuses on the figure of the vine, whether limited to the figure proper (15:1–6) or encompassing the whole of its initial presentation (15:1–8). The second major section (15:7–11 or 15:9–11) then focuses on the theme of love and the corresponding theme of keeping the commands as the basic condition for abiding in such love, though in the former case the proposed delineation of this middle section remains amorphous, given its inclusion of 15:7–8. Finally, the third major section focuses on the theme of

9. See, e.g., Lightfoot, 280–83; Brown, 2:665–68. The former argues for John 15:7, and the latter opts for 15:6.

10. Brown (2:665–66) specifically credits the earlier work of M.-E. Boismard ("L'évolution du thème eschatologique dans les traditions johanniques," RB 68 [1961] 507–24), in this regard.

11. Within this pattern 15:11 functions both as a transition between 15:7–10 and 15:12–17 and as a summary of 15:7–10. First, the two major components present seven different themes or expressions in common: Jesus' words or commands (15:7, 17), efficacious prayer (15:7, 16), bearing fruit (15:8, 16), the choosing of the disciples (15:8, 16), Jesus and the Father (15:9, 15), Jesus' love for the disciples (15:9, 15), and love for Jesus equaling the keeping of the commands (15:10, 12, 14). Second, each major component also contains examples of inclusions: (a) 15:7–10, with an emphasis on abiding in Jesus or in his love (15:7, 9–10), and (b) 15:12–17, with a repetition of the love command.

12. See, e.g., Wellhausen, 68–69; Bernard, 2:477–85; Bover, 16, 86, 95–96.

the disciples' love for one another, marked off by the inclusion of 15:12 and 15:17. The second section ultimately functions as a transition between the first and third sections: whereas the theme of love connects this central section to the final section, that of abiding connects it to the first section.

The preceding scholarly discussion points to two central questions regarding the literary structure and development of this unit. The first question concerns the role of 15:8 in the unit—whether a first break should be acknowledged at this point, as most claim, or whether such a break actually precedes or follows 15:8 itself. The second question has to do with the presence of a further break after 15:8, if a first such break has been posited at 15:8 or earlier. I agree with the majority position: only one break should be acknowledged at 15:8.

I agree with the majority position, as well as with the current of the third minority position that says a break is to be affirmed at 15:8 and not before or after. Such a division affirms the close unity and development of the figure of the vine (introduced in 15:1–2 and dominant through 15:8, with a brief reappearance by way of conclusion in 15:16). On the one hand, a break prior to 15:8 is unconvincing. Neither the proposed delimitation of the figure proper to 15:6(7) nor the parenetic interest posited for all of 15:7(8)–17 should override the clear continuation of the imagery of the vine through 15:8 and the introduction of the theme of love beginning with 15:9–10. On the other hand, a break after 15:8 itself is also unconvincing. Once again, neither the inclusion formed by the love command in 15:12–17 nor the proposed primacy of the theme of abiding within 15:1–10(11) should override the continued development of the figure of the vine through 15:8 itself and the immediate introduction of the theme of love in 15:9–10. In conclusion, 15:1–8 should be seen as the first major section of 15:1–17.

I also agree with the majority position and the second minority position that if a break is acknowledged at 15:8 or earlier, no further break need be posited before 15:17. Such a division acknowledges the close unity and development of the theme of love, introduced in 15:9 and dominant through 15:17. Again, the focus on the love of the disciples for one another and the inclusion formed by the disclosure of such a command in 15:12 and 15:17 should not override the continued development of the theme of love through all of 15:9–17, though the inclusion points to a minor break in the development of these verses. In conclusion, 15:9–17 should be seen as the second major section of 15:1–17.

This proposal for a twofold division of 15:1–17 can be defended from a structural point of view. Both major sections of the unit reveal a similar threefold development in the form of an inclusion.

In each major section the beginning subsection (15:1–2, 9a–b) sets forth the fundamental relationship that binds Jesus and the disciples to one another. Each subsection, furthermore, mentions the figure of the Father and assigns him a specific role with regard to this relationship. In addition, each beginning subsection introduces the central thematic concerns of each section, so the relationships in question—Jesus/the disciples, Jesus/the Father, and the Father/the disciples—are described in terms of these central themes.

Once the central theme of each section has been introduced and the relationship between Jesus and the disciples described accordingly, the middle and focal subsection of each major section (15:3–7, 9c–11) introduces and develops the controlling theme of the unit as a whole— namely, the theme of abiding and, more specifically, a call to the disciples to abide in their given relationship with Jesus as described in the first subsection. In other words, once the fundamental relationship between Jesus and the disciples has been set forth in the first subsection, a direct appeal to the disciples—very effectively summarized in the corresponding imperatives of 15:4a and 15:9c—to abide in such a relationship immediately follows. This call also specifies how the disciples are to abide in their given relationship with Jesus, thus describing in turn the proper role of the disciples as disciples of Jesus.

Finally, after the call to abide has been issued and the proper role of the disciples as disciples of Jesus outlined, the third and final subsection of each major section (15:8, 12–17) returns to its corresponding first subsection for further development, thus accounting for the basic pattern of inclusion that further marks off these two major sections within the unit. In so doing, the final subsection develops the relationship between Jesus and the disciples described within the beginning subsection in the light of the intervening call to abide. Whereas in the first major section this development is brief and specific, in the second major section, as the striking difference in length shows (15:12–17), this development is more expansive and complex.

The proposed parallelism between these two major sections should not be seen, as Bultmann would have it, in terms of a variation of 15:1–8 in 15:9–17—of a continued exposition of the imperative of 15:4a by means of 15:9c—but rather as a reaffirmation and expansion of 15:1–8 in 15:9–17. The parallelism reaffirms the call for the disciples to abide in Jesus as branches in the vine by abiding in his word by means of a further call to abide in the love of Jesus and the chain of love by carrying out his commands, above all the preeminent command of love for one another as Jesus himself had loved them.

LITERARY-RHETORICAL ANALYSIS

The proposed literary structure and development of this second unit of discourse can be summarized by the following structural outline, which this section will develop in detail:

> I. Abiding in Jesus, the vine (15:1–8)
> II. Abiding in the love of Jesus (15:9–17)

First Major Section (John 15:1–8)

The first major section of the second unit of discourse, 15:1–8, describes the theme of abiding in Jesus, the vine. In keeping with the threefold pattern of inclusion proposed for each major section, the literary structure of this section can be outlined as follows: (1) the vine, the vinedresser, and the branches (Jesus, the Father, and the disciples [15:1–2]); (2) a call to the disciples to abide in Jesus as branches in the vine (the bearing of fruit [15:3–7]); and (3) the abiding and fruitful disciples and the Father (15:8).

The beginning subsection, 15:1–2, introduces the central theme of this section, the figure of the vine, and in so doing provides a first, indirect description of the relationship between Jesus and the disciples: Jesus as the vine and the disciples as the branches. In so doing, the first subsection introduces the character of the Father and assigns him a specific role within the figure as the vinedresser of the vine; this establishes a direct relationship not only between Jesus and the Father but also between the disciples and the Father. The central subsection, 15:3–7, develops the first call to the disciples to abide in their given relationship with Jesus—the overarching and controlling theme of the unit as a whole—by expanding the imagery of the figure introduced in 15:1–2: it is the proper role of the disciples as disciples of Jesus to abide in Jesus as branches in the vine by abiding in his word and thus bearing much fruit. The final subsection, 15:8, returns to the beginning description of the relationship between Jesus and the disciples in 15:1–2 for further development in the light of the call to abide of 15:3–7. This development is brief and specific. The direct relationship between the Father as vinedresser and the disciples as branches posited in 15:1–2 is now pursued from the point of view of the fruitful branches, of those disciples who heed the call of 15:3–7 and abide in Jesus.

Literary Genre

This chapter so far has referred to the extended use of imagery from viticulture in this first section as a figure—the figure of the vine. Such a characterization is adequate to describe the nature of the sustained imagery developed in these verses, while also broad and ambiguous enough to by-pass the traditional problems that have marked the scholarly discussion. Two such problems can be identified. First, the nature and development of this figurative language in 15:1–8 has given rise to an ongoing debate regarding its proper classification. In the light of the synoptic material, many have characterized this development as a parable, whereas others have called it an allegory. Other, less frequent designations include symbolism or symbolic teaching, metaphor, comparison, and similitude. Second, within such a debate there is a recurring failure to provide a satisfactory (and in some cases, even elementary) description of the various literary terms employed for the classification or identification in question, terms that themselves are fluid in meaning and scope.

In the more recent past there have been some attempts to move beyond this traditional impasse by focusing on the important question of classification or identification. For example, R. Borig has argued that these verses (15:1–10) constitute a *Bildrede* (figurative discourse), a uniquely Johannine form of expression that brings together both parabolic and allegorical elements. Borig describes this literary form as not metaphorical but literal—Jesus is indeed the true vine.[13] Similarly, Brown has characterized these verses (15:1–6) as a *mashal*—a designation said to cover in the Jewish tradition all figurative illustrations without further distinctions—though Brown says this *mashal* emphasizes, as usual in the Fourth Gospel, the allegorical element.[14] Finally, D. Wead has argued that these verses (15:1–8) represent an extended metaphorical discourse, a peculiarly Johannine form of expression in which a metaphor is followed by lengthy development in discourse form, with great freedom to move between the literal and the figurative realms (e.g., 4:8–15; 6:27–58; 10:1–16). Each discourse is different and follows its own characteristics; in this case, Wead points out a marked increase in allegorical content.[15]

The more traditional categories of parable, allegory, and the like, employed in terms of their common Synoptic usage, are inadequate to describe

---

13. Borig, *Weinstock*, 21–23. Borig specifically acknowledges his debt in this regard to E. Schweizer (*Ego Eimi: Die religionsgeschichtliche Herkunft und theologische Bedeutung der johanneischen Bildreden, zugleich ein Beitrag zur Quellenfrage des vierten Evangeliums*, FRLANT 38 [Göttingen: Vandenhoeck & Ruprecht, 1965]), from whom he adopts the concept of a *Bildrede*. In direct contrast to a comparison or an allegory, where image and explanation are juxtaposed, the Johannine figurative discourse brings image and explanation into the closest possible union so that the end result is literal speech: Jesus lays claim thereby to the title of "the vine."

14. Brown, 1:390–91; 2:668–69. Brown specifically acknowledges his debt in this regard to the work of M. Hermaniuk (*La parabole évangélique* [Louvain: Louvain University Press, 1947]).

15. D. Wead, *The Literary Devices in John's Gospel*, Theologischen Dissertationen 4 (Basel: Friedrich Reinhardt Kommissionsverlag, 1970) 74–83, 92–94.

the figurative development in the first section. The more recent classifications need further revision as well. First, the inclusive designation of *mashal*, which encompasses different types of figurative development under one classification, blurs the distinctive character of the various types in question. Second, the specific conception of *figurative discourse* as literal speech is too restrictive. The vine is not a traditional or established title, with set connotations, being claimed by Jesus, but rather is an implicit comparison meant to shed light on the nature of the relationship between Jesus and the disciples. Finally, I agree with Wead, though I would not use the term *metaphorical discourse*, since I see 15:1–8 as part of a larger unit of discourse comprising all of 15:1–17 in which the metaphor comes into play once again at the end. Therefore, 15:1–8 exemplifies a highly developed sustained metaphor with a high degree of correspondence between the object and the term of comparison. This accounts for both the parabolic and allegorical traits traditionally associated with this figure.[16]

The central or grounding metaphor within this figure is that of Jesus as the vine, introduced at the beginning (15:1a) and reiterated in the course of its subsequent development (15:5a). The metaphor's high degree of development can be observed in its extended use of related imagery from viticulture: the references to both the vinedresser and the branches, the description of the vinedresser's role in relation to the branches (pruning and removing), the focus on the proper function of the branches in relation to the vine (abiding and the bearing of fruit), the delineation of the two different types of branches (those bearing much fruit and those bearing no fruit), and the description of the ultimate fate awaiting the two kinds of branches (bearing more fruit and removal from the vine). The metaphor's high degree of correspondence can be observed in the following elements of the development: the metaphorical identifications of the vine, the vinedresser, and the branches; the explicit comparisons or similes of 15:4 and 15:6 concerning the proper function of the branches in relation to the vine and the ultimate fate awaiting the unfruitful branch, respectively; and the metaphorical descriptions of what both pruning and bearing fruit entail.

This sustained metaphor of Jesus as the vine also reveals a frequent interchange between the literal and metaphorical levels, between the imagery of viticulture and the relationship between Jesus and the disciples. The literal level is foremost in the first subsection (15:1–2), and the metaphorical level emerges as dominant within the final subsection (15:8). In the middle subsection (15:3–7) the metaphorical level is foremost within its beginning and

16. See G. B. Caird, *The Language and Imagery of the Bible* (Philadelphia: Westminster, 1980) 144–71. On metaphor, see P. Wheelwright, *Metaphor and Reality* (Bloomington: Indiana University Press, 1968) 70–91; T. Hawkes, *Metaphor*, The Critical Idiom 25 (London: Methuen, 1972).

concluding components (15:3, 7), whereas the literal level proves dominant within the central component (15:4–6).

In conclusion, the first major section describes the relationship between Jesus and the disciples in terms of a sustained metaphor taken from the field of viticulture. Its grounding metaphor is that of Jesus as the vine, and its focus becomes, in keeping with the overarching theme of the unit as a whole, the need for the disciples to abide in Jesus, as branches abide in the vine, by bearing fruit.

The Vine, the Vinedresser, and the Branches: Jesus, the Father, and the Disciples (John 15:1–2)

The first subsection (15:1–2) introduces the central theme of the section, the figure of the vine; provides the first description of the relationship between Jesus and the disciples in terms of this theme; and assigns a specific role to the Father within such a relationship. First, two successive metaphorical identifications of Jesus and the Father are given in terms of imagery from viticulture (15:1). Second, a description of the Father's role within this imagery is provided, introducing several more elements of the sustained metaphorical development (15:2). This first subsection, therefore, is primarily developed on the literal rather than metaphorical level.

The Vine and the Vinedresser: Introduction and Identification (John 15:1)

John 15:1 introduces the metaphorical identifications as coordinate members of a compound sentence. First, the grounding metaphor of Jesus as "the vine" is introduced by the familiar "I am" formula of the Gospel (15:1a).[17] The first related element from viticulture then is immediately associated with the figure of the Father—the Father as "the vinedresser" of the vine (15:1b).[18] The most salient feature of these identifications is the use of the adjective "true" (ἀληθινή) in the description of Jesus as "the vine," especially given its clearly emphatic position after the noun. Jesus is specifically introduced thereby as "the true vine."[19] The status and role of Jesus as a vine is thereby affirmed at a fundamental level: he is the only true vine, and there is no other.

17. This "I am" saying, with a repetition in 15:5a, is the last one in the farewell (see 14:7).
18. As in the first unit (13:31–32), the second unit also begins with a declaration concerning the relationship between Jesus and the Father. This unit, however, does not pursue this relationship except in 15:9c–10, where it is used solely as a grounding and exemplar for the relationship between Jesus and the disciples.
19. For similar uses of the adjective, see 1:9 ("the true light") and 6:32 ("the true bread from heaven"). Cf. 4:32; 8:16.

The emphatic presence of this adjective in this initial metaphorical identification of Jesus has been invariably regarded as affirming Jesus' claims vis-à-vis any other such claims. The identification of such competing claims has depended largely on a further identification of the provenance of this metaphor of the vine, that is, on the symbolic function of the vine. The literature contains two distinct lines of interpretation, which argue for either a Jewish or a gnostic-Mandaean provenance.[20]

The first, far more common position traces the symbolism of 15:1–8 to the traditional Jewish description of Israel as the vineyard or vine of God; the tradition is both biblical (e.g., Isa 5:1–7; 27:2–6; Hos 10:1; 14:7; Jer 2:21; 5:10; 6:9; Ezek 15:1–8; 19:10–14; Ps 80:8–16) and pseudepigraphical (e.g., 2 Esdr. 5:23). Several recurring motifs of such a description have been used to argue for such provenance: God as the keeper of the vine, an emphasis on fruitfulness, and the promise of punishment or destruction for lack of fruitfulness. Indeed, it is the frequent portrayal of Israel as an unproductive vine within this tradition that is often identified as the context for the emphatic description of Jesus as the "true" vine in 15:1–8; in other words, Jesus has replaced Israel as the faithful and fruitful vine of God.[21]

The more recent interpretation, of far more limited appeal, looks to the figure of the vine as developed in the Mandaean literature (e.g., *Right Ginza* 59:39–60:2; 181:27–28; 301:11–14; 325:4–327:23) for the proper background of the symbolism in 15:1–8. Again, several recurrent motifs of this figure have played a decisive role in the choice of this provenance: the use of the "I am" formula, the vine as the tree of life whose very fragrance gives life, and the branches and shoots of the vine as the souls who receive life only through union with the tree. As such, a context for the emphatic description of Jesus as the "true" vine in 15:1–8 has been suggested: as the only messenger from the world above, only Jesus can provide true life through his revelation in the world below.[22]

The proposed Jewish background is not only more acceptable, given the elements in common with the development of this figure in 15:1–8, but to the point, given the sustained conflict with the Jews that lies at the heart of the plot of the Gospel. Within such a general context this emphatic insistence on Jesus as the "true" vine of God would be proper and effective. At the same time, given the salient lack of any explicit differentiation

20. See Borig, *Weinstock*, 79–192. For a eucharistic reading, with the wine of the eucharist as the source for the metaphor, see Bernard, 2:477–78; Loisy, 417–18.
21. See, e.g., A. Jaubert, "L'image de la vigne (Jean 15)," in *Oikonomia: Heilsgeschichte als Thema der Theologie. Oscar Cullmann zum 65. Geburtstag gewidmet*, ed. F. Christ (Hamburg: B. Reich, 1967) 93–99.
22. See Schweizer, *Ego Eimi*, 39–41; Bultmann, 529–32; Schulz, 194–95; Lattke, *Einheit*, 162–63.

of the disciples from the world at large in this unit of discourse, does such
an emphatic affirmation of Jesus as the one and only true vine have additional connotations or rival claims in view? The final section of this chapter will return to this question.

The Role of the Vinedresser in Relation to the Vine: The Vinedresser and the Branches (John 15:2)

After the introductory metaphorical identifications of Jesus and the Father,
the subsection continues with a description of the role of the Father as "the
vinedresser" of the vine (15:2).[23] Such a description is developed by further
related imagery from viticulture:

1. "The branches" of the vine, introducing thereby a formal distinction
   and an indirect relationship between the vine itself and the branches
   (between Jesus and the disciples).
2. "The bearing of fruit" of the branches, thus introducing the proper
   role of the branches in relation to the vine (of the disciples as disciples of Jesus).
3. The "removing" or "pruning" of the branches by the vinedresser, further introducing thereby a direct relationship between the branches
   and the vinedresser (between the disciples and the Father).

The description is carefully constructed. First, an explicit distinction
between those branches that do not bear fruit (15:2a–b) and those that do
(15:2c) allows a sharp antithetical development of the role of the Father as
vinedresser, since the two types of branches are accorded radically different treatments by the vinedresser. Second, this antithetical development
reveals a parallel structure consisting of the following three elements:

1. A suspended nominative detailing the type of branch in question—
   first, the unfruitful branch (15:2a) and, then, the fruitful branch
   (15:2c$_1$).[24]

---

23. In a study of proverbial material in the Fourth Gospel, K. Dewey ("*Paroimiai* in the
Gospel of John," *Semeia* 17 [1980] 81–99) lists this delineation of the Father's role in
15:2—with a possible continuation in 15:6 and a conjectural introduction somewhat like
"There is a vinedresser"—as one of thirty-four items in the Gospel that function proverbially
within the text (p. 84). This description of 15:2 represents a traditional statement whose
basic meaning is being extended and applied to a new situation altogether.
24. For anacoluthon after πᾶς, see BDF, 466.3. For anacoluthon in general, see Smyth,
3004–8, esp. 3006, with regard to its effects, intended or unintended. In John 15:2 force
becomes the predominant effect. The double use of the suspended nominative at the beginning and the personal pronoun at the end sharply emphasizes the different fates awaiting the
two types of branches.

2. The specific role of the vinedresser with respect to each type of branch in question—"removal" of the unfruitful branch (15:2b) and "pruning" of the fruitful branch ($15:2c_{2-3}$).
3. The personal pronoun as the direct object of each verb, thus resuming the suspended nominative at the beginning of each description.

Finally, the verbs used to describe the respective actions of the vinedresser with regard to the two different types of branches constitute an effective example of paranomasia (αἴρει/καθαίρει).[25]

Two unmatched elements within this antithetical parallelism should be noted. First, the description of the unfruitful branch (15:2a–b) contains an example of the frequent interchange between the literal and metaphorical levels in these verses—a prepositional phrase indicating the proper location of the unfruitful branch in Jesus himself ("in me") rather than in the vine as such. Second, the description of the fruitful branch (15:2c) has a concluding subordinate clause indicating the purpose behind the Father's pruning of the fruitful branch, "so that it may bear more fruit" ($15:2c_3$), thus indicating the need—underscored by the use of the present subjunctive—for all branches in the vine to bear fruit unceasingly or otherwise face the certainty of removal from the vine. The first element introduces the first description of the relationship between the disciples and Jesus (branches in the vine), and the second emphasizes an essential feature of this relationship, the need for ongoing fruitfulness on the part of the branches in the vine.

The first subsection (15:2) plays an important programmatic role within the first major section and its continued development of the metaphor of the vine. First, the direct relationship posited between the vinedresser and the branches, the Father and the disciples, is pursued in the final subsection (15:8). Second, the indirect relationship introduced between the vine and the branches is immediately pursued in the central subsection (15:3–7) and developed in terms of the many elements of the imagery used in the description of the Father's role.

A Call to the Disciples to Abide in Jesus
as Branches in the Vine:
The Bearing of Fruit (John 15:3–7)

The second subsection (15:3–7) focuses on the relationship between the vine and the branches, between Jesus and the disciples, and introduces the overarching theme of the unit: a call to the disciples, as branches, to

25. The use of paranomasia draws attention to not only the two contrasting roles of the Father involved but also the corresponding fates of the branches in question.

abide in Jesus, the vine. Two major components can be outlined: (1) a re-affirmation of the present status of the disciples as disciples of Jesus, of their given relationship with Jesus (15:3), and (2) a call to the disciples to abide in Jesus, in that relationship that is already theirs, and thus preserve and insure their given status as disciples of Jesus (15:4–7). In this second subsection the metaphorical level emerges as dominant at both the beginning and end (15:3, 4a–b, 7), whereas the literal level is foremost at its very center (15:4c–6).

The Relationship between Jesus and the Disciples: Reaffirmation and Origins (John 15:3)

The middle subsection (15:3–7) begins with a reaffirmation, in direct address, of the relationship between Jesus and the disciples. This first component is pursued mainly on the metaphorical level. The only exception is the use of the adjective *clean* (καθαίροι)—drawn from the same root as the verb *to prune* used in the description of the Father's role with regard to the fruitful branches and thus taking on the more specific meaning of "pruned" as well ("you are already pruned")—to describe the present status of the disciples. This reaffirmation proceeds as follows: the basic status of the disciples with regard to Jesus is described (15:3a), and the fundamental reason (the origins) for such a given status follows (15:3b). In effect, the beginning statement of 15:3 characterizes the disciples as already "clean" or "pruned" because of the "word" (λόγος) that Jesus has spoken to them, with the obvious implication that the disciples have already heard and accepted this "word" of Jesus.

Thus, the relationship between the disciples and Jesus is now reaffirmed on the basis of their own acceptance of, or belief in, his "word," a term that encompasses at this point the whole of Jesus' teaching and revelation, especially given the use of the perfect tense (λελάληκα) in this regard—a perfect of completed action pointing to the full ministry, including "the hour," as already accomplished. It is such an acceptance and belief, therefore, that qualifies the disciples as "clean" or "pruned" and, thus, in terms of the imagery from viticulture (cf. 15:5b), as "branches" of the vine to begin with. In other words, the branches represent the disciples as those who have accepted or believed in Jesus' revelation and teaching, who have been "cleansed" or "pruned" by the word of Jesus.[26]

---

26. This use of the term "word" is similar, therefore, to that of 14:22–23 in the first unit; see chap. 2, n. 77. For a similar use of the adjective "clean," see 13:9–11. However, in the present unit the dialectic of being "clean" and yet in need of further "washing" disappears, so the disciples are now addressed—as both the use of the adverb "already" and the perfect of completed action with regard to Jesus' revelation suggest—as fully "clean," as having already attained full understanding and belief.

A comparison of the status of the disciples in 15:3 with that of the first unit is useful. Whereas in the first unit the disciples are consistently portrayed as unable to understand the full meaning of Jesus' declarations concerning his impending departure and yet are repeatedly assured that such an understanding would be forthcoming, in the present unit such an understanding is presupposed—the disciples are already "clean" or "pruned" because they have received the word of Jesus. Therefore, the dialectic between a present partial understanding and a future full understanding is gone. Such a shift is accompanied by a corresponding shift in the standpoint of the speaker. Whereas the first unit points to a Jesus who speaks as both about to undergo the climactic events of "the hour" and as having done so except for its final components, the present unit reflects a Jesus who speaks as if already glorified with the Father.

The Call to the Disciples to Abide in Jesus (John 15:4–7)

The subsection continues (15:4–7) with an extended call to the disciples to abide in Jesus, in that relationship they already possess—the overarching theme of the unit as a whole. Three major components can be identified: (1) the call proper (15:4a–b); (2) a description of what such abiding in Jesus entails ("bearing fruit" as the proper role of the disciples as disciples of Jesus [15:4c–6]); and (3) a promise to the disciples who respond to the call and abide in Jesus, who bear fruit and thus fulfill their correct role as disciples of Jesus (15:7). A distinctive inclusion frames the call: the concluding promise (15:7) parallels an earlier promise extended within the call proper (15:4b).

The call proper (15:4a–b), which continues the direct address of 15:3, is brief. It is a compound sentence with two coordinate members, yielding a formula of mutual abiding. The first member conveys the call as such (15:4a: "abide in me"), and the second extends a promise to those disciples who respond to the call (15:4b: "and I [will abide] in you").[27] This formula is programmatic. Whereas the call itself introduces the overarching theme of the unit, extensively developed in the second component (15:4c–6), the promise anticipates the second promise of the third and final component (15:7), setting up thereby the inclusion that frames the call as a whole. The call proper continues the metaphorical level adopted with 15:3, though the term "abiding" is also used on the literal level and thus serves as a point of transition to the predominant use of this level in 15:4c–6.

27. The formula is abbreviated insofar as the verb of the second member is omitted. The aorist imperative of the first member functions as the equivalent of a dependent, conditional clause: "If you abide in me, then I [will abide] in you." For the formula of mutual abiding, see 6:56; see also 1 John 3:24; 4:13, 15, 16.

Therefore, although the relationship between Jesus and the disciples, first acknowledged and affirmed in 15:1–2, is reaffirmed in 15:3 on the basis of their previous belief in, and acceptance of, Jesus' word, a call (15:4a) is now issued to the disciples to abide in Jesus, in that vine whose branches they represent and in that word they have accepted. Such a rapid succession of affirmation and call to abide implies that a certain role is expected and required of the disciples as disciples of Jesus, the fulfillment of which ultimately insures their status as disciples, their relationship with Jesus. The addition of a conditional promise at this point (15:4b) reinforces such a call and expectation insofar as the promise presents the fulfillment of this role as an essential condition for Jesus' own continued abiding in the disciples: if they abide in him and in his word, he abides in them. In other words, the extension of the promise itself at this point makes it clear that the relationship between Jesus and the disciples is by no means final and irrevocable but may well come to a complete and radical end.

The call proper is followed by a description of what such abiding in Jesus means and entails for the disciples: bearing fruit as the proper role of the disciples as disciples of Jesus, as branches in the vine (15:4c–6). This description incorporates the many related terms from viticulture introduced in the delineation of the Father's role as vinedresser in 15:2 and, in so doing, returns for the most part to the literal level of the development. The description follows a pattern of inclusion: the outer components describe the proper role of the disciples (15:4c–d, 5c–6), and the central component provides two metaphorical identifications of elements from the figure (15:5a–b).

The first outer component (15:4c–d) initially presents abiding in Jesus as the essential condition for that activity or behavior proper to the disciples of Jesus, the bearing of fruit, by using a simile or direct comparison (καθώς/οὕτως) between the relationship of a branch with regard to its vine and that of a disciple with regard to Jesus. The beginning comparative clause (15:4c) returns, therefore, to the literal level of the development, specifically recalling the role proper to a branch as outlined in 15:2 (the bearing of fruit) and developing it further by including the essential condition for such fruitfulness as specified in the preceding call of 15:4a–b (abiding): "as the branch can bear no fruit by itself unless it abides in the vine." The metaphorical application of this role to the disciples in the main clause (15:4d) continues the direct address of both 15:3 and 15:4a–b: "so neither can you unless you abide in me." Thus, in effect, only a proper response to the call of 15:4a–b, a continued abiding in Jesus, is said to make possible that role proper to, and expected of, the disciples as disciples of Jesus—the bearing of fruit.

The comparison reveals a careful literary construction. Both the comparative clause (the example of the fruitful branch) and the main clause (the application to the fruitful disciple) consist of a beginning statement to the effect that the activity in question, the bearing of fruit, is impossible for both branches and disciples in and of themselves ($15{:}4c_1$, $4d_1$) and a subsequent conditional clause that presents abiding in either the vine or Jesus as the essential condition for the fulfillment of such a role ($15{:}4c_2$, $4d_2$). The comparison is therefore forceful and to the point:[28] fruitfulness is as impossible for the branches as for the disciples without abiding in the vine, that is, in Jesus.

The central component (15:5a–b) provides two explicit metaphorical identifications of elements from the developing figure. First, as in 15:1, a beginning "I am" saying again introduces Jesus as "the vine" (15:5a), though this time without the further emphasis on his specific status as "the true vine." Second, the disciples are identified as "the branches" of the vine (15:5b), thus making explicit what the prepositional phrase of 15:2a ("in me") indirectly conveyed. This double and repeated identification at this point, between the twofold delineation of the proper role of the disciples, clarifies that what is true in the realm of viticulture is also true in the relationship between Jesus and the disciples.

The second outer component (15:5c–6) again presents abiding in Jesus as the essential condition for the disciples' fulfillment of that activity proper to them as disciples of Jesus, the bearing of fruit. The development now, however, differs from that of the first outer component. Instead of a direct comparison or simile with the relationship of a branch in relation to its vine, here is a direct contrast between the disciple who heeds the call and the disciple who does not. This returns to the sharp distinction of 15:2 between the two different types of branches. In so doing, this second description of what abiding in Jesus means and entails continues to be developed for the most part on the literal level.

The contrast reveals a careful literary construction as well. Both elements of the contrast—the portrayal of the disciple who heeds the call (15:5c–d) and the portrayal of the one who does not (15:6)—contain the same two basic components: (1) a beginning reprisal of the essential condition for bearing fruit already set forth in 15:4c–d (abiding in Jesus), from both a positive point of view ($15{:}5c_{1-2}$: "the one who abides in me and I in him/her") and a negative point of view (15:6a: "if someone does not abide

---

28. Although the beginning statement is omitted in the main clause, it is in effect reprised and summarized by the use of the adverb οὐδέ at that point, thus rendering the comparison itself even more forceful and pointed. Furthermore, insofar as both conditional clauses employ the present tense of the subjunctive, the need for ongoing fruitfulness, already stressed in 15:2, is now subtly recalled and further emphasized.

in me"),[29] and (2) a delineation of the consequences of each option, briefly formulated in the former case (15:5c$_3$: the bearing of much fruit) but presented in greater detail in the latter (15:6b–c: a fivefold process leading from separation or removal to burning). Within the second element of each portrayal, therefore, the literal level comes to the fore within this final component of the inclusion. The contrast is again forceful and pointed: not only is fruitfulness impossible without abiding in Jesus, the vine, but also a failure to abide will have radical consequences indeed.

It should be noted that the portrayal of the abiding disciple in 15:5c–d contains an additional component with no parallel in that of the unabiding disciple, namely, a strong concluding statement that the disciples can do nothing without Jesus (15:5d). This concluding statement functions within this first portrayal as a further grounding for the results outlined in 15:5c$_3$, the bearing of much fruit, and therefore can be seen as a variation of the essential condition set forth in 15c$_{1-2}$ (mutual abiding of the disciple and Jesus in one another; not being able to do anything without Jesus).[30] As such, this concluding statement forms an inclusion framing the portrayal of the abiding disciple, whose purpose it is to emphasize the condition necessary for such positive results to take place—the bearing of much fruit depends solely on a continued adherence to Jesus, howsoever expressed.

Furthermore, it should be noted that a comparison of the results outlined in both portrayals of the contrast shows two important differences. On the one hand, the contrast itself does not involve fully parallel counterparts: whereas the first portrayal is concerned with immediate consequences, the second deals with final or ultimate consequences. Thus, like 15:4c–d, the first portrayal describes—with the poignant addition of the adjective "much"—the immediate consequences of abiding in Jesus for the disciples, essentially following the example of the fruitful branch described in 15:2c: the bearing of much fruit as the proper role of the disciples as disciples of Jesus. However, instead of providing the immediate results of the corresponding failure to abide as described in 15:2a–b (the bearing of no fruit), the second portrayal mentions the ultimate fate awaiting such a disciple: the fivefold process beginning with removal from the vine and ending with destruction by burning (cf. 15:2b), the proper counterpart of which would

29. In 15:5c$_{1-2}$ the reprise is in terms of a participial phrase that incorporates the promise attached to the call of 15:4a, "he who abides in me and I in him," thus reproducing the formula of mutual abiding of 15:4a–b. For this peculiar type of anacoluthon, where the substantival participle can be said to function conditionally, see BDF, 468.2–3. In 15:6a a similar conditional clause is used, though now with the indefinite pronoun τις as subject. Neither case, therefore, employs direct address.

30. The statement itself also represents a variation and reaffirmation of the beginning statements to be found in both clauses (though only fully so in the comparative clause) of 15:4c–d. Indeed, the statement can be seen even more specifically as an expansion of the prepositional phrase "of or by itself" (ἀφ' ἑαυτοῦ) from the beginning statement of 15:4c. This statement, furthermore, briefly resumes direct address to the disciples.

be the "pruning" mentioned in 15:2c.[31] Such an uneven comparison of consequences strongly emphasizes the severe fate that awaits the disciple who fails to heed the call of 15:4a–b and does not abide in Jesus—not just a failure to bear fruit but actual removal from the vine of Jesus.

On the other hand, as indicated above, the contrast also shows a marked difference in length. The portrayal of the consequences awaiting the disciple who abides is brief (the bearing of much fruit), but that of the disciple who does not abide is developed in a series of five steps of increasing intensity: separation or removal from the vine, withering, being gathered together, being thrown into the fire, and burning. Such a description goes well beyond that of the unfruitful branch in 15:2a–b, which mentions only removal from the vine.[32] Such an extended description of consequences places even greater emphasis on the severe prospect awaiting the unabiding disciple, especially given the crescendo effect of the description's components and its position at the end of the contrast—not just removal or separation from Jesus but certain destruction as well.

The middle subunit of 15:4c–6, it should be noted, describes the proper role of the disciples as disciples of Jesus in strictly literal terms—the bearing of fruit. The meaning of such fruitfulness at the metaphorical level, however, can be readily determined from the context, in terms of both the essential condition outlined for such fruitfulness to take place and the preceding reaffirmation of the relationship between Jesus and the disciples of 15:3, with its clear statement of origins. The bearing of fruit, therefore, involves the act of abiding in Jesus itself, and such an abiding involves an abiding in the "word" that Jesus has spoken. In other words, a proper response to the

31. The use of the adjective "much" ($\pi o\lambda \acute{u}v$) within the delineation of results of the first portrayal could be interpreted as a conflation of the immediate consequences (the bearing of fruit) and ultimate consequences (the pruning of the vine by the Father, so that it can bear "more" fruit) of the description of the fruitful branch in 15:2c, so both the action of pruning and its result would in fact be presupposed and comprehended by the use of "much" at this point (the bearing of "much" fruit). If this were the case, the contrast would not be at all uneven, involving in both portrayals a comparison of the ultimate consequences already outlined in 15:2. Although this is a defensible position, the other reading is more satisfactory overall. Thus, it is with the mention of the ultimate fate awaiting the failure to abide within the second portrayal that mention of the ultimate fate awaiting the abiding disciples is introduced in both the promise of 15:7 and the final subsection of 15:8.

32. Only the first step ("cast out"), therefore, parallels the measure attributed to the Father as vinedresser in 15:2a, though the specific terminology involved is different ($\alpha \H{\iota}\rho \epsilon\iota/\grave{\epsilon}\beta\lambda\acute{\eta}\theta\eta$ $\H{\epsilon}\xi\omega$). The remaining four steps, then, constitute a further literal development of this first step, introduced as it is by the second example of a comparative particle in this subunit of 15:4c–6, "like ($\acute{\omega}\varsigma$) a branch." An eschatological interpretation of this metaphorical development (Bernard, 2:481; Barrett, 475), especially with regard to its final step (the burning of the branches) should not be ruled out in principle (e.g., J. N. Sanders, *A Commentary on the Gospel According to St. John*, ed. B. A. Mastin, HNTC [New York: Harper & Row, 1968] 338; Lindars, 489). In other words, it is possible that the ultimate result of separation from Jesus may be portrayed thereby in the traditional terms of final damnation (Matt. 13:36–43; see also 1 John 2:8, 18; 3:2–3). Such an interpretation would not be the primary one, however.

call to abide in Jesus of 15:4a–b entails at a fundamental level a continued abiding of the disciples in that relationship with Jesus that is already theirs as branches of Jesus the vine, and in that word of Jesus that they have already accepted and by which they have already been cleansed or pruned and have become branches in the vine of Jesus—a continued belief in, acceptance of, and adherence to the whole of Jesus' revelation and teaching.

The description of what the call to abide in Jesus entails leads directly to the extension of a specific promise to those who do heed the call and thus bear much fruit: whatever they wish and ask for will be granted (15:7). This promise not only brings 15:4–7 to a definite, proper end but also expands the earlier promise conveyed by the call proper in 15:4b. In so doing, the promise also resumes the metaphorical level of the beginning call of 15:4a–b.

On the one hand, following immediately upon the dire portrayal of the ultimate fate awaiting the unabiding or unfruitful disciple, the sudden extension of such a comforting promise to those who do abide and bear fruit is clearly meant to serve as an additional argument on behalf of this latter option: not only does a failure to abide lead to very undesirable consequences, but also a continued abiding will result in a rich reward indeed. On the other hand, this attractive promise reinforces and expands the earlier promise attached to the beginning call of 15:4a–b: Jesus' continued abiding in those who respond to the call will result in other specific benefits and rewards as well, such as the hearing and granting of all their requests. As a result, the call to abide ends on a positive, reassuring note: fruitfulness will have manifold dividends.[33]

---

33. The promise is formulated in terms of a future more vivid condition, whose protasis presents abiding in Jesus as the basic condition for the fulfillment of the promise (15:7a) and whose apodosis contains the promise itself (15:7b). From a formal point of view, therefore, the promise is particularly effective for its concluding position and function within 15:4–7. First, the beginning delineation of abiding in Jesus as the essential condition for fulfillment parallels similar usage in both outer components of 15:4c–6. Second, such a delineation prior to the formulation of a promise also parallels similar usage in the call proper of 15:4a–b. Not only is a recurring form within 15:4–7 again employed at its conclusion, therefore, but also the strong emphasis on abiding of the entire subunit is clearly continued thereby. One particular feature in the formulation of this condition at this point should be noted. In addition to the familiar formulation "if you abide in me," one also finds the coordinate statement "and my words (τὰ ῥήματα) abide in you." Although such a statement appears to be another example of a formula of mutual abiding similar to those of 15:4a–b and 15:6, such a reading would be problematic here. The two components of the statement are better read as parallel or synonymous: the abiding of Jesus' words in a disciple is but another way of expressing the abiding of a disciple in Jesus and his word. As such, this formulation of abiding as the basic condition can be said to draw directly on the previous use of "word" in 15:3 and to call attention thereby to the fact that abiding in Jesus entails the continued abiding of Jesus' "words"—that is, the entirety of his teaching and revelation—in the disciple. Given the compound structure of this particular formulation of the condition, it can also be said to place added emphasis on abiding as the basic condition at the conclusion of these verses.

A comparison with the similar promise extended in the first unit of discourse (14:12–14) is useful. In 13:31–14:31 this promise immediately follows the explanation of Jesus' departure in terms of his relationship to the Father and is thus extended to those who accept such christological teaching (14:4–11, 12–14). In the present unit of discourse, however, the promise is specifically made not so much to those who come to believe in Jesus as specified, since such a relationship is already in effect and presupposed, but rather to those who abide in, who continue to hold on to, what they already believe with regard to Jesus.[34] The conditions for the fulfillment of this promise have clearly changed, therefore, from the first unit to the second; once again, the earlier dialectic of partial and full understanding has disappeared.

The Abiding or Fruitful Disciples and the Father (John 15:8)

The final subsection (15:8) returns, by way of conclusion, to the initial description of the relationship between Jesus and the disciples of 15:1–2 and develops it further in the light of the intervening call to abide of 15:3–7. The direct relationship between the Father and the disciples introduced within such a description in terms of the Father's role as vinedresser with respect to the disciples as the branches of the vine, whether unfruitful or fruitful, is now further pursued from the point of view of those disciples who respond to the call, who abide in Jesus and bear much fruit. The subsection is developed largely on the metaphorical level. In fact, 15:8 ends the sustained metaphor of the vine, except for a brief final reprise at the end of the second major section.

The relationship itself is now formulated in terms of the proper role of the disciples with regard to the Father. By bearing much fruit—by heeding the call to abide in Jesus and fulfilling their proper and correct role as disciples of Jesus—the Father is said to be glorified by the disciples.[35] It should be noted, furthermore, that this literal description of the role of the disciples in relation to Jesus (first introduced in 15:2 and used repeatedly

34. Other points of comparison should be noted: (a) The emphasis of 14:12–14 on asking in Jesus' name is omitted; there is no procedure outlined for the asking itself. (b) The similar emphasis of 14:12–14 on Jesus' role as both addressee and grantor of such requests completely disappears as well; again, there is no mechanism outlined for the fulfillment of the promise. In the example of 15:17, therefore, the emphasis rests exclusively on the need for the disciples to abide in Jesus and in his words.

35. Such glorification of the Father by the disciples (a dative of personal agency) recalls the initial declaration of the first unit (13:31–32), where the Father is also said to be glorified by Jesus. In other words, just as Jesus' fulfillment of his appointed mission glorifies the Father, according to the first unit, so does the fulfillment by the disciples of their proper role (to bear much fruit) glorify the Father, according to this second unit. Cf. 21:19.

in 15:4–7) is now followed by a coordinate statement explicitly identifying such fruitfulness with continued discipleship: the disciples, by bearing much fruit and thus proving themselves to be disciples of Jesus, glorify the Father.[36]

As the conclusion to the first major section, this final description of the relationship between the Father and the disciples is appropriate and effective. On the one hand, the description summarizes at the metaphorical level the thrust of the call to abide in Jesus of 15:3–7, making explicit what had remained implicit in the literal description of the disciples' role: the fulfillment of the disciples' correct role as disciples of Jesus, the bearing of fruit, presupposes and entails discipleship itself (a continued abiding in Jesus and his word and a continued belief in, acceptance of, and adherence to all of Jesus' teaching and revelation). On the other hand, the description directly expands the first such description of 15:1–2 in the light of the intervening call to abide. It is only by heeding the call to abide in Jesus and his word and thus bearing much fruit that the disciples also glorify the Father, who then, in keeping with the role already outlined in 15:2, prunes them so they can go on bearing more fruit and glorifying him unceasingly. In other words, the fulfillment of the disciples' proper role with regard to the Father as the vinedresser of the vine presupposes and entails the fulfillment of their proper role with regard to Jesus himself, the vine. Only when they are fruitful—when they abide in Jesus and his word—do the disciples glorify the Father and can the Father in turn proceed with his own role of pruning them.

This concluding development of the relationship between the Father and the disciples is meant to reassure the disciples with regard to their status and role as disciples of Jesus. As in the case of Jesus' own ministry and mission, their own fruitfulness as disciples is now presented as a glorification of the Father himself. As such, this characterization of the relationship has essentially the same purpose as that of the earlier promises

---

36. The precise formulation of this statement is textually uncertain. The manuscript tradition is deeply divided between the aorist subjunctive γένησθε (p[66vid] B L X Θ Π al) and the future indicative γενήσεσθε (ℵ A K Δ Φ al). I favor the latter as the more difficult reading, since the former can be readily explained as an attempt to make the statement dependent upon the preceding ἵνα and thus coordinate with the other verb form, φέρητε. However, the presence of the future indicative need not be seen as either a new sentence (which would be problematic in its present context) or as referring back to the beginning demonstrative pronoun and thus coordinating with ἐδοξάσθη (which would be unusual given the intervening position of the epexegetical clause). Instead, such a future indicative can be seen as a rare instance where the future follows a subjunctive within a clause (see BDF, 369.2–3). The ἵνα clause thus presents two coordinate and parallel members: to bear much fruit is to carry out the proper role of a disciple of Jesus. The meaning of γίνεσθαι here would thus be closer to either "to show truly" or "to prove to be" and therefore in keeping with the preceding call of 15:4–7.

extended to those who abide, namely, further support and enticement for the choice of this option. Given this characterization's position at the end of the section and immediately following the formulation of the second promise in 15:7, it is particularly effective in this regard: abide in Jesus and his word and glorify the Father.

The first major section (15:1–8) focuses on the relationship between Jesus and the disciples. This relationship, pursued in terms of a sustained metaphor with Jesus as the vine and the disciples as its branches, is presented in two basic movements. In the first, the relationship itself is acknowledged and reaffirmed. Jesus has already revealed his word to the disciples, has already made known to them the fullness of his teaching and revelation; in other words, their given status as branches in the vine is granted. In the second movement, a call is issued to the disciples to abide in Jesus, that is, in the relationship they already possess and in the word that is already theirs by bearing much fruit. In other words, as branches of the vine, the disciples must be fruitful—must abide in Jesus and in his word—or be summarily removed from the vine. The main emphasis of the first major section clearly lies on this call to abide. Thus, this section presents discipleship as impossible without fruitfulness, and it describes fruitfulness itself as presupposing and entailing at its most fundamental level abiding in Jesus and his word.

Second Major Section (John 15:9–17)

The second major section of the second unit of discourse, 15:9–17, explores abiding in the love of Jesus. The literary structure of this second section can be readily outlined as follows, in keeping with the threefold pattern of inclusion proposed for each major section: (1) The chain of love: the Father, Jesus, and the disciples (15:9a–b); (2) a call to the disciples to abide in the love of Jesus, in the chain of love (the carrying out of Jesus' commands [15:9c–11]); and (3) the expansion of the chain of love (the disciples and the command of love for one another [15:12–17]).

The beginning subsection (15:9a–b) introduces the central theme of this section, love, and provides a second, direct description of the relationship between Jesus and the disciples—the love of Jesus for the disciples. In so doing, the first subsection also introduces the character of the Father and assigns him a specific role within such a relationship by grounding the love of Jesus for the disciples in the Father's own love for him, introducing thereby a chain of love with both a direct relationship between the Father and Jesus and an indirect relationship between the Father and the disciples. The central subsection (15:9c–11) develops the second call to the disciples to abide in their given relationship with Jesus, the controlling theme of the unit as a whole: it is the proper role of the disciples as disciples of Jesus to abide in his love, in the chain of love, by carrying out his commands. Finally, the concluding subsection (15:12–17) returns to the beginning description of the relationship between Jesus and the disciples of 15:9a–b for further development in the light of the call to abide of 15:9c–11.

This subsection's development of 15:12–17 is expansive and complex. As in 15:8, the indirect relationship introduced in 15:9a–b between the Father as the first link in the chain of love and the disciples as those loved by Jesus is now described from the point of view of those disciples who heed the call of 15:9c–11, who abide in the love of Jesus and the chain of love. The chain of love itself is extended in a new direction altogether through the disclosure of a specific command of Jesus as preeminent, namely, Jesus' command to the disciples to love one another as he had loved them. In effect, not only is the theme of love extended thereby to the relationship among the disciples themselves, but also such love for one another is directly grounded here in Jesus' own love for them, just as the first subsection had grounded the latter in the Father's love for Jesus. Such a development goes beyond that of 15:8, since a proper counterpart would amount to a further extension of the figure of the vine to address the relationship among the branches themselves. Finally, this new development pursues the beginning relationship between Jesus and the disciples within the chain of love with regard to both the specific character of Jesus' love for the disciples and the status of the disciples as those loved by Jesus within the chain of love.

The Chain of Love: The Father, Jesus, and the Disciples (John 15:9a–b)

The first subsection (15:9a–b) introduces the central theme of the section, love; further describes the relationship between Jesus and the disciples in terms of this theme; and assigns a role to the figure of the Father within such a relationship. Some differences in comparison with 15:1–2 should be noted: (1) the introduction of the central theme is much briefer, already preparing the way for a much longer final subsection; (2) the element of contrast is eliminated altogether; (3) the relationship between Jesus and the disciples is presented directly rather than indirectly; and (4) the relationship between the Father and the disciples is presented indirectly rather than directly.

The subsection involves a simple comparative sentence. The main clause (15:9b) describes Jesus' relationship to the disciples ("so also have I loved you"), and the comparative clause (15:9a) posits a similar relationship on the part of the Father with regard to Jesus ("as the Father loved me"). As a result, the former relationship is grounded in, and patterned after, the latter, and the Father is related to the disciples indirectly by means of his own relationship of love with regard to Jesus.

First, both relationships of love—that of Jesus for the disciples and that of the Father for Jesus—are formulated in terms of aorist indicatives (ἠγάπησεν/ἠγάπησα), best characterized as constative aorists, so both loves are presented from a fully completed or accomplished perspective. Jesus' love for the disciples, therefore, encompasses the whole of his mission and ministry, including the final events of "the hour." As such, this beginning perspective closely parallels that of the first major section— namely, the relationship between Jesus and the disciples is described from the point of view of a glorified Jesus.[37] Second, although Jesus' love for the disciples is grounded in, and patterned after, that of the Father for him, the remainder of the section does not pursue this at all;[38] in fact, the relationship between the Father and Jesus is only briefly developed (cf. 15:10) in the section as a whole. In both 15:1–8 and 15:9–17, therefore, the relationship between the Father and Jesus is mentioned at the beginning but either completely (15:1–8) or largely (15:9–17) bypassed in the remainder of the section.

The first subsection also plays an important programmatic role within the second major section and its continued development of the theme of love. The indirect relationship posited between the Father and the disciples is pursued in the final subsection of 15:12–17. Also, the direct relationship introduced between Jesus and the disciples is developed—along with the direct relationship posited between Jesus and the Father—in the central subsection of 15:9c–11 and then further pursued in the final subsection.

A Call to the Disciples to Abide in the Love of Jesus, in the Chain of Love: The Carrying out of Jesus' Commands (John 15:9c–11)

The second subsection (15:9c–11) focuses on the relationship between Jesus and the disciples and introduces the controlling theme of the unit: a

37. Such an understanding of Jesus' love for the disciples is much closer to that of 13:34–35 than that of 14:21 in the first unit. Whereas the latter example refers to Jesus' return to the disciples at the conclusion of "the hour," the former encompasses, by means of a similar constative aorist, the whole of Jesus' ministry and mission, including the events of "the hour." However, whereas in this unit the whole of "the hour" is comprehended, in the first unit its final events still appear as outstanding.

38. The love of the Father for Jesus is not mentioned at all in the first unit (cf. 14:31a). Elsewhere in the Gospel it is presented either in terms of the Father's willingness to entrust Jesus with the whole ministry of revelation (3:35; 5:20) or, more specifically, in terms of a response to Jesus' fulfillment of the appointed end of that ministry (10:17; see chap. 2, n. 98). As a constative aorist, therefore, the present reference clearly comprehends both aspects of this love.

call to the disciples to abide in the love of Jesus, in the chain of love. This
call follows the same threefold development of 15:4–7: (1) the call proper
(15:9c); (2) a description of what such abiding in the love of Jesus implies
and entails (obedience to Jesus' commands as the proper role of the disciples as disciples of Jesus [15:10]); and (3) a promise to the disciples who
respond to the call and abide in the love of Jesus, who carry out the ·
commands of Jesus and thus fulfill their correct role as disciples of Jesus
(15:11). Several differences in comparison with 15:3–7 should be noted.
The second call is more compact, again preparing the way for a much
longer final subsection. There is no initial reaffirmation of the relationship
between Jesus and the disciples. Again, the element of contrast is omitted
altogether.

The Call to Abide (John 15:9c)

The call proper (15:9c) is even briefer than that of 15:4a–b ("abide in my
love"), with no conditional promise attached. Once again, although the
relationship between Jesus and the disciples is acknowledged and affirmed
in 15:9a–b, a call (15:9c) is issued to the disciples to abide in the love of
Jesus, in the chain of love. Such a rapid succession of affirmation of union
and call to abide again implies that a certain role is required and expected
of the disciples as disciples of Jesus, a role that ultimately preserves their
status as disciples and their relationship with Jesus.

Abiding in the Love of Jesus:
Meaning and Implications (John 15:10)

The call proper is followed by a description of what such abiding in the
love of Jesus entails for the disciples: obedience to Jesus' commands as the
expected role of the disciples as disciples of Jesus, as members of the chain
of love (15:10). In comparison to 15:4c–6, in 15:10: (1) the description is
more concise; (2) it is only preliminary and will be extended in the final
subsection; and (3) it reintroduces the direct relationship between Jesus
and the Father described in the first subsection.

The description itself is formulated in terms of a future more vivid
condition (15:10a–b). The apodosis (15:10b) provides the immediate result of a positive response to the call (abiding in Jesus' love). The protasis
(15:10a) outlines the essential condition for such abiding to take place and
thus describes what the disciples must do to preserve their given status
in the chain of love (carry out the commands of Jesus [τὰς ἐντολὰς
μου τηρήσετε]).[39] Just as Jesus' love for the disciples was grounded in, and

---

39. The development of this description is similar to that of 15:4c–6, where conditional
clauses also play a major role (15:4c–d, 6; cf. 15:5c–d). The major difference in this regard

patterned after, that of the Father for him in the first subsection, so now
the role that is proper to, and expected of, the disciples themselves is also
grounded in, and patterned after, Jesus' own role in relation to the Father
(15:10c).[40] In other words, just as Jesus' status within the chain of love has
been preserved and ensured by his own obedience to the Father's commands, so is the disciples' own status within the chain of love to be preserved and ensured by their own obedience to Jesus' commands.[41]

At first, this second description of the correct role of the disciples
seems to duplicate the first delineation of this role in 15:3–7. In other
words, if "the commands" of Jesus are seen as a synonymous term or
expression for the "word" that Jesus has spoken and that the disciples
have already accepted, this second description of their role as disciples of
Jesus, as those loved by Jesus and members of the chain of love, simply
repeats the thrust of the first major section: it is only by abiding in Jesus
and his word, in the whole of his teaching and revelation, that the disciples carry out his commands and abide in his love, in the chain of love. In
that case, the main function of this second major section would be to
reaffirm and reinforce the main thrust of the first major section by a
variation in formulation. However, as already indicated, this second call
to the disciples should also be seen as preliminary; the call has in mind a

concerns the use of "abiding" itself. Whereas in 15:4c–6 abiding in Jesus (or its counterpart)
is used in the protasis as the essential condition for fruitfulness (or its counterpart), in 15:10
abiding in the love of Jesus is used in the apodosis as the immediate result of keeping Jesus'
commands. As a result, the descriptions of what abiding implies for the disciples are undertaken from different perspectives in the two major sections. The use of an aorist subjunctive
in the protasis emphasizes the disciples' behavior as a whole rather than the need for the
unceasing fulfillment of the commands.

40. The comparative element (15:10c), which covers both protasis and apodosis, is
more developed here. Because the love of the Father for Jesus is not detailed at all in
15:9a–b, it is the fact of such love rather than its mode that is of primary importance in
describing Jesus' own love for the disciples. However, in 15:10c the specific mode of
Jesus' abiding in the love of the Father is disclosed and is thus of primary importance in
describing the disciples' own mode of abiding in the love of Jesus, as the description of
15:10a–b shows. In both instances, furthermore, the comparison implies not only a patterning after but also a grounding in; that is, all subsequent relationships within the chain
of love are patterned after previous relationships that have given rise to, or have made
possible, the chain of love itself.

41. Such a role—obedience to the commands—has already been predicated of both
Jesus (14:31a–c) and the disciples (14:15, 21a) in the first unit, thus providing an implicit
grounding and patterning of the role of the disciples upon the role of Jesus. Such behavior is
also used in the first unit as a definition of love for the Father on the part of Jesus and love for
Jesus on the part of the disciples. The present unit brings to the fore the element of comparison and presents the role itself (the carrying out of, or obedience to, the commands) from a
slightly different perspective, namely, as a description of what abiding in the chain of love
entails rather than as a definition of the love that is due the higher link in the chain. The end
result, of course, is the same (to abide in the love of the Father is to love the Father; to abide
in the love of Jesus is to love Jesus). The difference lies in whether one chooses to emphasize
the ascending aspect of the chain (as in the first unit) or the descending aspect of the chain
(as in the present unit).

specific command of still to be disclosed in the third subsection that follows. As such, this second call, while certainly reaffirming and reinforcing the thrust of the first call, also expands it, by way of anticipation, in a different direction altogether.

A Promise to the Abiding Disciples (John 15:11)

The call to abide ends with a promise to those disciples who heed the call, who carry out the commands of Jesus and abide in the chain of love (15:11). This promise is now introduced by the second example of the recurring concluding formula of the discourse, "These things I have said to you," pointing the way to the approaching conclusion of the unit.[42]

The promise is formulated in terms of "joy" (χαρά). Such joy is presented, to begin with, as the ultimate purpose behind the preceding call to abide and thus as the specific reward to be expected from the disciples' abiding in Jesus' love, from carrying out his commands and thus preserving and insuring their given status in the chain of love. This joy is described from two different, though parallel, perspectives conveyed by means of coordinate members within the same purpose clause: the perspective of Jesus (an extension of his own joy to the disciples) and that of the disciples (a fulfillment of their own joy). Just as Jesus' own joy is based on the fulfillment of his proper role as the messenger of God, so will the disciples' own joy be made perfect only through their own fulfillment of their proper role as disciples of Jesus, thus matching or reproducing Jesus' own joy in themselves.

A comparison of this promised joy with the joy already described in the first unit with respect to the disciples (14:28) is again useful. In both cases the joy of the disciples is ultimately based on their obedience to Jesus' commands. However, whereas in the first unit joy is presented as the direct result of a full understanding concerning Jesus' teaching and revelation (cf. 20:20), in the present unit joy presupposes such an understanding and is thus presented instead as a direct result of a proper fulfillment of the disciples' role as disciples of Jesus, as members of the chain of love.[43]

---

42. The formula's function at this point can be described from two different, though interrelated, perspectives: (a) the formula brings the central subsection to a close by introducing the promise extended to all those who respond to the call to abide; (b) the formula also signals, by way of anticipation, the conclusion of the unit as a whole.

43. The element of comparison is missing altogether in the first unit, since there is no mention of Jesus' joy. In fact, in the Gospel as a whole Jesus' joy or rejoicing has been presented entirely from the point of view of the completion of his mission, with special emphasis on the role of the chosen disciples within that mission (4:36; 11:15; see chap. 2, n. 92). This case, therefore, preserves that basic focus, but with special emphasis on Jesus' relationship to God. Cf. 1 John 1:1–4.

The Expansion of the Chain of Love:
The Disciples and the Command of Love for
One Another (John 15:12–17)

The final subsection (15:12–17) returns, by way of conclusion, to the beginning description of the relationship between Jesus and the disciples of 15:9a–b for further development in the light of the intervening call to abide of 15:9c–11. This development is again more complex than that of 15:8, as the length of the subsection indicates. Three specific directions can be outlined: a further, and now direct, development of the relationship between the Father and the disciples; an extension of the chain of love itself by means of a focus on the relationship among the disciples themselves; and a further description of the relationship between Jesus and the disciples. The subsection follows an overall chiastic development in the form of an ABCBA pattern. The outer, parallel components (A) identify a specific and preeminent command of Jesus to the disciples: to love one another as he had loved them (15:12–13, 17). The inner, parallel components (B) outline the proper role of the disciples as the "friends" or loved ones of Jesus (15:14, 16), and the central component (C) explains the nature of their status as Jesus' "friends" (15:15).[44]

Jesus' Command of Love for One Another
(John 15:12–13)

The first outer component (15:12–13) identifies a preeminent "command" of Jesus in two steps: (1) the identification of the command (15:12) and (2) a further development of its comparative element (15:13). The identification is presented in terms of an epexegetical ἵνα clause, "that you love one another" (15:12b$_1$), in apposition to a demonstrative pronoun within the introductory main clause, "this is my command" (15:12a).[45] Within the explanatory clause, furthermore, a comparative clause is added whereby such love for one another is grounded in, and patterned after, Jesus' own love for the disciples—"as I have loved you" (15:12b$_2$). This identification then is expanded immediately by a general definition of love

44. In an insightful study of 15:13, M. Dibelius ("Joh 15:13: Eine Studie zum Traditionsprobleme des Johannesevangeliums," in *Festgabe für Adolf Deissman zum 60. Geburtstag* [Tübingen: Mohr-Siebeck, 1927] 168–86; repr. in *Botschaft und Geschichte*, ed. G. Bornkamm [Tübingen: Mohr-Siebeck, 1953] 1:204–20) argues that these verses are developed by a chainlike association whose links represent variations of the theme of love. Although such a chainlike association is undeniable, the subsection reveals a much more complex pattern of composition.

45. Both final subsections begin with examples of this construction (cf. 15:8). The present subsection further employs this construction in the immediate expansion of 15:13, as well as in the second formulation of the command in 15:17.

beyond equal—to lay down one's life for one's friends (15:13).[46] Because such love clearly characterizes the love of Jesus for his disciples, this definition functions at this point as an elaboration of the preceding comparative clause of 15:12.

The preeminence accorded to this one command of Jesus—underscored by both the use of the definite article and the emphatic use of the possessive pronoun—expands the preceding description of 15:10 regarding what abiding in Jesus' love implies. To abide in the love of Jesus, in the chain of love, the disciples must above all obey this command to love one another, that is, show love for the other members of the chain of love. Once again, the description of 15:10 should be seen as preliminary, so a full reading of it is impossible without the incorporation of 15:12–17 within it.

The identification of this one command of Jesus as preeminent, which its repetition in 15:17 sharply reinforces, expands the chain of love introduced in 15:9a–b in the light of the call to abide of 15:9c–11. The descending character of this chain of love is suddenly redirected in a horizontal fashion: the disciples as the last link in the chain must continue and expand the chain itself by loving one another. With this extension of the chain of love, the second major section proceeds in a radically new direction, beyond the relationship between Jesus and the disciples that formed the primary focus of the first major section. At the same time, this new direction, with its focus on the relationship among the disciples themselves, remains integrated into the relationship between Jesus and the disciples insofar as the fulfillment of this one command of Jesus to love one another insures the abiding of the disciples in the love of Jesus (in the chain of love).

With the expansion of the definition of 15:10 and of the chain of love of 15:9a–b, the call to abide of the present section takes on a different character than that of 15:1–8. It no longer emphasizes, as did 15:3–7, a continued belief in, acceptance of, and adherence to Jesus and his word, but rather an ongoing fulfillment of a practical or ethical directive within the community of the disciples. Similarly, the proper role of the disciples as disciples of Jesus is no longer described primarily in terms of a correct relationship to Jesus but instead in terms of a correct relationship to their

46. This definition has all the characteristics of a traditional proverb whose meaning is being extended to a new situation altogether (K. Dewey, *"Paroimiai,"* 89, 96), especially since such a concept of the highest love is well known in the wider Greco-Roman culture as well (see, e.g., G. Stählin, *"Phileô,"* TDNT 9 [1974] 151–54). The present formulation of the proverb points to a stylistic adaptation into its new, Johannine context—e. g., the use of the epexegetical clause in apposition to a preceding demonstrative pronoun and the expression "to lay down one's life for" (10:17–21; 13:37–38).

fellow disciples. Again, the former dimension is not abandoned but expanded by more specific focus: above all, love for one another.

The comparative element in the formulation of this one command of love makes clear that the expansion of the chain of love is as closely tied to its preceding link as that link was tied to the first link of the chain: as the Father loved Jesus, so Jesus loved the disciples; as Jesus loved the disciples, so the disciples must love one another. Consequently, just as Jesus' love was grounded in, and patterned after, that of the Father for him, so is this love of the disciples for one another grounded in, and patterned after, that of Jesus for them.

The major difference in this regard, however, is the presence of the proverb of 15:13 immediately after the comparative statement of 15:12. Whereas the section does not pursue the mode of the Father's love for Jesus at all, it does describe that of Jesus' love for the disciples, with emphasis on the climactic act of his ministry—his death for the sake of his "friends" or "loved ones."[47] Therefore, it is not only the fact of Jesus' love that is important, but also its mode. It is not immediately clear, however, how the disclosure of this mode of love in 15:13 affects the element of comparison within the command of love, because the love of the disciples for one another is not further pursued in this section and because the disciples are not differentiated from an unbelieving and hostile world in the unit. In other words, what exactly does it mean for the disciples to love one another as Jesus loved them, given the explicit description of this love in terms of Jesus' death and the lack of any further information concerning the disciples' own love? Several interpretations are possible: (1) a literal reading, with an implicit warning (if need be, to lay down one's life for one's fellow disciples); (2) a metaphorical reading (total service or self-giving, as symbolized by such death); or (3) both. I favor the last option, as the conclusion to the chapter will explain.

The presence of the comparative element as a whole ($15:12b_2$–13) in this first formulation of the love command provides a further description

47. The expression "to lay down one's life for" was used in the first unit by Peter (13:36–38) and is also used elsewhere in the Gospel with respect to Jesus himself (10:11–13, 14–18); see chap. 2, n. 40. On the one hand, the expression's application to Jesus at this point is consonant with its previous use in John 10. Jesus' death on behalf of the disciples, his "friends" or "sheep," is not only in keeping with the Father's command or mission for him (15:10; 10:18e) but also describes in a special way the nature of this mission. On the other hand, the expression's use here sheds further light on Peter's alternative proposal in the first unit. In and of itself the proposal exemplifies the thrust of the proverb, namely, Peter's offer to give up his life for Jesus. The problem, therefore, lies not with the proposal itself but with its underlying ramifications, namely, Peter's failure to understand the nature of Jesus' mission and his unwitting resolve to upset the plan of God in his preventing or circumventing the fulfillment of that mission.

of the relationship between Jesus and the disciples introduced in 15:9a–b. In describing Jesus' love for the disciples in terms of his death on their behalf, the comparative element describes such love in terms of the final act of the mission entrusted to Jesus by the Father and hence in terms of the final component of the "commands" from the Father with which Jesus has been entrusted and that he has obediently kept (15:10; see also 10:17; 14:31). As such, a further explanation of the nature of Jesus' love for the disciples first posited in 15:9a–b is provided in the light of the call to abide of 15:9c–11: such love is preeminently characterized by Jesus' own death for them.[48]

A comparison with the first unit is helpful at this point. The use of the term "command" in 15:12 (and of the verb form in 15:17) to refer specifically to this one practical directive of Jesus to his disciples comes closer to that of 13:34–35 (where the "new" command of love for one another is first introduced) than to that of 14:15 and 14:21a, the definitions of love for Jesus (where the reference encompasses all of Jesus' teaching and revelation—not only the teaching concerning his own status and role in relation to the Father but also all practical directives, including the command of love for one another).[49] Indeed, not only is the "new" command of 13:34–35 also promulgated with the same element of comparison attached to it—whereby such love is grounded in, and patterned after, that of Jesus' for them—but also the fulfillment of this one command is likewise presented as the proper role of the disciples as disciples of Jesus in relation to one another.[50]

---

48. The extension of 15:13 renders the preceding aorist of the comparative proper (15:12b$_2$) a culminative aorist. Similarly, in developing and expanding the love of Jesus for the disciples first posited in 15:9a–b, the extension of 15:13 also interprets that previous aorist as culminative—it is on Jesus' death and the results of that death for the disciples that the emphasis is now clearly placed. For culminative aorist, see, e.g., H. Dana and J. Mantey, *A Manual Grammar of the Greek New Testament* (New York: Macmillan, 1962) 196.

49. See chap. 2, nn. 37, 64. The shift in meaning from the second subsection—where the meaning of "commands" is close to that of 14:15 and 14:21a—to the third subsection, from a reference to the whole of Jesus' teaching and revelation to the designation of a practical or ethical directive, should not be seen as an abandonment or replacement of the earlier meaning but rather as an extension of this earlier meaning, which now receives preeminent attention. See 1 John 2:7–8; 3:22–24.

50. Further similarities should be noted: (a) the command of 13:34–35 is also given twice, forming thereby a clear inclusion; (b) both 13:34 and 13:35 use an epexegetical clause (a ἵνα clause in 13:34 and a conditional clause in 13:35)—the only two examples of this construction in the first unit. Differences should be noted as well: (a) the specific designation of this command as "new" in 13:34–35; (b) the lack of a definite article in the formulation of the command; (c) the presentation of the command as the distinctive sign of discipleship to outsiders (13:35); and (d) the absence of any explanation concerning the mode of Jesus' love in the comparative element of 13:34c, a love which is highlighted by the surrounding inclusion.

The Disciples' Role as Jesus' "Friends" (John 15:14)

The three interior components, 15:14–16, address the status and role of the disciples as Jesus' "friends," as members of the chain of love.[51] The subsection therefore proceeds to develop the comparative element of 15:12b$_2$–13 rather than the command proper of 15:12b$_1$, thus again shifting the focus away from the relationship among the disciples themselves to the relationship between Jesus and the disciples.

The first inner component, 15:14, describes the proper role of the disciples as "friends" of Jesus in terms of a present general condition: "if you do what I command (ἐντέλλομαι) you."[52] Such a description represents a reformulation of the preceding description of abiding in Jesus' love (15:10). At the same time, given the immediately preceding promulgation of the love command as the preeminent command of Jesus, such a reformulation now has this one command specifically and explicitly in view, and not just by way of anticipation, as in 15:10. In other words, the correct role of the disciples as Jesus' "friends" or "loved ones" is first described in terms of obedience to the one command of love for one another. Thus, their given status in the chain of love will only be preserved through an ongoing fulfillment of this command.

The Disciples' Status as Jesus' "Friends" (John 15:15)

The central component, 15:15, explicitly identifies the disciples as Jesus' "friends" by a metaphorical contrast with their previous status as "servants" or "slaves" (δοῦλοι).[53] The contrast is carefully developed. An assessment of the present applicability of each metaphorical designation (15:15a, c: no longer "servants" . . . but "friends") is followed by the reason for such a proper or improper applicability (15:15b, d: lack of understanding; fullness

---

51. These interior components, in effect, further develop the term "friends" from the proverb of 15:13. Such a characterization of the disciples is unique to this unit; see 3:29 (John); 11:11 (Lazarus). Cf. 19:12; 3 John 15.

52. The verb form is now used instead of the noun form, and the verb ποιεῖν—in the present subjunctive, clearly emphasizing the need for continuous fulfillment of the command—now replaces τηρεῖν as well. This formulation comes very close to that of 14:31b–c, where Jesus is also said "to do as the Father has commanded." The use of a plural neuter relative pronoun (ἅ) need not point beyond the one command of love for one another, especially since the second formulation of the love command in 15:17 proceeds to introduce this one command in apposition to a preceding plural neuter demonstrative pronoun (ταῦτα).

53. For a similarly metaphorical use of the term δοῦλοι, though with different connotations, see 8:34–36; 13:16. In 13:16, another traditional proverb whose meaning has been extended to a new situation altogether (K. Dewey, "Paroimiai," 96; cf. John 15:20), the term is used as a proper metaphorical designation for the disciples in relation to Jesus—the disciples, as "servants," are to do what Jesus, as "master," did. In 8:34–36 the term is used, as in 15:15, as an improper metaphorical designation for the Jews in relation to Jesus. However, not only is its proper contrast in 8:34–36 with "freedmen" rather than "friends," but it also entails an open, hostile rejection of Jesus instead of a lack of knowledge or understanding.

of revelation).[54] Thus, what distinguishes the disciples' present status as "friends" from their former standing as "servants"—and by extension, what distinguishes the disciples from those who still qualify under the latter designation—is the fact that they have received and accepted the whole of Jesus' teaching and revelation as entrusted to him by the Father.[55] In other words, the given status of the disciples in the chain of love, as those loved by Jesus, is due to their own reception and acceptance of Jesus' teaching and revelation.[56] The same reason is given for their present status as "friends" of Jesus and as "branches" in the true vine of Jesus—their belief in, and acceptance of, Jesus and his word.

The Disciples' Role as Jesus' "Friends" (John 15:16)

The second inner component, 15:16, expands the description of the proper role of the disciples as Jesus' "friends." While completing the unit, it incorporates elements from both the present major section and the first.

54. The formulation of the basic reason, which in both cases has to do with Jesus' revelation to the disciples, is presented from two different points of view, that of the disciples in 15:15b and that of Jesus in 15:15d. Whereas in 15:15b the disciples are said to be "servants" no more because a "servant" does not know what "the master" does (implying, of course, that the disciples do know what Jesus does), in 15:15d the disciples are said to be Jesus' "friends" because he has made known to them all that he heard in the presence of the Father. The contrast between "servants" and "friends" can thus be understood from an epistemological perspective (lack of understanding/full understanding) or a christological perspective (partial revelation/full revelation), both of which are ultimately parallel and coterminous. The first reason of 15:15b represents yet another traditional proverb that has been adapted to a new situation altogether (K. Dewey, *"Paroimiai,"* 97)—as a description of the relationship between Jesus and the disciples prior to the time of full revelation and understanding. The development of the term "friends" by means of its metaphorical counterpart "servants" was probably occasioned by the author's use of this other proverb of 15:15b—of itself unrelated to that of 15:13—and the further realization of its applicability to the further explanation of the status of the disciples as Jesus' "friends." The second reason of 15:15d reflects standard Johannine terminology and thinking (8:26, 40; 17:26).
55. Just as the expansion of the comparative element in 15:13 describes Jesus' love for the disciples in terms of the final act of the mission entrusted to him by the Father and thus in terms of the final component of the "commands" from the Father that Jesus obediently fulfilled, so the explanation of 15:15d now describes Jesus' love for the disciples in terms of his mission as a whole and thus in terms of all the "commands" from the Father that he has obediently kept (15:10; 12:49–50). Similarly, just as the extension of 15:13 renders the preceding aorists of 15:12b$_2$ and 15:9b culminative aorists, so now this explanation of 15:15d renders them constative aorists. This explanation of 15:15d, as well as its indirect counterpart of 15:15b, makes it clear again that the given status of the disciples as Jesus' "friends," as members of the chain of love, presupposes a full understanding and acceptance of Jesus' claims. Thus, the dialectic between present and future, and between partial and full, understanding of the first unit disappears altogether.
56. With this contrast of 15:15, household terminology is employed in the second unit to describe the disciples as a whole (the disciples as "friends" rather than "servants" of the "master" because the latter has revealed all about the "Father" to them. Such terminology, however, differs from that of the first unit (the disciples as "little children" rather than "orphans" because the "son" was going away to prepare "dwelling places" for them in "the Father's house" and would then return with the "Father" to make their "dwelling place" in their midst).

In effect, the delineation of the role of the disciples itself ($15{:}16b_2$) is preceded by a further description of their status as "friends" ($15{:}16a{-}b_1$) and followed by a promise to those who properly carry out their role as "friends" (15:16c).

To begin with, the status of the disciples as "friends," as those loved by Jesus, is further clarified by a sharp contrast outlining the origins of such friendship and love: it was not the disciples who "chose" Jesus but rather Jesus who "chose" the disciples ($15{:}16a{-}b_1$). In other words, the contrast clarifies that although the disciples became "friends" of Jesus and members of the chain of love through their own acceptance of Jesus' teaching and revelation, they were "chosen" by Jesus for such a status.[57]

The proper role of the disciples as "friends" is further developed by the addition of a third coordinate member to the preceding contrast; here such a role is attributed to Jesus himself from the very beginnings of the relationship ("and I appointed you") and expanded by a purpose clause with three elements arranged in an ascending sequence: "so that you might go forth, bear fruit, and that your fruit might endure."[58] The sustained metaphor of the vine makes a brief final appearance with the last two elements. The metaphor of "bearing fruit" is extended to cover the proper role of the disciples described in the present section: bearing fruit also entails the fulfillment of the one preeminent command of love for one another. To this extent the second description parallels the first description of 15:14. The metaphor also brings with it the correct role of the disciples as described in 15:1–8: bearing fruit entails a continued belief in Jesus and his word. To this extent the second description goes beyond the first description of 15:14. The renewed use of the figure at the end of the unit is effective. It encompasses at this point the basic thrust of both major sections: not only does the "bearing fruit" include a

57. Such a description of the disciples is by no means unique to the present unit (see 6:70; 13:18), though in both cases the designation is given with reference to the exclusion of Judas Iscariot from the circle of disciples.

58. As in 15:14, all three elements are given in the present subjunctive, emphasizing again the need for an ongoing fulfillment of the disciples' assigned role. Although the sequence of these three elements creates a powerful heightening effect, I do not see its individual components as pointing to three distinct facets of the disciples' role as "friends." This is especially true of the emphasis sometimes placed on the first element of the sequence as pointing to the missionary task of the disciples in the world (see, e.g., Lagrange, 408; Bernard, 2:489). Instead, I see these three components as pointing emphatically to the role of the disciples as a whole and thus encompassing the thrust of both major sections of the unit (abiding in Jesus' word; fulfillment of the love command). Two further observations are in order. First, the sequence represents a mixture of thematic material from both sections. Whereas the first element can be readily connected with the designation of the disciples as "friends," the second and third elements return to the imagery from viticulture of the first section. Second, the introduction of a different subject in the third element introduces an awkwardness into the sequence as a whole.

continued acceptance of, belief in, and adherence to Jesus' teaching and revelation by the disciples as "branches" in the vine but also an ongoing fulfillment of the command to love one another as Jesus' "friends" or "loved ones." The figure here also grounds both of these fundamental aspects of abiding in the origins of Jesus' relationship with the disciples as his chosen ones.

Finally, the same promise extended in the first section to those who bear much fruit by abiding in Jesus and his word is now extended, by a result clause (15:16c), to those who bear fruit by carrying out the command to love one another and thus fulfilling their proper role as "friends" and members of the chain of love: the promise that all their requests will be granted.[59] Like 15:1–8, therefore, the second major section closes with a special incentive to the disciples to exercise their proper role as "friends," namely, a promise whereby they are now brought into direct relationship with the Father, the first link of the chain of love.[60]

In addressing the status of the disciples as Jesus' "friends," the interior components of 15:14–16 further develop the relationship between Jesus and the disciples introduced in 15:9a–b in the light of the intervening call to abide of 15:9c–11. The relationship itself is further described: (1) the love of Jesus for the disciples is further explained in terms of his full revelation of the Father to them, and (2) the status of the disciples as those loved by Jesus is further explained in terms of both their characterization as Jesus' chosen friends and the role assigned to them from the beginning of the relationship (to bear fruit). The indirect relationship with the Father introduced in 15:9a–b also is now further developed from the point of view of those who respond to the call and abide in Jesus'

---

59. Certain differences in formulation should be noted. The Father is now presented as both addressee and grantor of such requests. Also, the proper procedure for making such requests is specified in terms of Jesus' name as an instrumental of manner. Indeed, the present reformulation of the promise explains in much greater detail the actual mechanism involved in the fulfillment of the promise—identification of the addressee, identification of the grantor, and delineation of the proper procedure for asking.

60. Insofar as the disciples can ask the Father and he will grant their petitions and requests, the relationship with the Father as the first link of the chain of love is indeed direct. At the same time, a degree of mediation on Jesus' part remains nonetheless, insofar as the asking itself must be done in his name. A comparison with the first unit is again useful (14:12–14; cf. 14:16, 26; see n. 34 above). On the one hand, the first unit reveals a similar mechanism for the fulfillment of the promise, though with certain differences as well: although the proper procedure for asking in terms of Jesus' name is the same (14:13, 14a), Jesus is also presented as both addressee (14:14) and grantor (14:13a, 14). Clearly, therefore, a major role is assigned to the Father in the mechanism of this promise within the second unit. On the other hand, whereas in the first unit the fulfillment of the promise is made conditional upon proper belief in Jesus, in the second unit its fulfillment depends not only on continued adherence to Jesus' revelation (as pointed out with regard to the formulation of the promise in 15:7), but also (given its present reformulation) on the fulfillment of an ethical directive within the community of believers.

love. A direct relationship with the Father is now posited by means of the promise concerning the unconditional granting of all their petitions as disciples of Jesus.

Jesus' Command of Love for One Another (John 15:17)

The second outer component, 15:17, closes the subsection with a further identification of the disciples' love for one another as the preeminent command of Jesus. This second formulation contains no mention of the comparative element so prominent in the first formulation; coming after the further development of the comparative element in 15:14–16, this second formulation simply reiterates the command proper, returning thereby, at the conclusion of the subsection, to the proper relationship of the disciples to one another. In so doing, this final component emphatically reaffirms the preeminence of this one command of Jesus, the understanding of the call of 15:9c–11 in terms of an ongoing fulfillment of a specific practical or ethical directive within the community of believers. This component also extends the chain of love of 15:9a–b in a radically new direction, with a focus on the relationship among the disciples themselves.

The second major section, 15:9–17, focuses on the relationship of the disciples to one another, though within the wider focus of the relationship between Jesus and the disciples. The section develops both relationships in terms of the theme of love.

The wider focus, the relationship between Jesus and the disciples, is presented in two basic movements, as in the first section. First, the relationship is acknowledged and reaffirmed: Jesus loved the disciples not only by making known to them all he had heard from the Father—the fullness of his revelation and teaching—but also by laying down his own life for them. In other words, the disciples' status as Jesus' chosen friends or loved ones in the chain of love is granted. Second, a call is issued to the disciples to abide in the love of Jesus, that is, in that relationship they already possess and in the chain of love by bearing fruit. In other words, as Jesus' chosen friends or loved ones, the disciples must be fruitful (must carry out and obey his commands) if they are to abide in the chain of love.

The primary focus, the relationship among the disciples themselves, is firmly anchored in both movements of this relationship between Jesus and the disciples. On the one hand, the disciples' love for one another as Jesus loved them is identified as the preeminent command of Jesus. In other words, as Jesus' chosen friends or loved ones, the disciples must be fruitful (must carry out and obey above all the command to love one another as Jesus had loved them) if they are to abide in the chain of love and in their given relationship with Jesus. On the other hand, this preeminent command of

Jesus is explicitly traced to the beginnings of the relationship itself. In other words, Jesus appointed the disciples to go out and bear fruit that abides, to love one another as he had loved them.

The second section, like the first, emphasizes the call to abide. Thus, it again presents discipleship as impossible without fruitfulness. However, fruitfulness itself is now said to presuppose and entail, at its most fundamental level, abiding in Jesus' love through an ongoing fulfillment of the command to love one another within the community of believers.

STRATEGIC CONCERNS AND AIMS

The preceding literary-rhetorical analysis of John 15:1–17 shows that the proposed second unit of discourse, like the first, can be regarded as a coherent artistic whole that is carefully developed from beginning to end. The second unit of discourse can also be seen as a coherent strategic whole with concerns and aims developed through the use of such a literary structure. The concerns of this unit of discourse are the internal affairs of the community of disciples after the departure of Jesus; the unit focuses on the proper relationship of the disciples to Jesus and to one another. These concerns are guided and informed by a number of interdependent aims, which yield a variety of strategic functions for the unit as a whole.

Exhortation and admonition replace the first unit's teaching and consolation as the primary functions of the second unit, and the exhortative function is more prominent than the admonitory. The exhortative function lies at the heart of both major sections. Both have a twofold call to the disciples to abide as disciples of Jesus: to abide in Jesus, the vine (in the first section) and to abide in the love of Jesus, in the chain of love (in the second section). In both cases, the implications of such abiding are clarified. In the first section the disciples are called upon to bear fruit by abiding in the word of Jesus, in the whole of Jesus' teaching and revelation. In the second section the disciples are further called upon to bear fruit by obeying the commands of Jesus, above all the preeminent command of love for one another. The disciples are thus explicitly urged to insure their status as disciples of Jesus: to hold on to their faith in Jesus himself and to practice unceasingly their fundamental principle for community relations. The focal exhortations of the unit, therefore, involve both the grounds for, and the praxis of, discipleship.

The admonitory function is also present in both major sections. It is explicit in the first and indirect in the second. In the first section the call to abide is accompanied by a severe, sustained portrayal of the consequences for the disciples of a failure to heed the call. The disciples are warned that those who do not bear fruit, who do not abide in Jesus and his word, will not only be removed from the vine but also undergo death and destruction. Although such warnings are not repeated in the second section, they apply to the second call as well: the disciples are also warned that those who do not bear fruit, who do not obey the commands of Jesus and love one another, will suffer the same consequences of removal, death, and destruction. The intended effect of such warnings is clear. The invocation of these dire consequences sharply reinforces the calls to abide. In other words, the disciples, despite their status as disciples of Jesus, have a specific role to fulfill, and a failure to fulfill this role means a complete loss of such a status. The choice facing the disciples is thus formulated in the sharpest terms possible: either hold on to what you have, or lose it altogether; either fulfill your proper role as disciples, or lose not only your discipleship but ultimately your life as well.

The second section also includes a more implicit warning. With the disclosure of the mode of Jesus' love for the disciples, the laying down of his life for them, the disciples are warned that the fulfillment of Jesus' preeminent command may well entail the laying down of their own lives for their fellow disciples; in other words, love for one another may ultimately demand death itself. The intended effect of this implicit warning is also clear. The calls themselves are presented thereby as being in keeping with the highest form of love possible, with the highest of human values.

Both functions clearly point to a situation where faltering or separation from the community appears as a real and immediate possibility to the disciples. Such faltering, moreover, clearly concerns both matters of belief (of abiding in the word of Jesus) and matters of praxis (of abiding in love for one another). However, the precise nature of the situation in question and the precise nature of the faltering involved remain undeveloped. There is rupture in the community, but neither its causes nor its concrete manifestations are evident. Thus, the disciples are urged to abide and severely threatened if they do not.

Again in contrast to the first unit, teaching and consolation emerge as the secondary or subordinate functions of the second unit. The didactic function is prominent in both major sections. On the one hand, teaching with regard to Jesus is minimal. Such teaching involves a presentation of a specific aspect of the relationship between Jesus and the Father as an exemplar for the relationship between Jesus and the disciples (abiding in the love of the Father, in the chain of love, given his obedience to the Father's commands) and the further presentation of Jesus' death as an example of love beyond equal and hence in accord with the highest of human values. On the other hand, each call to abide is accompanied by teaching concerning the status and role of the disciples as disciples of Jesus. The first section elaborates this relationship in terms of the figure of the vine, with the disciples as branches in the vine of Jesus (the disciples as already pruned by the word of Jesus, by the whole of his revelation and teaching). The second section describes the relationship in terms of love, with the disciples as Jesus' loved ones in the chain of love (the disciples as the chosen friends of Jesus, to whom he has made known all that he heard from the Father, for whom he laid down his own life, and to whom he assigned the role of bearing fruit from the beginning of the relationship). The didactic function thus provides a basic foundation for the exhortative function. Each reaffirmation of the disciples' status as disciples of Jesus sets the stage for the call to abide. As branches in the vine of Jesus or as his chosen friends, the disciples have an assigned role to fulfill as disciples of Jesus.

The consolatory function is also present, though to a much more limited extent, in both major sections and provides an effective counterpart to the admonitory function. In both sections the call to abide is accompanied by a brief portrayal of the consequences awaiting a positive response to such calls.

In the first section the disciples who abide in Jesus and his word are extended a series of promises: they will glorify the Father, be further pruned by the Father so that they go on bearing fruit and glorifying him unceasingly, and receive whatever they wish and ask for. The second section extends this final promise to those disciples who abide in the love of Jesus by carrying out his commands and loving one another: the Father will grant whatever they ask for in the name of Jesus. The intended effect of such promises is clear. Such positive consequences make the calls to abide more enticing. In addition, the didactic function can be said to possess an underlying consolatory dimension insofar as the unit recalls for the disciples who they are as disciples of Jesus.

Finally, an important polemical function must be acknowledged. This function has a prominent internal dimension and a much less prominent external dimension. On the one hand, a differentiation of the disciples from the world at large is present, though by no means as explicit or as sustained as in the other units of the farewell. Thus, while the claims of the world are attacked, the disciples' own claims as disciples are affirmed. In the first section the emphatic characterization of Jesus as the true vine points to a contrast with outsiders, especially given the symbolic use of the vine in the Jewish literary tradition. Such a contrast again identifies the Jews as the primary representatives of an unbelieving world. In the second section the description of the former status of the disciples as slaves echoes this contrast, given the use of the term "slaves" to characterize the unbelieving Jews of chapter 8. The comparative element attached to the love command also points to a contrast with outsiders, given the twofold reference to Jesus' own death on behalf of the disciples and the possibility of their own deaths in their love for one another. This contrast with outsiders, however, is subdued in this unit; it is presupposed but remains largely in the background.

On the other hand, a sharp, sustained differentiation among the disciples themselves now comes to the fore. The claims of some disciples are attacked, and the claims of others are affirmed. This contrast is sharp in the first section, where the disciples are divided into two categories: those who bear fruit and abide in Jesus and his word, and those who do not. The contrast extends into the second section: those who bear fruit and abide in the love of Jesus and love for one another, and those who do not. The contrast entails, therefore, matters of belief as well as matters of praxis: a continued adherence to the word of Jesus, to the whole of his teaching and revelation, as well as a continued fulfillment of his preeminent command of love for one another.

As a result, the disciples do stand out as disciples of Jesus in the world, a world that is ultimately associated with the Jews as its preeminent representatives. Despite the evidence to the contrary, therefore, the external dimension of this function makes it clear that it is the disciples who represent the ways and values of God in the world. However, not all disciples stand out in the world or bear fruit as disciples of Jesus. Consequently, the disciples must stand out in the world by bearing much and constant fruit or lose their status as disciples. The internal dimension of this function makes it very clear, therefore, that not all disciples represent the ways and values of God in the world, that some disciples are abandoning the true vine of Jesus and the chain of love.

The problem of faltering, therefore, can be considered from two different but related perspectives. On the one hand, the faltering in question can be seen in the light of the external dimension of this function: the disciples as caving in to the pressures from an unbelieving, hostile world and as failing to abide in the word of Jesus, in the command of love for one another, or both. The failure to abide in the love command, in effect, can be seen as a failure by the disciples to lay down their lives for their fellow disciples, following the example of Jesus—a failure to show love beyond equal among the chosen friends of Jesus. However, given the lack of an explicit differentiation of the disciples from the world in this unit, such a context is only in the background.

On the other hand, the faltering can be seen in the light of the internal dimension of this function: the disciples as (1) unfaithful or (2) in disagreement regarding matters of belief and praxis and as failing to abide in the word of Jesus and/or in the command of love for one another. The love command can then be seen as a failure to show total service or self-giving among the chosen friends of Jesus. This context is immediate, at the forefront of the concerns of this unit. Once again, however, the unit does not pursue the specific character of the situation in question. Again, I do not rule out the former dimension concerning the world; in fact, abiding pressure from the world can indeed exacerbate the internal problems of the community. In the end, therefore, the polemical thrust is twofold: distant with respect to the world at large, and immediate with respect to the community as such.

The character of this unit as a strategic whole points to a twofold rhetorical situation or view of the implied readers by the implied author. On the one hand, the disciples are viewed as being in serious danger of rupture and dissolution and hence as in need of urgent exhortation and admonition. The possibility of faltering—of failing to carry out their proper role as disciples of Jesus, whether in terms of belief, praxis, or both—is seen as real and immediate. At the same time, the disciples are still viewed as being under pressure from the world at large. On the other hand, the disciples are also viewed in a positive light. Their status as disciples of Jesus—as the branches in the vine of Jesus that the word of Jesus has already pruned, as the chosen friends or loved ones of Jesus to whom he has revealed the Father in full and for whom he gave up his life—is presupposed and affirmed. Their role as disciples of Jesus—the bearing of fruit in terms of continued belief and sustained praxis—is traced to the beginning of their relationship with Jesus. Their status as disciples of Jesus is differentiated from that of the world at large. It was this twofold rhetorical situation, with its perceived socioreligious exigencies, that called forth the complex and effective response conveyed by this second unit of discourse.

4

THE WORLD WILL HATE YOU!
JOHN 15:18–16:4a

STRUCTURAL OUTLINE

A. The hatred of the world for the disciples (15:18-21)
   1. Hatred: Similar response of the world to the disciples and Jesus (15:18–19)
      a) Description: The hatred of the world (15:18)
         (1) Hatred of the world for the disciples (15:18a)
         (2) Previous hatred of the world for Jesus (15:18b)
      b) Rationale (15:19)
         (1) The love of the world for its own (15:19a-b)
         (2) The hatred of the world for the disciples (15:19c-e)
   2. Persecution and acceptance: Similar responses of the world to the disciples and Jesus (15:20-21)
      a) Rationale and description: The persecution and acceptance of the world (15:20)
         (1) Rationale: Earlier saying of Jesus—A servant as not greater than the master (15:20a-b)
         (2) Description of responses (15:20c-f)
            (a) Negative response: Persecution (15:20c-d)
            (b) Positive response: Acceptance (15:20e-f)
      b) Rationale for persecution of the world (15:21)
         (1) Jesus' name (15:21a)
         (2) Rejection of Jesus' status vis-à-vis the Father (15:21b)
B. The hatred of the world for Jesus (15:22-25)
   1. Description: The hatred of the world (15:22-24)
      a) Rejection of Jesus' revelation as sin and hatred (15:22-23)
         (1) Previous status of the world: Without sin (15:22a-b)
         (2) Present status of the world (15:22c-23)

(a) World as sinful (15:22c)

(b) Hatred of Jesus and the Father (15:23)

b) Rejection of Jesus' works as sin and hatred (15:24)

(1) Previous status of the world: Without sin (15:24a-b)

(2) Present status of the world: Hatred of Jesus and the Father (15:24c)

2. Rationale: Scriptural citation (15:25)

C. The hatred of the world for the disciples (15:26—16:4a)

1. Rationale (15:26-27)

a) The witness of the Spirit-Paraclete (15:26)

(1) Origins of the Spirit-Paraclete (15:26a)

(2) Role of the Spirit-Paraclete (15:26b-c)

b) The witness of the disciples (15:27)

(1) Role of the disciples: Witness to Jesus (15:27a)

(2) Rationale (15:27b)

2. Description: Concrete examples of the hatred and persecution of the world (16:1-4a)

a) Purpose of Jesus' present disclosures (16:1)

b) Persecution of the disciples (16:2-3)

(1) Concrete examples of persecution (16:2)

(a) Expulsions from the synagogues (16:2a)

(b) Killings (16:2b)

(2) Rationale (16:3)

c) Purpose of Jesus' present disclosures (16:4a)

THE PROPOSED BEGINNING FOR THE THIRD unit of discourse within the farewell speech depends on the delineation of the second unit. Given the previous adoption of 15:1–17 as the second unit of discourse, 15:18 is the point of departure for the third unit. The determination of a proper conclusion for this new unit of discourse is problematic, as it was in the case of John 15:1–17.

JOHN 15:18–16:4a AS A THIRD UNIT
OF DISCOURSE

Three traditional and well-represented positions can again be discerned in the literature: (1) a designation of 15:18–16:4a as the second major unit of discourse within John 15–16; (2) a designation of a somewhat smaller unit, usually consisting of either 15:18–27 or 15:18–25, by those who posit a wide number of such units in these chapters; and (3) a designation of a considerably longer unit, often encompassing all of 15:18–16:15, by those who argue for fewer units in these chapters. As in the case of John 15:1–17, furthermore, only two of these positions (a unit encompassing 15:18–16:4a or longer) continue to be represented in the more recent literature, thus confirming the growing tendency pointed out in chapter 3 of this work to increase the length of the proposed units of discourse within chapters 15–16.

The most frequent position, the designation of 16:4a as another major break in these chapters and the resulting identification of 15:18–16:4a as the second unit of discourse within John 15–16, is grounded in two critical observations. First, the sustained emphasis on the hatred of the world for the disciples, introduced in 15:18, is not continued at all past 16:4a. Second, after 16:4b the theme of Jesus' forthcoming departure and the explicit ambience of farewell are further developed through the remainder of chapter 16.[1]

A far less common position is to argue for a major break prior to 16:4a, either at 15:27 or 15:25, depending on where the Paraclete saying of 15:26–27 is placed. In the latter case, the teaching of 15:26–27 with regard to the Spirit-Paraclete is removed from the immediate concern of 15:18–25, the hatred of the world for the disciples, and directly related instead to the further teaching on the Spirit-Paraclete that follows in the first part of chapter 16. In the former case, the teaching of 15:26–27 remains firmly united to 15:18–25 on the following grounds: both the hatred of the world for the disciples and the role of the Spirit-Paraclete in regard to the disciples are introduced in 15:18–27 and elaborated in more concrete terms in the following unit of discourse extending through the first half of John 16.[2]

A more frequent position opts for a major break after 16:4a, usually at 16:15, thus yielding a much larger unit comprising 15:18–16:15. The basic grounding for this position involves the same argumentation observed in the previous position, though with different results: (1) the teaching on the Spirit-Paraclete of 15:26–27 should not be separated from the further teaching of 16:7–15, and (2) the vindication of the

---

1. See, e.g., Heitmüller, "Johannes," 832–33; Lagrange, 398–99, 409; Strathmann, 208, 212; van den Bussche, 113–14; Wikenhauser, 290–93; Brown, 2:692–93; Schulz, 200–202. In the more recent literature, see Kaefer, 277–78. Among those who argue for John 15:1–16:4a as a unit of discourse, many point to 15:18–16:4a as a major section within it: Huby, 68–69; Behler, 129–31; Schnackenburg, 3:91–93. In the more recent literature, see Simoens, 145–46, 148 (with an ending at John 16:3).
2. For a break at John 15:25, see, e.g., Hoskyns, 479–86; Morris, 682. For a break at John 15:27, see, e.g., Westcott, 216, 222; Barrett, 478, 493; Haenchen, 2:133–42. Aside from Haenchen, this position has not been revived in the more recent literature.

disciples vis-à-vis the world by the Spirit-Paraclete (16:7–11) should not
be divorced from the hatred of the world for the disciples described in
15:18–25 and 16:1–4a, because it is meant to be their main consolation
in the face of such hatred.[3]

Two other divisions after 16:4a have also been suggested in the literature from time to time. A major break has been posited at 16:6, thus closely
connecting the demonstrative pronoun "these things" of both 16:4b and
16:6a with the previous disclosures concerning the coming hatred and persecution of the world, especially given the reference in 16:6 to the sorrow
of the disciples. This proposed break keeps all the subsequent teaching
on the Spirit-Paraclete as part of the same unit of discourse.[4] A break at
16:11 has also been proposed. Here the Spirit-Paraclete's role of judgment
in relation to the world described in 16:7–11 is seen as the proper climax
to the severe opposition of the world to the disciples described through
16:4a.[5]

The first position, the majority position in the literature, is preferred by
far to the other two: John 15:18–16:4a should be seen as the second unit
of discourse within chapters 15–16. The critical observations that follow
argue against either a further subdivision of 15:18–16:4a or its incorporation into a larger unit of discourse.

The reference to the concrete expressions of the hatred of the world for
the disciples to be found in 16:1–4a gives these verses a sense of conclusion. There is a climactic disclosure of the specific means by which such
hatred will be carried out. The additional disclosure of the purpose behind all such warnings regarding the coming opposition of the world further heightens this strong sense of closure. At the same time, the renewed
reference after 16:4b to the forthcoming departure of Jesus—its meaning
and its consequences for the disciples—also provides a definite sense of a
new departure or beginning, a renewed focus on the final events of Jesus'
mission and ministry.

In 16:1 and 16:4a the recurring concluding formula of the discourse,
"These things I have said to you," appears twice. This twofold appearance

3. See, e.g., Loisy, 424–33; Dodd, 410; Lightfoot, 255; Lindars, 486; B. Lindars, "The
Persecution of Christians in John 15:18–16:4a," in *Suffering and Martyrdom in the New
Testament: Studies Presented to G. N. Styler by the Cambridge New Testament Seminar*, ed.
W. Horbury and B. McNeil (Cambridge: Cambridge University Press, 1981) 48–69, esp. 54–
55. In the more recent literature, see Becker, 236–41; Becker, *Johannes*, 2:486–87. Loisy,
Lightfoot, and Becker point to John 15:18–16:4a (along with 16:4b–15) as a major section
within the unit. Those who argue for a major break at either 15:25 or 15:27 frequently posit a
further break at 16:15; see, e.g., Hoskyns, 485–87; Morris, 695–701; Barrett, 483–84.
4. See, e.g., Durand, 323, 332–38; Durand, 410. Durand (pp. 338–44; *Saint Jean*,
426–31) argues for another unit of discourse comprising John 16:7–15.
5. See, e.g., Bultmann, 547–48. Again, John 15:18–16:4a is seen (along with 16:4b–11)
as a major section within the unit.

signals, for the first time in the farewell, a direct or immediate break rather than a break of anticipation (cf. 14:25; 15:11). In addition, these two successive examples of the formula provide a distinctive and effective frame for the concluding subdivision of the unit, the subsection of 16:1–4a.[6]

The two traditional arguments on behalf of the proposed division point out a distinct shift after 16:4b in the overarching and controlling theme of 15:18–16:4a. On the one hand, the primary focus of 15:18–16:4a on the external affairs of the community—on the proper and correct relationship of the disciples to the world, with a pointed and sustained emphasis on the fundamental opposition of the world to the disciples as disciples of Jesus— ends with 16:4a. To be sure, chapter 16 contains further references to the coming travails of the disciples in and from the world (16:6, 20–22, 32–33); however, such references are few and brief, do not explicitly mention the active opposition of the world, and are more closely tied to the forthcoming departure of Jesus. Indeed, even the conviction of the world by the Spirit-Paraclete described in 16:7–11 is not directly related to the preceding description of the world's behavior toward the disciples themselves. On the other hand, 16:4b further develops the overarching and controlling themes of 13:31–14:31: the fundamental meaning of Jesus' departure and its consequences for the disciples.

The remainder of chapter 16 also resumes the motif of conversation between Jesus and the disciples, which has been absent since the beginning of chapter 15. In fact, as the next chapter will argue, 16:5b–6 contains a first formulation of this motif, insofar as Jesus himself describes and addresses the reaction of the disciples to the beginning recollection of the forthcoming departure. In other words, after 16:4b the uninterrupted address of Jesus to his disciples that extends through all of chapter 15 and into the beginning of chapter 16 comes to an end and is replaced by a series of reactions on the part of the disciples to the ongoing declarations of Jesus.

The tone of Jesus' address to the disciples again shifts after 16:4b:

1. The primary tone of warning and exhortation of 15:18–16:4a is replaced by a primary tone of consolation and teaching.
2. Although the contrast between the disciples and the world is continued, it is by no means as sharp or intensive as that of 15:18–16:4a.
3. Although the disciples continue to be portrayed as those who believe in Jesus and are about to receive the Spirit-Paraclete, they are now further portrayed as those who, despite their present failure to

---

6. This break is further reinforced by the repetition of the formula in 16:6a, at the beginning of the next unit (see chap. 2, n. 5; chap. 5, n. 12).

understand, will eventually come to a full understanding of Jesus'
mission and message and thus become the sole recipients of Jesus'
farewell promises.

4. The possibility of the disciples' faltering, depicted as real though distant in 15:18–16:4a, is now described as inevitable though temporary,
insofar as such a stumbling is specifically tied to their anticipated
behavior during the climactic events of "the hour," to their prophesied
scattering and abandonment of Jesus (16:32–33).

The standpoint of Jesus as speaker of the discourse also shifts in the
remainder of chapter 16. The Jesus who speaks as if the climactic events of
"the hour" were already behind him, except for the coming of the Spirit-
Paraclete (his announced successor to and among the disciples) and his final
journey or return to the Father, becomes a Jesus who speaks once again as
both about to undergo the climactic events of "the hour" and as already
having done so, except once again for its final events.

Therefore, 15:18–16:4 should not be further subdivided. Although both
15:25 and 15:27 do represent breaks in the farewell speech, neither constitutes a major break serving as a literary marker for a self-contained unit of
discourse. Such breaks are minor breaks, pointing to either a major section
(as in the case of 15:25) or to a subsection of a major section (as in the case
of 15:27) within this third unit of discourse. Furthermore, 15:18–16:4a
should not be included within a larger unit of discourse; the ties in question
point not to one and the same unit of discourse but to the various links that
connect two major units of discourse to one another within the ongoing
farewell speech. In particular, given its prominent role in such argumentation, the teachings on the Spirit-Paraclete of 15:26–27 and 16:4b–15 have
different thrusts; each thrust is tied in a specific way to its own immediate
context, though of course ultimately related to the other as well within the
farewell speech as a whole. In conclusion, 16:4b constitutes a proper ending to the second unit of discourse within chapters 15–16, and therefore,
15:18–16:4a should be regarded as the third self-contained and coherent
unit of discourse within the farewell speech as a whole.

LITERARY STRUCTURE AND DEVELOPMENT

The literature contains four recurring possibilities for the overall organization of 15:18–16:4a. To a large extent, the discussion centers on the
specific location and role assigned to the Paraclete saying of 15:26–27
within the unit.

The majority position argues for a threefold division of these verses,
with the Paraclete saying of 15:26–27 at the center. At the beginning of

the unit is an introductory, general major section on the hatred and persecution of the disciples by the world (15:18–25). A concluding and more
concrete major section, again concerned with the hatred and persecution
of the disciples by the world, is at the end of the unit (16:1–4a). In the
middle, then, the Paraclete saying of 15:26–27 serves as a sharply contrasting and much-needed word of comfort and consolation in the midst of
such dire announcements.[7] Schnackenburg, who exemplifies this position,
sees 15:18–25 as providing the basic reason for the hatred of the world,
15:26–27 as insuring the continued revelation of Jesus through the
witness of the disciples even in the face of such hatred, and 16:1–4a as
pointing to the specific quarters of such hatred to be encountered by the
disciples in the course of their continued witness to Jesus' revelation.

One minority position argues for a twofold division consisting of 15:18–
27 and 16:1–4a, with the Paraclete saying of 15:26–27 formally linked to
15:18–25 as a self-contained major section. As a result, this position elimi-
nates the major division posited by the majority position between a general
and a more concrete presentation of the hatred of the world for the disciples
(brought about by the central position assigned to the Paraclete saying
of 15:26–27). A good example of such a proposal is that of Becker, who
regards 15:18–16:4a as a major section within 15:18–16:15. Becker argues that whereas 15:18–27 is primarily concerned with the world and its
hatred for the disciples, 16:1–4a focuses on the disciples themselves and
their reaction to this hatred of the world. The same pattern, he continues,
can be found in 16:4b–15: whereas the Spirit-Paraclete is developed from
the point of view of the world in 16:4b–11, it is developed in 16:12–15
with respect to the community.[8] Both major sections of the unit, therefore,
reveal the same pattern of thought: first, the world; then, the community.

The second minority position formally links the Paraclete saying of
15:26–27 to 16:1–4a as a self-contained major section, again eliminating
the separation posited in the majority position between the more general
and the more concrete presentations of the world's hatred in 15:18–25 and
16:1–4a, respectively. However, a threefold division is proposed nonetheless, insofar as 15:18–25 is no longer regarded as a self-contained major
section but is divided instead into two such sections, consisting of either
15:18–20 and 15:21–25 or 15:18–21 and 15:22–25. Thus, the second
minority position maintains a threefold rather than twofold division.[9]

7. See, e.g., Lagrange, 409, 412, 415; Schulz, 201; Kaefer, 277–78. Among those who
argue for a self-contained major section within a larger unit of discourse, see, e.g., Bover, 16,
108–9, 118, 123; Schnackenburg, 3:93; Lindars, 486, 493–98. Among those who posit a
wide number of smaller units, see, e.g., Bernard 490, 498, 500.
   8. Becker, *Johannes*, 2:24–25.
   9. For the former division, see, e.g., Bultmann, 547–48; for the latter, see Simoens,
145–50.

Simoens, who provides the most thorough example of this position, argues for an overall inclusion.[10] The outer components (15:18–21; 15:26–16:3) provide the same explanation for the hatred of the world for the disciples— the failure to know the Father as the one who sent Jesus (15:21; 16:3)—and the central component (15:22–25) exposes this hatred as hatred of the Father and inexcusable sin.

The third minority position, like the majority approach, differs from the other two in regarding the Paraclete saying of 15:26–27 as a self-contained major section. However, as in the second minority position, 15:18–25 is formally divided into two self-contained major sections, once again consisting of either 15:18–20 and 15:21–25 or 15:18–21 and 15:22–25. Consequently, this third minority position opts for a fourfold division of the unit as a whole.[11] The most thorough position in this regard is that of Brown, who argues for a rough chiastic pattern in the form of ABBA. The outer components (15:18–21; 16:1–4a) deal with the world's hatred for the disciples and attribute such hatred to the world's failure to recognize the Father in Jesus; the inner components (15:22–25; 15:26–27) address the sin and guilt of the world that result from such hatred. Moreover, whereas the first central component (15:22–25) focuses on the guilt and sin of the world, the second (15:26–27) introduces the figure of the Spirit-Paraclete, who is then presented in 16:4b–33 as the one who reveals such guilt and sin on the part of the world.[12]

This scholarly discussion points to two central questions regarding the literary structure and development of this unit. The first question has to do with the proper location and role of 15:26–27 within the unit, and the second concerns a proposed division within 15:18–25. I agree with the second minority position: a first break should be posited at 15:21 and a second break acknowledged at 15:25.

I agree with the second and third minority positions that 15:18–25 should not be considered a self-contained major section but rather should be divided into two such major sections. In effect, a clear shift can be observed within these verses with respect to the target of the world's

10. The proposed structure for this final major section of the unit—the overall pattern of inclusion—parallels the proposed structure for the unit's first major section, 15:1–11 (see chap. 3, n. 8). Such parallelism, however, is only a part of a more extensive and complex structure for 15:1–16:3 as a whole: an overall inclusion in which these two parallel major sections serve as the framing components, and 15:12–17 serves as the central component and the pivot of the entire unit.

11. For the former division, see, e.g., Wikenhauser, 290–93; for the latter division, see, e.g., Brown, 2:692–95.

12. Brown, 2:695. As Brown himself acknowledges, the chiastic pattern is only present by way of anticipation in the central components, since the Paraclete saying of 15:26–27 does not directly address the issue of the world's sin and guilt; it is only in the light of 16:4b–11 that such a reference can be posited.

hatred. Such a shift ultimately grounds and accounts for this formal division: whereas the first major section is primarily concerned with the disciples of Jesus, the second major section focuses exclusively on Jesus himself. This shift (as I see it) begins with 15:22 rather than 15:21, thus yielding two major sections, 15:18–21 and 15:22–25. To argue, as both the majority and the first minority positions do, that the function of 15:18–25 (plus 15:26–27, in the latter case) is to present not only a general description of the hatred of the world but also the underlying reason for such hatred is to bypass this important shift in the given targets of such hatred. In conclusion, 15:18–21 and 15:22–25 should be seen as the first and second major sections within 15:18–16:4a.

I also agree with the second minority position that 15:26–27 should be formally linked with 16:1–4a. On the one hand, the formal association with 15:18–25 proposed by the first minority position completely bypasses the harsh connection established thereby between 15:26–27 and 15:22–25. The former verses have little to do with the hatred of the world toward Jesus described in the latter; indeed, 15:26–27 is primarily concerned with Jesus' disciples rather than with Jesus himself. In this regard, it is difficult to understand Becker's contention that all of 15:18–27 is concerned with the world and its hatred for the disciples; such a judgment is not true of 15:26–27, where the main concern is with the community of disciples. On the other hand, the relative independence accorded to 15:26–27 as a self-contained major section by both the majority position and the third minority position completely bypasses as well the explanatory function of these verses within the unit. The Paraclete saying of 15:26–27 does have a consolatory function, as the majority position argues, but such a function remains subordinate to its didactic function within the unit. Similarly, a position like Brown's is only correct by future reference and anticipation, since in and of itself 15:26–27 has nothing to do with the sin of the world and its judgment. As such, 15:26–27 should be seen as providing the basic rationale for the specific acts of hatred and persecution against the disciples described in 16:1–4a and thus as an integral and formal part of these verses. Therefore, 15:26–16:4a should be seen as the third major section within 15:18–16:4a.

This proposal for a threefold division of 15:18–16:4a can gain a more solid foundation when viewed more formally. I agree with Simoens that an overall pattern of inclusion can be discerned within this unit, though I would describe such an inclusion from a different perspective.

First, the framing major sections (15:18–21 and 15:26–16:4a) do focus on the hatred of the world for the disciples as well as explain such hatred as stemming from the fact that the Father was not perceived or recognized in Jesus (15:21; 16:3). However, these observations, while correct, do not go far enough. The given rationale for the existence of such opposition from the world is far more extensive and complex than that of the proposed repetition of the one fundamental reason given in 15:21 and 16:3; in fact, the unit provides a large number of such reasons. Furthermore, a clear structural pattern can be discerned within both of these major sections, whereby each description given of the opposition of the world to the disciples is immediately accompanied by a corresponding reason for such an opposition. As a result, the warnings concerning the coming opposition of the world are closely linked throughout to the different explanations for such opposition.

Second, the central major section (15:22–25) does expose the hatred of the world for the disciples as hatred of the Father and inexcusable sin. Again, however, such an observation, although correct, does not go far enough. In direct contrast to the framing major sections, this central section focuses exclusively on the hatred of the world for Jesus himself, a hatred that is already mentioned by way of preparation and anticipation in the first major section of 15:18–21. Thus, whereas the disciples are presented as the main target of this hatred in the framing major sections, it is their master who emerges as such a target in the central section. Furthermore, the same structural pattern to be discerned in the framing major sections can be observed within this central section: the description of the opposition of the world to Jesus is accompanied by a corresponding reason for such an opposition.

Third, the structural pattern operative in all three major sections is reproduced or paralleled by the overall pattern of inclusion that governs the unit as a whole. The description of the hatred of the world for the disciples elaborated in both 15:18–21 and 15:26–16:4a is ultimately grounded and accounted for in terms of the previous hatred of the world for the disciples' master—a hatred that is then further presented as hatred for the Father himself, as inexcusable sin, and as hatred without cause.

Fourth, this threefold division also reveals a further structural pattern, namely, a narrowing or concretization of the opposition of the world to the disciples. Such a pattern is generally seen as a movement from a broad to a more concrete depiction of such an opposition in the unit. However, a threefold development is present in the unit, so the narrowing actually begins with the first major section itself (from hatred to active persecution) and then becomes concrete in the final major section (from active persecution to radical social dislocation and killings). Such a pattern is absent, however, from the central major section, where the hatred of Jesus is described throughout in general terms. Within the overall inclusion, therefore, is also found an ascending description of the forthcoming opposition of the world to the disciples, with an effective climax in the concrete predictions of 16:1–4a.

LITERARY-RHETORICAL ANALYSIS

The proposed literary structure and development of this third unit can be summarized in terms of the following structural outline. The literary-rhetorical analysis to come will develop this outline in detail:

I. The hatred of the world for the disciples (15:18–21)
II. The hatred of the world for Jesus (15:22–25)
III. The hatred of the world for the disciples (15:26–16:4a)

First Major Section (John 15:18–21)

The first outer component of the overall inclusion governing this unit, 15:18–21, focuses on the hatred of the world for the disciples. In the light of the first recurring structural pattern mentioned above, whereby each description of the opposition from the world is accompanied by a corresponding rationale for such an opposition, the literary structure of this first major section can be ascertained. In fact, two successive examples of this pattern occur (15:18–19, 20–21), with the rationale (15:19, 21) directly following the given description of the opposition (15:18, 20) in both cases. Such a twofold occurrence of this pattern within 15:18–21 points immediately to the second structural pattern mentioned above, namely, the concretization with regard to the opposition of the world to the disciples. Thus, in effect, such a process begins already within the first major section of the unit—from a general description of such an opposition in terms of hatred in 15:18–19 to a more concrete description in terms of persecution in 15:20–21.

Two further observations are in order. First, although this first major section focuses on the opposition of the world to the disciples, such an opposition is patterned after, and grounded in, the opposition of the world to Jesus himself in both 15:18–19 and 15:20–21. As such, the description concerning the forthcoming opposition is formulated in both cases in terms of a similar response to the disciples and Jesus on the part of the world.[13] Second, the description of the opposition of the world in 15:20–21 unexpectedly includes an explicit reference to a certain acceptance of the disciples by the world, again formulated in terms of a similar response to the disciples and Jesus. This structure can be outlined as follows: (1) hatred: similar response of the world to the disciples and Jesus (15:18–19); and (2) persecution and acceptance: similar responses of the world to the disciples and Jesus (15:20–21).

13. The primary focus of this first major section on the disciples is clear from the formulation of both major rationales employed: "because of this the world hates you" (15:19e); "but all these things they will do to you on account of my name" (15:21a).

Hatred: Similar Response of the World to the Disciples and Jesus (John 15:18–19)

Description: The Hatred of the World for the Disciples (John 15:18)

The unit's first description of the opposition of the world (15:18) is given in terms of "hatred" (μισεῖν). This description is conveyed by a first-class condition that also introduces the comparative element regarding Jesus and the disciples already mentioned above. The protasis immediately raises the issue of the hatred for the disciples on the part of the world (15:18a), and the apodosis points out how such hatred had also been directed at Jesus beforehand (15:18b).[14] As such, this beginning description clearly implies that, given the earlier hatred of Jesus by the world, a similar hatred of the disciples on the part of that same world should not be surprising. Furthermore, in the light of both the following rationale of 15:19 and all the other rationales of the unit, this hatred of the disciples by the world should not be regarded as just a theoretical possibility but rather as a definite and inescapable reality.

Rationale for the Hatred of the World for the Disciples (John 15:19)

The beginning reference to the hatred of the disciples by the world is immediately followed in 15:19 by a basic rationale that explains both the reason for such hatred and the clear implication that such hatred should not be surprising to the disciples. This rationale has to do with the status of the disciples vis-à-vis the world and is developed in terms of a fundamental contrast in the attitude of the world toward those who belong to it and those who do not: whereas the former are said to be loved by the world (15:19a–b), the latter are said to be hated by it (15:19c–e). This rationale, furthermore, presents such hatred as a definite and inevitable reality: "because of this the world does hate you" (15:19e).

Both components of the contrast reveal a parallel structure. First, the reason for the attitude of the world in question is given (15:19a, 19c–d); then, the specific response of the world in each case is described (15:19b, 19e).[15] First, the reason as such is developed in terms of fundamental

---

14. The comparative element is introduced in the apodosis by the verb form γινώσκετε, which can be read as either a present indicative ("you know that") or a present imperative ("know that"); ultimately, to be sure, either meaning is possible (see Brown, 2:686; Morris, 678; Bultmann, 549, n. 1; Barrett, 480). However, given the fact that such a hatred and rejection of Jesus by the world has been constant throughout the public ministry, I favor the specific nuance that the indicative would convey at this point—not so much a question of imparting new information but rather a question of calling upon a common and shared knowledge.

15. The specific formulation of each component, however, is different. On the one hand, the attitude of the world toward those who are not "of it" is phrased in terms of a

status vis-à-vis the world: either being "of the world" (ἐκ τοῦ κόσμου) or not (15:19a, 19c). The second formulation, however, expands this reason to include the fundamental status of the disciples in regard to Jesus himself and, therefore, the reason why the disciples properly qualify as not "of the world"—Jesus chose or called (ἐξελεξάμην) them (15:19d)[16] "out of the world" (ἐκ τοῦ κόσμου).[17] Second, the corresponding response of the world is then simply presented in terms of love or hatred: "the world" loves "its own" (τὸ ἴδιον)[18]—that is, those who are "of it" (15:19b). However, the world hates the disciples (ὑμᾶς)—that is, those who are not "of it" because they have been chosen or called by Jesus "out of it" (15:19e). Given such a call and resulting status, therefore, the hatred of the world for the disciples should be understandable and, again, not surprising.

---

contrary-to-fact condition (15:19a–b). Thus, its protasis provides the reason for the attitude of the world in question (15:19a, with specific reference to the disciples [ἦτε]), and the apodosis describes that attitude (15:19b, with a general reference to "its own" rather than the expected "you" [ὑμᾶς]). On the other hand, the attitude of the world toward those who are "of it" is conveyed by an epexegetical ὅτι clause in apposition to a following demonstrative pronoun in the main clause (15:19c–e). Thus, the ὅτι clause (15:19c–d) gives the reason for the attitude of the world in question, and the main clause describes that attitude (15:19e).

16. The characterization of the disciples as "chosen" or "called" by Jesus provides a close link to the preceding unit of 15:1–17 (15:16), though a difference in application should also be noted. In 15:1–17 Jesus' choosing of the disciples not only explains the origins of their relationship to him as disciples (chosen prior to their belief and acceptance of his revelation) but is also specifically tied to their proper role as his disciples (chosen for the bearing of fruit, as defined in the unit). Here, however, such a choice is explained in terms of the disciples' fundamental differentiation from the world and "its own" and is given as a basic reason why they must endure the inevitable hatred from that world. A further comment is in order. The strong element of determinism that such a characterization carries with it in 15:16, where the choice of the disciples by Jesus is presented as clearly preceding their own belief in him, is not as explicit in 15:19, where the attendant circumstances of such a choice are not further pursued. To be sure, however, such an element should be presupposed here as well. See also chap. 3, n. 57.

17. The use of the preposition ἐκ to describe both fundamental status vis-à-vis the world (15:19a, 19c) and fundamental status vis-à-vis Jesus (15:19d) should be noted. Whereas the former can be best described as a genitive or ablative of source, indicating provenance and affiliation, the latter represents a genitive or ablative of separation, indicating the reason for such an affiliation and provenance. As such, this latter usage should be regarded as logically and temporally prior to the former: because they were "chosen out of the world," the disciples can in no way be said to be "of it" or "from it." Although both usages of this phrase can be found elsewhere in the Gospel narrative, in neither case—aside from chap. 17—are they used again with reference to Jesus' disciples. As ablative of source, see 8:23; 18:36; cf. 17:14, 16. The example of 8:23 is relevant here: the disciples are like Jesus (who is "not of this world") and unlike the Jews (who are "of this world"). As ablative of separation, see 13:1; cf. 17:6, 15.

18. Just as Jesus has "his own" (10:3, 4, 12 [used adjectivally with "sheep," given the metaphorical context]; 13:1), so does the world. The example of 1:11 is ironic (cf. also 4:44): those who qualified by birth as Jesus' "own"—a clear reference to the Jews—did not receive him or believe in him but instead ultimately became the primary representatives of the world (cf. 16:2–3). On the love of the world, see 3:19 (darkness); 12:43 (the glory of human beings); cf. 12:25.

What is surprising is this beginning reference of 15:18–19 to the hatred of the world for the disciples at this point in the narrative. Nowhere in the preceding narrative are the disciples of Jesus said to be hated by the world, not even within the first unit of 13:31–14:31, where the disciples are sharply and systematically differentiated from the world so that all that is promised to the former is categorically denied to the latter. Similarly, such hatred on the part of the world is not mentioned again in the narrative that follows (cf. 17:14, however). Thus, in effect, this beginning description and warning of hatred toward the disciples in 15:18–19—a warning that sets the tone for the entire unit that follows—is unique in the Gospel.

The element of comparison within this description (the previous hatred of Jesus by the world), however, is not surprising. In fact, the negative reaction of the world toward Jesus has already been characterized twice in such terms in the preceding narrative (3:20; 7:7). In 3:20, within the conclusion to the conversation between Jesus and Nicodemus (3:16–21), the negative reaction toward the coming of "the light" into the world ($3:19a_1$) is described as hatred of "the light" ($3:19a_2$–20; further characterized therein in terms of love of "darkness" and not coming to "the light"). In 7:7, within the conclusion to Jesus' second major journey to Galilee of chapter 6 (7:1–9), the negative reaction of his own brothers toward him is explained in terms of their fundamental association and identification with the world: whereas the world does not hate Jesus' brothers (7:7a), it does hate him (7:7b–c). In both examples, therefore, hatred of Jesus implies a rejection of his mission and claims.[19] As such, the comparative element of 15:18b summarizes this sustained reaction of the world toward Jesus and his mission. This element also begins to explain what hatred for the disciples means and entails—a rejection of their own mission and claims.

The specific formulation of such hatred for Jesus within this comparative element immediately raises the question concerning the precise standpoint of Jesus as the speaker of the discourse. First, the use of the perfect μεμίσηκεν in 15:18b unquestionably represents a perfect of completed action, especially given the presence of the prepositional phrase that modifies

---

19. In both examples the hatred of Jesus is grounded in the "evil works" of the world (3:19b–20; 7:7c). The contrast provided by 3:21 (he who "does the truth" comes to "the light") shows that such "evil works"—and therefore such hatred—refer to unbelief and rejection. Such a rationale is repeated several times in this unit as grounds for the opposition of the world to both the disciples and Jesus (e.g., 15:21, 22–24).

it, "before you."[20] Such a perfect, however, can be understood from two different perspectives: (1) as pointing to and summarizing the basic recurring attitude of the world toward Jesus up to this point in the narrative (for example, 3:20; 7:7) or (2) as pointing to and encompassing the reaction of the world toward the whole of Jesus' mission, including the main events of "the hour" still outstanding at this point in the narrative. It is the latter meaning, I believe, that is intended; that is, the reference to the previous hatred of Jesus by the world presupposes and includes the climax of such hatred, suffering and death by crucifixion, so the Jesus who speaks and now warns his disciples of a similar hatred for them on the part of the world is a Jesus who has already undergone and surpassed the full hatred of the world. As such, the standpoint of Jesus as speaker in 15:18–16:4a parallels that of 15:1–17.

Persecution and Acceptance: Similar Responses of the World to the Disciples and Jesus (John 15:20-21)

The second description in the unit of the opposition of the world to the disciples (15:20) is in terms of "persecution" (διώκειν). As indicated above, however, its development differs from that of the first description of 15:18. First, the description of the opposition in 15:20c–d is followed by a similar, though contrasting, description of a certain acceptance of the disciples in the world (15:20e–f). The description is also preceded by a rationale that grounds both the opposition to, and acceptance of, the disciples (15:20a–b). A second rationale at the end, as in the case of 15:19, specifically grounds the opposition to the disciples on the part of the world, bypassing the contrasting element of acceptance introduced by way of expansion within the description itself (15:22).

Rationale and Description: The Persecution and Acceptance of the World (John 15:20)

The second description of opposition introduced in 15:20c–d at first seems to begin with an inversion of the structural arrangement found in 15:18–19—namely, the rationale for the opposition (15:20a–b) followed by a new description of it (15:20c–d). However, further examination shows that the rationale of 15:20a–b is meant to comprehend both the description of opposition of 15:20c–d and that of acceptance of 15:20e–f. In other words, the disciples will meet with the same response as Jesus in both respects.

20. The use of the perfect tense also conveys the sense of an abiding or enduring hatred of Jesus, a hatred that can be expressed after his departure or death only in terms of hatred for his disciples, for those who bear and preach his name (15:21).

The rationale of 15:20a–b consists of a specific recalling (μνημονεύετε)[21] for the disciples of a previous "saying" of Jesus to them.[22] The saying in question (13:16) is found in the preceding narrative unit of the foot washing (13:1–20) and is thus encountered here a second time in verbatim, though much abbreviated, fashion.[23] The saying uses household imagery similar to that employed in the preceding unit of 15:1–17, where the status of the disciples as "friends" of the "master" is further explained in terms of a metaphorical contrast with their previous status as "servants" or "slaves." It reminds the disciples that they, as "servants," are not greater than Jesus, the "master."[24] The immediate purpose of this reminder, given the context of hatred just elaborated in 15:18–19, would seem to be one of reinforcing the preceding rationale of 15:19 and preparing the way for the context of persecution to be outlined in 15:20c–d. However, the saying clearly prepares the way for both the negative and positive reactions that follow in 15:20c–d and 15:20e–f, respectively.

These two reactions are developed, as in the case of the first description of 15:18, in terms of first-class conditions that incorporate the element of comparison mentioned above regarding the similar fates of both Jesus and the disciples. In both cases the apodosis raises the question of the reaction of outsiders to the disciples (15:20d, 20f). Furthermore, in both cases the

21. The verb in the introductory formula can be read, as in 15:18b, as either a present indicative ("you remember") or a present imperative ("remember"). Although both meanings are again ultimately possible, I believe the latter is preferable in this case. The disciples are specifically asked to recall a previous saying of Jesus that is deemed to be very appropriate in this developing context of warnings concerning hatred and persecution from the world. Although the verb itself occurs elsewhere only in 16:4b–33 (vv. 4, 21), such a procedure immediately calls to mind one of the basic roles assigned to the Spirit-Paraclete in the first unit—to recall for the disciples Jesus' sayings and teachings (14:26). As in so many other respects, therefore, the roles of Jesus and the Spirit-Paraclete are clearly parallel in this regard as well. A subtle difference in the exercise of such a role should be noted nonetheless: whereas the recalling of the Spirit-Paraclete results in a fuller understanding of the sayings and teachings, the recalling of Jesus here results in a different application of the same saying in another context.

22. This usage of the term λόγος with reference to a specific saying of Jesus is not unusual in the Gospel (2:22; 4:50; 6:60; 7:36; cf. 18:36).

23. The expansion of this saying in 13:16b₂, which abandons the household language of 13:16b₁ ("servant"; "master") and reformulates the principle in question in terms of missionary language ("apostle"; "sender"), is dropped altogether. The saying recalled, like both 15:13 and 15:15b, is a traditional proverb whose meaning is being applied to a new situation altogether. It is the second such extension of this traditional proverb within the Gospel itself (see K. Dewey, "Paroimiai," 96–97).

24. The recurrence of such household language at this point provides another concrete link to 15:1–17, though the difference in application should be noted again. Whereas in 15:15 the characterization of the disciples as "servants" has a negative connotation (an improper metaphorical description for the disciples' status in relation to Jesus, given the contrast with the term "friends"), here such a characterization possesses a positive connotation (a proper metaphorical designation for the status of the disciples with regard to Jesus). See chap. 3, n. 53.

protasis begins by pointing out how both of these reactions had also been directed at Jesus himself beforehand (15:20c, 20e).[25] The basic function of the two descriptions of 15:20c–d and 15:20e–f is also similar to that of 15:18: to assuage the surprise of the disciples. However, a difference in their corresponding applications should be noted. The first description of 15:18 implies that, given the earlier reaction of the world to Jesus, a similar reaction to the disciples should not be surprising (a comparison that is subsequently explained in the rationale of 15:19 in terms of the disciples' having been chosen by Jesus and their resulting status vis-à-vis the world). The two descriptions of 15:20c–d and 15:20e–f function as direct examples or conclusions of the principle enunciated in the preceding rationale of 15:20a–b: given the earlier reactions of outsiders to the "master," similar reactions to his "servants" should not be surprising. There is a further affinity with 15:18: given the rationale of 15:21, as well as the truth of the conditional clauses in question, these reactions are to be regarded not as theoretical possibilities but as inevitable realities.

The two reactions in question, as indicated above, sharply contrast. The negative reaction is formulated first, thus giving rise to the second description of the opposition of the world to the disciples, now phrased in terms of "persecution" rather than "hatred" (15:20d). The positive reaction follows immediately and is formulated in terms of "carrying out or obeying the word" (τὸν λόγον τηρεῖν) of the disciples (15:20f). In the light of the preceding rationale of 15:20a–b, then, the comparative element points out in each case how (1) given the earlier persecution of Jesus as master, a similar persecution of the disciples as his servants is only to be expected (15:20c), and (2) given the earlier acceptance of the master's "word," a similar acceptance of the disciples' own "word" is also to be expected (15:20e). A further similarity with the first description of 15:18 should be noted at this point. The use of the constative aorist (see notes 26 and 27 below) in the comparative element should be seen as including the climactic events of "the hour" itself, so once again the temporal standpoint of Jesus as speaker is that of a Jesus who has already undergone and surpassed the full persecution of the world and has already fully revealed his "word" in and through these climactic events themselves.

The intended contrast can be more narrowly defined. In the case of 15:20c–d, the hatred of the world for the disciples has a more

25. Specific differences in formulation between 15:18 and 15:20c–d, e–f should be noted: (a) The respective functions of protasis and apodosis have been inverted. In 15:18 the protasis outlined the reaction of the world, and the apodosis introduced the comparative element. (b) The reactions of 15:20c–d, e–f are not attributed to the world as such; indeed, the term "the world" disappears altogether from 15:20–21. Within 15:20–21 itself, the source of these reactions remains unidentified in the third person plural forms of the verbs in question, though the context clearly points to the world as the source.

circumscribed expression, thus giving rise to the structural pattern of concretization already outlined: the hatred of the world for the disciples—a hatred that has already been shown to include a rejection of the disciples' own mission and claims—is now said to include an active element of "persecution" as well.[26] In the latter case of 15:20e–f, an unexpected development takes place, given the unfolding context of opposition in the unit: the disciples can also expect some acceptance of their "word" (that is, some belief in Jesus through their own mission and claims).[27] As such, the contrast points out that "persecution" involves—both by way of structural opposition to "carrying out or obeying the word" and a structural preservation of the specific denotation of the term "hatred" mentioned above—not only a rejection of the disciples' claims concerning Jesus but also a rejection that is openly and actively hostile. It will then be the role of the third step in this pattern of concretization to clarify how active and hostile this rejection will be.

26. Like the earlier references to hatred, this reference to the persecution of the disciples by the world is surprising at this point in the narrative. Nowhere else in the preceding (or following, for that matter) narrative are the disciples said to be persecuted by the world, although, to be sure, a definite element of fear can be detected on their part both prior to and after the farewell (11:8, 16; 20:19). Again, however, the comparative element within this second description (the previous persecution of Jesus by the world) is not surprising; the negative reaction of the world—specifically attributed to the Jews—has been characterized once in such terms in the preceding narrative (5:16). Thus, in the narrator's conclusion to the healing of the lame man in chap. 5 (5:16–18), Jesus is said to be persecuted by the Jews on two counts: a violation of the Sabbath law and his claims with regard to God. Furthermore, such a persecution is described as entailing a desire by the Jews to put Jesus to death. The persecution of Jesus, therefore, clearly involves both rejection of his claims and active hostility. Although the term "persecution" does not appear elsewhere in the narrative, several references to this desire to kill Jesus and several actual attempts on his life indicate that such an active persecution by the world remains constant throughout the public ministry (7:1, 14–31 [vv. 19, 20, 25]; 8:39–40, 59; 10:31, 39; 11:8, 45–54, 55–57). Furthermore, the use of the aorist tense in this regard—a constative aorist—should be seen as incorporating not only all of these various references and attempts but also the climax of such a persecution (namely, Jesus' death on the cross), so the standpoint of Jesus here is that of a Jesus who has already undergone and surpassed the full persecution of the world.

27. The use of the term "word" here is different from that of 15:20a–b. "Word" no longer refers to a specific saying of Jesus but rather to the whole of Jesus' ministry and revelation—a denotation already encountered in both 15:1–17 (v. 3) and 13:31–14:31 (vv. 23–24) and common as well elsewhere in the Gospel (4:41; 5:24; 8:31, 37, 43, 51–52; 12:48). The use of "word" here in combination with the verb τηρεῖν parallels that of 13:31–14:31; namely, to keep or fulfill the word of Jesus means, in part, to accept his claims and believe in him (see chap. 2, n. 77). The use of the aorist in this regard should be seen, as in the case of the preceding negative reaction, as incorporating not just Jesus' revelation up to this point but also its climax in the final events of "the hour." Thus, the standpoint of the speaker is once again that of a Jesus who has already undergone and surpassed "the hour." As such, the use of "word" here is closer to that of 15:1–17 than that of 13:31–14:31 insofar as it reflects a full acceptance and understanding on the part of those who have believed rather than a dialectic of present and future understanding. The acceptance of the disciples' own "word" is not found elsewhere in the Gospel, though the acceptance of Jesus' "word" certainly is: some, including the disciples themselves, have believed.

A comparison of the application in 15:18–16:4a of the basic principle given in 15:20a–b with the previous use of the principle in 13:1–20 is interesting. In 13:16 this proverb is given to ground and justify a pattern of behavior on the part of the disciples with regard to one another, a behavior symbolically represented by the washing of one another's feet as Jesus washed theirs and whose proper execution is presented as absolutely necessary for them to be characterized as "blessed." In 15:20a–b, however, the same proverb is used to ground and justify certain responses to the disciples on the part of the world as they fulfill their appointed mission. Thus, whereas the application of this proverb in 13:1–20 reflects the intraecclesial character of the foot washing, its application in 15:18–16:4a reflects the extraecclesial orientation of this third unit as a whole.

Rationale for the Persecution of the World (John 15:21)

The positive reaction of outsiders to the disciples is abandoned as unexpectedly as it was introduced in 15:20e–f. In fact, 15:21 resumes the unfolding context of opposition from the world, and the idea of a possible acceptance disappears altogether from the remainder of the unit.[28] The second rationale to be found within 15:20–21 now follows; unlike the earlier one of 15:20a–b, the rationale of 15:21 applies only to the negative reaction of 15:20c–d.[29] The positive reaction of 15:20e–f is thereby entirely bypassed, and the negative reaction of 15:20c–d receives a double grounding or justification: whereas the first grounding of 15:20a–b was general in scope, the second one of 15:21 is more specific and restricted. As such, this second grounding, 15:21, resumes the basic structural pattern of a description of opposition followed by a corresponding rationale for such an opposition.

Thus, the "persecution" that the disciples will experience from the outside is now explained not only in the more general terms of the master/servant metaphor but also in the more specific terms of a fundamental rejection of Jesus' claims with regard to the Father. This second rationale

28. The unexpected and fleeting inclusion of the positive reaction of 15:20e–f can be said to possess a twofold aim. On the one hand, the resulting juxtaposition of negative and positive reactions prepares the way for the explicit reference to the appointed mission of the disciples in 15:26–27. Thus, although the disciples can expect sharp opposition from the world, just as Jesus did, they can also expect to meet with some degree of acceptance, just as Jesus did. On the other hand, this stated possibility of acceptance does function as a word of comfort in the midst of prophecies of woe: despite the opposition, some belief will emerge.
29. It has been argued that the second reaction of 15:20e–f is not at all positive and thus provides no contrast to the preceding negative reaction of 15:20c–d; in fact, this reaction is said to confirm and reinforce the latter, since Jesus' "word" was, in effect, not kept or accepted (Loisy, 425; Lagrange, 410–11; Macgregor, 292). I believe, however, that the proposed formulation of a positive reaction and the resulting contrast it produces with the preceding formulation of a negative reaction are not only intended but very effective.

is developed in two basic steps, the second of which directly prepares the way for the second major section, 15:22–25.[30] First, an accusative causal with the preposition διά provides a beginning explanation—on account of Jesus' name (that is, because the disciples believe in Jesus, bear his name, and continue to proclaim his message to the world).[31] Second, a following ὅτι clause expands this beginning explanation—because of the outsiders' failure to recognize Jesus' sender (that is, because of their rejection of Jesus' claims regarding his status and role vis-à-vis the Father as presented by the disciples in and through their own mission).[32]

This second rationale, 15:21, is similar to the earlier rationale in 15:19 regarding the hatred of the world for the disciples insofar as it too explains the reason for the persecution of the disciples by the world, further explains why the disciples should not regard such a persecution as surprising, and presents such a persecution as an inevitable reality ("these things they shall do to you"; 15:19a₁. At the same time, the emphasis differs slightly. Whereas the rationale of 15:19 focuses on Jesus' choice of the disciples "out of the world" and their resulting status in relation to the world, the rationale of 15:21 emphasizes both the status (the rejection by the world of Jesus' name, a name that his "chosen" disciples bear and represent) and the role (the rejection by the world of Jesus' claims vis-à-vis God, claims that his "chosen" disciples continue to preach in the course of their own appointed mission) of the disciples in relation to the world.

In the end, this second warning of 15:20–21 concerning the inevitable persecution that the disciples will encounter from the world reinforces and sharply expands the first warning of 15:18–19 concerning the inevitable hatred of the disciples by the world. Thus, the opposition of the world to the disciples will be not only severe but also active. It will involve not only a total rejection of their own mission and message but also open hostility. At the same time, this second warning of 15:20–21 introduces a clear and strong, though fleeting and undeveloped, word of comfort in the

30. The rationale is introduced by the formula "These things they shall do to you" (used again in 16:3, though in a shorter form, with respect to the preceding and final description of the opposition of the world to the disciples of 16:2). The demonstrative covers only the negative reaction of 15:20c–d, given the nature of the subordinate causal clause that follows; however, insofar as the hatred of the disciples is comprehended within this theme of persecution, the pronoun also covers the first reaction outlined in 15:18–19.

31. For the possession of Jesus' name as signifying belief in Jesus and for the consequences of such a possession, see 1:12; 3:18; 20:31; cf. 2:23. A further consequence of the possession of Jesus' name has also been outlined in the two preceding units of discourse (14:13–14; 15:16; see also 16:23, 24, 26): the disciples will receive whatever they ask for in the name of Jesus. The present unit adds yet another consequence: because of Jesus' name, the disciples will be hated and persecuted.

32. On acceptance or rejection of Jesus as acceptance or rejection of "the one who sent him," see, e.g., 5:23–24; 7:25–29; 12:44–45; 13:20; 14:24–25. On rejection of the disciples as rejection of Jesus, who sent them, see 13:20.

midst of woes: there will be some acceptance of the disciples' mission and message. Nevertheless, though somewhat deflected by this positive word of comfort, the ominous tone of opposition predominates—indeed, in heightening fashion—within this first major section of the unit.

Aside from a brief, undeveloped word of comfort pointing to some acceptance of the disciples in and by the world, the first major section describes in heightening fashion the opposition that the disciples will encounter from the world: hatred (15:18–19) and persecution (15:20–21). Both kinds of opposition (and an acceptance as well) are patterned after, and grounded in, an earlier opposition to (and acceptance of) Jesus by the world. This earlier opposition (and acceptance) is presented from the point of view of the completion of the hour, so as the speaker, Jesus addresses his disciples as one who has already undergone and surpassed the climax of this opposition. Thus, the disciples as addressees are warned as those who have already accepted the whole of Jesus' revelation and have fully believed in him (except for the bestowal of the Spirit-Paraclete). Finally, these warnings of hatred and persecution are accompanied by a variety of rationales that are meant to account for such an opposition and thereby assuage its inevitable severe impact upon the community of disciples: for example, the disciples as "not of the world" but as "chosen" by Jesus "out of the world"; the disciples as "servants" who are not greater than the "master" (Jesus); the disciples as bearing Jesus' name and preaching his claims vis-à-vis God through their own mission and ministry; and the failure of the world to see the Father as the one who sent Jesus.

Second Major Section (John 15:22–25)

With 15:22 the primary focus of 15:18–21 on the disciples as the target of the world's hatred is replaced by an exclusive focus on Jesus himself as the earlier target of such hatred. This new focus continues through 15:25, thus clearly outlining the central section of the overall pattern of inclusion governing the unit. Such a shift is not unexpected; in fact, as the analysis of the first major section of 15:18–21 has shown, in both descriptions of the forthcoming opposition of the world to the disciples this opposition is explicitly patterned after, and grounded in, an earlier opposition of the world to Jesus himself. In the present section, therefore, this earlier opposition to Jesus is specifically pursued and described.

This central section follows the recurring structural pattern present in the unit as a whole: each description of the opposition of the world is accompanied by a corresponding rationale for such an opposition. In contrast with the first major section, however, such a pattern appears only once in this central section, though in the same sequence: the description of the

opposition of the world to Jesus (15:22–24) is followed by a corresponding
rationale for such an opposition (15:25).

Description: The Hatred of the World
for Jesus (John 15:22–24)

The description itself of the opposition of the world to Jesus in 15:22–24 is
more complex than either description of opposition in the first major section. Although the second major section contains only one description of
opposition, it is given a twofold formulation. Opposition to both fundamental aspects of Jesus' ministry is presented. In 15:22–23 the opposition is
described from the point of view of a rejection of Jesus' revelation and in
15:24, from the point of view of a similar rejection of Jesus' works. In both
cases the opposition is described again, as in the case of the first description
of 15:18–19, in terms of "hatred."[33]

The two formulations of the opposition have a similar structure. Each
formulation, first of all, is developed in terms of a sharp contrast between
the status of the world prior to the coming of Jesus (15:22a–b/15:24a–b)
and after the coming of Jesus (15:22c–23/15:24c). Second, the first part of
each contrast, the delineation of the status of the world prior to Jesus'
coming, is phrased in terms of a mixed contrary-to-fact condition. Third,
the second part of each contrast, the delineation of the status of the world
after the coming of Jesus, describes the resultant opposition of the world to
that coming in terms of hatred not only of Jesus himself but also of the
Father.

The contrary-to-fact conditions that constitute the first part of the contrast and describe the status of the world prior to the coming of Jesus present
a parallel development. First, the protasis of each condition sequentially
describes the coming and ministry of Jesus in terms of its two fundamental
aspects, thus accounting for the double formulation of the opposition: first,
Jesus' ministry in terms of his "speaking" or revelation (15:22a); then, the
ministry in terms of his "works" (15:24a).[34] Second, each apodosis describes

33. However, as in the second description of 15:20–21, the opposition is not ascribed
to "the world" as such; indeed, that term does not appear at all in this central section of
15:22–25. Once again, the opposition remains unidentified in the third person plural forms
of the verbs in question, though the context clearly points to the world as the source of such
an opposition and indeed begins to point above all to a specific group within the world.

34. Both protases employ the aorist tense. John 15:22a contains a reference to the coming
as such (ἦλθον), as well as to the revelation itself (ἐλάλησα). John 15:24a omits the reference to
the coming and instead refers only to the works themselves (ἐποίησα); however, this reference
is briefly expanded by a relative clause whose purpose is to accentuate the unique character of
such "works"—"works" that no one else had done (15:24a₂). For a similar division of the
ministry in terms of its two fundamental aspects, see 14:10–11. For a similar description of
Jesus' "works" as being without parallel, see, e.g., 9:32; cf. 14:12. On the use of λαλεῖν to
refer to Jesus' revelation, see, e.g., 3:11, 34; 7:17; 8:26, 28, 38; 12:49–50; cf. 15:3.

the status of the world in the absence of such a ministry in exactly the same terms: without Jesus' revelation and works the world would have no "sin" (15:22b, 24b).[35]

The use of contrary-to-fact conditions to describe the status of the world prior to Jesus' coming implicitly points out not only the current status of the world but also the fundamental reason for such a status. In effect, the world may be said to have "sin" because it rejected the coming and the ministry of Jesus both in terms of his revelation or claims and his unique works; thus, "sin" is clearly defined thereby as the overall rejection of Jesus' coming and ministry.[36]

What is implicit in the first part of the contrast becomes explicit in the second part, and what is presented at first from a negative point of view in the former is developed in the latter in strong positive terms. Thus, following each contrary-to-fact condition is a description of the reaction of the world to the coming of Jesus and thus a description of the status of the world after Jesus' coming (that is, its present status). Each of these descriptions, furthermore, is introduced by the strongly adversative formula "but now" (νῦν δέ), which thereby establishes an emphatic sign of contrast. In both cases this description is given in terms of "hatred"; however, the first formulation (15:22c–23) is longer and more developed than the second (15:24c).

The first description consists of a twofold statement. The first part of this statement (15:22c) describes the present status of the world in terms of "sin." This provides a direct contrast to the world's former status as outlined in 15:22b: whereas before it "had no sin," now it has "no excuse" for its "sin."[37] The implications of the beginning statement are clarified in the second part of this description (15:23). Such sin is due to the reaction accorded to the coming of Jesus and his ministry of revelation as outlined

35. Both apodoses employ the imperfect tense of the verb "to have" (εἴχοσαν) with the noun "sin" as its object, thus accounting for the mixed nature of these unreal conditions. The use of the imperfect in this regard makes it clear that the condition of "sin" in which the world presently finds itself is continuing and permanent, as the subsequent delineations of the status of the world after Jesus' coming will explicitly confirm.

36. Such an understanding of "sin" can be found elsewhere in the Gospel narrative, with particular reference to the Jews as those who reject Jesus and are thus guilty of sin (8:21, 24, 34 [with the verb ποιεῖν]; 9:41 [also with the verb ποιεῖν]; 19:11). Indeed, the example of 9:41, the final declaration of Jesus to the Pharisees of chap. 9, is similar to the first formulation of 15:22–23.

37. This specific formulation in variation serves not only to characterize the present status of the world in terms of sin but also to advance such a characterization one step further by emphasizing the nature of this sin—this hatred and rejection—as having no valid excuse (πρόφασιν). The term "excuse" itself is employed nowhere else in the Johannine writings and only seldom in the New Testament as a whole, though always with the quite different denotation of a pretext or false excuse (Mark 12:40 par.; Acts 27:30; Phil 1:18; 1 Thess 2:5).

in 15:22a, a reaction that is first described as one of "hatred" for Jesus and then extended to the one who sent him—"hatred" for the Father as well. A chiastic structure can be observed in this first formulation of the opposition of the world to Jesus: just as the first statement of 15:22c is to be directly connected with the apodosis of the contrary-to-fact condition in 15:22b (no sin; no excuse for sin), so is the second statement of 15:23 to be directly connected with the protasis of 15:22a (without or prior to Jesus' coming and revelation; hatred of Jesus).

The second description omits any reference to the present status of the world with regard to sin and limits itself instead to a statement concerning the reaction of the world to the coming of Jesus and his ministry of works as outlined in 15:24a (15:24c). Given the nature of that reaction, however, the present status of the world is unmistakably revealed again, though only implicitly so, as one of "sin." The given statement consists of a compound sentence: the world "has seen" (ἑωράκασιν), a direct reference to Jesus' works mentioned in 15:24a, and has hated (μεμισήκασιν) him and his Father. Once again, therefore, this reaction is described in terms of hatred for Jesus and is also extended to the one who sent him, the Father. Thus, although the chiastic structure of the first formulation is not preserved in the second formulation of opposition, there is an even more direct connection between the protasis of the contrary-to-fact condition of 15:24a and the statement of 15:24c (without or prior to Jesus' unique works/ a seeing of these works and hatred of Jesus).

Both formulations of the opposition of the world to Jesus, therefore, present such an opposition in terms of a rejection of the latter's ministry of revelation, both with regard to his words and his works. Furthermore, both formulations describe such a fundamental rejection in terms of "hatred," not only of Jesus but also of the Father.[38] Finally, such hatred and rejection are ultimately characterized as "sin," and indeed a sin for which the world has no valid excuse, given the fact and nature of that ministry.

This twofold description of the world's opposition to Jesus in terms of hatred returns to the first such description of the world's opposition to the disciples—and to Jesus—in the first major section (15:18–19). The description also reiterates the fundamental meaning and implications of the opposition, though now, because of the contrast within each formulation, it uses more explicit and detailed terms: "hatred" means an overall rejection of Jesus' coming and ministry, of both his claims and unique

---

38. Although the rejection of Jesus as a rejection of the Father who sent him is a common theme in the Gospel (see n. 32 above), such a chain of rejection is never formulated in terms of hatred elsewhere in the Gospel. In fact, these are the only references to hatred of the Father on the part of the world.

works.[39] The element of persecution or active hostility introduced in the second description of the world's opposition to the disciples—and, again, to Jesus—of 15:20-21 is thus not explicitly continued within this central section, though it is presupposed by, and comprehended in, the given hatred of the world for Jesus.

This double formulation of opposition, especially given the contrast developed within each formulation, is very effective. For example, because the rejection of Jesus is presented twice—first from the point of view of his fundamental message and then from the point of view of his unique signs—the opposition is portrayed as complete. Similarly, because the rejection is described both times in terms of hatred not only of Jesus but also of the Father, the opposition is further portrayed as having the most severe and far-reaching consequences. Finally, because the rejection is characterized as sin both times (not only by way of the contrast but also once in an explicit way), the opposition is also portrayed as undeserved and culpable (indeed inexcusably so, as the second formulation clearly asserts). As a result, this central section develops the earlier opposition to Jesus on the part of the world in the sharpest negative terms possible: such hatred was total, amounted to hatred of God, and resulted in inexcusable sin.

Such a stark portrayal of the opposition possesses a strong positive element as well. This portrayal reassures the addressees—who now represent the specific target of such hatred and its active element of persecution, as the first major section of the unit has clearly shown—concerning their own status in the world. In accepting Jesus' coming and ministry, they have shown that they are not part of the world and, as such, can in no way be said to hate God or to have sin.

Rationale for the Hatred of the World for Jesus (15:25)

The twofold description of the opposition of the world to Jesus (15:22-24) is followed immediately, in keeping with the recurring structural principle

39. That first description of 15:18-19 conveys the meaning of such hatred only indirectly, that is, through the use of the comparative element elsewhere in the Gospel (hatred for Jesus as a rejection of Jesus' mission and message). The second description of 15:20-21 develops such a meaning more fully through the theme of persecution. First, the acceptance of Jesus' or the disciples' "word" (the whole of that message and mission) is presented as the contrasting reaction of the world to that of persecution. Second, the concluding rationale of this second description grounds such persecution on the failure of the world to recognize the one who sent Jesus—God the Father—in Jesus. In both instances, therefore, what is implicit in 15:18-19 is made far more explicit: persecution involves, to begin with, a rejection of Jesus' fundamental message and claims. This central section, then, gives the basic meaning and implications of hatred in even greater detail: a rejection of Jesus' coming in terms of its two fundamental aspects, the ministry of "speaking" or revelation and the ministry of unique "works."

of the unit, by a corresponding rationale for such an opposition (15:25). This rationale, however, differs greatly from the two previously encountered in 15:18–21. The rationale in 15:25 consists of a scriptural citation— the only such citation in the whole of the farewell discourse—to the effect that the previously described hatred of Jesus on the part of the world represents the fulfillment of a scriptural prophecy and is thus in keeping with God's own plan of salvation and revelation.[40]

Two elements of this rationale should be noted. First, the use of the adverb δωρεάν, best translated here as "without cause,"[41] to describe the hatred in question within the citation itself can be said to be directly related to, and anticipated by, the previous description of the sin of the world in 15:24c as "without valid excuse." In other words, the citation confirms as well the undeserved and culpable nature of such a hatred for Jesus. Second, although in and of itself the citation begins to point to a specific group in the world as the agent of such hatred, the introductory formula confirms the identification of this group by referring to the citation itself as coming from "their Law."[42] In other words, the Jews begin to emerge as the primary and preeminent representatives of an unbelieving and rejecting world.

40. The source of the citation is usually identified as either Ps 35:19 or Ps 69:5, with some preference given to the latter because of its use as a messianic psalm elsewhere in the Gospel (John 2:17), as well as in the rest of the New Testament (Mark 15:36/Matt 27:48; Matt 27:34/Luke 23:36; Rom 11:9–10; 15:3; Heb 11:26; Rev 3:5; 13:8, 16:1, 17:8). The verb form here, however, is found in neither the Greek nor the Hebrew text (which the Greek translates literally) of these two proposed sources, both of which employ the present active participle (οἱ μισοῦντες) rather than the aorist indicative. Allusion is also frequently made to both Pss. Sol. 7:1 (where the same verb form can be found, though with the personal pronoun "us" rather than "me" as direct object) and Ps 119:161 (where the aorist indicative of the verb to persecute [ἐμίσησαν] is used instead). The use of the aorist here can indeed be characterized as a "free reminiscence" of one such passage (see, e.g., E. D. Freed, Old Testament Quotations in the Gospel of John, NovTSup 11 [Leiden: E. J. Brill, 1965] 94–95). However, the use of the aorist can also be regarded as a deliberate and appropriate adaptation of either Ps 35:19 or Ps 69:5 to the immediate context of 15:22–24, which presents the earlier opposition of the world to Jesus from the point of view of a Jesus who has already undergone and surpassed the climax of that opposition and hatred.

41. The adverb may exhibit different denotations: "gratis" or "as a gift" (e.g., Matt 10:8); "in vain" or "to no purpose" (e.g., Gal 2:21); and "without cause," which is most appropriate here. In other words, given the fact and character of Jesus' mission of revelation from the Father, such hatred from the world was without cause and unjustified.

42. The introductory formula, elliptic in character (see BDF, 448.7), is the longest in the Gospel and occurs nowhere else. Two of its main components, however, can be found elsewhere in the Gospel. For a similar use of "word" (λόγος) to refer to and introduce a quotation from the Scriptures, see 12:38; for a similar use of "Law" in this very broad sense in such formulas, again with the possessive pronoun "their" modifying it, see 10:34. Such an attribution serves not only to identify the Jews as the main agents of such hatred in the world but also to establish a distinct sense of distance between this opposing group and the addressees as disciples of Jesus.

THE WORLD WILL HATE YOU!

This rationale further underlines and advances both the negative and the positive aspects of the preceding portrayal of the opposition of the world. On the one hand, the hatred and rejection of Jesus are further described thereby as being not only without cause but also in keeping with the plan of God as revealed in the Scriptures. That is, such hatred was foreseen and inevitable. On the other hand, the addressees are further assured thereby that their own hatred and rejection by the world as followers of Jesus are likewise not only in keeping with the plan of God but also without cause.

The temporal mode of reference of Jesus as speaker within this entire middle section remains the same as that of the first major section; namely, the hatred of the world described therein presupposes and includes the climax of such hatred, the final events of "the hour." Such a standpoint is reflected in the components of this middle section; for example, the contrary-to-fact conditions used to describe the status of the world prior to Jesus' coming, both in terms of the aorist indicatives employed in the protases of both conditions (ἦλθον; ἐλάλησα/ἐποίησα) and the implication conveyed by the apodoses to the effect that the world now finds itself in sin; the statements that describe the status of the world after Jesus' coming, whether in the explicit accusation of sin of the first contrast (οὐκ ἔχουσιν) or the explicit description of the world's reaction to Jesus of the second contrast (ἑωράκασιν; μεμισήκασιν);[43] and the formulation of the scriptural citation that provides the rationale for such hatred (ἐποίησαν). In other words, this is a hatred that has already been fully expressed and carried out, and this is, once again, a Jesus who has already undergone and surpassed the climax of such hatred.

This second and central major section shifts the focus of the unit away from the opposition of the world to the disciples to its earlier opposition to Jesus himself. Such an opposition is described in terms of hatred and given a twofold formulation insofar as Jesus' mission is sequentially presented in terms of its two fundamental components, his message and his works. Furthermore, this opposition is presented from the point of view of the completion of "the hour," so as the speaker, Jesus addresses the disciples as one who has already encountered and surpassed the fullness of the

43. As in the case of the perfect tense employed in the comparative statement of 15:18b (see n. 20 above), the use of the perfect here conveys not only the sense of a hatred of Jesus that has already run its full course but also the sense of an abiding hatred of Jesus that now finds concrete expression in a hatred of his disciples, those who continue his mission of revelation in the world. It should be noted in this regard that the corresponding description of the world's reaction to Jesus of the first contrast is presented instead in terms of a timeless declaration via the use of the gnomic present (μισῶν; μισεῖ).

world's hatred. Finally, the one rationale provided describes such hatred as fulfilling, and thus being in keeping with, the Scriptures.

From the point of view of both the target and the mode of such hatred, the shift represented by this central major section has been well anticipated in the first section. On the one hand, in both descriptions of the opposition of the world to the disciples outlined in the first section, such an opposition is not only patterned after, but also grounded in, the earlier opposition of the world to Jesus himself, which is similarly presented from the point of view of the completion of "the hour." On the other hand, the second such description anticipates what such hatred means, namely, the failure to believe in Jesus' claims vis-à-vis the Father. This second major section, therefore, develops and expands the opposition to Jesus already introduced in the first major section: the world hated Jesus by rejecting the whole of his ministry (both his message and his works) and in so doing hated the one who sent him, the Father, as well. The second section, however, does not explicitly include the element of active hatred or persecution raised in the second description of the first major section.

The second section, therefore, can be said to continue the fundamental aims of the first section and to anticipate those of the third and final section. Indeed, the second section serves as an extended rationale for the preceding warnings of 15:18–21 and those to follow in 15:26–16:4a, further accounting thereby for the forthcoming opposition and attempting to assuage its inevitable severe impact on the community of disciples. From a negative point of view, such an opposition is portrayed in severe terms, especially given the radical nature of the rejection involved: inexcusable sin, hatred of the Father, hatred without cause, and a fulfillment of the Scriptures. From a more positive point of view, such a portrayal of the opposition against Jesus can be readily extended to the opposition against his disciples as well, thus strengthening them with regard to their own status in relation to an unbelieving and hostile world and reaffirming them with regard to their own status in relation to Jesus and God the Father, who sent him.

Third Major Section (John 15:26–16:4a)

John 15:26–16:4a renews the focus on the hatred of the world for the disciples and thus represents the concluding outer component of the overall inclusion controlling this unit. The focus here on the disciples is more intensive than that of 15:18–21, because the hatred of the disciples is now no longer explicitly modeled after, or grounded in, an earlier hatred of Jesus himself. The reason for this change of emphasis in the presentation of the same focus is not difficult to ascertain. The explicit comparisons of 15:18–21 were meant in part to prepare for the main focus of the central section on the hatred of Jesus. Once such a hatred for Jesus has been properly explained in the central section of the unit, there is no perceived need in the final section to stress the comparative element of the first section. In effect, such a patterning and grounding have been clearly established and can be presupposed in any further mention of the hatred of the world for the disciples.

The structure for the second outer component follows, with variations, the structural pattern outlined for the unit as a whole: each description of the opposition of the world is accompanied by a corresponding rationale. As in the preceding central section, such a pattern appears only once in the final section. However, its basic sequence is now reversed for the first time in the unit; the corresponding rationale is given first (15:26–27), and the description of the opposition from the world follows (16:1–4a). Such a reversal is more than a simple stylistic variation. A rhetorical effect is intended as well, in which the concluding note of the unit becomes the highly intensified warnings concerning this opposition and its possible consequences for the body of disciples. Two other important variations will be described in the following examination of the description.

This renewed focus on the disciples is accompanied by the reappearance of another major structural pattern of the unit: concretization concerning the opposition of the world to the disciples is advanced another, final step. Thus, the first such description (15:18–19) presented the opposition to the disciples in terms of hatred; it implied a rejection of the disciples' own mission and claims concerning Jesus. The second description (15:20–21) further presented the opposition in terms of persecution; an active element of hatred was added to the given rejection of the disciples' mission and claims, now explained in greater detail as well. The central section of the unit (15:22–25) again described the earlier opposition to Jesus himself in terms of hatred and explicitly defined such hatred in terms of a complete rejection of Jesus' own mission and ministry, his message and his works (thus outlining in even greater detail what such hatred entails for the disciples as well). Finally, the concluding section further concretizes the opposition to the disciples themselves and describes the active element of persecution in terms of two specific channels, namely, radical social dislocation by means of expulsions from the synagogue and killings.

Rationale for Concrete Examples of Hatred and Persecution of the World (John 15:26–27)

The third Paraclete saying of the farewell discourse, 15:26–27, has often been regarded as a self-contained major section within this unit. This division is proposed by both the majority position (where it becomes the central major section) and the third minority position (where it emerges as the third of four such sections). Because the saying has nothing to add about the opposition of the world to either Jesus or his disciples, it is frequently regarded as a lone word of consolation in the midst of dire warnings and hence as a distinct major section within the unit.

However, a close analysis of the unit as a whole shows that the saying need not be regarded as a self-contained major section. On the one hand, as the introduction to this chapter has argued, the saying can be seen as fitting the first recurring structural pattern of the unit, in which each description of the opposition of the world, whether with regard to Jesus or his disciples, is accompanied by a specific rationale. Within this final major section, therefore, 15:26–27 provides such a rationale for the following description of 16:1–4a: it is the continued witness of the disciples to Jesus in and to the world that will bring about the severe response of the latter, as detailed in 16:2. On the other hand, though the saying does represent a word of consolation in the midst of woes, it is by no means the sole consolation in the unit. Others can be found in the preceding major sections; for example, (1) the inclusion of a positive reaction to the disciples on the part of the world in contrast to the primary one of "persecution" (15:20e–f) and (2) the characterization of the hatred of the world for Jesus (and, by extension, the characterization of its hatred for the disciples as well) as not only inexcusable sin but also hatred of the Father (15:22–25). When viewed from such a perspective, therefore, the third Paraclete saying of 15:26–27 emerges as an integral part of the final major section of the unit and, more specifically, as the rationale for the final description of the opposition of the world to the disciples of 16:1–4a.

This prophetic saying of 15:26–27, as the rationale for the final warnings that follow, presents a twofold structure centering on the continued "witness" to Jesus in the world after his own departure from it. Such witness is associated, first, with the promised figure of a Spirit-Paraclete (15:26) and, then, with the disciples themselves (15:27). However, such a twofold witness is in no way presented as either sequential or juxtaposed but instead as constituting one and the same witness; the explicit identification of the disciples as the sole recipients of the Spirit-Paraclete within the first part of the saying itself (15:26a) makes this clear.

The Witness of the Spirit-Paraclete (John 15:26)

The first part of the saying, the witness of the Spirit-Paraclete (15:26), reveals a twofold development. First, the origins and coming of the Paraclete are described (15:26a); second, the fundamental role of the Paraclete, and hence the purpose for the coming itself, is outlined (15:26b–c).[44]

---

44. The same two components can be found, in the same order, in the two previous Paraclete sayings of the first unit. In both 14:16–17a and 14:26, the origin is given first (14:16a–b, 26a–c) and then the role (14:16c–17a, 26d).

To begin with, therefore, the coming of the Paraclete (15:26a) is described in terms of sender (Jesus), recipients (the disciples), and source (the Father). Such a description of the circumstances surrounding the coming of this figure accomplishes several purposes: (1) it subordinates the Paraclete directly to Jesus as sender; (2) it establishes the origins of the Paraclete with the Father in the world above; and (3) it distinguishes the disciples in the world as the Paraclete's sole recipients and possessors. All these functions will resurface in the remainder of this saying, so this beginning description of the Paraclete's coming and origins directly prepares the way for what follows.[45]

Once the coming itself has been described, the role of the Paraclete is set forth (15:26b–c) in the form of an inclusion. Its outer components outline such a role (15:26b$_1$, 26c), with the first component pointing the way to the second. Its central component repeats the origins of the Paraclete with the Father in the world above (15:26b$_2$).

First, then, the Paraclete is characterized as "the Spirit of truth" (τὸ πνεῦμα τῆς ἀληθείας),[46] and thus is directly associated with the fundamental meaning, disclosure, and proclamation of the truth.[47] This first delineation of the Paraclete's role is followed immediately by a second reference to, and identification of, its source—the Paraclete as "coming from" the Father—thus restating and confirming the previous identification of

45. All these functions of the beginning description of origins can be found as well in the corresponding descriptions of 14:16–17a and 14:26, though, to be sure, with some variations in formulation. For example, although both of these sayings present the Father rather than Jesus as the sender of the Paraclete, the subordination of the latter to Jesus can be observed nonetheless in either the identification of Jesus as the one who asks the Father to send the Paraclete (14:16a$_1$) or in the characterization of such a sending by the Father as being in Jesus' name (14:26b$_2$). Similarly, these sayings convey the origins of the Paraclete with the Father in the world above not by an ablative of source like that conveyed here by the use of the prepositional phrase "from the Father" but rather through the designation of the Father as the sender of the Paraclete (14:16a$_2$, 26b$_2$). Given the very close relationship between Jesus and God the Father in the Johannine tradition, not much emphasis should be placed on the different identifications of the sender of the Paraclete in these two units of discourse. Finally, although the disciples themselves are mentioned as recipients only in the description of 14:16a, in both cases these sayings follow as promises upon the essential condition of love for Jesus on the part of the disciples; furthermore, the disciples are mentioned explicitly in the delineation of the Paraclete's role in both sayings (14:16b, 26d).
46. The characterization of the Paraclete as "Spirit" (15:26b$_1$) can also be found in the two previous sayings of 14:16–17a and 14:26. Its particular designation here as "the Spirit of truth," however, is exactly the same as that of the first saying (14:17a), whereas the second saying characterizes the Paraclete instead as "the holy Spirit" (14:26b). The emphasis here, therefore, lies once again not so much on the origins of the Paraclete in the world above (as in the second characterization of 14:26) but rather in its role with regard to the truth and thus Jesus (as in the first characterization of 14:16–17a).
47. On the meaning and consequences of such a designation for the Paraclete, see chap. 2, n. 67. Most important in this regard is the subordination to Jesus as "truth" that such a designation implies. Such a subordination is very much in keeping with both the previous description of Jesus as sender and the subsequent description of the Paraclete's role as one of witness concerning Jesus.

15:26a.[48] Finally, the earlier delineation of the Paraclete's role as the Spirit of truth is further clarified and expanded in terms of "witnessing" (15:26c)[49]—as the Spirit of truth, the Paraclete will witness with respect to Jesus—thus outlining the Paraclete's connection to the meaning, disclosure, and proclamation of the truth.[50] Therefore, this description of the Paraclete's role among the disciples serves not only to subordinate the Paraclete directly to Jesus once again but also to emphasize the Paraclete's own origins with the Father. The second delineation of this role, furthermore, sets the stage, through the theme of "witnessing," for the subsequent delineation of the disciples' own role with regard to Jesus as the recipients of the Spirit-Paraclete (15:27).

48. This second identification of origins is introduced by a relative clause modifying the given characterization of the Paraclete as "the Spirit of truth" and represents an expansion of the first identification of 15:26a. Thus, in effect, the simple ablative of source with the preposition παρά is now accompanied by the present indicative of the verb to come or to proceed from (ἐκπορεύεται), thereby stressing even more the origins of the Paraclete with the Father in the world above. The use of this verb to indicate origins with, or provenance from, the Father is unique in the Johannine literature (cf. 5:29).
49. This is the first and only time the theme of "witnessing" appears in the farewell discourse. In the remainder of the narrative, Jesus' own witness may refer to specific events (4:44; 13:21; cf. 2:25; 3:28; 12:17; 19:35); for the most part, however, it refers to his mission and ministry as a whole (3:11, 32–33; 5:31; 7:7; 8:13–14, 17–18; 18:37; cf. 18:23). Furthermore, certain other figures or things are also said to witness concerning Jesus and his mission: John the Baptist (1:7–8, 15, 19, 32, 34; 3:26; 5:33–34), the Samaritan woman (4:39), the Father (5:32; 8:18), the Scriptures (5:39), and Jesus' own works (5:36–37; 10:25). Witnessing, therefore, implies an open confession in, and/or a proclamation of, Jesus' own claims concerning his status and role with regard to the Father. Such a task is now specifically assigned to the Spirit-Paraclete and, through the Spirit-Paraclete, to the disciples themselves. This secures the continuation of Jesus' own mission of "witnessing" for the time after his departure; that is, his message will continue to be put forward in his absence.
50. This description of the role of the Paraclete in terms of "witnessing" to or concerning Jesus differs markedly from the corresponding formulations to be found in the two sayings of 13:31–14:31. It is in the role assigned to the Paraclete, therefore, that the main difference between the present saying of 15:26–27 and those of the first unit lies. First, although the Paraclete's role is similarly characterized in the first unit as "the Spirit of truth," the first saying (14:16–17a) describes it simply in terms of a permanent stay—in contrast to that of Jesus—among the disciples (14:16b). Then, the second saying (14:26) pursues the previous characterization of the Paraclete as "the Spirit of truth" in greater detail: in the course of its permanent stay among the disciples, the Paraclete will engage in a twofold, interrelated task, namely, teaching the disciples all things and recalling for them all that Jesus himself said during his ministry (14:26d). In other words, the task of the Spirit-Paraclete with regard to the truth is explicitly defined in terms of the group itself, leading the disciples to a complete understanding of Jesus' ministry and revelation.
This third saying (15:26–27), therefore, extends the function of the Paraclete one step further: insofar as the Spirit-Paraclete witnesses concerning Jesus, it continues to present Jesus' revelation to the world at large. In other words, its task with regard to the truth is now explicitly defined not so much in terms of action within the group but rather in terms of action toward outsiders (although through the group itself, as 15:27 makes clear). As such, the Paraclete's given task here is in keeping with the central focus of the unit, namely, the severe opposition that the disciples will encounter as a result of such an outward thrust in and to the world.

The Witness of the Disciples (John 15:27)

The second part of the saying, the witness of Jesus' own disciples (15:27), also presents a twofold development. The disciples' own proper and expected role as disciples is outlined (15:27a), and a further reason is provided for the assignment of such a role (15:27b). First, having been identified as the sole recipients of the promised Spirit-Paraclete, the disciples are now assigned the role previously assigned to the Paraclete itself: they too will witness concerning Jesus (15:27a).[51] Second, such witness will take place not only because the Spirit-Paraclete will be in their midst but also because they have been with Jesus "from the beginning" (ἀπ' ἀρχῆς)—that is, from the beginnings of the ministry through the climactic events of "the hour."[52]

Thus, it is only in and through the disciples, those who have been with Jesus from the beginning, that the Spirit-Paraclete will witness to Jesus in and to the world after the latter's departure from the world. The disciples are assured that their own continued witness to Jesus in the world will be directly guided by another figure from above. This reinforces the distinctive character of the disciples in the world; they, who were with Jesus all along, will be the sole recipients of Jesus' successor.

It has already been observed that this Paraclete saying functions as an additional word of comfort within the unit. That consolation can now be better defined in terms of a promised successor to Jesus. Such a successor is described as having the same origins as Jesus: the Paraclete will come from the Father in the world above. The successor is also described, like Jesus himself, as being fundamentally associated with the truth—its meaning, revelation, and proclamation. In other words, the Paraclete is characterized as the Spirit of truth. Such a successor is further assigned the same role as Jesus, though in clear subordination to Jesus. The Paraclete (sent by Jesus) will witness in and to the world (like Jesus himself). In so doing, however, the Paraclete will witness concerning Jesus; that is, it will continue Jesus'

51. The previous two sayings of 13:31–14:31 mention the disciples in the course of their formulations of the Paraclete's role (14:16b, 26c). This third saying mentions the disciples only after formally outlining the role of the Paraclete. However, given the earlier identification of the disciples as the recipients of the Paraclete in the beginning description of its coming (15:26) and the formulation of their own role in the same terms as that of the Paraclete at this point, it is clear that the Paraclete will carry out its assigned role of witnessing through the disciples' exercise of their own assigned role of witnessing. These two activities of witnessing concerning Jesus, therefore, are neither sequential nor juxtaposed, but parallel.

52. This concluding characterization of the disciples' own relationship to Jesus is not found elsewhere in the Gospel, where the term ἀρχή is used to refer either to Jesus' origins with the Father (1:1, 2; cf. 8:44) or to the beginnings of his own ministry in the world (6:64; 8:25). However, cf. 16:4b, where this term (with the preposition ἐκ) is used to refer to the mode of Jesus' revelation to the disciples from the beginning of their relationship (cf. 2:11). In the Johannine letters, this same expression (the term ἀρχή with the preposition ἀπό) appears repeatedly not so much with respect to the relationship itself but rather with regard to proper and correct teaching (1 John 1:1; 2:7, 24; cf. 2:13–14 and 2 John 5–6).

mission through an ongoing presentation of his message and claims in and to the world after his departure. The disciples thus are assured that their own witness in and to the world will be directly sustained and guided by another figure from above, the Spirit-Paraclete who will, as Jesus' successor, take his own place among them.

With this promise of the Spirit-Paraclete, however, the temporal standpoint of the unit shifts. In the first two major sections the standpoint of Jesus as speaker was clearly that of a Jesus who had already gone through the final events of "the hour," except for his final return to the Father, and the situation of the disciples reflected in turn their own full acceptance of, and belief in, Jesus as seen through the eyes of "the hour." The presence of this Paraclete saying in the unit qualifies the standpoint of Jesus as speaker. This is a Jesus who has gone through the climactic events of "the hour," except for both the bestowal of the Spirit-Paraclete upon the disciples as his own successor among them and his final return to the Father. The situation of the disciples is also more narrowly described. They are about to receive the Spirit-Paraclete, who will bring them to full faith and understanding, allow their own mission to take place, and serve as Jesus' successor in their midst after his final return to the Father.

Finally, it has already been mentioned as well that the mission of the disciples in and to the world that this saying grounds and affirms through the theme of "witnessing" has echoes elsewhere in the unit. Perhaps even more important than these echoes, however, is the relationship that can be posited between the saying itself and the rest of the unit. It is precisely because of such a witness to Jesus, guided by the Spirit-Paraclete as Jesus' own successor among the disciples, that the latter are warned about the direct consequences of such a mission in and to the world. The disciples, like Jesus himself at an earlier time, will meet with some acceptance, but opposition will prevail (and a harsh opposition indeed, characterized in terms of hatred and persecution). In fact, the saying itself also functions as a concrete introduction, by way of rationale, to the final formulation of such an opposition in the unit.

Description: Concrete Examples of the Hatred and Persecution of the World (John 16:1–4a)

The final, most severe description of the opposition of the world to the disciples is presented in the form of an inclusion (16:1–4a). The outer components provide the immediate purpose behind not only the warnings of this concluding major section but also those of the first section (16:1, 4a). The central component specifically outlines the basic modes of such an opposition on the part of the world (16:2–3).

The framing statements of purpose ultimately refer to all the warnings of the unit, not just those of this final major section. It is better, therefore, to begin by analyzing the final description of opposition as contained in the central component. It is developed in two steps: a statement of the warnings proper (16:2) followed by the formulation of another rationale for the given opposition (16:3). This final description of the opposition, furthermore, contains two further variations of the overall structural pattern of the unit. First, the description provides a second rationale for the opposition. Second, within the description is a double formulation of the opposition, not by repetition but by escalation and intensification.[53] Like the reversal of its basic sequence within this third major section, these other variations of the overall structural pattern are not simply stylistic but also have a rhetorical intention. The second rationale reiterates the fundamental reason for such an opposition at the end of the unit, and the double formulation directly and starkly outlines, again at the end of the unit, what the disciples should inevitably expect in their own witnessing in and to the world.

To begin with, then, the statement of the warnings proper (16:2) continues the pattern of concretization observed throughout the unit by revealing the specific ways in which the active element of persecution against the disciples, introduced in 15:20–21, will be carried out by the world. Two such modes of persecution are outlined in a clearly ascending fashion reinforced by the intensive use of the adversative conjunction ἀλλά, "indeed," at the beginning of the second mode. The first is described directly and succinctly: the disciples should expect a forced separation from their respective synagogues (16:2a).[54] The second is presented in a more indirect

53. A second rationale is also included in the second description of the opposition to the disciples within the first major section (15:20–21). However, whereas the first rationale (15:20a–b) extends to both the positive and negative reactions of the world to the disciples that follow, the second rationale (15:21) applies exclusively to the latter, the statement of opposition. In the present instance, however, both the first (15:26–27) and second rationales (16:3) apply to the same statement of opposition. Similarly, a double formulation of opposition is also found within the central major section, whereby successive affirmations of hatred for Jesus are grounded on the different fundamental aspects of his mission (15:22–23, 24). In the present instance, however, such a double formulation of the opposition is given not only in terms of its different channels but also in ascending fashion, thus conveying a sense of an escalating opposition as well.

54. This first warning consists of a simple predictive future, employing the verb to make (ποιήσουσιν) with a double accusative—that of the receiver of the action (the disciples, "you") and that of the condition brought about by the action "un-synagogued" (ἀποσυναγώγους)— best rendered as "they shall expel you from the synagogues." Such a procedure has already been mentioned in the Gospel. In 9:18–23 the reticence of the parents of the man born blind is explained on the basis of an agreement by the authorities to the effect that anyone who acknowledges Jesus as Messiah would be "un-synagogued" (with the verb γίνεσθαι); this is precisely what happens to the man born blind in 9:24–34 (v. 34). In 12:36b–43, within the narrator's summary of Jesus' preceding ministry, such reticence is attributed to some of the Jewish authorities themselves, and a severe judgment is passed on such behavior (12:43). An immediate sign of hatred and persecution, therefore, is an expulsion of the disciples from their

and expansive way: the disciples should expect even death at the hands of the world (16:2b). Ironically, such death is presented as an offering to God on the part of the world, so the world, while believing to worship God through such actions, shows that it actually hates God and is guilty of an inexcusable sin.[55] As a result, the disciples are warned that the hatred and persecution of the world will entail not only expulsions from the synagogues but also death itself.

Such a statement of warnings further confirms the thrust of the central major section by more precisely identifying the source of such hatred and persecution. In effect, the given formulation of the first mode of persecution outlined in 16:2a reaffirms the attribution already conveyed by the introductory formula of the scriptural citation of 15:24. Thus, just as the hatred of the world for Jesus is presented therein as being in accord with "their Law," so now the disciples are warned that they are to expect, first, forced separation from "the synagogues"; in other words, the Jews again emerge as the primary representatives of an unbelieving and hostile world. It is from that quarter, therefore, that the disciples, like Jesus before them, can expect hatred and persecution.

A second rationale for such behavior on the part of the world (16:3) is attached to the statement of warnings proper. This rationale reformulates the earlier rationale within 15:20–21, the first warning of an active hatred or persecution against the disciples. Thus, in further accounting for the acts of persecution outlined in the preceding warning of 16:2, this second rationale within the final major section repeats the previous rationale of 15:21

---

respective "synagogues," with all the social dislocation that such an expulsion implies. For a connection of such an agreement with the much broader Benediction against the Heretics, see J. L. Martyn, *History and Theology in the Fourth Gospel*, 2d ed., rev. and enl. (Nashville: Abingdon, 1979) 24–62. See further in this regard R. Kimelman, "*Birkat Ha-Minim* and the Lack of Evidence for an Anti-Christian Jewish Prayer in Late Antiquity," in *Jewish and Christian Self-Definition*, 3 vols., ed. E. P. Sanders (Philadelphia: Fortress, 1981) 2:226–44; W. Horbury, "The Benediction of the *Minim* and Early Jewish-Christian Controversy," *JTS* 33 (1982) 19–61.

55. The second warning, introduced by the conjunction ἀλλά with a clear emphatic and ascensive sense (BDF, 448.6), is developed differently than the first. Instead of a simple predictive future, one finds a beginning reference to an "hour" (ὥρα) that is coming (with a futuristic present) and a description or explanation of this "hour" by means of a ἵνα clause with a definite temporal quality (BDF, 382.1). This clause contains an example of indirect discourse. The subject of the clause conveys the warning proper via the use of a substantive participle with the distributive adjective πᾶς—"whoever or every one who kills you." Thus, a further and more secure sign of hatred and persecution will be that of death itself at the hands of the world; in effect, the disciples will also experience in the course of their own witness to Jesus the climax of hatred and persecution that Jesus himself experienced (15:22–25). The irony that accompanies such a death is specifically conveyed by the indirect discourse that follows: the perpetrators will believe (δόξῃ) that such deeds against Jesus' disciples will constitute the offering of service or worship to God (λατρείαν προσφέρειν). The irony is even stronger if the reference is to the sacrificial cult as such. See H. Strathmann, "*Latreuō, Latreia,*" *TDNT* 4 (1967) 58–65.

used with regard to persecution in general: such behavior arises out of a failure on the part of the world to accept both Jesus and, through Jesus, God the Father.[56] The two rationales of 15:26–27 and 16:3 within this third major section are closely linked. It is in the witness of the disciples, sustained and guided by the presence of the Spirit-Paraclete among them, that the claims of Jesus as the unique messenger of God will be made in and to the world (15:26–27), and in its violent rejection of those claims and their proponents the world will reveal its continued failure to know Jesus and God the Father as the one who sent him (16:3), despite the world's protestations to the contrary (16:2b). The presence of this second rationale at the close of the section and the unit serves as a direct reminder to the disciples of the world's fundamental inability to perceive Jesus' role and identity.

Surrounding this final description of opposition from the world, then, are the two statements of purpose that serve as the outer components of the inclusion governing the whole of 16:1–4a (16:1, 4a). Both statements of purpose are introduced by the recurring formula, "These things I have said to you," which serves as a distinct concluding marker within the farewell speech as a whole. The statements outline the basic purpose not only for the concrete warnings of 16:2–3 encased within them but also for the more general warnings and explanations of the two preceding major sections. The demonstrative pronoun ταῦτα, therefore, covers not just the final declarations of 16:1–4a but all the declarations of the entire unit of discourse, including those of 16:1–4a.

The two statements of purpose are integrally related; the second such statement of 16:4a can be seen as providing the basic grounds for the first statement of 16:1. Furthermore, whereas the first statement is succinct, the second is more developed. Thus, to begin with, the concrete, severe

---

56. Indeed, the introduction to the rationale itself is the same introduction as that of 15:21, except that the disciples as the target of these actions are not explicitly mentioned here. The textual tradition contains several attempts to introduce the personal pronoun and thus the target of these actions; the strongest of these consists of the simple incorporation of a dative of indirect object (ὑμῖν: ℵ D L Ψ pl). However, not only is the textual evidence for omission strong (A B K pl) but also the addition can be readily explained in terms of assimilation to 15:21. With regard to the introductory formula, the demonstrative pronoun should be seen as encompassing not only the specific actions described in 16:2 but also, at this point, the previous reactions outlined in 15:18–21. With regard to the rationale itself, the double step present in 15:21—the reference to Jesus via the prepositional phrase and the reference to the Father via the causal clause—is eliminated in favor of a single declaration combining both references via a similar causal clause. Thus, both Jesus and the Father (now identified as such rather than as Jesus' sender) are now presented as the direct object of the same verb *to know* in the causal clause (now used as constative aorist rather than as a gnomic present). Just as the double step of 15:21 served as a specific transition to the central major section of 15:22–25, so does the single declaration here reflect specific developments within that central section (15:23, 24c).

warnings of 16:2–3 are prefaced by a brief statement to the effect that the disclosure of such forthcoming events is meant to prevent the disciples from "stumbling" (that is, from falling away from, or abandoning, the group in the face of such opposition).[57] After these warnings have been outlined, a concluding statement explains that such disclosures are to be recalled at the time of the events' occurrence; thus, it explains how such "stumbling" can be avoided.[58] In other words, both the foretelling and foreknowledge of this active opposition from the world and the subsequent

57. The beginning statement of purpose consists of a simple verb form, in the negative, within the purpose clause that follows the introductory formula: "so that you do not stumble" (μὴ σκανδαλισθῆτε). Such an exhortation to the disciples—to those who have fully accepted Jesus' word and who witness to that word in and to the world—is unique in the Gospel. The only other reference to "stumbling" is that of 6:61, but the referent there is not the group of disciples as such (6:67–72) but instead the multitude that witnessed the miracle of the feeding across the Sea of Galilee (6:1–15), followed Jesus back to Capernaum (6:22–24), and then engaged in conversation with him (6:25–59) regarding his claims concerning his status and role in regard to the Father. Such "stumbling" is therein described from a double and ascending perspective: on the basis of Jesus' claims thus far in the conversation or on the basis of his manner of death still to come in the narrative (6:62–65). The multitude in question "stumbles" over the former, in this case, and abandons Jesus en masse prior to the death itself (6:66). The "stumbling" of the disciples envisioned in 16:1, however, is different: their "possible stumbling" is not on the basis of the claims or of Jesus' own death, but rather on the basis of the opposition they are to encounter from a hostile and rejecting world.
58. The concluding statement of purpose includes both a beginning temporal clause and a clause containing indirect discourse framing the main verb within the purpose clause that follows the introductory formula: "so that, when their hour arrives, you recall them, that I spoke to you [of them]." The temporal clause refers back to the coming "hour" that introduced the second warning of 16:2 concerning possible death at the hands of the world; in this way, however, the coming "hour" is expanded to include both the possibility of death and the expulsions from the synagogues, as the use of the accompanying pronoun αὐτῶν indicates.
Two points need further comment. First, the presence of the genitive of the personal pronoun is not universal in the textual tradition, with regard to either this latter one modifying "hour" or the one functioning as a genitive of root idea with the main verb of the purpose clause. Some manuscripts remove the first but leave the second; some leave the first but remove the second; and some remove both. However, the backing for the double presence of these pronouns is strong (p[66vid] A B θ Π° 33 al), and the omission of either one is easier to explain than its inclusion as a way of avoiding such close and unnecessary repetition. Second, although the use of the term "the hour" is prominent and important in the Gospel, its use here is unique. Whereas "the hour" elsewhere refers primarily to some aspect of Jesus' hour of glorification (2:4; 4:21, 23; 5:25, 28; 7:30; 8:20; 11:9; 12:23, 27; 13:1; 19:27; cf. 16:21, 25, 32; 17:1), this is the only instance where "the hour" refers to the hatred and persecution of the disciples by the world. Thus, although "the hour" is directly associated with the modes of persecution to be used against the disciples, it is indirectly connected with the disciples themselves, thus expanding its basic meaning in the Gospel: as Jesus had his appointed "hour," so will his disciples.
The exhortation proper to the disciples resumes the theme of "recalling" from the first rationale of 15:20a–b within 15:20–21 (see n. 21 above). A somewhat different temporal perspective is to be observed between these two applications of the same theme (whereas in 15:20–21 the recalling takes place within the context of the warning itself, in 16:4 such a recalling is meant to take place after the context of warning and within the context of historical fulfillment). In both cases, however, the recalling itself functions as a way of softening the negative impact of the persecution of the world (just as in 15:20a–b the disciples are asked to recall a previous saying of Jesus as a way of grounding the eventual twofold reaction of

recollection of such foretelling and foreknowledge at the actual occurrence of the opposition are presented thereby as an effective means of assuaging the inevitable shock of the disciples at the sight of such developments and thus of preventing their "stumbling" in the face of such encounters with the world. In the light of the unit as a whole, furthermore, these concluding statements of purpose make it clear that a full knowledge of the opposition of the world—a knowledge that encompasses such an opposition in all of its various causes and dimensions, its unsparing severity, and its inevitability—is meant to help the disciples in coping with the consequences of their witness to Jesus in and to the world.

In the third and final major section, the focus of the unit returns to that of the first major section, the opposition of the world to the disciples themselves. The nature of the opposition continues to be described in ascending fashion, so the general warning of persecution of 15:20–21 now yields to the more concrete warnings of expulsions from the synagogues and even death itself (16:2). However, such an opposition is now no longer directly patterned after, or grounded in, the earlier opposition to Jesus himself, as in the first two delineations of 15:18–21. Thus, concretization intensifies, whereas patterning, which served as a direct introduction to the central section of 15:22–25, is now set aside, though certainly presupposed in the light of the preceding central section.

Given the previous exposition of the central section concerning the opposition of the world to Jesus himself, such explicit patterning or grounding is unnecessary at this point in the unit. Again, the earlier section as a whole can be said to function as an extended rationale for both the preceding general warnings of 15:18–21 and their more concrete extension in 15:26–16:4a. In other words, it is because the world rejected Jesus as it did that it proceeds to take the same measures against those who believe in him and continue his mission in and to the world. Whereas in 15:18–21 such a grounding was directly anticipated, in 15:26–16:4a such a grounding is presupposed.

As in the two preceding major sections, this more concrete description of opposition on the part of the world is presented from the point of view of the

---

the world to them [acceptance/persecution], so in 16:4a the disciples are asked to recall, in the heat of the persecution, the present disclosures of both 16:2 and the unit as a whole as a way of avoiding "stumbling"). As in the previous case of 15:20a–b, furthermore, this recalling of 16:4a has nothing to do with a deeper understanding of Jesus' sayings or teachings through the figure of the Spirit-Paraclete, as posited in the first farewell unit.

The concluding ὅτι clause introducing indirect discourse simply specifies that the recalling involves not only the specific measures in question as conveyed through the personal pronoun but also the fact that Jesus disclosed them ahead of time. It makes explicit what would otherwise remain implicit.

completion of "the hour." A slight qualification also is introduced through the presence of the Paraclete saying of 15:26–27. The disciples are warned as those who already have accepted Jesus' revelation and believed in him and now are about to receive the Spirit-Paraclete, thus bringing them to full belief and understanding. Jesus warns the disciples as one who is both about to impart his successor to and among them and about to leave for the Father.

Like the previous warnings of 15:18–21 concerning hatred and persecution, these further warnings of explusions from the synagogues and killings are accompanied by additional rationales that are meant to account for such measures and that thus help assuage their inevitable severe blow on the body of the disciples: (1) the disciples as witnessing to Jesus in and to the world with the help and support of the Spirit-Paraclete among them and (2) the continued failure of the world to accept Jesus' claims concerning his status and role in relation to the Father. Finally, this section adds a twofold statement of purpose explaining the reason for such disclosures to the disciples. Such statements cover not only these final warnings but the unit as a whole, thus pointing out the fundamental purpose for this third unit of discourse— to prevent stumbling or faltering by means of foretelling, foreknowledge, and recollection.

STRATEGIC CONCERNS AND AIMS

John 15:18–16:4a can also be seen as a unified and coherent strategic whole that interacts with its literary structure and development. This third unit of discourse is concerned with the external affairs of the community of disciples after the departure of Jesus. It focuses on the proper relationship of the disciples to outsiders, to the world at large. Such strategic concerns are guided and informed by a number of interdependent aims, which yield a variety of strategic functions for the unit as a whole. Admonition and exhortation emerge as the primary functions of this unit, like the second unit. However, the admonitory function now becomes more prominent and pervasive than the exhortative. Didactic, consolatory, and polemical functions are secondary.

The admonitory function can be discerned in the first and third major sections of the unit, where the forthcoming relationship between the disciples and the world is described in terms of inevitable, severe, and unrelenting opposition to come from the world. The disciples are, in effect, explicitly and repeatedly warned with regard to the nature and circumstances of this forthcoming opposition; in fact, such opposition is progressively circumscribed by the structural pattern of concretization. The opposition of the world is sequentially described in terms of (1) hatred, the first and broadest description, encompassing all subsequent concretizations but denoting above all the rejection by the world of the disciples' mission and claims concerning Jesus; (2) persecution, the intermediate description, introducing an active element of hostility within such hatred and rejection; and (3) expulsions from the synagogues and killings, the final and most concrete description, disclosing the specific modes for the active persecution arising from such hatred and rejection.

This ongoing concretization of the opposition of the world is thus presented in an ascending pattern, not only in terms of the sequence as a whole but also in terms of its final component in and of itself; in effect, the element of active hostility and outright violence increases dramatically as the concretization continues. As a result, the disciples are warned more and more severely about the nature of the opposition to come from the world outside, a world that will not only refuse to accept their mission and claims but also take active, drastic measures against them.

The exhortative function is limited to two brief statements within the final major section: the explicit declarations of purpose of 16:1 and 16:4a. This function, however, ultimately involves the unit as a whole, insofar as these declarations of purpose extend to and encompass the entire unit and its various disclosures and warnings. As a frame to the final, most concrete, and most severe warning of opposition, therefore, the disciples are told, by these two explicit declarations of purpose, that they are to recall such warnings and disclosures when the envisioned time of opposition arrives and thereby prevent their stumbling or falling away from the community. In other words, in the face of the forthcoming opposition, the disciples are urged to endure as disciples of Jesus in the midst of an unbelieving and hostile world and to avoid succumbing to the inevitable onslaught from the world by recalling all these farewell predictions and disclosures. A comparison with the preceding unit of discourse is helpful. Although the possibility of stumbling or faltering supplies the explicit purpose for the disclosures of the unit as a whole, in the end this possibility is by no means as strongly entertained, developed, or addressed as it was in 15:11–17. One finds, for example, neither urgent and repeated calls to abide nor a portrayal of the dire consequences to follow for those who surrender to the world and its pressures. The envisioned stumbling remains a possibility that is important and real but remote and infrequent as well.

The didactic function is present in not only all three major sections of the unit but also the unit as a whole, given the specific role of the central major section within the unit. As such, this function can be examined from both a circumscribed and a general perspective.

In keeping with the recurring structural pattern present in all three major sections of the unit, each warning regarding the forthcoming opposition from the world in the two outer major sections is immediately accompanied by at least one corresponding rationale for such an opposition; the second and third warnings provide two such rationales. Although each of these rationales is attached to a specific warning, in the end they are inter-changeable and can be applied not only to the other warnings of the unit but also to the series of warnings as a whole. Consequently, the forthcoming opposition from the world is ultimately explained from a variety of interdependent perspectives: (1) the fundamental status of the disciples with regard to Jesus and the world (the disciples as those who are not "of the world" because they were "chosen" by Jesus "out of the world," who bear the name of Jesus); (2) the basic role of the disciples with regard to Jesus and the world (the disciples as those who have been with Jesus "from the beginning" and who witness concerning him in and to the world after his departure); and (3) the disciples' duplication of Jesus' fate in the world, given such status and role (the disciples [or "servants"] as not greater than Jesus [their "master"], with the continued failure of the world to recognize the Father in Jesus through their own mission in and to the world). Because of such a privileged status and role, as well as the previous treatment accorded to Jesus by the world, the forthcoming opposition is ultimately presented as comprehensible and inescapable.

This internal structural pattern is reflected in the overall structure of the unit: the central major section functions as an extended rationale for the ascending series of warnings developed in the framing major sections. The opposition of the world to Jesus was mentioned in the first section as both a rationale for the opposition to the disciples themselves and a comparative pattern whereby the fate of the disciples is explicitly modeled after that of Jesus. The central section pursues this opposition in much greater detail. As a result, the forthcoming opposition against the disciples themselves receives a more solid grounding.

First, the opposition to Jesus is presented, as in the case of the first warning to the disciples, in the most general terms of "hatred" and is described in terms of a complete rejection of his entire mission and ministry. Second, such hatred is further presented as having severe consequences for the world: the hatred constitutes sin; such sin is inexcusable; and such hatred involves hatred of the Father as well. Third, following the internal structural pattern mentioned above, such hatred (now further described as without cause) is given specific rationale as a fulfillment of the Scriptures and thus in keeping with the plan of God. Given the disciples' own status and role in and to the world (a continued witness to Jesus), the forthcoming opposition of the world to them can only constitute once again inexcusable sin, hatred without reason, a fulfillment of the Scriptures, and hatred of the Father on the part of the world. Similarly, given the explicit grounding of this forthcoming opposition on the earlier opposition to Jesus himself, such an opposition is again presented as comprehensible and inescapable.

From both its circumscribed and general perspectives, therefore, this didactic function presents the forthcoming opposition from the world as understandable and inevitable by providing a complete account or explanation of its underlying causes. As such, the didactic function remains subordinate to the admonitory and exhortative functions: given such understanding and foreknowledge, the disciples should only expect the worst and endure accordingly as disciples of Jesus.

The consolatory function, which is directly at work in the first and third major sections (where the opposition of the world to the disciples is developed) is more limited. In the first section the consolation is brief and undeveloped. Within the second warning regarding the forthcoming opposition from the world, the persecution of the world is directly contrasted with a certain acceptance from the world. In the third section, within the rationale that grounds the third warning as a whole, this consolation is much more developed. The disciples will be the sole recipients and possessors of the Spirit-Paraclete (Jesus' successor to and among them); this Spirit-Paraclete will witness concerning Jesus after his departure; and it will do so in and through the disciples themselves and their own continued witness to Jesus. This function is also indirectly present in the second major section: insofar as their fate is grounded in and parallels that of Jesus, the disciples are ultimately assured that for the world such opposition is tantamount to inexcusable sin and hatred of God.

This consolatory function serves as a direct and deliberate counterpart to the admonitory function. Thus, despite the world's severe and unrelenting opposition against them, the disciples are reassured that their own mission in and to the world will not be without proper help from above in the form of the Spirit-Paraclete as Jesus' successor in their midst and that their mission will indeed meet with some success, some acceptance, some belief. This reassurance blunts the unsettling nature of the repeated warnings and provides the disciples with encouragement to go on in the face of such adversity. The didactic function can be said to possess a consolatory dimension as well: knowledge of the underlying causes of the opposition is meant to mollify its effects upon the disciples.

Finally, a polemical function is also important, as the emphasis on the forthcoming opposition of the world makes clear. The disciples are explicitly and repeatedly differentiated from the world at large so that their own claims are affirmed, and those of the world are questioned and attacked. This function operates in all three major sections and is closely linked throughout to both the admonitory and didactic functions.

In the first section the process of differentiation begins with the rationales for the forthcoming opposition. Jesus has called the disciples out of the world, and as a result, they now bear his name and are no longer of the world, no longer belong to the world. As such, the disciples, unlike the world, know the Father, the one who sent Jesus. The second section contains a brief allusion to the identity of this world of unbelief and hostility. The scriptural citation that serves as rationale for the hatred of the world against Jesus is introduced in terms of "their Law," thus pointing to the Jews as the preeminent representatives of the world. Such a world is accused of inexcusable sin and hatred of the Father, attitudes that further distinguish it from the community of disciples. The third section concludes the process of differentiation with a further identification of the disciples as those who have been with Jesus from the beginning and a more explicit reference to the source of the forthcoming opposition. The concrete description of the radical social dislocation that will take place in terms of expulsions from the synagogues again points to the Jews as the primary representatives of the world, as those directly responsible for the drastic measures to be taken against the disciples of Jesus. Such a world, furthermore, is ironically portrayed at the end as undertaking all such actions against the disciples as an offering to God—the very God whom Jesus and the disciples reveal and proclaim.

Consequently, the disciples stand out as disciples of Jesus in the midst of an unbelieving and extremely hostile world—a world that reacts with violence and mounting aggression against them and that is primarily represented by the Jewish synagogue. Despite all the evidence to the contrary, therefore, the polemical function assures the disciples that it is they who represent the ways of God in the world, who offer proper worship to God in and through Jesus.

The character of this unit as a strategic whole points to a twofold rhetorical situation, or view of the implied readers by the implied author. On the one hand, the disciples are viewed as in need of urgent admonition and exhortation. In the face of inevitable, severe, and unrelenting opposition from the world, the possibility of their stumbling or faltering—of their caving in to these overwhelming pressures from the outside in the course of their mission in and to the world—is seen as real. On the other hand, the disciples are also viewed in an overall positive light, as being still essentially united. Their status and role as disciples of Jesus—as those called by Jesus, those who bear the name of Jesus, and those who witness to Jesus—are presupposed and affirmed. Their status and role in the world are also sharply set off against an unbelieving, hostile world. Thus, though the possibility of faltering is seen as real, it does not yet appear to be an everyday reality. In the end, this twofold rhetorical situation, with its perceived socioreligious exigencies, called forth the complex and effective response contained within this third unit of discourse.

5

IT IS BETTER FOR YOU THAT I LEAVE!
John 16:4b-33

STRUCTURAL OUTLINE

A. Jesus' departure and the disciples (16:4b-15)
 1. Jesus' disclosure of departure and its destination (16:4b-5a)
     a) Jesus' previous silence concerning the departure (16:4b-c)
     b) Jesus' present disclosure of departure and its destination (16:5a)
 2. The disciples' reaction to Jesus' disclosure of departure and its destination (16:5b-6)
     a) Disciples' silence concerning Jesus' destination (16:5b-c)
     b) Disciples' sorrow concerning Jesus' departure (16:6)
 3. Jesus' departure and its consequences for the disciples (16:7-15)
     a) Jesus' departure and the Spirit-Paraclete (16:7)
         (1) Jesus' departure as beneficial for the disciples (16:7a-b)
         (2) Rationale: The coming of the Spirit-Paraclete (16:7c-f)
     b) The role of the Spirit-Paraclete (16:8-15)
         (1) The Spirit-Paraclete and the world (16:8-11)
             (a) Spirit-Paraclete's coming as condition (16:8a)
             (b) Spirit-Paraclete's role vis-à-vis the world: Conviction of the world (16:8b)
             (c) Rationale (16:9-11)
         (2) The Spirit-Paraclete and the disciples (16:12-15)
             (a) Present situation of the disciples (16:12)
             (b) Future situation of the disciples (16:13-15)
B. Jesus' departure and return and the disciples (16:16-24)
 1. Jesus' disclosure of departure and return: The coming situation of the disciples (16:16)
     a) Disclosure of departure: Disciples' inability to see Jesus (16:16a)
     b) Disclosure of return: Disciples' renewed ability to see Jesus (16:16b)

2. The disciples' reaction to Jesus' disclosure of departure and return
   (16:17-18)
   a) Question concerning Jesus' disclosures of departure/return and
      destination of departure (16:17)
   b) Question concerning time references (16:18a-b)
   c) Disciples' acknowledgment of failure to understand (16:18c)
3. Jesus' departure and return: Further consequences for the disciples
   (16:19-24)
   a) Jesus' knowledge of the disciples' reaction (16:19)
   b) Consequences of Jesus' departure and return for the disciples
      (16:20-24)
      (1) Jesus' departure and the disciples (16:20a-b)
          (a) Sorrow as the attitude of the disciples (16:20c)
          (b) Joy as the attitude of the world (16:20d)
      (2) Jesus' departure and return and the disciples (16:20c-22)
          (a) Identification of the disciples' contrasting attitudes:
              Sorrow/joy (16:20c-d)
          (b) Example of the child-bearing woman (16:21)
          (c) Identification of the disciples' contrasting attitudes:
              Sorrow/joy (16:22)
      (3) Jesus' return and the disciples (16:23-24)
          (a) The disciples and Jesus (16:23)
          (b) The disciples and the Father (16:24)
C. Jesus' revelation and the disciples (16:25-33)
   1. Jesus' disclosure of nature and content of revelation (16:25-28)
      a) Nature and content of Jesus' revelation (16:25)
         (1) Present revelation as in figures (16:25a)
         (2) Future revelation as without figures and open (16:25b)
      b) Future situation of the disciples: Granting of requests to the Father
         in Jesus' name (16:26-27)
      c) Content of Jesus' revelation: Disclosure of identity (16:28)
         (1) Disclosure of Jesus' origins (16:28a)
         (2) Disclosure of Jesus' destination (16:28b)
   2. The disciples' reaction to Jesus' disclosure of the nature and content of
      his revelation (16:29-30)
      a) Characterization of Jesus' present revelation as open (16:29)
      b) Characterization of Jesus as the one come from God (16:30)
   3. Jesus' departure and its consequences for the disciples (16:31-33)
      a) Negative consequences of the departure (16:31-32a)
         (1) Question regarding the disciples' belief in him (16:31)
         (2) The future situation of the disciples: Dispersion and
             abandonment of Jesus (16:32a)

b) Positive consequences of the departure (16:32b-33)
   (1) Jesus' relationship to the Father (16:32b)
   (2) Jesus' reassurance of the disciples (16:33)

THE PROPOSED BEGINNING FOR THE FOURTH unit of discourse within the farewell speech depends on the delineation of the third unit. Because of the preceding adoption of 15:18–16:4a as the third unit of discourse, 16:4b becomes the point of departure for the fourth unit. The determination of a proper conclusion for this new unit of discourse is not as problematic as that of the second or third unit of discourse, but there is no definite consensus.

JOHN 16:4b-33 AS A FOURTH UNIT OF DISCOURSE

Two traditional positions are well represented in the literature. The first and more frequent position by far, the designation of 16:33 as the final major break in these chapters and the corresponding identification of 16:4b–33 as the third unit of discourse within John 15–16,[1] is based on two critical observations:

1. The reappearance, for the first time since the first unit, of the themes of Jesus' departure from and return to the disciples in these verses.
2. The reappearance, again for the first time since the first unit, of reactions to Jesus on the part of the assembled disciples.

The second and much less common position posits a major break at 16:15, thus formally dividing the remainder of chapter 16 into two distinct units of discourse made up of 16:4b–15 and 16:16–33, respectively.[2] Several common arguments justify such a division:

1. The exclusive focus of 16:4b–15 on the figure of the Spirit-Paraclete, which is not continued at all past 16:16.

1. Among those who posit a major break at 16:4a, see, e.g., Wellhausen, 71–75; Lagrange, 398–99, 417; Huby, 68–69, 91; Bover, 16, 127 (beginning with John 16:5); Behler, 177, 280; Brown, 2:709, 727–29; Schnackenburg, 3:123–25. In the more recent literature, see Painter, 536–40; Simoens, 151–52 (beginning with John 16:4a itself).
2. Among those who argue for a major break at 16:4a, see, e.g., van den Bussche, 120–27; Strathmann, 208. A similar division usually obtains among those who extend the preceding unit of discourse through 16:15, with 16:4b–15 as a major section within a larger unit of discourse (see chap. 4, n. 3).

2. The corresponding focus of 16:16–33 on Jesus' departure from, and return to, the disciples, as well as its focus on the further consequences of such a return, which are presented in terms of a transition from a situation of sorrow and lack of understanding to one of full understanding and joy.
3. The reappearance of the disciples in 16:16–33, with uninterrupted speech of Jesus through 16:15.

The critical observations that follow argue on behalf of 16:4b–33 as the fourth unit of discourse within John 15–16. The prophecy regarding the scattering of the disciples and their abandonment of Jesus at the climactic time of "the hour," the twofold exhortation to peace and joy, and the triumphal declaration of Jesus' victory over the world in 16:32–33 bestow on these verses a sense of conclusion not found anywhere else in chapter 16 after 16:1–4a. This sense of closure is immediately reinforced by the distinctive farewell prayer that follows in chapter 17, with its unmistakable sense of a new beginning, a new point of departure.

The recurring concluding formula of the discourse, "These things I have said to you," does not appear anywhere near 16:15; however, it appears in 16:25 and 16:33. As in 14:25 and 15:11, the first example (16:25) signals by anticipation the forthcoming conclusion of the unit; similarly, as in 16:1 and 16:4a (with a further reinforcement in 16:6), the second example (16:33) directly signals such a conclusion. In addition, this double presence of the formula at the end of the unit provides, as in 16:1–4a, a distinctive and effective frame for the concluding subdivision of the unit, in this case the final major section of 16:25–33.

I agree with the first traditional argument on behalf of a proposed division at 16:33 but would formulate it differently. The overarching and controlling themes of the first unit reappear in this fourth unit, but such themes are not the departure and return of Jesus but rather the fundamental meaning of the departure and the consequences of this departure for the disciples. Thus, whereas in 16:4b–15 the consequences of the departure focus on the figure of the Spirit-Paraclete, in 16:16–33 such consequences concern the figure of Jesus himself. It is, in effect, because of all such consequences that the forthcoming departure is said to be of advantage to the disciples and that the disciples themselves are portrayed as undergoing a fundamental transition from a situation of sorrow and lack of understanding to a situation of joy and full understanding.

I also support the second traditional argument on behalf of such a division, though again with a different formulation. The explicit reactions of the disciples to the ongoing disclosures of Jesus do reappear only after

16:16 (indirectly, to one another and away from Jesus, in 16:17–18; directly, in 16:29–30). At the same time, however, the unit contains yet another reaction of the disciples at 16:5b–6, though it is described by Jesus himself as speaker and is thus even more indirect than that of 16:17–18. As such, in 16:4b–33 the motif of conversation or dialogue between Jesus and the disciples reappears, for the first time since the first unit, though the motif is developed very differently in this final unit. With 16:4b–33, therefore, Jesus' uninterrupted speech that characterized the whole of 15:1–16:4a comes to an end, and the disciples again play a major role as interlocutors of Jesus.

No major shift in the tone of Jesus' address to the disciples can be detected within 16:4b–33:

1. The same primary tone of consolation and teaching prevails throughout.
2. A pronounced contrast between the disciples and the world is sustained from beginning to end.
3. The disciples are positively portrayed throughout as those who, despite their present failure to understand the message of farewell and their anticipated scattering and abandonment of Jesus at the crucial time of "the hour," will eventually come to a full understanding of Jesus' mission and message and thus become the sole recipients of the farewell promises extended.

The overall tone of the fourth unit is thus similar to that of the first unit.

No major shift in the standpoint of Jesus as speaker of the discourse can be detected within 16:4b–33. As in the first unit, this is a Jesus who is both about to undergo the climactic events of "the hour" and who has already surpassed "the hour" except for its final events (the bestowal of the Spirit-Paraclete—Jesus' promised successor to and among the disciples—and Jesus' final return to the Father). The fourth unit, however, places much more emphasis on the Jesus who is about to face the climax of "the hour."

Consequently, I would argue against the proposed further subdivision of 16:4b–33 that although 16:15 does signal a break in the farewell speech, it is not a major break pointing to a self-contained unit of discourse but instead a minor break pointing to a major section within this fourth unit of discourse. In conclusion, 16:33 constitutes a proper ending to the third and final unit of discourse within chapters 15–16; therefore, 16:4b–33 should be seen as the fourth self-contained, coherent unit of discourse within the farewell speech.

LITERARY STRUCTURE AND DEVELOPMENT

The scholarly literature contains four recurring ideas about the organization and arrangement of 16:4b–33. Two are majority positions and the other two, minority positions. A great deal of the discussion focuses on the perceived centrality of 16:15 within the unit.

The basic difference between the two majority positions is whether there is a break within 16:4b–33 in addition to 16:15. The first position argues against another such break and posits two major sections consisting of 16:4b–15 and 16:16–33. The second majority position proposes a further break after 16:15, usually at 16:24, yielding thereby three major sections consisting of 16:4b–15, 16:16–24, and 16:25–33.

In the first majority position the arguments for a twofold division of 16:4b–33 duplicate by and large the arguments for another major division of the farewell at 16:15; in other words, such a division is affirmed, but now only as a subdivision within 16:4b–33. Thus, the first major section of the unit is seen as developing the figure of the Spirit-Paraclete (16:4b–15), and the second major section is said to focus on Jesus' own return to the disciples (16:16–33).[3] The most thorough example of such a proposal is that of Brown, who argues for an overall chiastic pattern in 16:16–33 with two subdivisions (16:16–23a, 23b–33). Each subdivision consists of the same three constitutive elements arranged in inverse order, thus yielding an ABCCBA pattern for the section as a whole: prediction of trial and of subsequent consolation (16:16, 31–33), intervening remarks of the disciples (16:17–19, 29–30), and promise of blessings to be enjoyed by the disciples (16:20–23a, 23b–28).

The second majority position argues for breaks at 16:15 and 16:24 on the following grounds: the twofold appearance of the recurring concluding formula of the farewell in 16:25 and 16:33 forms an unmistakable inclusion; 16:25 itself has a definite air of finality, serving thereby as an introduction to the conclusion of the unit; and a different emphasis is posited within 16:25–33, namely, an explicit focus on the belief of the disciples with respect to Jesus' own relationship to the Father.[4] Becker further refines the preceding argumentation. Each subdivision, he argues,

---

3. See, e.g., Behler, 177, 196; Brown, 2:709–11, 727–29. Among those who extend the preceding unit of discourse through 16:15, see, e.g., Morris, 695, 701; among those who argue for 16:4b–15 as a self-contained unit of discourse, see, e.g., van den Bussche, 120–21, 127–28; Strathmann, 208–19.

4. See, e.g., Lagrange, 417, 425, 429; Huby, 68, 91. Both begin the unit, however, with 16:5, and Huby extends the first section through 16:16. Among those who extend the preceding unit of discourse through 16:15, see, e.g., Becker, *Johannes*, 2:499–506; among those who divide chaps. 15–16 into a wide number of self-contained units of discourse, see, e.g., Wikenhauser, 293, 296–97, 298–99; Schulz, 202–8.

is clearly demarcated by the use of a contrasting pair of themes: sorrow and joy in 16:16–24; hidden and open revelation of Jesus in 16:25–33.

Although this threefold division of 16:4b–33, with breaks at 16:15 and 16:24, is by far the most common proposal within this position, it is by no means the only one. In fact, the most thorough explanation of this unit as a self-contained unit of discourse with three constitutive major sections, proposed by Simoens, offers a different division altogether.[5] Simoens sees this unit of discourse as arranged in the form of an overall inclusion, with 16:4–20 and 16:25–33 as its outer components and 16:21–24 as the central component. Thus, the second break at 16:24 is preserved, and the first break at 16:15 is posited instead at 16:20. Simoens explains that the framing components describe the passage of the disciples from sadness to joy, and the central component portrays this passage through the image of the childbearing woman. As a whole, therefore, "the hour" of Jesus is described from the point of view of its immediate and ultimate consequences: initial sadness will give way to joy and peace.

Both minority positions affirm the breaks at 16:15 and 16:24. However, both recognize other breaks as well. The first minority position posits one further break, to yield four major sections altogether. The second minority position acknowledges two or more such breaks, giving rise to five or more major sections within the unit.

The argument offered by the first minority position on behalf of a fourfold division involves a proposed break at 16:11. Such a break is taken to point to another major section within the unit, thus yielding the following four major sections: 16:4b–11, 12–15, 16–24, 25–33. As such, the first minority position rests on a willingness to introduce a major division within the promise of the Spirit-Paraclete itself.[6] Schnackenburg argues in this regard that the unit itself deliberately sets off the external role of the Spirit-Paraclete with regard to the world in 16:8–11 against its internal role within the community of 16:13–15 by means of the intervening comment of 16:12, so the Paraclete saying of 16:13–15 should be seen as constituting a distinct and self-contained major section.

The second minority position usually affirms not only the additional break at 16:11 but also other such breaks, yielding a considerable array of brief subdivisions.[7] Such a proliferation of subdivisions, however, does not

5. Simoens, 151–73, esp. 162–67.
6. See, e.g., Schnackenburg, 3:125. Among those who divide John 15–16 into a wide number of self-contained units, see, e.g., Westcott, lxv–lxvi, 216 (with a first division consisting of John 16:1–11).
7. For a sixfold division, see, e.g., Bover, 126–27, 137–38, 152–53, 162, 165–66, 173 (John 16:5–11, 12–15, 16–22, 23–24, 25–28, 29–33). For a similar sixfold division among those who argue for a wide number of self-contained units within John 15–16, see, e.g., Bernard, 2:503–23 (John 16:5–7, 8–15, 16–19, 20–24, 25–28, 29–33). A fivefold division

necessarily imply the complete lack of an overall structural design. In fact, J. M. Bover provides a thorough explanation for the presence of so many subdivisions within 16:4b–33. Bover argues that given the fundamental theme of Jesus' departure in this unit, the different subdivisions represent different ways of consoling the disciples in the light of this departure, all of which can be seen as variations on the two central themes of consolation (the coming of the Spirit-Paraclete; the return and spiritual presence of Jesus).

The preceding scholarly discussion points to two central questions regarding the literary structure and development of this unit. The first question is whether a first break should be recognized at 16:15. The second is whether the discourse material after 16:15 should be further subdivided. The second majority position is correct (in my opinion): a first break should be acknowledged at 16:15 and a second break at 16:24.

A division at 16:15 (and not before) acknowledges and affirms the close unity of the Paraclete material. This material is introduced by 16:4b–6, where the forthcoming departure of Jesus is reiterated, its fundamental meaning is disclosed, and its first consequences for the disciples (all negative) are described. Then, by way of reaction to this introduction, the positive consequences of the departure are directly and extensively pursued in 16:8–15 in terms of the Spirit-Paraclete and tied to the introduction itself by means of 16:7. In other words, given the twofold role assigned to the Spirit-Paraclete (16:8–15), Jesus' forthcoming departure can indeed be described as being of unquestionable benefit to the disciples (16:7). To posit a break prior to 16:15 (as proposed by both minority positions) or after 16:15 (as argued by Simoens within the second majority position) is to bypass the close unity of the Paraclete material, as well as its immediate relationship to the theme of Jesus' departure. In conclusion, 16:4b–15 should be seen as the first major section within 16:4b–33.

After 16:15, a second break is in order at 16:24; once the Paraclete material comes to an end, a further division should be acknowledged in the discourse material that follows. The twofold appearance of the recurring concluding formula of the discourse provides an effective inclusion for the final major section of the unit (16:25–33). In addition, although beginning with 16:16 the consequences of the departure focus on Jesus and his return rather than on the figure of the Spirit-Paraclete, within 16:16–33 itself this return is developed from two different perspectives in 16:16–24 and 16:25–33. In 16:16–24 the return is pursued from the point of view of its further consequences for the disciples and their initial

---

can be found among those who extend the preceding unit of discourse well into John 16; see, e.g., Hoskyns, 481–93 (John 16:5–6, 7–11, 12–15, 16–24, 25–33). A similar division can be found among those who argue for a wide number of self-contained units within John 15–16; see, e.g., Lindars, 498–515 (John 16:4b–11, 12–15, 16–24, 25–28, 29–33).

reaction to the forthcoming departure: the sorrow and lack of understanding that the departure occasions will be directly counteracted by the perfect joy and full understanding that will ensue immediately upon the return. In 16:25–33 the return is developed instead from the point of view of Jesus' revelation of the Father, a revelation that will not take place fully or openly until the return itself. As such, the return is used as a point of departure for a basic summary of the relationship between Jesus and the Father. Finally, Becker points out that beginning with 16:25 a different pair of contrasting themes is employed. The contrast of sadness and joy is used in 16:16–24 to develop the beginning announcement of departure and return, whereas the contrast of speaking in figures and openly is used in 16:25–33 to describe the character of Jesus' revelation of the Father prior to and after the return.

The first majority position, by not positing another break after 16:15, fails to see the significant shift represented by the statement of 16:25. However, any attempt to posit more than one such break after 16:15, as proposed by the second minority position, bypasses the two different developments of the theme of Jesus' return within these verses. In conclusion, 16:16–24 should be seen as the second major section and 16:25–33, as the third and concluding major section of 16:4b–33.

This proposal for a threefold division of 16:4b–33 can be provided with an even more solid grounding from a formal point of view. An overall threefold linear and progressive development—consisting of an introductory, a central, and a concluding major section—can be detected.

This unit contains a compositional element that has been widely recognized in the literature and actually employed, though to a limited extent, in the delineation of its literary structure—namely, the renewed reactions of the assembled disciples to the ongoing declarations of Jesus. On the one hand, the reappearance of such reactions in 16:17–18 and 16:29–30 for the first time since the first unit has been used repeatedly to argue for a close similarity between this unit and the first unit, a similarity that is not seen as lessened by the distinct shift from individual to collective reactions in this fourth unit of discourse. On the other hand, the chiastic structure proposed by Brown for 16:16–33 shows how this compositional element can also be construed as having an important structural function: these two reactions become the middle components of the proposed chiastic structure.

This compositional element is present as well within the first major section of 16:4b–15. Therefore, 16:5b–6 represents another example, like those of 16:17–18 and 16:29–30, of a reaction on the part of the disciples to the ongoing disclosures of Jesus in this unit. A difference in the formulation of this first reaction of 16:5b–6 accounts for the fact that it is never listed as such along with the other two. Whereas the other two represent, in their respective ways, direct interventions on the part of the disciples themselves, the reaction of 16:5b–6 is conveyed indirectly by Jesus himself, who describes, as the speaker of the discourse, this initial reaction of the disciples.

This difference, however, is neither significant nor surprising, since the other two reactions of 16:17–18 and 16:29–30, though more direct, are nevertheless different from one another as well. Whereas the former consists of questions among the disciples themselves and away from Jesus, the subject of which is immediately known and repeated by Jesus himself (16:19), the latter involves a direct confession of faith in and to Jesus on the part of the disciples. Despite such differences in formulation, all three passages in question can be classified as reactions of the disciples to the ongoing declarations of Jesus. Thus, all three passages have direct structural implications.

All three major sections of 16:4b–33, therefore, contain a reaction on the part of the disciples, and this reaction forms the central component of a threefold structure within each section. All three sections, then, contain a threefold cycle consisting of (1) a beginning declaration of Jesus (2) followed by a reaction of the disciples to this beginning declaration and (3) a further declaration of Jesus in the light of this intervening reaction. Within this overall arrangement, furthermore, a number of other structural patterns can be further identified.

A second such pattern concerns the sequence of the reactions themselves and reveals a threefold dimension. First, these three reactions have been arranged in an ascending pattern of explicit portrayal of the disciples: from indirect description by Jesus, to a more direct focus on their own deliberations away from Jesus, to direct address on their part to Jesus. Second, within this ascending pattern a progressive sense of irony can be detected as well. Although the disciples are sharply criticized at first for not asking, the more they ask or speak in what follows, the more they fail to understand; this finally leads to a prediction of (temporary) demise on their part following immediately upon their open and direct confession of faith. Finally, there is an ascending element of promise as well: the more the disciples fail to understand, the more they are told that after "the hour" they will understand and have no further need to ask.

A third structural pattern involves the overall sequence of the three major sections or cycles as a whole. The controlling themes of the unit— the fundamental meaning of the departure and its consequences for the disciples—are developed in a similarly progressive fashion in the course of the unit, so the overall arrangement of these three major sections should be seen as linear and progressive. The thematic development of this fourth unit is similar to that of the first unit, therefore, but also very different.

In the first, introductory section of 16:4b–15, the forthcoming departure of Jesus is recalled and reaffirmed from the beginning. The departure's fundamental meaning is immediately and briefly disclosed in terms
of the relationship between Jesus and the Father—"the one who sent
him" as the destination of the departure—further subtly introducing the
question of Jesus' origins with the Father. Then, in addition to a couple of
negative consequences, the positive consequences of such a departure for
the disciples are outlined at great length in terms of the Spirit-Paraclete,
Jesus' successor to and among the disciples. Finally, within the exposition
of the Spirit-Paraclete's role as Jesus' successor, the meaning of the departure is again briefly pursued in terms of the relationship between Jesus
and the Father: the Father as the ultimate source of Jesus' revelation.

The second, central section of 16:16–24 again gives a few troubling
consequences of the departure for the disciples. It also extensively pursues
the positive consequences in terms of Jesus' own return to the disciples
and the consequences of such a return for them—perfect and inalienable
joy; full understanding; and direct access to the Father, with universal
granting of all their requests and petitions. The meaning of the departure,
however, is not developed at all in this central major section.

The third, concluding major section of 16:25–33 again describes a few
negative consequences of the departure for the disciples. The positive
consequences are also developed in detail, as in the second major section,
in terms of Jesus' own return to them and the consequences of this return
for them—an open revelation of the Father; direct access to the Father,
with universal granting of all their requests and petitions; the love of the
Father because of their full belief and love; and victory over the world.
With the emphasis on the open and forthcoming revelation concerning the
Father, the fundamental meaning of the departure is now addressed at
greater length in terms of the relationship between Jesus and the Father:
(1) an excellent summary of Johannine teaching on Jesus, now fully and
explicitly incorporating (for the first time in the farewell) the question of
Jesus' origins with the Father, introduced in the first section and (2) a
climactic, though abbreviated, reaffirmation of the mutual presence of
Jesus and the Father in each other.

A final structural pattern involves the threefold structure and development of each major section or cycle. Each section follows an overall
pattern of inclusion similar to that already encountered in 14:4–14, the
second subsection of 14:1–27, whereby the linear and progressive development of the overarching themes of the unit is extended to, and carried
out within, each section itself. The beginning declaration of Jesus introduces the teaching in question; the intervening reaction of the disciples
provides, by way of their failure to understand the ongoing disclosures of

Jesus, an occasion for further teaching on the part of Jesus; and finally, the concluding declaration of Jesus provides such further teaching by expanding upon the beginning declaration in the light of the intervening reaction of the disciples.

LITERARY-RHETORICAL ANALYSIS

The literary structure and development of this fourth unit can be summarized by the following structural outline, which will be developed in detail in the following literary-rhetorical analysis:

I. Jesus' departure and the disciples (16:4b–15)
II. Jesus' departure and return and the disciples (16:16–24)
III. Jesus' revelation and the disciples (16:25–33)

First Major Section (John 16:4b–15)

The first major section (16:4b–15) concerns Jesus' departure and the disciples. In accordance with the threefold pattern of inclusion proposed for each major section, the literary structure of this first section can be outlined as follows: (1) Jesus' disclosure of departure and its destination (16:4b–5a), (2) the disciples' reaction to Jesus' disclosure of departure and its destination (16:5b–6), and (3) Jesus' departure and its consequences for the disciples (16:7–15).

Jesus' Disclosure of Departure and Its Destination (John 16:4b–5a)

The brief beginning declaration of Jesus consists of two contrasting statements, both concerning his forthcoming departure and related disclosures (16:4b–5a). The contrast revolves around the previous silence/present disclosure concerning such disclosures on Jesus' part. Whereas the first statement both acknowledges and accounts for Jesus' silence concerning "these things" during the course of the public ministry (16:4b–c),[8] the second statement makes a full and direct reference at this point, within "the hour" itself, to the forthcoming departure (16:5a).

8. Whereas the silence itself is acknowledged in 16:4b, 16:4c provides the reason for such silence. This first statement further exemplifies the recurring formulas of departure in the farewell, the first such example since the first unit and the first of several in this unit (16:12, 16, 25; see chap. 2, n. 33). With regard to form, this example follows the pattern of 14:25—namely, the use of an expression (a causal clause) indicating the coming break in the relationship with the disciples, "because I was with you" (here used in conjunction with a subsequent and explicit affirmation of this break [16:5a]). With regard to purpose, this example, like 14:25, also draws a distinction involving the disciples themselves, but now in terms of their relationship to Jesus prior to and during "the hour" itself.

In the first statement (16:4b–c), the reach of the beginning demonstrative pronoun, "these things"—that is, the extent and scope of the disclosures in question—should be seen as both general and specific. On the one hand, the pronoun encompasses not only the preceding third unit of 15:18–16:4a (with all its warnings regarding the forthcoming opposition of the world) but also the whole of the preceding speech up to this point (that is, all the preceding disclosures of 13:31–16:4a regarding the meaning of the departure and its consequences for the disciples). On the other hand, the pronoun also has a more specific reference. In the light of the contrast itself, such a reference has to do above all with the previous announcement of the forthcoming departure as such. In other words, the silence of Jesus with regard to the departure itself during the entire public ministry—and ultimately, with regard to all that such a departure implies as well—is thereby acknowledged (16:4b) and explained on the basis of Jesus' continued presence among them during this time (16:4c).[9] In the second statement of 16:5a, then, the forthcoming departure is announced again and its destination immediately disclosed in terms of Jesus' origins: Jesus goes to "the one who sent him."[10] As such, the beginning declaration of Jesus explains that given his ongoing presence among the disciples during the public ministry, there was no need for such disclosures at an earlier time; now that this stay is rapidly drawing to a close, however, such disclosures become imperative.

In recalling and reaffirming the forthcoming departure and its destination, this beginning declaration of Jesus reintroduces, from the beginning of the unit, one of the two controlling themes of the first unit of discourse—the fundamental meaning of Jesus' departure. In so doing, the unit returns to the beginning announcement of the departure in 13:33a–b (in the first unit).

The Disciples' Reaction to Jesus' Disclosure
of Departure and Its Destination
(John 16:5b–6)

The reaction of the disciples to the beginning declaration of Jesus is briefly conveyed only by Jesus as the speaker of the discourse (16:5b–6). The

---

9. For a similar use of the prepositional phrase "from the beginning" to refer to the beginnings of the relationship between Jesus and the disciples, see 15:27, though with the preposition ἀπό rather than ἐκ; see chap. 4, n. 52. A difference in application should be noted. Whereas 15:18–16:4a uses this phrase as a further grounding for the continued witness of the disciples to Jesus in and to the world, this unit uses it to characterize the extent of Jesus' silence toward the disciples concerning the departure.

10. The term used for the departure as such (ὑπάγω) is common in the first unit (13:33, 36; 14:4, 5, 28; see 16:10, 17). However, the description of the destination as "the one who sent me," unique in this unit, is not common in the first unit (14:24).

description of this initial reaction consists of two supplementary statements. The first statement of 16:5b–c not only points out the silence of the
disciples in the face of the announced departure but also critiques it (and
given the preceding contrast of 16:4b–5a, this critique is ironic). Whereas
Jesus' silence concerning the departure was justifiably confined to the time
of the public ministry, the silence of the disciples takes place at the time of
the departure itself, so they fail to raise the important question of its destination.[11] In the second statement of 16:6, such silence on their part is also
said to be accompanied by a sorrow that has overwhelmed their hearts and
that is tied directly to the preceding disclosures ("these things") presupposed by, and reaffirmed in, 16:4b–5a (16:6).[12]

These two components of the first reaction are interrelated. Sorrow over
the disclosures regarding the departure prevents any further inquiry on the
part of the disciples concerning the departure itself, even though its reassuring destination has been explicitly identified; hence, the immediate consequences of the announcement of the departure presupposed by, and
reaffirmed in, 16:4b–5a are clearly negative. As such, this first description
of the disciples' reaction reintroduces from the beginning of the fourth unit
the second overarching theme of the first unit—the consequences of the
departure for the disciples.

There can be no doubt that the first aspect of the disciples' reaction—the
silence concerning the departure and, more specifically, the destination
of this departure—conflicts directly with Peter's question of 13:36 following a similar announcement of the forthcoming departure in 13:33; in other
words, Peter has already asked precisely that question of Jesus. This conflict
between the two units is significant. In fact, this first part of the reaction

---

11. The disciples' failure "to ask" Jesus is expressed in terms of the verb ἐρωτᾶν. Within
the farewell thus far, this verb is used only with reference to the relationship between Jesus
and the Father (14:16; cf. 17:9, 15, 20). Although such a connotation is also present in this
unit (16:26), the verb is now used to characterize the ongoing dialogue between Jesus and
the disciples (cf. 9:2): from their present failure to ask him (16:5); to a subsequent, though
reluctant, wish to ask (16:19); to Jesus' promise of no need for asking in the future (16:23),
which is misunderstood by the disciples (16:30).

12. The grounding in the preceding disclosures is formulated in terms of the recurring
concluding formula of the discourse "because I have said these things to you." This is the
only time the formula is not found as a main clause and does not anticipate or signal the end
of a unit of discourse. Its specific use here—at the beginning of a unit of discourse and as
part of a subordinate causal clause—reinforces the preceding twofold occurrence of the
formula at 16:1–4a and thus is another, emphatic sign that one unit of discourse has ended
and another has started.

This second description introduces the theme of sorrow (λύπη), an important theme
within the second section (16:20–24). Given this initial reaction on the part of the disciples,
the remainder of the unit can be seen as an attempt to help the disciples overcome such
heartrending and paralyzing sorrow, beginning immediately with the extended promise of
the Spirit-Paraclete itself. Such sorrow parallels, in effect, the first unit's reference to their
troubled and fearful hearts (14:1a, 27d).

deliberately signals a completely different development of the same controlling themes from the first unit. It is not so much the case, therefore, that
the conflict in question is really not a conflict at all, but rather that
the conflict is intended to call attention to a different development of the
same fundamental themes from the earlier unit. Therefore, upon returning
to the initial announcement of the departure in 13:33a–b, the fourth unit
develops it altogether differently than does 13:33c–38, deliberately bypassing thereby the previous question of Peter.

Jesus' Departure and Its Consequences for the Disciples (John 16:7–15)

Jesus next explains to the disciples how his departure is ultimately of great
benefit to them (16:7–15). In other words, he begins to outline the positive
consequences of the departure reaffirmed in 16:4b–5a and thus to provide
a direct counterbalance to the negative consequences already portrayed
in the initial reaction of the disciples. This extensive explanation focuses
almost exclusively on the figure of the Spirit-Paraclete. Two basic steps can
be distinguished: (1) a brief introduction explaining the beneficial character of such a departure for the disciples, insofar as the departure constitutes
the essential condition for the coming of the Spirit-Paraclete to the disciples
(16:7), and (2) an extended exposition of the twofold role of the Spirit-
Paraclete as Jesus' successor among the disciples (16:8–15).

Jesus' Departure and the Spirit-Paraclete (John 16:7)

The exposition of the positive consequences of the departure for the
disciples begins in 16:7 with an introductory statement closely connecting all the Paraclete material that follows to the theme of the departure
(its meaning and consequences) introduced in 16:4b–6. This statement
reveals two basic components. To begin with, it affirms the positive character of the departure (16:7a–b):[13] the departure is declared to be of
unquestionable advantage to the disciples.[14] The statement then explains
this positive character in terms of the departure as the condition for
the presence of the Spirit-Paraclete among the disciples (16:7c–f). Two

13. In this first step the statement regarding the positive character of the departure
(16:7b) is introduced by an emphatic assertion regarding the truth of such a statement (16:7a),
so the former clearly stands in apposition to the latter and explains what the "truth" in question
is all about. Such an introduction is unique in the Gospel and further emphasizes the beneficial
nature of the forthcoming departure for the disciples.
14. The use of the impersonal verb συμφέρει to describe the beneficial character of the
departure provides a sharp, ironic contrast to its only other use in the Gospel, on the lips of
Caiaphas (11:41; cf. 18:14). Jesus' departure is indeed of unquestionable advantage, though
not at all as the high priest would have it but rather only for those who believe in him.
Another term for the departure (ἀπελθεῖν), found only in this unit and limited to this
statement, is introduced at this point.

contrasting conditional sentences are used to convey and emphasize this direct relationship between the departure and the Spirit-Paraclete. The first condition describes the relationship from a negative point of view (no departure means no coming of the Spirit-Paraclete [16:7c–d]), and the second condition provides its positive formulation (departure does mean the sending of the Paraclete [16:7e–f]). The positive consequences of the departure are thereby set forth directly and effectively.[15]

The Role of the Spirit–Paraclete (John 16:8–15)

Once the beneficial character of Jesus' departure has been explained as the essential condition for the coming of the Spirit-Paraclete, the role of this figure is pursued in detail (16:8–15). The development of this role reveals two distinct, though interrelated, dimensions: first, the role of the Spirit-Paraclete with regard to the world is described (16:8–11); then, the role of the Spirit-Paraclete with regard to the disciples themselves is outlined (16:12–15). Although these two roles seemingly involve two different groups, one must remember that in the introductory statement of 16:7 the Spirit-Paraclete is promised specifically to the disciples, so even its first role in relation to the world of 16:8–11 should be understood as taking place in and through the disciples themselves. In addition, the development of these two roles shows, for the most part, a similar structure. The juxtaposition of these two roles of the Spirit-Paraclete within this first section is meant to provide immediate reassurance and consolation to the disciples in the light of the forthcoming events and their own initial reaction to them.

The exposition of the role of the Spirit-Paraclete with regard to the world in 16:8–11 reveals three basic components:

1. In a basic repetition and reaffirmation of 16:7, the coming of the Spirit-Paraclete to the disciples is briefly presented again as the essential condition for the fulfillment of the role that follows (16:8a).
2. The role itself is then briefly described (16:8b).
3. Finally, a more extensive rationale is provided for the undertaking of this role by the Spirit-Paraclete (16:9–11).

15. Within this antithetical development an effective variety in formulation can be observed. For example, in referring to the departure, each protasis employs a different term. The negative formulation of 16:7c reprises that of 16:7a–b (ἀπελθεῖν), and the positive formulation of 16:7e introduces yet a third such term for the departure (πορεύομαι), which is frequently used in the first unit, as well as in the present unit (14:2–3, 12, 28; 16:28). Similarly, in outlining the contrasting consequences, each apodosis describes the Paraclete from a different perspective. Whereas 16:7d simply refers to its failure "to come," 16:17f describes Jesus as "sending" it. This latter formulation provides an immediate link with 16:5a. The Paraclete's own relationship to Jesus parallels in fact that of Jesus to the Father— as the latter sent Jesus, so will Jesus send the Paraclete to the disciples.

A brief participial phrase ("when it has come") specifies the basic condition for the fulfillment of the task about to be unfolded. In so doing, it repeats by way of introduction the basic message of 16:7—what follows will take place only when the Spirit-Paraclete comes and hence only when Jesus departs as already announced (16:8a)—thus preparing the way for a more concrete reaffirmation of the ultimate fruitfulness of this departure.

The first role of the Paraclete then is described in terms of an ἐλέγχειν of the world in three different areas: with regard to sin, righteousness, and judgment (16:8b).[16] The search by Johannine scholars for a meaning of this Greek verb that can properly encompass and accurately render all three areas has proved to be problematic.[17] The verb encompasses a wide range of meanings, which can yield in turn a similarly wide range of interpretations regarding the precise nature of this first role of the Spirit-Paraclete with regard to the world. Thus, for example, A Greek-English Lexicon of the New Testament (BAGD) lists four different denotations for this verb: (1) to bring to light, expose, set forth, demonstrate, or prove; (2) to convict or convince someone of something or to point out something to someone (within which category 16:8 is placed); (3) to reprove or correct; and (4) to punish or discipline. Similarly, A Greek-English Lexicon (LS) provides two major groupings (with no reference whatever to 16:8): (1) to put to shame or disgrace and (2) a second grouping encompassing all the following connotations: to cross-examine or question, to accuse or be convicted, to test or bring to the proof, to prove, to refute or confute, to put right or correct, to get the better of, to expose, or to decide a dispute. An examination of the other usages of this verb in the Gospel (3:20; 8:46) shows that it has already been employed with two different denotations. In 3:20 the term is used (in the negative) in direct contrast to the verb to reveal; thus, a meaning of "exposing" or "bringing to light" is in order ("that his works may not be exposed"). In 8:46 the term occurs in a question pointedly addressed by Jesus to the unbelieving Jews, best rendered along the lines of "convicting" ("Who among you will convict me of sin?"). In the end, any interpretation of this term at this point must take into

16. The delineation of this first role consists of two essential components: (a) the identification of the role as such (16:8b₁) and (b) a threefold listing of the specific areas or respects in which the fulfillment of this role will be carried out (16:8b₂). The listing consists of three consecutive prepositional phrases joined by the connective καί and functioning as a genitive of reference with the preposition περί. This threefold listing is arranged in terms of an ascending type of development, which becomes even sharper when repeated and expanded in the concluding rationale that follows.

17. The literature in this regard is vast; for a good summary, see D. A. Carson ("The Function of the Paraclete in John 16:7–11," JBL 98 [1979] 547–60). A proper working principle is proposed (pp. 548–49): given the pronounced structural symmetry of the passage, whatever meaning is adopted should lend itself to a consistent application throughout the entire passage.

account the extended rationale that follows the delineation proper of this first role of the Paraclete (16:9–11).

The concluding rationale for this first role of the Spirit-Paraclete repeats in the same order each prepositional phrase from 16:8, that is, each area or respect associated with the specific role assigned to the Paraclete (16:9a, 10a, 11a). The rationale then follows each of these phrases with a ὅτι clause that is in some way meant to shed further light on each of these areas or respects (16:9b, 10b, 11b). It also brings all three statements closely together by means of a μέν/δέ/δέ pattern attached to the prepositional phrases. As such, the entire rationale can be said to stand—by way of ellipsis, expansion, and further clarification—in apposition to the preceding statement of the definition proper (16:8b).

This development of the rationale reveals other important structural characteristics. First, each ὅτι clause that follows each repetition of the prepositional phrases, each restatement of area or respect, lays down a correct definition of each term:[18] a true understanding of "sin" in terms of a failure to believe in Jesus (16:9b),[19] a true understanding of "righteousness" in terms of the Father as the vindicating destination of Jesus' departure (16:10b),[20] and a true understanding of "judgment" in

---

18. In each case this correct definition is provided from a different perspective: "sin," from the point of view of the world (they do not believe in Jesus); "righteousness," from the point of view of Jesus (his departure to the Father and separation from the disciples); and "judgment," from the point of view of the ruler of this world (Satan is already condemned).

19. The first clause is a simple statement with a gnomic present and phrased in the negative ("because they do not believe in me"). For sin as unbelief, see, e.g., 8:21–24; 9:40–41; 15:22–25 (cf. 1:29; 19:11); for the world as a realm of unbelief and rejection, see, e.g., 1:9–10; 3:19; 7:7; 8:23.

20. The second clause is compound. In the first member is a repetition of 16:5a ("because I go to the Father")—a further reference both to the departure (again in terms of ὑπάγειν) and its destination, now explicitly identifying "the one who sent me" as "the Father." In the second member is an expansion of 16:5b–6 ("and you will see me no more")— another consequence of the forthcoming departure for the disciples, namely, separation of Jesus from the disciples. First, the reference to "righteousness" is unique in the Gospel; this concept plays no role whatsoever in the ongoing debates with the Jewish authorities. However, the use of the corresponding adjective (5:30; 7:24) sheds further light on the present definition: "righteous" judgment as being in keeping with God's will. As such, the definition of 16:10 adds that such "righteousness" also extends to, and includes, Jesus' forthcoming departure and separation from the disciples, as its destination readily shows. God the Father as the destination vindicates both the departure and the separation from the disciples that it entails, showing that such events are indeed in keeping with God's will. Second, the expansion of the initial consequences of the departure plays a similar role to that of 13:33c–e, the first negative consequence of the departure, in the first unit. Jesus announces a seemingly definitive and final separation in both cases. However, subsequent disclosures in each unit revise this initial impression by describing such a forthcoming separation as temporary (13:36; 14:3, 18–21, 23, 28; 16:16–24). This expansion of the consequences of the departure thus prepares the way directly for the second major section (16:16–24), which pursues the theme of Jesus' return to the disciples.

terms of the condemnation of the ruler of this world (16:11b).[21] Second, the
sequence of these three areas or respects reveals a crescendo in development—from a wrong fundamental stance with regard to God ("sin"), to a
proper fundamental stance with regard to God ("righteousness"), to a fundamental and definitive evaluation of such attitudes or stances ("judgment").
Third, given the final and climactic reference to "judgment" within the
sequence, the exposition of this first role of the Spirit-Paraclete with regard
to the world possesses, from beginning to end, a definite forensic dimension.

If the preceding interpretation of the rationale is correct and the subordinate clauses can indeed be seen as providing a proper meaning for each
area or respect in question, then the subordinate clauses themselves cannot be regarded as explicative (as definitions or explanations of what the
world means and understands by these terms) but instead should be seen
as causal (as the grounds upon which the ἐχέγχειν of the Paraclete vis-à-vis
the world takes place).[22] As such, these subordinate clauses must also be
regarded as standing in direct and sharp contrast to the world's own understanding of sin, righteousness, and judgment as presupposed and conveyed by the prepositional phrases themselves. Of course, however, such
definitions on the part of the world remain undeveloped in this passage
and can only be supplied from the rest of the Gospel.[23] In other words,

---

21. The third clause is a simple statement in the passive voice ("because the ruler of this
world has been condemned"). The use of the perfect here (κέκριται; see also 3:18) points to
such an event as already accomplished. For Satan as "the ruler of the/this world," see 12:31;
14:31. For the use of "judgment/to judge" with a negative denotation, see, e.g., 3:17–19;
12:31, 47–48 (all with reference to the world); 5:22–30. The present definition brings
together these two themes of the Gospel. Satan's demise as "the ruler of this world" is now
reformulated in terms of the negative use of "judgment/to judge"—"the ruler of this world"
has been "condemned."

22. So argues, quite correctly, Carson, "Paraclete," 558–62. Carson, however, does not
see the full force of this element of contrast present in the rationale as a whole because of his
adoption of the meaning "to convince" or "to bring to a self-conscious recognition" for this
role of the Paraclete vis-à-vis the world. Such a decision tones down considerably the nature
of the contrast: the subordinate clauses contain not that on the basis of which the world is
proved or declared guilty but that which the world is brought to see as it admits its own guilt.

23. First, what the world regards as "sin" can be supplied from the nature of its reactions
to Jesus: directly, a violation of the law by healing on the Sabbath (9:16, 24-25; cf. 5:16;
18:30–31); indirectly, blasphemy (5:17–18; 10:31–33), leading the people astray (7:12, 47),
demonic possession (7:20; 8:48–52; 10:19–21), and deserving death on account of Jesus'
claims with regard to God (19:27). Second, what the world regards as "righteousness" can
only be supplied by way of opposition to what is regarded as "sin," since this concept plays only
a minor role in the remainder of the Gospel. Such righteousness should also be conceived in
terms of conformity to God's will and thus as including both a proper observance of the law and
a radically different approach altogether to the figure of the Messiah in terms of origins, role,
and relationship to God. Finally, what the world regards as "judgment," in the negative sense
of condemnation, can be indirectly supplied from the course of action adopted with regard to
both Jesus and his disciples. In the case of Jesus, these actions are persecution and repeated
attempts on his life (5:17–20; 8:59; 10:31); the official decision to kill him in order to save the

these clauses do throw light on these three areas or respects, but only by way of contrast and opposition—that is, by indicating what the proper definitions of these terms are in relation to those of the world and thus providing the fundamental grounds for the given action of the Spirit-Paraclete with regard to the world.

Such an understanding of the rationale in terms of a fundamental contrast between what might be called the values of the world and the values of God with regard to sin, righteousness, and judgment in turn places delimitations on the meaning of the verb ἐλέγχειν as used in the definition of the role proper in 16:8b. In other words, the specific denotation to be adopted must adequately convey the role of opposition and confrontation vis-à-vis the world that such a contrast implies on the part of the Spirit-Paraclete. In the light of the semantic possibilities outlined above, the first role of the Spirit-Paraclete could be interpreted in one of four ways.

First, the Spirit-Paraclete can be seen as "exposing" or "bringing to light" the values of the world, as in the example of John 3:20. However, although this meaning is certainly presupposed and envisioned by this first task of the Spirit-Paraclete, it cannot serve as the primary meaning for two reasons. First, the values of the world are not concealed but become fully and immediately evident during both the ministry of Jesus and that of the disciples. Second, in and of itself such an exposé of the world would fail to convey any sense of consequences for the world on account of its values, thus bypassing altogether the distinctive meaning of *judgment* as "condemnation."

Second, the Spirit-Paraclete can be interpreted as "proving" to the world or "convincing" the world that its given values are erroneous and false. However, from a Johannine perspective the world as a whole remains for the most part—as the very designation for Satan of 16:11 shows—a realm of profound unbelief and hostility, for which no hope of repentance or salvation is ever expressed.[24]

The third possible role of the Spirit-Paraclete involves "reproving," "correcting," or "refuting" the values of the world through the revelation and dissemination of the values of God. However, although this meaning is also presupposed and envisioned as part of this first task of the Spirit-Paraclete, it alone is inadequate as the primary meaning. Such a correction would ultimately obtain only within the realm of the disciples themselves as

---

people and forestall the destruction of the nation (11:45–53); and the actual execution of this decision through his arrest, trial, and crucifixion. In the case of the disciples, the third unit of discourse is to the point. The actions include persecution and even death at the hands of the world—indeed, a death that will be interpreted by that world as a sacrificial offering to God.

24. So argues Carson, "Paraclete," 558. Actually, Carson argues for "to convict," but this meaning is in the end equated with "to convince."

those who accept and submit to such a reevaluation of these values. This correction would spare the world of any consequences on account of its given values, thus again bypassing, like the previous case of "exposing," the distinctive negative meaning of "judgment" as "condemnation."

Fourth, the Spirit-Paraclete can be seen as "convicting" the world on the basis of the values that it holds and exercises, as in the example of John 8:46. This is the option to be preferred in my opinion. Given the fundamental difference between the values of the world and those of God as already revealed by Jesus, it will be the specific role of the Spirit-Paraclete to convict, to prove guilty, an unbelieving and hostile world. Only this option, therefore, fully conveys the important element of contrast so central to the structure of the rationale and hence the element of opposition and confrontation so central to this first role of the Spirit-Paraclete.

Such an interpretation of this first role proves to be appropriate as well with regard to the two other structural characteristics of this passage mentioned earlier. First, a basic task of "convicting" the world would fully convey the forensic dimension of the saying as a whole. In a clear context of judgment, the Spirit-Paraclete will "convict" the world because of its fundamental values and their total opposition to those revealed by God through Jesus. Second, this basic task of "convicting" the world also would be effectively developed by the threefold, ascending presentation of the fundamental values in question. In a clear context of judgment, the Spirit-Paraclete will "convict" the world with regard to "sin" (the world's understanding and exercise of what constitutes an incorrect fundamental stance with regard to God); with regard to "righteousness" (the world's understanding and exercise of what constitutes a correct fundamental stance with regard to God); and, ironically, with regard to "judgment" itself (the world's understanding and exercise of what constitutes a definitive evaluation of these fundamental stances and attitudes).[25] The Spirit-Paraclete's "conviction" of the world is thereby portrayed as taking place on all fronts in a methodical fashion and hence as totally comprehensive.

25. A sharp sense of irony informs this entire passage. The world does not hesitate to accuse both Jesus and his disciples of sin, to claim righteousness with regard to God, and to render negative judgment on both Jesus and the disciples. In the end, however, the world will be exposed, reproved, and convicted by the Spirit-Paraclete on the basis of the true values of God: the fundamental sin of unbelief on the part of the world (a world that fails to acknowledge and believe in the one sent by the Father), the fundamental righteousness of Jesus in relation to God (a Jesus whose departure and separation from the disciples represent the climax of his mission and a return to the Father, who sent him and entrusted him with that very mission), and the fundamental judgment already rendered against the demonic power who rules the world (a demonic power that through Jesus' glorification has already been condemned). In other words, it is those who claim to be on the side of God and to represent the values of God who will be convicted by the true values of God as revealed by Jesus and proclaimed by the Spirit-Paraclete after Jesus.

A question inevitably arises at this point as to how this first task of the Spirit-Paraclete is to be accomplished. Given the implicit promise contained within the introductory statement of 16:7—the announced coming of the Spirit-Paraclete to the circle of disciples—this task of "convicting" the world must be seen as taking place in and through the disciples themselves, that is, in and through their own mission and "witness" in and to the world. As such, this first task of the Spirit-Paraclete represents a further development of the third Paraclete saying of 15:26–27 within 15:18–16:4a. Three specific aspects of this expansion can be identified.

First, the previous chapter pointed out that the third Paraclete saying of 15:26–27 advances the role of the Spirit-Paraclete among the disciples in a different direction from that outlined in the first unit (14:16–17a, 26). Thus, in this third saying of 15:18–16:4a the envisioned mission of the disciples in and to the world is specifically identified with, and grounded in, the role assigned to the figure of the Spirit-Paraclete: in and through the circle of the disciples, the Paraclete, the Spirit of truth, will "witness" to Jesus (that is, will continue to present Jesus' claims to the world after his departure from it). Second, chapter 4 also pointed out that this Paraclete saying serves, within the third major section of the unit (15:26–16:4a), as a rationale for the forthcoming opposition of the world to the disciples. It is precisely as a response to the disciples' mission and continued witness to Jesus (15:26–27) that the world will take severe measures against them (16:1–4a). In fact, the unit as a whole anticipates by way of warning the basic consequences of this mission: the disciples will encounter exactly the same reception in the world that Jesus encountered during his own mission and ministry; although there will be some acceptance of their claims on Jesus' behalf, they will meet with overwhelming rejection and opposition at the hands of the world because of their continued witness to Jesus. Third, chapter 4 also argued that this Paraclete saying further serves as a word of comfort to the disciples in the midst of such dire warnings. It is the Spirit-Paraclete who, as Jesus' successor in their midst, will inform and sustain their mission in and to the world.

In each of these three aspects, the specific development provided by this first role assigned to the Paraclete of 16:8–11 can be easily discerned. First, the mission of the disciples in and to the world as sustained and informed by the Spirit-Paraclete is now given a decidedly forensic thrust. Again, in and through the circle of the disciples and their very "witness" to Jesus in the world, the Spirit-Paraclete will "convict" the world with regard to its fundamental values. Second, such a sharpened role can be seen as emerging directly from the fundamental values of the world described in the course of 15:18–16:4a. Given the world's overwhelming rejection of, and opposition to, the mission of the disciples (a response that matches that directed against Jesus himself during his own mission), it will be proved guilty by the Spirit-Paraclete. Third, such a sharpened forensic role can only serve as an added and much-needed source of comfort to the disciples for the time after the departure. In the face of such forthcoming rejection and opposition, the disciples will not be left defenseless. In fact, the Spirit-Paraclete, as Jesus' successor, will not only inform and sustain their mission in and to the world but will also convict the world because of its fundamental response of unbelief and opposition to that mission.

Through this first role of "convicting" the world, another important facet of Jesus' mission and ministry is continued by both the Spirit-Paraclete and the disciples. In other words, their role of "convicting" the world (a role that follows upon, and is correspondingly addressed to, the given rejection and opposition of the world) can be seen as corresponding to the role of "judging" the world that is so central to Jesus' own mission and ministry (a role that is presented in terms of negative judgment or condemnation and that also follows upon and addresses the given rejection and opposition on the part of the world). Both "convicting" and "judging" emphasize a forensic interpretation of the encounter between those not "of the world" and an unbelieving and rejecting world, though from slightly different perspectives. Whereas Jesus is said "to condemn" the world, functioning in the role of judge, those who continue Jesus' mission are said "to convict" the world, acting in the role of prosecutor.[26] In both cases, the end result is the same: the fundamental values of the world are shown as standing in total opposition to those of God despite all claims to the contrary, and judgment is found for the prosecution.

The exposition of the second role of the Spirit-Paraclete follows immediately upon the first (16:12–15). Once its role with regard to the world—a role whose fulfillment is seen as taking place in and through the circle of the disciples themselves—has been set forth, the attention shifts from the world to the disciples and the role of the Spirit-Paraclete among them. The exposition of this second role reveals two major components. The first provides both a smooth transition from the delineation of the first role to that of the second and a direct introduction to the nature of the second role itself. The second component outlines the role as such. These two

26. "To convict" is never used with regard to Jesus' role vis-à-vis the world (cf. 3:20), and "to condemn" is never used to describe the role of either the Spirit-Paraclete or the disciples vis-à-vis the world. The distinction implies subordination, and the declaration of 12:47–48 is helpful in this regard: it is Jesus' "word" as proclaimed by the Spirit-Paraclete in and through the disciples that renders negative judgment on the world. For Jesus' role of judging, see n. 21 above; for this role as entrusted to him by the Father, see 3:17; 5:22–23, 27; 8:15–16; 12:47.

components can be identified as follows: (1) a description of the present situation of the disciples with regard to the teaching of Jesus (16:12) and (2) a description of the future situation of the disciples with regard to such teaching, upon the coming of the Spirit-Paraclete (16:13–15). In other words, the role of the Spirit-Paraclete within the community of disciples is pursued in terms of a fundamental contrast in their situation vis-à-vis the teaching of Jesus between the time preceding and the time following the Paraclete's presence with the group. Furthermore, the delineation of the role proper in 16:13–15 reproduces the threefold development observed above with regard to the first role.

The present situation of the disciples is given in 16:12. As indicated above, this first component of 16:12–15 serves as both transition and introduction. With 16:11 the delineation of the first role clearly ends; the grounds for the conviction of the world by the Spirit-Paraclete have now been explained. With 16:12, therefore, the delineation of the second role begins. However, instead of a simple repetition of the same threefold pattern here, one finds another formula of departure, the second within the unit itself (cf. 16:4b–5a).[27] The use of such a formula at this point is effective from a structural point of view. While avoiding an immediate duplication of the threefold pattern, the formula provides a different and specific context for the subsequent exposition of the Spirit-Paraclete's second role in 16:13–15 and the resumption of the threefold pattern within this second subdivision, thus creating a smooth and appropriate transition.

In allowing for such a transition, this first component of 16:12–15 also prepares the way for the following description of the Spirit-Paraclete's role among the disciples themselves. This introductory function can be observed both in terms of its actual formulation and its role as a formula of departure within the unit itself.

On the one hand, the formula turns to the relationship between Jesus and the disciples at the time of the farewell itself and posits a basic contrast between two fundamental aspects of it. Whereas Jesus is said to have "many things" still to say to his disciples (16:12a), the latter are described as being unable "to bear" such disclosures at this point (16:12b). In other words, although Jesus' mission of revelation with regard to the disciples is by no means complete, a continued revelation at this point is regarded as pointless

27. See n. 8 above. With regard to form, this formula follows, as in the case of 14:30a–b, a variation of the third type of formulation (namely, the use of temporal adverbs—two, in effect, "still" and "now"—alluding to a forthcoming break in the relationship with the disciples). With regard to purpose, this formula, like 14:25, presents a contrast between the present and future situation of the disciples. In fact, as in 14:25, a formula of departure is used again to introduce a Paraclete saying.

because of the disciples' fundamental inability not only to understand but also to endure the impact of such disclosures.[28]

On the other hand, the formula also looks back to the previous formula of 16:4b–5a and forward to the formulas of 16:16 and 16:25. If the present formula is seen in terms of 16:4b–5a, a shift in the line of argumentation can be discerned: just as the beginning declaration of 16:4b–5a specifies that there was revelation that would not be dispensed by Jesus until the present time of "the hour," so does the present declaration point out that there is further revelation that cannot be dispensed until the time after "the hour" itself, given the disciples' inability to "bear" such revelation at this point. If the present formula is seen in the light of the formulas of 16:16 and 16:25, a further development of this shift in the line of argumentation can be discerned. The future disclosure of this revelation and the corresponding reaction of the disciples to it are explicitly pursued in both 16:16 and 16:25, as well as in the sections of the unit that these formulas introduce. Thus, the present departure formula of 16:12 moves the discussion beyond the (present) revelation of the departure and related events to the (future) revelation that will follow upon the completion of such events.

The use of such a departure formula at this point provides an effective introduction to what follows. In raising the issue of an undisclosed revelation that cannot be "borne" by the disciples at this point in the ministry of Jesus, the formula prepares the way for the subsequent exposition of the second role of the Spirit-Paraclete, which will be defined in terms of such a revelation. Thus, the Spirit-Paraclete will bring about the essential change in the situation and status of the disciples that will allow them "to bear" (to comprehend and endure) such disclosures. This change is then further developed in the next two major sections of the unit.

The future situation of the disciples is delineated by 16:13–15. This second component of 16:12–15 duplicates the threefold development of the first role outlined in 16:8–11. Thus, the same three basic steps occur in the exposition of the Spirit-Paraclete's role among the disciples: (1) a brief repetition and reaffirmation of the essential condition for this role to be fulfilled (16:13a), (2) a more developed description of the role itself (16:13b–e), and (3) a similarly extended rationale for the precise undertaking of this role by the figure of the Spirit-Paraclete (16:14–15).

---

28. Such a metaphorical use of the term βαστάζειν is unique in the Gospel (cf. 10:31; 12:6; 19:17; 20:15). Such usage also reveals two different, though closely related, connotations: an inability to grasp the undisclosed revelation at this point (in connection with the failure of the disciples to understand the ongoing disclosures of Jesus) and an inability to endure the weight or impact of such revelation (in connection with both the theme of sorrow and the theme of opposition from the world).

To begin with, a brief temporal clause ("but when it [that one] comes") specifies the essential condition for the second role of the Paraclete about to be unfolded, thus repeating by way of introduction the basic thrust of 16:7: what follows will take place only when the Paraclete comes to the disciples and therefore only when Jesus goes to the Father as announced (16:13a). Like the previous example of 16:8a, therefore, such a restatement of 16:7 sets the stage for yet another reaffirmation and underlining of the ultimate fruitfulness of the departure.

The delineation of the role itself is in the form of an inclusion (16:13b–e). Two interrelated descriptions of the role (16:13b–c, 13e$_2$) frame a central component providing a basic rationale for such a role (16:13d–e$_1$). The outer components do not simply parallel one another; rather, the first component leads to, and is further explained by, the second. The central component not only grounds this twofold description of the second role but also leads to, and is further explained by, the rationale proper that follows in 16:14–15. The following discussion will examine the delineation of the role itself and then proceed to the intervening rationale as an entry into the third component of the subdivision, the rationale proper.

The first description of the role (16:13b–c) has a twofold structure: a succinct identification of the role as such (16:13b) and a first explanation of what such a role entails (16:13c). Attached to the introductory temporal clause is an expansion of this clause in direct apposition to the demonstrative pronoun "that one," and hence with direct reference to the figure of the Spirit-Paraclete (16:13b). This expansion simply characterizes the Paraclete as "the Spirit of truth," thus providing an initial succinct description of its role among the disciples. Such a description of the Paraclete has already been employed in two of the four preceding Paraclete sayings (14:16–17a; 15:26–27; cf. 14:25–26), so the connection between the Paraclete and "truth" is firm by now in the farewell speech: the Spirit-Paraclete continues Jesus' own mission with regard to the truth (its meaning, disclosure, and proclamation). The use of such a characterization at this point looks back to the formula of departure of 16:12 and its observation that "many things" remain to be disclosed to the disciples. In other words, given its identification as the "Spirit of truth," it is the Paraclete who begins to emerge as the one who will continue Jesus' unfinished mission of revelation to the disciples. A further explanation of this initial characterization and role follows in 16:13c: the Spirit-Paraclete will "lead or guide" (ὁδηγήσει) the disciples "in [ἐν] the whole truth."[29] Again, such a description looks back to the contrast

29. This is the only use of the expression ὁδηγήσει in the Gospel. Its origins and present application, however, can be readily surmised in terms of the first unit of discourse. In 14:4–6 Jesus is characterized as "the way" to the Father. This characterization is immediately followed by two other characterizations of Jesus as "truth" and "life," which explain

of 16:12: it is indeed the Spirit-Paraclete who will proceed with Jesus' undisclosed revelation to the disciples after his departure from them.

The second description of the role (16:13e$_2$) then explains more precisely what such a "leading or guiding" implies: it will be the role of this figure "to proclaim or disclose" (ἀναγγελεῖ) to the disciples the "things to come" (τὰ ἐρχόμενα).[30] Again, such a description points back to the contrast of 16:12: it is the Spirit-Paraclete who will reveal the "many things" that the disciples could not have understood or endured prior to Jesus' departure. Such a direct connection between the Spirit-Paraclete's role among the disciples and the contrast of 16:12 will become increasingly evident and explicit in the two rationales that account for the undertaking of such a role.

The first of these rationales constitutes, once again, the central component of the inclusion formed by the two descriptions of the Spirit-Paraclete's role (16:13d–e$_1$). Thus, lying directly between the more general characterization of this role in 16:13b–c and its subsequent concretization in 16:13e$_2$ is an initial description of the source of the

---

precisely why and how Jesus represents and functions as the sole "way" to the Father (14:6b). In the present unit, the role of the Paraclete as Jesus' successor to and among the disciples is specifically presented, by means of a cognate, as an expansion of Jesus' own identity and role as "the way": after Jesus' departure, the Paraclete will "lead or guide" the disciples in "all the truth." As such, the subordination of the Paraclete to Jesus remains clear: whereas Jesus is "the way" to the Father, the Paraclete "leads or guides" the disciples in or along that way; whereas Jesus is "the way" because he is "the truth," the Paraclete leads or guides the disciples in "all the truth" as the Spirit of truth.

One finds a wide number of textual variants with regard to the prepositional phrase "in the whole truth." The most important substitutes the preposition εἰς with the accusative for ἐν with the dative. I find persuasive Metzger's (*Commentary*, 247) position that the former usage was probably introduced by copyists who regarded it as more idiomatic after the verb in question. It would be more difficult to explain the use of ἐν with the dative as a scribal addition (א D L W Θ 33 565 1071 al). In the end, however, a decision in either direction is insignificant; any difference in meaning would be slight.

The meaning of this prepositional phrase has various dimensions, involving disclosure, direction or orientation (meaning and understanding), and proclamation with respect to such "truth." The meaning of the adjective πάσῃ ("the whole"; "all the") modifying "truth"—the only such occurrence in the Gospel, and in fact the only instance where the noun "truth" is modified at all—can be explained as follows. The Spirit-Paraclete will fulfill not only the role already assigned to it in 14:26 (teaching and recalling, with reference to what Jesus has revealed during the ministry) but also the role demanded by the preceding statement of 16:12 (meaning, disclosure, and proclamation, with reference to what Jesus has left unrevealed during the ministry). In other words, the Paraclete will "guide or lead" the disciples in "the whole truth," whether disclosed or yet to be disclosed.

30. Such a role is unique in the Gospel. Its origins and present application can be readily surmised from the role claimed by Jesus in 4:23–26: it is he, as Messiah, who "discloses or proclaims all things" now, not in the future. With 16:12 such a statement is qualified, since the role is now extended as well to the Messiah's successor: it is the Spirit-Paraclete who will "disclose and proclaim the things to come," which Jesus refrains from revealing at this point. Although such a role implies a clear prophetic or predictive dimension, it should also be seen as patterned after that of Jesus himself and thus as revelatory in the wide sense of involving disclosure, meaning, and proclamation.

Spirit-Paraclete's own "truth," of the revelation it will make known (16:13d–e₁). This initial description is presented by way of contrast. The source of the Spirit-Paraclete's truth is not internal or from within but rather external and from without; the Spirit-Paraclete does not "speak" of its own accord or on its own authority (16:13d) but "speaks" only what it "hears" or on the basis of someone else's authority (16:13e₁).³¹ Therefore, it is the Spirit-Paraclete's ultimate and complete dependence on an external source—as yet undisclosed—for such "truth" and revelation that grounds its own assigned role among the disciples themselves (namely, both its "leading or guiding" of the disciples "in the whole truth" and its "proclaiming or disclosing" to them "the things to come").

This first rationale within the inclusion itself fulfills several important functions. First, from a structural point of view, it provides a smooth transition between the two framing descriptions of the role itself. In effect, one can detect within the rationale the same movement from the more general to the more concrete that is evident in the outer components. The first part of the contrast points out in a general way that the "truth" previously mentioned in the first delineation is not the Spirit-Paraclete's own. The second part refers to this "truth," in the course of positing its external provenance, in terms of a neuter plural relative pronoun (ὅσα), thus preparing the way for the use of the neuter plural substantival participle "the things to come" in the second delineation that follows. Second, this initial rationale begins to confirm the connection suggested above with the formula of departure of 16:12 insofar as it posits an unidentified, external source of revelation for the figure of the Spirit-Paraclete itself. Finally, in positing such an external source of revelation, this first rationale anticipates directly the rationale proper of 16:14–15, where such a source will be explicitly identified, thus establishing beyond question the proposed connection with the contrast of 16:12.

The second and extended rationale, 16:14–15, is developed in terms of two basic components. First, following directly upon the delineation of the Spirit-Paraclete's role with regard to the disciples, it gives a corresponding delineation of its role with regard to Jesus himself. This provides a first, indirect identification of the external source already claimed for the truth and revelation to be disclosed by the Spirit-Paraclete, namely, Jesus (16:14a). Second, just as a rationale is provided for the Spirit-Paraclete's

---

31. The contrast is sharply reinforced by the strong adversative ἀλλά and focuses on the verb *to speak* (λαλεῖν) as encompassing the twofold role assigned to the Spirit-Paraclete in the outer components of the inclusion: not of its own accord/whatever it hears. As such, the role of the Spirit-Paraclete is patterned directly after that of Jesus himself, whose activity is not only comprehensively described in terms of "speaking" but also commonly presented by the same contrast (variously expressed) not of himself/what he has seen and heard (3:11, 31–32a, 34; 7:17–18; 8:26, 28, 38; 12:49–50; 14:10).

role among the disciples, so now a corresponding rationale is also given for its role with regard to Jesus. Within this rationale, Jesus is explicitly identified as the external source in question. An ultimate source for Jesus himself also is named: the Father (16:14b–15). This rationale, furthermore, unites these two roles of the Paraclete, its role with regard to both Jesus and the disciples.

To begin with, the role of the Spirit-Paraclete with regard to Jesus is briefly described: the Spirit-Paraclete will glorify Jesus. This immediately points to Jesus as the external source (16:14a). Then the rationale for this role, for this glorification of Jesus on the part of the Spirit-Paraclete, takes the form of an inclusion. The outer components explicitly identify Jesus as the Spirit-Paraclete's own source of revelation (16:14b, 15b), and the central component further identifies the Father as the ultimate source of revelation for Jesus himself (16:15a). In addition, the outer components not only point directly to Jesus as the external source of the Spirit-Paraclete's "truth" and revelation but also repeat the Spirit-Paraclete's basic role among the disciples themselves as formulated in the second description of 16:13e$_2$.[32] In so doing the outer components ground the role of the Spirit-Paraclete with respect to Jesus in the fulfillment of its role with respect to the disciples—in "proclaiming or disclosing" to the latter what it "receives" from Jesus himself, the Spirit-Paraclete glorifies Jesus.[33] In so doing, furthermore, the outer components place the

32. These two descriptions parallel each other, with only minor stylistic variations in formulation. First, both outer components posit Jesus as the source in question by rephrasing the second part of the preceding rationale and contrast of 16:13d–e$_1$. Instead of "to hear," one now finds the verb to take or to receive (λαμβάνειν); instead of a relative pronoun, one now finds a prepositional phrase with ἐκ as a genitive of source, "from what is mine" (thus, the Spirit-Paraclete "shall receive or take from what is mine [what Jesus has]"). Second, both outer components repeat the role of the Spirit-Paraclete with regard to the disciples as described in 16:13e$_2$, that is, by the verb ἀναγγελεῖ (thus, the Spirit-Paraclete "shall proclaim or disclose to you [the disciples]" what it "shall receive or take" from Jesus).

33. Although the verb to receive (λαμβάνειν) is often used in the Gospel with the sense of "to accept" (e.g., 1:12; 3:11, 32–33), the connotation conveyed here—the reception of revelation or "truth" from a higher link in the chain of revelation in order to pass it on to others—is not duplicated elsewhere either with regard to the Spirit-Paraclete or to Jesus (cf. 10:18). The closest parallels in this regard concern the disciples and Jesus (1:16), the disciples and the Spirit-Paraclete (7:39; 14:17; 20:22), and the Baptist and God (3:27).

This is the only time in the Gospel that the role of the Spirit-Paraclete is defined as glorifying Jesus. However, both the role itself and its mode of fulfillment have been encountered in two of the preceding units of discourse: in 13:31–32 with regard to Jesus, and in 15:8 with regard to the disciples. All three instances basically expand and apply a principle enunciated at the beginning of Jesus' extended stay in Jerusalem of 7:11–10:39, namely, the contrast provided by 7:18. Whereas the one who "speaks" of himself or on his own authority "seeks his own glory," the one who "seeks the glory" of the one who sent him is true and righteous. This contrast is particularly relevant with regard to the present description of the Spirit-Paraclete's role vis-à-vis Jesus, given the similar terminology employed to describe the Spirit-Paraclete at this point. In other words, all those who are "sent" in the chain of revelation "glorify" their senders by carrying out their assigned tasks.

previously disclosed role of the Spirit-Paraclete with regard to the disciples within the wider perspective of its own fundamental role with regard to Jesus himself: in carrying out the former role, the Paraclete fulfills the latter as well.

As a whole, this second rationale—the rationale proper within the threefold sequence—provides a more secure grounding than the initial rationale for the specific role assigned to the Spirit-Paraclete with regard to the disciples. Both the explicit identification of Jesus as the external source in question and the nature of the relationship posited between Jesus and the Spirit-Paraclete in and through the latter's execution of its assigned role among the disciples ground this role at a fundamental level. In "leading or guiding" the disciples "in the whole truth" and in "proclaiming or disclosing" to them "the things to come," the Spirit-Paraclete will disclose and proclaim the "truth" that comes from Jesus himself and, in so doing, fulfill its own role with regard to the source of such "truth" and revelation (namely, the glorification of Jesus). The further identification of the Father as the ultimate source of Jesus' truth and revelation provides an even more fundamental grounding. In carrying out its assigned role both among the disciples and with regard to Jesus, the Spirit-Paraclete will disclose the "truth" that comes not just from Jesus but from God the Father himself.[34]

Such a fundamental grounding confirms beyond any doubt the proposed connection with the departing formula of 16:12. In other words, what must of necessity remain undisclosed on the part of Jesus even at the time of "the hour" eventually will be disclosed by the Spirit-Paraclete beginning with the completion of "the hour." The Spirit-Paraclete will receive such "truth" and revelation from Jesus himself and will make it known to the disciples. Such a fundamental grounding, moreover, properly identifies the entire chain of "truth" and revelation: the Father, Jesus, the Spirit-Paraclete, the disciples, and the disciples in and to the world.

Just as the first role of the Spirit-Paraclete outlined in 16:8–11 represents an expansion and development of the role previously outlined in 15:18–16:4a, so does this second role of 16:12–15 represent a further expansion and development of the role previously outlined in 13:31–14:31. Three specific aspects of this expansion and development can be immediately identified. First, the analysis of the first unit pointed out that the role ascribed to the Spirit-Paraclete among the disciples is concerned with the meaning, disclosure, and proclamation of "truth" (14:16–17a)

---

34. This identification of the Father as the ultimate source of truth and revelation is conveyed by a copulative sentence that equates what Jesus has (ἐμά) with all that the Father himself has (πάντα ὅσα ἔχει)—that equates what is of Jesus with what is of the Father. Such complete identification of Jesus' revelation and message with the Father's is common in the Gospel and is expressed in a wide variety of ways (e.g., 5:19–30; 8:27–28).

and that such a role involves two interrelated tasks—a "teaching" and a "recalling" (14:26) that continue Jesus' own teaching after his departure and that allow the disciples to come at last to a full, though ongoing and open-ended, understanding of Jesus' mission and message. Second, the analysis of the first unit also pointed out that the fulfillment of such a role would reverse the pattern of the disciples' obvious failure to understand and thus serve as the means by which many of the other promises of the unit would begin to be fulfilled. Third, the analysis pointed out that this promise of the Spirit-Paraclete as a successor to Jesus and its given role within the circle of the disciples directly advances the strategy of reassurance and consolation of the disciples in the light of the departure. In all three respects the expansion and development represented by this second role assigned to the Spirit-Paraclete in 16:12–15 can be summarized.

To begin with, whereas the role of the Spirit-Paraclete in the first unit is exclusively concerned with the teaching and revelation of Jesus while in the world and leads to a deeper understanding of that teaching and revelation, the role of the Spirit-Paraclete in the present unit is formulated in terms of the preceding contrast of 16:12: the Spirit-Paraclete will be concerned as well with that teaching and revelation of Jesus that remained deliberately undisclosed during the ministry itself, making such "truth" known and available to the disciples after the ministry is over. Furthermore, just as the process of "teaching" and "recalling" envisioned in the first unit is ongoing and open-ended, in keeping with the unending presence and abiding of the Spirit-Paraclete among the disciples, so is this process of "proclaiming and disclosing" envisioned in the present unit. In effect, the concept of "truth" has been significantly expanded. Although in both cases the figure of the Spirit-Paraclete remains completely subordinate to Jesus, "truth" is no longer limited to the revelation of Jesus during his mission and ministry (the further understanding and interpretation of which it now becomes the task of the Paraclete to guide and direct) but is extended to include further revelation by Jesus after the end of his mission and ministry, the "whole truth" (the disclosure of which it now becomes the task of the Paraclete to disclose and proclaim).

Second, whereas in the first unit the failure of the disciples to understand the full character and implications of Jesus' message and mission (a characteristic of the circle of disciples as a whole from the beginning of the narrative) becomes evident with regard to the disclosures regarding the meaning and consequences of the departure itself, in the present unit that failure to understand is specifically cited in the departing formula of 16:12 as the very reason for a limited revelation on Jesus' part during the ministry. Consequently, although the role of the Spirit-Paraclete remains formally the same in both units in this regard (counteracting this failure of the disciples to understand the mission and message of Jesus), the scope of the role undergoes significant expansion in the present unit. This theme of the disciples' failure to understand fully is no longer limited to the actual revelation of Jesus (the full perception of which begins to take place only upon the coming of the Spirit-Paraclete at the very end of "the hour") but extended to revelation that remains undisclosed during the ministry (the disclosure of which begins to take place only upon the coming of the Spirit-Paraclete at the completion of "the hour").

Finally, the strategy of consolation undergoes a significant development as well. Whereas in the first unit the promise of full understanding in the future by means of the Spirit-Paraclete as Jesus' successor in the midst of the disciples constitutes a central element in the strategy of consolation and reassurance of the disciples, in the present unit such reassurance and consolation is focused primarily on the further proclamation and disclosure that the Spirit-Paraclete as Jesus' successor would receive from Jesus himself (and the Father) and impart to the disciples. The reassurance of the disciples is no longer limited to an ongoing change of perception promised within the first unit itself (a change of perception that allows for the fulfillment of many of the other promises given in the unit) but is extended to a future leading or guiding of the disciples in the world by means of further revelation from above (a revelation that is made possible precisely by such a change of perception on their part).[35]

Such a description of the Spirit-Paraclete's role among the disciples in 16:12–15 cannot but have a direct and immediate effect on the previous description of its role with regard to the world in 16:8–11, a role that is conceived as being carried out in and through the circle of the disciples themselves. In other words, it is only because the Spirit-Paraclete will "lead and guide" the disciples "in the whole truth" and will "proclaim and disclose" to them "the things to come"—a "truth" that it receives from Jesus and the Father and then passes on to the disciples, and a "truth" that remained deliberately undisclosed in part during Jesus' own ministry—that the disciples will be able to "convict" the world on the basis of its definitions and practices of righteousness, sin, and judgment (definitions and practices that differ from those of Jesus and God, from those that inform and characterize "truth" itself). Consequently, in the course of their mission and proclamation of this "truth" in and to the world, guided and informed by

35. The earlier role assigned to the Spirit-Paraclete in the first unit is in no way displaced or abandoned by the further role assigned in the present unit. In fact, the latter includes the former: the Spirit-Paraclete will not only disclose and proclaim the "many things" left unsaid by Jesus during the ministry but also, in so doing, will direct the disciples to a proper understanding thereof. In other words, the "leading and guiding," along with the "disclosing and proclaiming," of the Spirit-Paraclete entail revelation, as well as a proper understanding of such a revelation (see n. 30 above).

the Spirit-Paraclete as Jesus' successor in their midst, the disciples will indeed be able to convict an unbelieving and hostile world.

Following the initial, negative reaction of the disciples in 16:5b–6 (a reaction characterized by complete silence and profound sorrow on their part) to Jesus' beginning reaffirmation of the forthcoming departure (16:4b–5a) is an extensive explanation on Jesus' part concerning the ultimate fruitfulness of such an inevitable and imminent departure (16:7–15). This entire explanation focuses on the figure of the Spirit-Paraclete, Jesus' promised successor to and among the disciples. It involves two different, though interrelated, functions of this successor: its role with regard to the world at large (16:8–11) and its role with regard to the disciples themselves (16:12–15).

In both cases, the promised presence of the Spirit-Paraclete in their midst serves as direct consolation and reassurance to the disciples in the face of the announced departure and their given reaction. It is the disciples who will ultimately convict an unbelieving and hostile world. Similarly, it is the disciples who will possess the full "truth" that comes from above, from God the Father himself, thus allowing them in effect to bring about the conviction of the world. The juxtaposition of these two Paraclete sayings is most effective. Its constitutive elements—the back-to-back sequence, the extensive length of each saying and of the subsection as a whole, the nature of the declarations and promises involved, and the close interrelationship of the two sayings—provide a secure grounding for the main point at issue, the ultimate fruitfulness of the forthcoming departure for the circle of disciples.

Second Major Section (John 16:16–24)

The second major section of the fourth unit of discourse, 16:16–24, describes Jesus' departure and return as these events affect the disciples. This section, like each major section of the unit, follows a threefold pattern of inclusion. Its literary structure can be outlined as follows: (1) Jesus' disclosure of departure and return: the coming situation of the disciples (16:16); (2) the disciples' reaction to Jesus' disclosure of departure and return (16:17–18); and (3) Jesus' departure and return: further consequences for the disciples (16:19–24).

Jesus' Disclosure of Departure and Return: The Coming Situation of the Disciples (John 16:16)

The beginning declaration of Jesus in the second section (16:16) is similar to that of the first section in several respects: it is brief; it is phrased in terms of a contrast; the contrast involves two different periods of time; and the time periods in question involve Jesus' impending departure and other related concerns. At the same time, there are two major differences. The first difference concerns the identification of the time periods in question. In 16:4b–5a the time periods involve the public ministry at large and "the hour"; in 16:16 such periods refer to two different stages within "the hour" itself (though the second period extends indefinitely beyond "the hour" as well), namely, the time beginning with the crucifixion and death and the time beginning with the resurrection. The second difference involves the description of these time periods. In 16:4b–5a the two periods are respectively characterized by silence/disclosure on Jesus' part concerning the events of the departure; in 16:16 the two periods are respectively characterized instead by inability/ability on the part of the disciples to see Jesus (or, to put it differently, by Jesus' absence from/presence with the disciples).

The contrast itself is conveyed by two coordinate members of a compound sentence. The first member returns to the theme of the departure from the previous section (16:16a), and the second introduces the theme of the return for the first time in the unit (16:16b). These themes, however, are not conveyed directly at this point (that is, by journey or travel terminology as such). They are conveyed indirectly, via the closely related theme of not seeing/seeing Jesus (that is, by direct, immediate, and closely interrelated consequences of Jesus' departure and return for the disciples).

The contrasting statements reveal a similar structure: a time reference followed by a prediction. Each statement is introduced by the temporal adverb "a little while" (μικρόν), which sets up the basic temporal sequence in question.[36] Indeed, given its position at the beginning of each statement, this twofold temporal designation emphasizes not only the importance of the sequence as a whole but also the brevity of the first (and negative) period or stage within the sequence.[37] Each statement then continues with a prediction on Jesus' part regarding the coming situation of the disciples in each period or stage of the sequence. The two predictions outline, in effect, very different situations for the disciples with regard to Jesus himself, thus sharply reinforcing the basic temporal sequence involved. These contrasting

36. The declaration represents a third example of a formula of departure in this unit (see nn. 8, 27 above). With regard to form, the present example combines the most common type of formulation (a variation of the expression "yet a little while") with the third type of formulation (the use of a temporal adverb, "no longer"): "a little while and no longer." With regard to purpose, the present example distinguishes again, as in 16:12, between the present and future situations of the disciples. The use of the adverb "a little while" at this point is unique insofar as it makes an explicit distinction within "the hour" itself (cf. 7:33; 12:35; 13:33; 14:19). To be sure, its previous use in 13:33 and 14:19 implies such a distinction; thus, its twofold use here makes explicit what is already implicit in the first unit.

37. Such brevity is reinforced by the use of another temporal adverb to modify the second example of 16:16b: "and yet again a little while."

situations are both described in terms of "seeing." To begin with, a time is said to be rapidly approaching when the disciples will no longer "see" (θεωρεῖτε) Jesus (16:16a); then, a period of time is said to soon follow when the disciples "will see" (ὄψεσθε) Jesus once again (16:16b).[38] Thus, the first situation envisioned in the contrast is portrayed in negative terms for the disciples, and the second is presented in a very positive light.

The formula therefore addresses the coming situation of the disciples in terms of the closely related contrast "not seeing/seeing." The first part of the contrast returns thereby to the theme of the departure after the long exposition of the twofold role of the Spirit-Paraclete as Jesus' successor among the disciples (16:7–15). It does so indirectly, however, by restating an immediate negative consequence of the forthcoming departure for the disciples that was already mentioned in passing within the first Paraclete saying of 16:8–11 (v. 10b).[39] The second part of the contrast immediately counteracts the first part in two ways. On the one hand, it continues to outline the positive consequences of the forthcoming departure, though now apart from the figure of the Spirit-Paraclete as such, who from this point on disappears altogether from the unit. Such positive consequences now entirely focus on the figure of Jesus—a prediction and promise is made to the effect that the disciples will see Jesus once again. On the other hand, the second part of the contrast underlines the ephemeral nature of the negative consequence outlined and emphasizes instead the lasting character of the positive consequence to follow—the disciples soon will see Jesus again. From both perspectives, furthermore, the original negative consequence posited in 16:10b is radically revised with this beginning declaration of 16:16.

This beginning declaration of Jesus, like the previous formula of departure of 16:12, points forward. Unlike the formula of 16:12, however, what it points forward to is not the figure of the Spirit-Paraclete but that of Jesus himself, though the two are thoroughly intertwined, as the second Paraclete saying of 16:12–15 has affirmed. This beginning declaration of Jesus, furthermore, points the way for the subsequent development of this middle major section. Jesus' departure and return will be addressed for the most part through other interrelated consequences of such a departure and return for the disciples.

---

38. For a similar use of the verb θεωρεῖν, see 14:15–17, 18–21. However, in both cases this earlier use refers to "the hour" as a whole and to a permanent situation on the part of the world after "the hour," whereas 16:16a refers to an ephemeral stage of the disciples within "the hour" itself. For its use in 16:10b, see n. 39 below. For a similar use of the verb ὁράω, see 20:18, 20, 25, 29; cf. 20:14. Such variation in terminology is simply stylistic.

39. The use of the verb in 16:16a, therefore, closely matches its previous use in 16:10b, especially given the common use of the temporal adverb "no longer."

The Disciples' Reaction to Jesus' Disclosure
of Departure and Return (John 16:17–18)

The reaction of the disciples to the beginning declaration of Jesus within this middle section (16:17–18) concerns 16:16 for the most part and does not pursue the preceding Paraclete sayings of 16:7–15. This reaction differs considerably from that portrayed in the first major section. First, the reaction here receives a much more extensive elaboration. Second, the reaction is no longer conveyed by Jesus as the speaker of the discourse but instead more directly, by a focus on a discussion that takes place within the group itself, away from Jesus. As such, it becomes clear that the disciples, in the light of the preceding disclosures, have begun to raise specific questions about the announced departure, thus moving beyond both their initial reaction of silence and Jesus' criticism of that reaction (16:5b). At the same time, this move on their part is presented ironically. The questions are confined to the group itself and not addressed to Jesus; also, these questions bring the disciples no closer to a proper understanding of the fundamental meaning of the departure and its consequences. Therefore, as the disciples become more involved with these ongoing disclosures on Jesus' part, they show an increasing failure to understand their meaning.

Beginning with an introductory formula that switches the focus of attention from the speaker to the group of assembled disciples (16:17a),[40] the reaction is described in terms of three steps presented in an ascending sequence. The first two steps consist of specific questions regarding the preceding disclosures of Jesus, and the third represents a concluding declaration concerning their own overall understanding of these disclosures.

The first step in the sequence (16:17) looks back not only to the immediately preceding declaration of Jesus in 16:16 but also to the beginning declaration of Jesus in 16:4b–5a (especially its second component of 16:5a, subsequently repeated with some variations in 16:10b). In effect, the disciples ask themselves at this point what the meaning of these two declarations can be and in so doing repeat, with only minor stylistic variations, both the preceding statement of 16:16 (16:17c–d) and the beginning statement of 16:5a concerning the departure and its destination (16:17e–f).[41] There

---

40. This introduction by the narrator serves two other purposes as well: (a) it points out that the reaction is not directed at Jesus but strictly confined to the group itself, and (b) it further describes the reaction as arising from "some" of the disciples within the group. The import of the latter distinction within the group should not be pressed too far, especially given the fact that by 16:29 the group speaks as a whole. I prefer to see it as an indication that some of the disciples are now willing to pursue the announcements and explanations in question, but others still prefer to remain silent, thus continuing the first reaction already described and criticized in 16:5b–6.

41. An introduction raises the basic question of meaning ("What is this which he is telling us?") so that the two repeated declarations stand in apposition to this basic question of 16:17b.

can be no doubt, therefore, that the preceding statement of 16:16 concerning the coming inability/ability to see Jesus is immediately connected by the disciples with the previous statements regarding Jesus' forthcoming departure to the one who sent him/the Father. In other words, this beginning declaration is clearly placed within the same frame of reference as the already announced departure, though neither statement is properly understood. The second step (16:18a–b) again looks back to the immediately preceding declaration of 16:16, but now the one question raised focuses on the time references within that statement—namely, on the twofold use of the temporal adverb "a little while" and the swift temporal sequence such a twofold use posits and predicts (16:18b).[42] The third and final step (16:18c) represents a self-assessment of the disciples' overall understanding with regard to Jesus' ongoing disclosures: a fundamental confession of ignorance concerning the departure itself, its announced and related consequences of 16:16, and the temporal sequence involved.[43]

The sequence, therefore, contains an effective, mounting progression from a failure to understand the departure and the return in terms of their direct, immediate, and interrelated consequences (the not seeing/seeing of Jesus); to a failure to understand the nature of the temporal sequence involved in the rapid succession of such consequences (a little while/again a little while); to a more comprehensive failure to understand the fundamental nature of these farewell disclosures as a whole. Silence and sorrow have now given way, as desired, to questions concerning the impending departure. Such questions, however, reflect and lead to a self-confessed inability on the part of the disciples to perceive the basic thrust of Jesus' remarks with regard to the departure and its consequences.

Jesus' Departure and Return:
Further Consequences for the Disciples
(John 16:19–24)

The third subsection of the second major section (16:19–24), like that of the first major section, is far more extensive than the first two. However,

42. This second step is also introduced, as in 16:17a, by a brief introductory formula on the part of the narrator that simply indicates a further declaration on the part of those disciples who had already spoken (16:18a). The question itself is given in 16:18b, and its precise formulation depends on the textual acceptance of the relative clause "which he is saying" as modifying the demonstrative pronoun. I favor exclusion: the omission of the clause has good backing (p^5 p^{66} ° D° W 565 al), and the addition itself can be readily explained in terms of assimilation to 16:17b. The question is thus straightforward, with the demonstrative as an adjective rather than a pronoun ("What is this little while?").

43. I take this final step to refer to all that precedes—both the temporal sequence as such (16:18a–b) and the wider declarations concerning inability/ability to see and the departure to the Father (16:17). Thus, this final step provides an effective climax to the reaction itself: the disciples simply do not know the import of any of these disclosures.

its plan of development differs from that of 16:7–15. First, it is necessary at this point to return the focus from the group of disciples back to Jesus. Second, it is also necessary to show how Jesus as speaker becomes acquainted with the disciples' reaction so that the further development of the beginning declaration can take place in the light of this reaction. Third, since the nature of the reaction itself changes at this point, the nature of such a further development changes as well.

This third subsection consists of two basic steps. The first step addresses the first two observations made above: the focus is returned to Jesus as speaker, who is also portrayed as being fully aware of the disciples' reaction (16:19). The second step deals with the third observation above: the development of the beginning declaration in the light of the intervening reaction—the consequences of Jesus' departure and return for the disciples (16:20–24).

Jesus' Knowledge of the Disciples' Reaction (John 16:19)

The return to Jesus as the speaker of the discourse is accomplished in such a way that Jesus is shown as knowing the exact nature of the preceding discussion among the disciples and hence as addressing the disciples accordingly. In 16:19a a statement from the narrator indicates that Jesus is fully aware of the questioning among the disciples—an insight into Jesus' mind—and of their desire to bring such questions before him (though the latter element has not been expressed in the exposition of this discussion).[44] Such a statement is to be immediately connected with the important recurrent motif in the Gospel of Jesus' comprehensive knowledge concerning all things and all human beings: he knows the precise preoccupations and questions of his own disciples at this time. Through the motif of foreknowledge, therefore, the focus returns to Jesus.

A direct address of Jesus to the disciples, by way of a question, reflects in a concrete way the full extent of his knowledge concerning their private reaction. With minor stylistic variations, he quotes their first question of 16:17b–d, so the beginning declaration of 16:16 is repeated practically verbatim a third time within the section (16:19b–e).[45] The importance

---

44. This desire is expressed by the verb ἐρωτᾶν, the same term used earlier with regard to Jesus' critical description of the disciples' silence in 16:5b–c. Thus, one is now informed by Jesus' own comprehensive knowledge of the situation that the disciples (or "some" of them, in any case) wish to bring their own "questioning" before Jesus at this point, but they fail to do so. From the previous attitude of "no questions," therefore, there is a definite movement toward "questioning"; however, such "questioning" is strictly limited to the confines of the group at this point.

45. Whereas 16:19b continues the narrator's introduction by anticipating Jesus' open rejoinder to the disciples, thus disclosing to them his full knowledge of the situation, 16:19c–e provides the question itself. The question has two parts: (a) the question proper (16:19c),

of this beginning declaration cannot be made more obvious; it has now been repeated and reaffirmed three times. Thus, tremendous emphasis is being placed on the temporal sequence put forward, both in terms of its inevitability (the two stages must take place) and its swiftness (the first, negative step will be followed quickly by the second, positive step). In other words, the departure is inescapable and absolutely necessary, but ultimately beneficial as well.

Consequences of Jesus' Departure and Return for the Disciples (John 16:20–24)

John 16:20–24 develops the introductory declaration of John 16:16 as a much fuller exposition of the consequences of departure and return for the disciples. It takes into account the disciples' failure to understand the reference to the coming sequence of departure and return in the direct and immediate consequences outlined for such a departure and return, the not seeing/seeing of Jesus in rapid sequence. This exposition focuses on the contrast sorrow/joy, thus returning to the theme of sorrow introduced at the beginning of the unit in the first reaction of 16:5b-6.

The exposition proceeds in three steps arranged again in an ascending pattern. First, further consequences of the departure are briefly outlined (16:20a–b). Such consequences are then contrasted directly and at greater length with those of the return (16:20c–22). Finally, further consequences of the return are delineated in much greater detail (16:23–24). Therefore, the development of this exposition (its internal movement from departure to return) reinforces not only the inevitability of the contrasting temporal sequence but above all the brevity of its first, negative stage in relation to the enduring character of its second, positive stage.

The first step of the development (16:20a–b) pursues only the first component of the beginning declaration of 16:16, namely, the reference to the forthcoming departure by means of the coming inability of the disciples to see Jesus (16:16a). This first step introduces the general contrast between sorrow and joy, along with a corresponding contrast between the disciples and the world.

This contrast is brief and to the point. It is introduced by the solemn formula "Amen, amen, I say to you."[46] The contrast itself is developed in an ABBA chiastic form; the contrasting attitudes serve as the framing

which raises the issue of the disciples' own questioning among themselves concerning Jesus' disclosures, and (b) the repetition of a specific object of this questioning, the declaration of 16:16 as a whole (16:19d–e). This repetition follows the version of the disciples in 16:17c–d rather than that of Jesus in 16:16.

46. This is the third example of this formula within the speech (13:38; 14:12) and the first of two examples within this unit (16:23; see n. 59 below). In every case the formula introduces a specific prediction of Jesus to the disciples.

252 THE FAREWELL OF THE WORD

components, and the central components identify the different groups in question. The disciples' attitude with regard to the departure is described in terms of sorrow (16:20a: weeping and mourning), whereas that of the world is described in terms of joy (16:20b: rejoicing).[47] The contrast also has a negative orientation. The use of two different expressions to convey the disciples' sorrow at the beginning of the contrast sharply underlines the severe character of this first stage of the sequence for the disciples. This emphasis is then pointedly reinforced by the opposite attitude of the world during the same period. Both in terms of internal disposition and external reinforcement, therefore, the first time period foretold in 16:16a is envisioned as difficult and trying for the disciples.

At the same time, this sharp contrast with the world of 16:20a–b should be read in the light of the previous portrayal of the world conveyed through the first Paraclete saying of 16:8–11. On the one hand, given the world's fundamental values with regard to sin, righteousness, and judgment and the fundamental opposition of such values to those of God, the joy the world experiences over the departure of Jesus should not be surprising. The execution of its judgment against Jesus will bring joy to the world, especially given the nature of such a judgment and departure. On the other hand, given the corresponding assurance that in the end it is the disciples, as those who represent the values of God, who will convict the world, such a reaction of joy (though real and painful) should also appear ironic—premature and misguided. The next two steps of the overall development, then, clearly point out that joy—indeed full and perfect joy—will be the lot of the disciples and not of the world. Therefore, although the contrast of 16:22a–b itself presents a negative view of the future situation of the disciples, the previous affirmations of 16:8–11 already point the way beyond it as well, and the steps that follow immediately reveal the true and lasting future situation of the disciples.

The second step of the development (16:20c–22) deals with both components of the beginning declaration of 16:16—that is, with the references to both the forthcoming departure and the return to follow soon thereafter (both the inability to see Jesus and the subsequent ability to see him again). As such, 16:20c–22 immediately begins to assuage the strong negative tone of the beginning contrast of 16:20a–b. This second part of the development is much more complex. The general contrast, sorrow/joy, is retained throughout. At the same time, the direct contrast with the world is dropped. As a result, the contrast sorrow/joy is developed only in

---

47. The attitude of sorrow is conveyed in terms of "weeping" (κλαύσετε) and "mourning" (θρηνήσετε). For the former, always in a context of death, see 11:31, 33; 20:11, 13, 15. Its use here, therefore, points in a specific, though implicit, way to the kind of "departure" envisioned, the death of Jesus. The attitude of joy is conveyed in terms of "rejoicing" (χαρήσεται), the only time in the Gospel that such a reaction is ascribed to the world.

reference to the disciples themselves; whereas sorrow continues to represent their characteristic attitude during the first stage of the sequence,
such sorrow yields to joy in the second stage. Finally, this new shift in
development takes the form of an inclusion. The outer components identify the contrasting attitudes of the disciples during these two different
stages (16:20c–d, 22), and the central element effectively describes this
same contrast by the use of a sustained metaphor (16:21).

The first outer component (16:20c–d) outlines the contrasting attitudes
of the disciples in both stages without much development. The first part of
the contrast reaffirms their previous attitude as outlined in 16:20a
(16:20c: "being distressed"). The second part points to a different situation
altogether as it describes the ultimate attitude of the disciples in the same
terms as that of the world previously outlined in 16:20b (16:20d: "joy").[48]
The message is unmistakable: sorrow over the departure will yield to joy
with the return.[49] The joy previously attributed to the world in 16:20a–b is
now openly revealed as premature, ephemeral, and ironic; in the end it
is the disciples who will possess true and proper joy.

The central component (16:21) repeats and affirms these contrasting
attitudes among the disciples by a sustained metaphor, a woman in childbirth.[50] The first part of the metaphor describes the woman's attitude
prior to the birth itself (16:21a–b) and the second part, her attitude after
birth (16:21c–d).[51] The sorrow that characterizes the first period turns to
joy in the second period, a joy that is described as having no recollection

48. The attitude of sorrow is now conveyed in terms of "being distressed" (λυπηθήσεσθε).
The attitude of joy is conveyed by a concise version of the contrast itself that focuses on the
transformation proper: "sorrow" (λύπη) "shall become or turn to joy" (εἰς χαράν). The contrast
is emphasized by the use of the strong adversative conjunction uniting the two clauses.

49. The expression of sorrow used within this contrast is limited to the present unit,
where it was used by Jesus at the beginning to describe the reaction of the disciples (16:6).
This initial reaction to the announcement of the departure is now used to characterize the
fundamental attitude of the disciples during the whole period of time that revolves around
the departure itself, beginning with its announcement and ending with the return. The use
of joy to characterize the subsequent attitude of the disciples is found elsewhere in the
Gospel (4:36; 20:20). The last example is particularly relevant, given its connection with
Jesus' return: the joy of the disciples will begin with the resurrection itself, when the
disciples will see Jesus again.

50. This sustained metaphor represents another traditional proverb whose meaning is being extended to a new situation altogether; see K. Dewey, "Paroimiai," 89, 97. The metaphor's
present formulation shows clear signs of adaptation to its present Gospel context as well, e.g.,
the reference to the arrival of the woman's "hour."

51. Both parts of the contrast reveal the same development. First, both begin with a
reference to the period in question by employing a temporal clause introduced by ὅταν:
"when a woman gives birth" (16:21a$_1$) and "when the child is born" (16:21c). Second, both
continue with a main clause describing the attitude of the woman during each of the periods
in question: "she has sorrow" (16:21a$_2$) and "she no longer remembers her distress because
of her joy" (16:21d$_1$). Finally, both conclude with a causal clause explaining the reason for
such an attitude in each period: "because her hour has come" (16:21b) and "because a
human being has been born into the world (16:21d$_2$)." The contrast is thus sharp from the
beginning to the end of the metaphor.

of the preceding sorrow.[52] Thus, this intervening metaphor introduces a greater emphasis on the resulting attitude of joy than on that of sorrow.

This metaphor is effective at this point because it describes in vivid and poignant terms the full process that awaits the disciples themselves in the near future (not only the rapid sequence of two stages but also the sharply different attitudes that characterize each of these stages), a process outlined in the surrounding components of the inclusion. The reference to the arrival of the woman's "hour," the reason given for her attitude of sorrow (16:21b), immediately connects the metaphor with "the hour" of Jesus and its approaching climactic events. What the woman experiences in her own "hour" the disciples will experience during Jesus' "hour" as well (sorrow at first, but then joy). Furthermore, the description of this ultimate joy on her part in terms of forgetting the preceding and necessary sorrow ($16:21d_1$) immediately connects the metaphor as well with a primary theme of this unit: the departure as ultimately beneficial for the disciples (16:7).

The metaphor is also important because the theme of birth is a recurrent Johannine theme. Its specific connotation here differs considerably from that found in the remainder of the Gospel. In the Gospel at large all those who come to believe in Jesus are properly called "the children of God" (1:13; 11:52; 21:5) and described as "having been born" of God (in contrast to human agency: 1:13) or of the Spirit (in contrast to the flesh; 3:3–8). In the metaphor of 16:21, however, the disciples as those who believe in Jesus are portrayed as undergoing a process of birth in terms of their reactions to the rapid sequence of Jesus' departure/return. Whereas in the present unit it is a fundamental shift in the attitude of the disciples that is compared to a process of birth, elsewhere it is the process of becoming a disciple that is formulated in terms of a birth. These two dimensions are by no means unrelated; in fact, both address the status of believers from different perspectives. On the one hand, the overall process of becoming a believer entails a process of birth from flesh to Spirit; on the other hand, this process of becoming a believer involves a more concrete process of birth from sorrow over Jesus' departure to joy at his return. In the end, of course, it is this return of Jesus that gives way as well to the coming of the Spirit-Paraclete, who in turn brings the disciples to full belief and understanding (that is, to their full status as children of God).

---

52. The description of the woman's sorrow is brief and continues the use of λύπη from 16:20d, though now as the object of the verb *to have*—namely, the woman "has sorrow." The description of the woman's joy is more complex. First, the description refers to the absence of any later recollection of such sorrow (16:33), now conveyed in terms of "tribulation" (θλῖψις, a word not found outside this unit of discourse). Second, the description grounds such absence of recollection in the woman's new attitude of "joy," again employing the term χαρά from 16:20d.

This metaphor, therefore, focuses the more general dimension of the believer's birth from God present in the Gospel on the more specific birth of the believer that takes place during "the hour" itself.

The concluding outer component of 16:20c–22 (16:22) again outlines the contrasting attitudes of the disciples in both time periods, though now with an even stronger emphasis on joy (following the thrust of the preceding metaphor). Thus, whereas the first part of the contrast briefly reaffirms the disciples' attitude of sorrow over the departure as previously outlined in 16:20b (16:22a: "having sorrow"),[53] the second part elaborates on their subsequent attitude of joy in the light of the return (16:22b–d: "rejoicing of the heart").[54] This elaboration includes both a preceding reason for such an attitude and a further description of the kind of joy that the disciples will possess. In effect, this joy of the disciples (16:22c) is grounded in the fact that Jesus will see them again (16:22b)—that is, in Jesus' return[55]— and is described as a possession that no one will be able to wrest from them (16:22d).[56]

Whereas this second step of the overall development (16:20c–22) begins with a balanced emphasis on the contrasting attitudes of the disciples in the light of Jesus' departure and return, it closes with a more pointed emphasis on their attitude in the light of the return. The beginning and balanced emphasis of 16:20c–d on sorrow/joy yields to a concluding emphasis on joy, first with the extended metaphor of 16:21 itself and then

53. This attitude of sorrow is conveyed in exactly the same way as in the first part of the metaphor of 16:21 (v. 21a–b): the noun is used with the verb *to have*. From a textual point of view, I favor the use of the present tense (p²² ℵ° B C K Wᶜ 054 28 565 700 al). It has strong support: the introduction of the future is in line with the many predictive futures used in the course of the contrast, and a present/future distinction in the contrast agrees well with the "now/but again" distinction also present in the contrast—a distinction that reinforces and accentuates the contrast between these two stages.

54. The formulation of the attitude of joy follows that of the first contrast of 16:20a–b— namely, the use of the verb *to rejoice* (χαρήσεται), but now with "the heart" of the disciples as the subject. As such, this expression of joy can be seen as formulating in positive fashion what the exhortations of 14:1a and 14:27d present in negative fashion. Such joy, however, is clearly restricted here to the time of the return, whereas the time of the departure is presented as inevitably marked by sorrow. In the first unit, by way of contrast, the disciples are urged not only to dispel all troubles and fears during the time of the departure but also to adopt an attitude of joy during this time (14:28).

55. Such a grounding returns to the beginning declaration of 16:16, thus making an explicit connection between the joy of the disciples and their ability to see Jesus again, now formulated from the point of view of Jesus himself ("I shall see you again").

56. Such a description of the future joy of the disciples strongly affirms its enduring character and hence the enduring character of the second stage of the sequence in relation to the first. However, the description also conveys an implicit warning: such joy will not go without opposition or conflict. Two other comments are in order. First, a link can be observed between this description of the disciples' joy and the preceding metaphor of 16:21: once attained, such joy is supreme (in her joy the woman no longer remembers her sorrow; the disciples cannot lose their joy). Second, as in 16:22a and for the same reasons, I believe that the use of the present tense with regard to the verb *to wrest away* is preferable (p²² p⁶⁶ᵛⁱᵈ ℵ A C Dᵇ K L 28 33 al).

with the final identification of 16:22. In so doing, this middle component of the development both reflects and prepares the way for the internal movement within the development as a whole, from its beginning exclusive focus on the consequences of the departure (16:20a–b) to its concluding exclusive focus on the consequences of the return (16:23–24). As the overall development progresses, therefore, the emphasis effectively shifts from the first time period of the sequence to the second.

The third and final step in the overall development of the beginning declaration of 16:16 (16:23–24) pursues only the declaration's second component, the reference to Jesus' return by means of the promised ability on the part of the disciples to see Jesus again (16:16b). This final step altogether bypasses the contrast of sorrow/joy, although the element of joy continues to play a prominent role. As a result, the sharp contrast among the disciples themselves, so central to the second step of the development in 16:20c–22, is replaced by a far more general contrast comparing the time of the ministry as a whole with the time of the return. The assuagement of the negative thrust of the beginning contrast of 16:20a–b (begun in 16:20c–22) climaxes in this final step of the development. Two basic parts can be discerned: a beginning description of the disciples' future relationship to Jesus (16:23a) and a subsequent description of the disciples' future relationship to the Father (16:23b–24).

The first step is brief (16:23a). A beginning formula (16:23a$_1$: "on that day") identifies the time period in question by pointing back to the second part of the contrast within 16:22 (16:22b–d), and it introduces a further consequence of the return for the disciples (16:23a$_2$).[57] This consequence, which involves the disciples' future relationship to Jesus, is formulated in terms of the disciples' second reaction of 16:17–18, though now by way of opposition: the disciples will ask nothing of Jesus.[58] In other words, all questioning of the sort encountered in 16:17–18—and hence the very failure to understand so evident in and through this questioning itself— will definitely end upon the return. Without a doubt, such an envisioned situation further grounds the joy that will characterize the disciples in that time period. Furthermore, such an envisioned situation implies that only then, in that second time period, will the departure be seen in its full and proper context, that of the return. This additional consequence of the return presented in 16:23a can be directly associated with the major thrust of the second Paraclete saying of 16:12–15; in effect, this

57. For a similar use of the formula, see 14:20; 16:26; cf. 6:39, 40, 44, 54; 12:48.
58. A further development of the theme of "questioning" takes place, therefore. The recently begun movement toward "questioning," though confined to the group itself, is now envisioned as coming to an end and as unnecessary with the return of Jesus (with the second stage of the sequence).

consequence brings together the sending of the Paraclete and the return of Jesus. Thus, the earlier promise that the Paraclete, the Spirit of truth, will come to the disciples after the departure and will lead them in the whole truth that comes from the Father and Jesus and the present promise that upon the return the disciples will have no need to ask further questions of Jesus can be seen as different dimensions of the same future situation of the disciples: it is the presence of the Spirit-Paraclete among them that will make all such questioning of the sort observed in 16:17–18 unnecessary. In other words, both the sending of the Spirit-Paraclete and the return of Jesus, with all their respective consequences, are closely related consequences of Jesus' departure.

The second element (16:23b–24) is longer. Yet another consequence of the return for the disciples is outlined, this time involving their future relationship to the Father. This consequence is presented by way of a further inclusion. The outer components describe the future situation of the disciples with regard to the Father (16:23b–c, 24b–c), and the central component outlines their present situation with regard to the Father (16:24a), providing a direct contrast to the situation envisioned in the outer components. This inclusion at the end of the section again effectively drives home the radically different character of the second stage of the sequence, the stage of the return. However, this final contrast among the disciples themselves is different from that of 16:20c–22, because the situation of the disciples portrayed in 16:24a encompasses not only the time period of the departure but also the whole of Jesus' ministry.

This final consequence of the return—introduced by the second example of the solemn formula "Amen, amen, I say to you" within this second major section[59]—concerns a promise that the Father will grant whatever the disciples ask for in Jesus' name. This is the fourth such promise within the farewell discourse (14:13–14 [with double formulation]; 15:7, 16), and it is just as strategically located here as it was in the earlier examples. In all cases this promise occurs at the end of a major section of discourse and therefore, regardless of the specific context in each case, receives a clear and pointed emphasis. The promise is thus used throughout the farewell as a key element in the consolation and comforting of the disciples.

The first outer component of the inclusion outlines the basic promise: whatever the disciples ask for in Jesus' name, the Father will grant to them (16:23b–c). Two elements of this promise should be noted. First, as in all other examples of this promise, the "asking" of the disciples is conveyed by the verb αἰτεῖν, thus pointing to a different sort of "asking" than that

---

59. The formula thus provides an overall inclusion for this third subsection of 16:20–24 (16:20a, 23b–24).

mentioned in the immediately preceding consequence of 16:23a–b and exemplified in 16:17–18.[60] Such "asking" involves requests, not questions; indeed, given the presence of the Spirit-Paraclete in the midst of the disciples, questions become unnecessary. Second, the specific addressee and grantor of such "asking" is identified as the Father.[61] This brings the disciples into a direct and fruitful relationship with the figure of the Father, who has already been identified in the unit as the destination of Jesus' departure (16:5a, 10b) and the ultimate source of Jesus' own truth or revelation, which the Spirit-Paraclete in turn receives and proclaims to the disciples (16:12–15). Therefore, this promise assures the disciples that upon Jesus' return they will be able to approach the Father directly and be given by the Father whatever they request in the name of Jesus. Such a promise again clearly consoles the disciples. The task of assuaging the negative thrust of the beginning contrast of 16:20a–b comes now to its full climax; the period of the return will indeed be a very positive one for the disciples.

The central component (16:24a) contrasts this envisioned situation with the disciples' given relationship to the Father during Jesus' ministry. Up to now the disciples have not "asked" for anything in Jesus' name; in other words, so far the disciples have neither approached the Father nor directly received anything from him. The contrast outlines even more sharply the positive nature of the second stage of the sequence, the time of the return.

The concluding outer component (16:24b–c) expands the first. It begins by reiterating the basic promise of 16:23b–c (16:24b),[62] and then it describes a further result of this future relationship with the Father for the disciples: their joy will be made perfect (16:24c). This pointedly

60. Such "asking" on the part of the disciples indirectly parallels Jesus' own relationship to the Father in this regard (see 11:22, 41–44). In the case of Jesus, however, such "asking" is also expressed several times by the verb ἐρωτᾶν (14:16; 16:26; 17:9, 15, 20).
61. The present formulation of the promise comes close to that of the third example of 15:16, except that whereas the present example is phrased in terms of a future more vivid condition, that of 15:16 forms part of a subordinate clause. Both contain the same elements in the same order: (a) the "asking" on the part of the disciples; (b) the identification of the Father as the addressee for such "asking"; (c) the proper procedure to be followed in such "asking," with reference to the name of Jesus by means of an instrumental of manner with the preposition ἐν; and (d) the identification of the Father as grantor, with the verb to give. The other examples of 14:13–14 and 15:17 reveal much greater differences.
62. The promise receives a different, more succinct formulation at this point: (a) Instead of a future more vivid condition, here one finds the compound statement "ask and you shall receive" (though the beginning imperative does function as a condition, the result of which is provided by the following predictive future). (b) The "asking" of the disciples (αἰτεῖτε) omits both the reference to the Father as addressee and the proper procedure for the "asking" itself. (c) There is no reference to the Father as grantor; there is only a reference to the disciples as those who will receive (λήμψεσθε). This effective variation in formulation avoids unnecessary repetition while repeating the basic promise in a nutshell.

reaffirms the positive role of the contrast developed in 16:20-22.[63] In addition to these two elements of repetition and expansion, the final outer component plays a threefold role in effectively concluding the inclusion of 16:23b–24, the subdivision made up of 16:20–24, and the entire second major section.

First, from the point of view of the inclusion, the final outer component again underscores the positive nature of the return. The disciples' relationship to the Father will undergo a drastic change; they will approach the Father directly and receive whatever they request. Second, from the point of view of the final subdivision, the focal contrast of sorrow/joy is now presented solely from the perspective of joy, thus completing the following:

1. The ongoing shift within the subsection itself from the time of the departure to that of the return—from the initial focus on the departure in 16:20a–b to the concluding focus on the return beginning with 16:23a.
2. The process of consoling the disciples with respect to the initial negative contrast of 16:20a–b. Not only will they not have any need "to question" Jesus further but also the Father will grant to them whatever they "ask for" in Jesus' name.
3. The presentation of the disciples' attitude at the time of the return—not only a joy unlike that of the world and a joy that no one will wrest from them, but also a joy fulfilled or made perfect.

Finally, from the point of view of the section as a whole, the inclusion's final outer component ends the further development of 16:16 in the light of the reaction of 16:17–18. Not only will the first stage of the sequence be transitory but also the second stage of the sequence will be enormously beneficial to the disciples. Given all the consequences of a renewed "seeing" of Jesus, such a period of time can be described as one of joy fulfilled or made perfect, despite the inevitability and sorrow of the first stage.

63. This further consequence of the return is conveyed by a subordinate result clause attached to the preceding reiteration of the promise concerning the disciples' future relationship to the Father. The theme of a joy fulfilled or made perfect occurs elsewhere in the Gospel and, in fact, has already been encountered in the second unit (3:29; 15:11; 17:13). Its use here, however, is different. Such joy is not dependent, as in 15:9c–11, on the disciples' fulfillment of their proper role as disciples but rather on a further consequence of Jesus' return, the future relationship of the disciples to the Father. Such a concept of joy differs as well from that of the first unit, which described joy as the direct result of a full understanding concerning Jesus' teaching and revelation (14:28; cf. 20:20). Although such an understanding is also presupposed in this unit (cf. 16:23a), perfect joy is presented as directly dependent on the kind of relationship that will ensue between the Father and the disciples. The understanding of joy in the present unit, therefore, has a distinctive emphasis.

A further declaration of Jesus begins the second major section (16:16–24) by reaffirming the forthcoming departure and then positing a subsequent and forthcoming return as well (16:16). Just as "in a little while" the departure is to take place, so also "in yet again a little while" a return will take place. As such, this beginning declaration continues the consolation and reassurance of the disciples, both through the promise of a return conveyed by this twofold sequence of departure/return and the timing envisioned for such a sequence, with the return following quickly upon the departure.

Then, in the light of the disciples' own admission concerning their inability to understand the meaning of Jesus' disclosures (16:17–18), such consolation is continued at greater length by a further development of the beginning declaration of 16:16 (16:19–24). Such consolation now focuses on Jesus himself, with the contrast joy/sorrow playing a key role. First, although the departure is characterized as a time of sorrow on the part of the disciples and of joy on the part of the world, the disciples are assured that their sorrow will turn to joy upon the return, a joy that no one will be able to wrest from them. Second, further promises are extended to the disciples for the time of the return. They will have no need to question Jesus any further, which implies a full understanding of Jesus' mission and ministry, as well as a direct and fruitful relationship to the Father whereby all their requests in Jesus' name will be granted by him. Third, in the light of such promises, the time of the return is further described in terms of perfect joy. In conclusion, despite the inevitable sorrow that the departure will bring, the disciples are reassured throughout that such sorrow will ultimately yield to perfect joy. Not only will the Spirit-Paraclete be sent to them but in fact Jesus himself will return to them, so the departure can again be characterized as being of unquestionable benefit to the disciples.

Third Major Section (John 16:25–33)

The third and final section of the fourth unit of discourse (16:25–33) focuses on Jesus' revelation and the disciples, and follows the threefold pattern of inclusion proposed for each major section of the unit. The structure of this section can be outlined as follows: (1) Jesus' disclosure of the nature and content of his revelation (16:25–28), (2) the disciples' reaction to Jesus' disclosure of the nature and content of his revelation (16:29–30), and (3) Jesus' departure and its consequences for the disciples (16:31–33).

Jesus' Disclosure of the Nature and Content of His Revelation (John 16:25–28)

The beginning declaration of Jesus in 16:25–28 is considerably longer than those of the first two major sections. Three major components can be outlined: (1) a brief exposition of the basic character and content of Jesus' revelation to the disciples (16:25), (2) a reiteration of the future relationship of the disciples to the Father previously outlined in 16:23–24 (16:26–27), and (3) a succinct disclosure of Jesus' full identity (16:28).

These three components represent a progressive, ascending elaboration of the relationship between Jesus and the Father. In the first component, 16:25, Jesus' revelation to the disciples is tied directly to the figure of the Father—it is the Father whom he proclaims. The second component, 16:26–27, repeats the future relationship of the disciples to the Father, already set forth at the end of the preceding major section. However, this relationship is now grounded directly in the disciples' own acceptance of Jesus' own relationship to the Father as revealed by him. In the last component, 16:28, this relationship of Jesus to the Father, which Jesus has revealed and which the disciples have accepted, is described in what amounts to an excellent summary of Johannine teaching on Jesus. This beginning declaration of 16:25–28, then, develops the fundamental meaning of the departure for the first time since 16:4b–15.

Nature and Content of Jesus' Revelation (John 16:25)

From a formal point of view, the first component of the beginning declaration (16:25) closely resembles its counterparts in 16:4b–5a and 16:16. It is brief; it conveys a basic contrast; this contrast concerns two different periods of time; and the time periods in question again involve the forthcoming departure of Jesus and other related events. Despite such formal similarities, however, the present contrast also has a distinctive thrust.

First, the time periods in question do not concern different stages within the period of "the hour" (as in 16:16) or the public ministry with regard to "the hour" (as in 16:4b–5a). The time periods now involve the full ministry up to and including the time of the departure itself vis-à-vis the period beginning with the concluding events of "the hour" and extending indefinitely thereafter (in other words, the period of Jesus' return). Second, the description of these time periods has nothing to do with the disciples' inability/ability to see Jesus (as in 16:16) or with silence/disclosure on Jesus' part concerning the forthcoming events of the departure (as in 16:4b–5a). These time periods are characterized instead in terms of the basic character of Jesus' revelation (concerning the Father) to the disciples, "in figures/openly." Finally, although the figure of the Father is also mentioned, as in 16:4b–5a, within the present contrast, this figure is no longer simply identified as the destination of the departure but rather as the very content of Jesus' revelation to the disciples.

The contrast itself is formulated in two separate statements. The reference to the full ministry is brief (16:25a), and the reference to the concluding events of "the hour" is more detailed. The latter describes the change involved from two different perspectives, thus emphasizing the second time period and its positive thrust for the disciples (16:25b–c).

In the first statement of 16:25a, the entire revelation of Jesus up to and including the disclosures of the present unit itself is described as being "in figures" (ἐν παροιμίαις).[64] In the second statement of 16:25b–c, Jesus' revelation at the time of the return, at the completion of "the hour," is first described negatively (by way of opposition to that of the full ministry) and then positively (in terms of his actual role with regard to the Father).[65] After "the hour,"[66] the revelation will no longer be "in figures" (16:25b); instead, Jesus will proclaim the Father "openly" (16:25c).[67] The contrast not only identifies the Father as the very content of Jesus' revelation to the disciples but, in so doing, begins to reveal the nature of Jesus' own relationship to the Father: it is Jesus who reveals or proclaims the Father. The contrast further specifies that this revelation of the Father by Jesus has a twofold temporal character. Up to the completion of "the hour," the revelation is "in figures"; after the completion of "the hour," it becomes "open." In other words, complete information concerning the Father will be given only after the return.[68]

64. The beginning demonstrative "these things" (as I see it) encompasses the present disclosures of the fourth unit, the ongoing disclosures of the farewell speech as a whole, and the disclosures of the entire mission up to the time of the return itself.

65. In this second statement, therefore, the two different descriptions of the change involved in the character of Jesus' ministry are themselves presented by way of contrast (negative/positive formulation) reinforced by the adversative use of the conjunction ἀλλά.

66. This reference to "the hour" must be interpreted in the light of the further consequences of the return outlined in 16:23–24. First, these consequences were introduced by the temporal reference "on that day," with direct reference to the time of the return and the renewed "seeing" of one another on the part of Jesus and the disciples (16:16b, 22b–d). Second, the same temporal reference is used immediately afterward, in 16:26, to introduce a further consequence of the return. This use of "the hour" with specific reference to the time of the return (cf. 16:21) is found only here in the Gospel narrative and follows the distinction already made within "the hour" in 16:16.

67. Jesus' role of revealing or proclaiming the Father is conveyed by the verb ἀπαγγελεῖν, found only here in the Gospel. However, given the previous use of the verb ἀναγγελεῖν in 16:12–15 to describe the Spirit-Paraclete's role of revealing or proclaiming the truth that comes from Jesus and the Father (4:25; cf. 5:33), the use of this cognate here brings close together the given tasks of Jesus and the Spirit-Paraclete for the time after the return. Jesus' "open" proclamation of the Father and the Paraclete's proclamation as the Spirit of truth clearly emerge as two dimensions of the same phenomenon.

68. The contrast "in figures/openly" is found only within the present unit. In a wider sense, the term παροιμία—used here as an instrumental of manner—is used of a proverb or maxim, as well as of an incidental remark or digression (cf. LS; F. Hauck, "paroimia," TDNT 5 [1967] 854–56). In the Gospel itself, the term is used elsewhere with reference to the sustained metaphor of the shepherd (10:6). Its use here goes beyond both of these meanings. The reference is not just to proverbs (e.g., 15:13, 15b, 20) or sustained metaphors (e.g., 15:1–8; 16:21) but encompasses the whole of Jesus' revelation of the Father: everything that he reveals about the Father prior to the return is, as it were, veiled or hidden, beyond understanding, and belonging to the world above (Dewey, "Paroimiai," 82). Consequently, I have chosen the phrase "in figures" to convey this wider connotation. The further use of the

This beginning contrast of "in figures/openly" has several important elements in common with the consequences of the return outlined in 16:23–24. For example, this contrast parallels that of 16:23b–24: once again, it is the full ministry (up to and including most of the events that make up "the hour") that is being compared with the final events of "the hour" (the return of Jesus and its aftermath). To be sure, the terms of the comparison have changed. The contrast no longer concerns the nature of the disciples' relationship to the Father (no requests of the Father up to the conclusion of "the hour"/the subsequent granting of all such requests by the Father) but the character of Jesus' revelation to the disciples. Similarly, in positing an "open" revelation to the disciples for the time of the return, this contrast resonates with the previous description of the disciples' future relationship to Jesus in 16:23a to the effect that they will have no need to ask any further questions of him. In effect, "open" revelation and no further questioning represent two aspects of the same situation. Finally, this beginning contrast begins a further development of the figure of the Father reintroduced in 16:23b–24: Jesus' revelation involves that figure whom the disciples will be able to approach directly and from whom they will receive all they ask for in Jesus' name. Therefore, the distinctive thrust of this beginning contrast is largely due to the influence of the immediately preceding formulation of the consequences of the return in 16:23–24. This beginning contrast incorporates some essential components of these consequences but develops them in a different direction.

This contrast represents the fourth example of a formula of departure within this unit (16:4b–5a, 12; 16:16).[69] Its assessment of the present relationship between Jesus and the disciples throws further light on these earlier formulas. With regard to 16:4b–5a, the present formula specifies that even the necessary disclosure of the forthcoming departure and its consequences during "the hour" itself remains "in figures" until the time of the return. Similarly, with regard to 16:12, the present formula specifies that in addition to the undisclosed revelation of Jesus, all revelation

contrasting term παρρησία—again as an instrumental of manner—confirms such a decision. In a wider sense the term points to frankness or outspokenness; freedom of action, license, or permission; and liberality or lavishness. In the Gospel itself the term is employed several times outside the present unit with varying connotations: with reference to freedom (7:13, 26; 11:54; 18:20), outspokenness (7:14; 10:24), and full rather than partial information (11:14). The last meaning comes closest to that of the present unit—complete rather than veiled information concerning the Father, and hence revelation that is "open" vis-à-vis "in figures."

69. See nn. 8, 27, 36 above. With regard to form, the present example, like 16:12, follows a variation of the third type of formulation: the use of a temporal adverb ("no longer") to anticipate the break in the relationship. As in 14:25, moreover, this formula is used in conjunction with the recurring concluding formula of the discourse, "These things I have said to you." With regard to purpose, the present example again posits a difference between the present and future situation of the disciples.

disclosed is given "in figures"; only at the time of the return, therefore, both what remains undisclosed and what is "in figures" will be disclosed "openly." Such revelation clearly presupposes the second Paraclete saying of 16:13–15—that is, the presence of the Spirit-Paraclete among the disciples and its assigned role of leading them into the whole truth, a truth that the Paraclete receives directly from Jesus and ultimately from the Father. Finally, with regard to 16:16, the present formula characterizes the time of Jesus' return, following the lead of 16:23a, as a time of "open" revelation when both what has been given "in figures" and what has not been given at all will be proclaimed "openly" (that is, explicitly and in full), so all questioning on the part of the disciples will end.

Like the earlier example of 16:16, furthermore, this final formula of departure points to what follows in the remainder of this final major section. It anticipates what follows not so much now in terms of joy but rather in terms of a proper understanding of the relationship between Jesus and the Father.

Finally, the contrast also represents a further example of the recurring concluding formula of the farewell discourse, "These things I have said to you."[70] As in 14:25 and 15:11, the formula is used at this point to anticipate the end of the unit; its further use in 16:33 to signal the end of the unit marks off by way of inclusion this final major section of the unit. All of what follows, therefore, begins to point toward the resumption of the final events of "the hour," a pointing that the prophecy of 16:32 renders concrete.

The Future Situation of the Disciples (John 16:26–27)

The beginning contrast of 16:25 pointed the way to the different character of Jesus' revelation of the Father beginning with the completion of "the hour" and, in so doing, reintroduced the question of the relationship between Jesus and the Father. The second component (16:26–27) again describes the future situation of the disciples with regard to the Father by reaffirming the concluding promise of 16:23–24: at the time of the return, the disciples will be able to approach the Father directly and to make requests of the Father in Jesus' name (16:23b–24). The relationship between Jesus and the Father is also further developed through a significant expansion of the earlier promise. The promise itself reveals the same basic structure as before: the reference to the "asking" of the disciples (16:26a) precedes the reference to the granting of their requests (16:26b–27). With minor variations, the former element remains basically the same.

---

70. In this case the concluding formula reflects and incorporates the use of the contrast "in figures/openly" in the beginning declaration of Jesus: "These things I have said to you in figures."

After an introductory formula specifies the time reference in question for the fulfillment of the promise ("on that day"), the "asking" of the disciples is again conveyed by the verb αἰτεῖν, with an accompanying repetition of the proper procedure to be followed in such "asking"—in Jesus' name (16:26a).[71] The reference to the granting of the disciples' requests, however, is expanded. The granting is now described indirectly rather than directly, and a fundamental reason is added for such an envisioned relationship to the Father on the part of the disciples (16:26b–27). Within this grounding the relationship between Jesus and the Father receives further amplification, thus preparing the way for the summary statement of the relationship that follows (16:28).

The granting itself is no longer described in terms of the Father's direct response to the disciples' requests, as in 16:23b, but instead is described indirectly, in terms of Jesus' own role vis-à-vis the Father with respect to his disciples. Jesus will not play an intermediary role with the Father on their behalf (16:26b). This implies that such a role will be unnecessary, that the disciples will be able to approach the Father directly, and that the Father will grant all such requests in Jesus' name.[72]

The grounding for such granting on the Father's part is twofold (16:27). First, the Father is said to love the disciples, thus accounting for the direct access promised to them, as well as for the envisioned universal granting resulting from such direct access to the Father (16:27a). Second, this love of the Father for the disciples is itself grounded in the disciples' own prior response to Jesus and his claims with regard to the Father: their love for Jesus and their belief in Jesus as "having come from God" (16:27b).[73] It is because of the disciples' love of Jesus and belief in Jesus, therefore,

71. The introductory formula is the same as that of 16:23a and is used again to introduce a further consequence of the return (see n. 66 above). As a result, the concept of "the hour" introduced in 16:25 is not continued; to be sure, the reference throughout is to the time of the return (16:22b–d). The promise does omit, as in 16:24b, the addressee for such "asking."

72. This description of the granting describes the future situation of the disciples with regard to the Father from a different point of view: there will be no need for Jesus "to ask" (ἐρωτᾶν) the Father on their behalf (to function as a direct intermediary). For such "asking" of the Father on behalf of the disciples, see n. 60 above. Given the presence and role of the Spirit-Paraclete among the disciples, one can understand why any further "asking" of the Father on Jesus' part is seen as unnecessary: in and through the Spirit-Paraclete the disciples will receive the promised "open" revelation of the Father and will be able to approach the Father directly.

73. Although the term "Father" has been employed throughout, both in 16:23–24 and 16:25–27a, the textual tradition is divided at this point between "Father" and "God," with strong support on both sides. I favor the use of "God" (p[5] אo,b A Θ 33 1079 al [all without the article]; C[3] K W 054 28 565 700 892 al [all with the article]; many instances of the early versions). It is easier to explain the use of "Father" in terms of assimilation to its immediately preceding and following use in 16:27a and 16:28a. Furthermore, a repeated shifting from one term to the other can be observed throughout these verses: from Father (16:23–24, 25–27a) to God (16:27b), to Father (16:28), to God (16:29–30), to Father (16:31–32).

that the Father loves them and will grant them, at the time of the return, whatever they ask for in Jesus' name.[74] This grounding also explains how Jesus reveals the Father, whether "in figures" or "openly"—Jesus proclaims the Father because Jesus himself has come from the Father.[75] In other words, the content of Jesus' revelation is thereby grounded on Jesus' own origins with the Father, and because the disciples have come to accept such origins, the Father will correspond by granting all their petitions once Jesus has left the disciples and returned to the Father, the previously disclosed destination of his departure.

The grounding provided by the expansion of 16:27 is interesting in the light of the disciples' own role within the unit itself. This promise presents the disciples' love for/belief in Jesus, as well as the Father's love for them, as an already existing and positive reality on the basis of which the disciples' future relationship to the Father is affirmed and secured.[76] At the same time, however, such love/belief on the part of the disciples is hardly satisfactory and, indeed, increasingly problematic, as their two reactions so far have shown and the third will confirm. Such tension can be explained in the light of the beginning contrast of 16:25, "in figures/openly." Given the circumstances of the ministry up to the time of the return (undisclosed revelation that the disciples cannot "bear"; inability to see Jesus, with resultant sorrow; and revelation "in figures"), the initial reaction of the disciples— though improper and misguided—is one of belief/love and thus is sufficient to warrant the Father's love and the promises outlined. Furthermore, given the circumstances envisioned for the time of the return (the coming of the Spirit-Paraclete, who will lead the disciples in the whole truth; a renewed seeing of Jesus, giving rise to perfect joy; and "open" revelation), the belief/ love of the disciples will be made perfect, so all the promises outlined will come to pass, and the Father's own love for them will be concretely manifested through the granting of whatever they ask in Jesus' name.

74. The line of argumentation here is similar to that of the first unit: (a) Belief in Jesus (14:11) and love for Jesus (14:15a, 21a, 23a–b, 24a) have positive consequences: very specific promises are attached once again to such love and belief. (b) Among such promises is that of the Father's own love for the disciples, for those who love Jesus (14:21b, 23c). In this unit, however, the Father's love is tied directly to the granting of the disciples' requests rather than to the abiding of the Father among them.

75. Jesus' origins with the Father are described in terms of an inceptive aorist with the verb ἐξέρχομαι and the preposition παρά as a genitive of source. The question of origins is only mentioned in passing in the first unit (14:24: "the Father who sent me"; cf. 14:16). The present unit subtly introduces this question of origins from the beginning (16:5a), and it plays a major role in the present exposition of the relationship. For the question of origins, see, e.g., 8:42; 13:13; 17:8.

76. The love of the Father is described in terms of a gnomic present indicative, as an already existing and enduring reality (16:27a). Similarly, the disciples' belief in and love for Jesus is presented in terms of perfect indicatives of completed action: again, as an already existing and enduring reality (16:27b).

In addition, the move from Jesus as revealer of the Father in 16:25 to Jesus as having come from the Father in 16:26–27 plays a double role within the unit itself. First, such a shift further develops the relationship between Jesus and the Father described in 16:4b–15, insofar as the question of the origins was already included in the beginning identification of the Father as the destination of the departure (16:b–5a: "the one who sent me") and insofar as the Father was also described therein as the source of Jesus' revelation (16:15). Second, this shift also anticipates and prepares the way for the final step in the present exposition of this relationship in 16:28, where both the origins and destination of Jesus are explicitly addressed. Thus, the question of origins, which was subtly introduced at the beginning, is explicitly pursued here in preparation for the closing statement of 16:28.

The Content of Jesus' Revelation: Disclosure of Identity (John 16:28)

The preceding explanation of Jesus' role as revealer of the Father in terms of his origins with the Father (16:25) leads directly to the final statement of this brief exposition regarding his relationship to the Father (16:28). This final statement, as mentioned above, provides an excellent summary of Johannine teaching on Jesus: a beginning description of his origins (16:28a) followed by a description of his destination (16:28b). This summary is composed in chiastic fashion (ABBA). In the outer components, $16:28a_1$ and $16:28b_2$, the Father is identified as the origins and destination of Jesus, respectively. In the central components, $16:28a_2$ and $16:28b_1$, the world is presented as the destination of Jesus' journey and his place of sojourn while he is away from the Father.

The first description, that of Jesus' origins, begins by reiterating, with minor variations, the christological development of 16:27: Jesus has come from the Father.[77] This second reference to the origins is followed by the destination behind such a separation from the Father: Jesus came into the world.[78] This first description, therefore, continues to address and expand the question of the origins subtly introduced in 16:4b–5a, at the beginning of the unit ("the one who sent me"). The second description,

---

77. This beginning reiteration of Jesus' origins is omitted altogether in several manuscripts (D W al). However, the textual evidence for inclusion is strong; and the omission can be seen as accidental, given the immediately preceding use of this statement in 16:27b. Further disagreement exists with regard to the use of the preposition; some manuscripts opt for παρά ($p^5 p^{22}$ ℵ A C^2 K 054 p^1) and others, for ἐκ (B C^o L X 33 al). I favor the former reading, since the use of the latter preposition can be explained in terms of assimilation to the compound verbs in the context.

78. Whereas the description of Jesus' origins follows that of 16:27, the description of his destination in the world is given in terms of a perfect indicative emphasizing existing state (ἐλήλυθα). The latter is common in the Gospel (1:9; 3:19; 6:14; 9:39; 11:27; 12:46; 18:37).

that of Jesus' destination, begins by reaffirming the forthcoming departure: Jesus now leaves the world. The identification of the destination for
this departure is also repeated: Jesus goes to the Father.⁷⁹ As such, this
second description brings to the fore once again the question of the destination already introduced in 16:4b–5a, 7, 10, 17.

As a whole, therefore, this summary provides an overall sense of Jesus'
journey and ministry, from beginning to end. In so doing it also provides
an overall sense of his relationship to the Father—the Father as his origins
and destination. Thus, Jesus reveals the Father because it is from the
Father that he comes and to the Father that he goes. It is with the Father
that he belongs, and he has come into the world to reveal the Father to the
disciples, at first "in figures" but then "openly."⁸⁰ This final statement of
the declaration not only concludes the exposition of the relationship between Jesus and the Father but also recapitulates the entire Johannine
message concerning Jesus and the Father.

The Disciples' Reaction to Jesus' Disclosure
of the Nature and Content of
His Revelation (John 16:29–30)

After the christological summary of 16:28, the beginning declaration of
Jesus gives way to the third and final reaction of the disciples (16:29–30).
This reaction is not unlike the previous one of 16:17–18. It is equally
extensive, is not conveyed by Jesus, and involves issues related to the
departure and thus moves beyond the initial silence of 16:5b–6 and Jesus'
criticism of that silence. However, two important differences should be
noted. First, the reaction is no longer confined to the group itself; the
disciples now address Jesus directly for the first time. Second, the reaction no longer raises specific questions; such questioning is replaced by
confident affirmation of understanding and belief on the part of the disciples, an affirmation that counterbalances their previous acknowledgment
of a failure to understand in 16:18c.

Despite such direct address and confident confession on the part of the
disciples, it becomes clear that they are no closer to a proper understanding of Jesus' ongoing disclosures. In fact, their failure to understand
emerges more sharply than before, so their portrayal becomes more
ironic. At the very time when they finally approach Jesus directly and

79. The term used for the departure itself (ἀφίημι), though not common, is used elsewhere (14:18). The term used with regard to the destination of the departure (πορεύομαι) is
far more common (7:35; 14:2, 3, 12, 28) and is used within the unit itself (16:7e–f).
80. It is clear that the use of "world" as Jesus' destination and place of sojourn while
away from the Father is neutral when compared with previous usage in both 16:8–11 and
16:20a–b. To be sure, given the origins and destination of Jesus, the reaction of the world to
which he comes and from which he is about to depart is presented thereby as sharply ironic.

with firm confidence, therefore, their own failure to understand becomes even more evident. Not only do they thoroughly misunderstand the character of Jesus' revelation, just disclosed, they also only partially comprehend the relationship between Jesus and the Father, just explained.

The reaction, introduced by the narrator (16:29a—the second such intervention; cf. 16:17a, 18a), consists of two major components in ascending order. These two components follow the basic sequence of the declaration of 16:25–28. To begin with, the disciples address themselves to the beginning statement of 16:25 regarding the twofold character of Jesus' revelation (16:29b). The disciples then turn to the question of Jesus' own relationship to the Father as elaborated in both the promise of 16:26–27 and the disclosure of 16:28 (16:30). In both instances the disciples speak with conviction, claiming to know at this point the full meaning and import of these declarations.

In the first step of the reaction, the disciples identify the present time within "the hour" and within the unit itself as the time envisioned by Jesus in 16:25 for the cessation of all revelation "in figures" and the beginning of the "open" revelation. It is "now," therefore, with the declaration of 16:25–28, that Jesus is said to speak "with openness" and to use "no figure" (16:29b).[81] Such a confident assertion on their part is misguided; it bypasses and misunderstands both the future reference of the coming "hour" to the time of the return and the connection between the time of the return and the "open" revelation (until "that day," all revelation is "in figures"). In the end, therefore, the surprising confidence of the disciples in this regard proves to be unfounded and ironic—Jesus in fact does not yet speak "openly."

This initial characterization of the present time as the time of the envisioned "open" revelation sets the stage for the second step of the reaction. The disciples now claim a full understanding of Jesus' status and role as presented in the preceding declaration. They make this claim in two parts: the first part provides a rationale for the claim (16:30a), and the second part outlines the claim itself (16:30b).

To begin with, therefore, the disciples immediately acknowledge that Jesus knows all things and consequently has no need for anyone to "question" (ἐρωτᾶν) him.[82] In other words, the rationale for the claim that follows

---

81. The reaction as a whole is introduced by the particle ἴδε, "you see," which draws attention to the statements that follow and hence to the disciples' new, presumed understanding of Jesus' farewell declarations. This first step of the reaction reproduces, with some stylistic variations and in inverse order, the twofold description of Jesus' revelation in the future of 16:25b–c. Such an inversion places even greater emphasis on the disciples' new, presumed understanding of Jesus' revelation within the unit itself and heightens the ironic element as well.

82. The use of the introductory temporal adverb "now" can be connected immediately with that of 16:29b—the presumed recognition of Jesus' "open" revelation is matched by the disciples' presumed knowledge of him.

is that because Jesus is now perceived as possessing all-encompassing knowledge, all "questioning" on the part of the disciples is known to him ahead of time and hence becomes unnecessary.[83] Such a rationale can be understood in the light of the disciples' second reaction of the unit and its aftermath (16:16–24). First, much "questioning" arose among the disciples after Jesus' declaration of 16:16 (16:17–18), a "questioning" that also extended to earlier declarations in 16:4b–15 and that led, in effect, to the climactic admission of a failure to understand in 16:18c. Second, although such "questioning" was not raised before Jesus himself, he did show that he was fully aware of it and even repeated for the disciples one of their fundamental questions (16:19). Third, in the course of the further exposition of 16:16 in 16:20–24, Jesus also promised that at the time of the return, all such "questioning" would end (16:23a). Consequently, once the disciples identify, following the remarks of 16:25–28, the present time ("now") as that of the "open" revelation, this first part of the claim becomes clear. In a retrospective analysis of what has transpired within the unit itself, the disciples "now" conclude, with certainty and confidence, that Jesus knows all things (16:17–18, 19) and that as a result there is no need for them to place their "questioning" before him (16:17–18, 23a), since he already knows the full thrust of their discussions and preoccupations.[84]

In the light of this realization, conveyed by the rationale, the disciples go on to proclaim their affirmation and understanding of Jesus' status and role as presented in 16:26–28. Given such knowledge on Jesus' part and its concrete results for their own situation, the disciples now express their full belief in Jesus as "having come from the Father."[85] In other words, in the light of Jesus' all-encompassing knowledge as demonstrated earlier, the disciples accept and proclaim the preceding identification of the Father as the origins of Jesus.

This second part of the disciples' reaction, like the first part, is improper and misguided in several respects. First, the future relationship of the

83. Cf. the very similar comment by the narrator in 2:23–25.

84. A final development of the theme of "questioning" takes place at this point. The "questioning" envisioned as coming to an end with the return of Jesus is now seen as having already taken place.

85. The claim repeats, with some variations, the formulation of 16:27b, 28a. The claim—consisting of a brief main clause ("we believe") and a following subordinate clause—is introduced by the prepositional phrase "in this," which in itself allows for two different interpretations: (a) "In this" is a dative of reference, and the subordinate clause is epexegetical, explaining the demonstrative in the phrase ("In this we believe, that you have come from God"). (b) "In this" is an instrumental of cause, and the subordinate clause is indirect discourse following the verb; thus, the referent of the demonstrative becomes the statement of 16:30a, and the statement of belief follows from the knowledge specified in the earlier declaration ("On account of this we believe that you have come from God"). As my own description of 16:30a as rationale already implies, I favor the latter alternative—given the course of the unit, Jesus' disclosure is accepted.

Father to the disciples, first described in 16:23b–24 and reiterated in 16:26–27, is completely bypassed. Second, the future relationship to Jesus, presented in 16:23a, is completely misunderstood. Their "questioning" will end not because the disciples suddenly realize that Jesus is already fully aware of all such "questioning" but instead because they themselves will fully understand the relationship between Jesus and the Father through the Spirit-Paraclete. Third, the given affirmation of, or confession in, Jesus' status and role is limited at this point. Thus, for example, although the disciples openly accept Jesus' origins with the Father, such acceptance is strictly based on a demonstration of his all-encompassing knowledge and does not really indicate whether they fully understand Jesus' origins at this point (that is, whether such an affirmation understands this provenance as the prologue of 1:1–18 presents it). Similarly, the confession has nothing to say about the remainder of Jesus' relationship to the Father, as summarized, for example, in 14:4–14. Indeed, even the important fact of the destination, repeated several times throughout the present unit and reintroduced in the self-disclosure of 16:28 itself, is totally bypassed—namely, the fact that Jesus' relationship to the Father involves a forthcoming departure from the world to the Father. In effect, such failure to address the full character of this relationship casts further doubt on the parameters of the given confession concerning origins.

In conclusion, the disciples' confident claim to knowledge and belief expressed here proves to be just as unfounded and ironic as their earlier claim to recognize the "open" revelation—such belief and knowledge are only partially correct. In fact, the present claim makes the earlier claim even more ironic: the disciples themselves are clearly unable to grasp even the partial revelation dispensed at this point. These full and confident affirmations, therefore, reveal an even greater lack of understanding than before. Sorrowful silence and an admission of ignorance finally give way to obvious misunderstanding.

Jesus' Departure and Its Consequences for the Disciples (John 16:31–33)

The preceding misunderstanding of the disciples leads directly to Jesus' final declarations of the unit (16:31–33). In the first two sections, these final declarations provide extensive development of the initial declaration in the light of the intervening reaction of the disciples. In this final section, the initial declaration of 16:25–28 receives further development as well, insofar as the portrayal of Jesus' relationship to the Father is continued; however, such a development is limited. These final declarations emphasize instead the climactic events of "the hour" to follow and, in so doing, anticipate the resumption of the narrative line. In emphasizing the events of "the hour," furthermore, these declarations focus on the forthcoming departure of Jesus, thus returning to the first disclosure of the unit in 16:4b–5a. Indeed, the further elaboration of Jesus' relationship to the Father is now presented in terms of Jesus' impending departure and the climactic events of "the hour."

The final declarations begin with a brief introduction by the narrator that shifts the focus away from the disciples to Jesus (16:31a; cf. 16:19). These declarations reveal two basic steps. In the first step the preceding reaction of the disciples, with its confident claims to belief and understanding, is directly addressed and severely undermined (16:31b–32a). In the second step the disciples receive a concluding, strong reassurance from Jesus, thus ending not only the section but the entire unit on a positive note, despite the negative tones of the initial criticism (16:32b–33). Thus, whereas the first part of the declarations undermines and demolishes, the second part reassures and builds up. In both parts the question of the forthcoming departure emerges as primary.

A twofold development can be observed within the first part of the declarations (16:31b–32a). The first element acts as an effective transition between the preceding reaction of the disciples and the subsequent prediction of Jesus. Jesus begins by addressing the concluding claim of the disciples to belief in him as "having come from the Father," though to be sure the other claims that led to such a climactic confession are addressed thereby as well. Jesus follows up such a claim to belief with a very brief question—"Now you believe?" (16:31b)—that sharply undermines the entire response of the disciples, not only questioning the claim to belief itself but also sharply underscoring the ironic nature of their response. The juxtaposition of firm confession and subsequent question (we believe/you believe?) immediately undermines the tone and thrust of the former claims. The use of the temporal adverb "now" at the beginning of the question should be seen as emphatic and as deliberately paralleling the disciples' own double use of "now" in their reaction (16:29b, 30a), thus further undermining the certainty of the given confession; the claims to present understanding and belief on their part are thereby entirely deflated. The prediction that follows continues this initial deflation of the claims.

Jesus' prediction involves the behavior of the disciples during the climactic events of "the hour" (16:32a). It is introduced by a formula that serves as its main clause and reorients the present perspective adopted by the disciples in their reaction of 16:29–30 to the future perspective expressed by Jesus in the initial declaration of 16:25–28. The formula is preceded by the demonstrative particle ἰδού, which parallels the earlier use of ἴδε by the disciples in 16:29b and hence calls specific attention to the future reorientation that follows, away from the present reading of the disciples. This reorientation is then presented by a renewed reference to "the hour that is coming," the same introductory formula used in 16:25b to describe the time of the "open" revelation.[86] The prediction itself is then conveyed by a temporal ἵνα clause attached to the introductory formula. This clause has two components that describe the same future event in causal fashion: the disciples will be dispersed, each to his own home,[87] and will leave Jesus alone.[88]

As a result, the previous claim of the disciples to proper belief and understanding is shattered. Such firmness and certainty will give way shortly to an abandonment of Jesus, whom they have just acknowledged as knowing all things and as having come from God.[89] In effect, the disciples' claims have been completely deflated, and the irony of the situation has been sharply underscored. Jesus' first response to this third reaction of the disciples does not so much parallel as mimic (for example, the use of the temporal adverb "now"; the reference to their own belief by way of a doubting question; the use of a demonstrative particle to call attention to the teaching in question; and the use of a prediction, a further demonstration of Jesus' all-encompassing knowledge) the disciples' own response, thus making the situation even more ironic.

The second part of the declarations, however, completely reverses this negative beginning. Once the claims have been deflated, strong reassurance and consolation follow (16:32b–33). Again, a twofold development can be observed in this latter part of the declarations, with the first element again serving as an effective transition from the prediction concerning the flight of the disciples to Jesus' parting message of peace to these same disciples, who are about to abandon him.

86. The formula is expanded at this point by the addition of a perfect of completed action—the hour is coming and has already arrived (ἐλήλυθεν; cf. 2:23; 5:25)—indicating the arrival of "the hour" as a whole (cf. 12:23) and reinforcing thereby the proximate nature of the events to come within "the hour" itself. In this regard, the concept of "the hour" receives two further connotations within the unit (cf. 16:21, 25; see n. 66 above): an event concerning the disciples prior to the departure itself and the entire period as such, respectively.

87. The dispersal is conveyed by the verb σκορπίζω in the passive voice and reinforced by the parenthetical comment that follows, "each to his own home" (εἰς τὰ ἴδια); cf. 10:7–18. The use of the passive voice may introduce a certain sense of inevitability to this predicted scattering, assuaging thereby the culpability of the disciples in this regard.

88. For a similar sequence of confession on the part of the disciples and deflation by Jesus, see 13:36–38. The strategic placement of such a sequence at the beginning and end of the speech points out that despite all the disclosures in question, not much progress has been achieved.

89. This prediction does not quite agree with what follows in the narrative. Not only is it hard to describe the disciples as "scattered," since they are formally released by Jesus (18:1–11) and two closely follow the final events (18:15–27; 19:25–27, 31–37), but also no disciple is described as having gone back "to his own home"—they are found together repeatedly in Jerusalem as a group (20:1–29).

This parting word of consolation and reassurance begins by providing a direct contrast to the anticipated reaction of the disciples with regard to Jesus within "the hour" through a description of the Father's own attitude toward Jesus throughout "the hour" (16:32b–c). This description, therefore, further develops the relationship between Jesus and the Father, already presented in 15:25–28, a final time. The resulting contrast reveals a chiastic arrangement with an inversion of the previously observed causal pattern: flight of the disciples, abandonment of Jesus (16:32a)/no abandonment of Jesus, and the presence of the Father with him (16:32b–c). In other words, although seemingly "left alone" by the flight of his own disciples, Jesus in fact is not "left alone," because the Father is with him. Thus, in effect, the previous portrayal of the relationship in 16:25–28 is advanced a step further. Not only does Jesus reveal the Father, given the identification of his origins and destination with the Father, but also the Father is always "with him" (16:32b–c)—an abbreviated version of the mutual presence of Jesus and the Father in each other.[90] As a result, the death on the cross becomes an essential and climactic component of Jesus' ministry of revelation—of disclosing the Father, from whom he came and to whom he returns.

This final expansion of the relationship fulfills a further twofold role as well. On the one hand, the reference to the mutual presence at this point brings out even further the ironic character of the situation. The firm claim to belief and understanding concerning Jesus is immediately followed by a further exposition of the relationship between Jesus and the Father—the Father is with Jesus. On the other hand, such a reference is reassuring as well; Jesus is never "left alone" by the Father, not even at the time of his death and departure from the world.

This word of consolation and reassurance concludes with a twofold message of strong affirmation (16:33). This message is introduced by the last example of the recurring concluding formula of the disclosure ("These things I have said to you"), thus signaling not only the end of the final major section (by way of inclusion with the earlier use of the formula in 16:25) but also the end of the entire unit of discourse. First, the purpose for all the preceding disclosures of the unit is portrayed in positive terms—that the disciples may have "peace" in Jesus (16:33a).[91] Second, the nature of this "peace" is then explained by way of a contrast: although the disciples will

90. The formula is abbreviated insofar as only the presence of the Father with Jesus is mentioned; that of Jesus in the Father is not. As in the first unit (14:10–11), this exposition of the relationship also comes to a climax with the teaching on the mutual presence, although the exposition in the first unit is different and more detailed.

91. The parallel with the first unit (14:25–27) is clear, especially given the explicit contrast drawn in both instances between the disciples and the world. In the first unit, the peace of Jesus is contrasted with that of the world; in the present unit, the peace of Jesus is contrasted with the tribulation from the world.

encounter "tribulation" in the world (16:33b),[92] a call to courage is nonetheless confidently issued on the basis of Jesus' own victory over the world (16:33c–d).[93] Thus, despite the forthcoming departure, the predicted flight of the disciples from Jesus prior to that departure, and the continued tribulation of the disciples in the world, the disciples are called to show courage and confidence. This courage and confidence are ultimately grounded in the belief that in and through the departure, it is Jesus who conquers the world (and not vice versa). Indeed, the previous expansion of the relationship between Jesus and the Father in 16:32b–c prepares the way directly for this final and confident expression of triumph. Given the nature of this relationship, "the hour" is a moment of victory (not defeat) and a source of courage and peace (not sorrow). This message of victory and courage is reinforced by the standpoint of Jesus as speaker at this moment. For only the second time in this unit, Jesus speaks not as someone who anticipates, but rather as someone who has already surpassed, the climactic events of "the hour." The victory is presented as already achieved, as already on hand.[94]

As in the two earlier sections, therefore, the final declarations of Jesus point out the ultimate fruitfulness of the departure. The final declarations, moreover, end not only the third section but the entire discourse on an extremely positive tone and footing. What lies ahead is without question for the benefit of the disciples. The victory of Jesus over the world ultimately grounds that of the disciples over the world as well, giving way to the time of the "open" revelation concerning the Father and a full and proper belief in Jesus as the revealer of the Father.

92. The use of "tribulation" (θλῖψις) to characterize the status of the disciples in the world is limited to the present unit and represents an expansion of the metaphor of 16:21—the woman in childbirth—used to describe the future situation of the disciples. This reference to the coming "tribulation" continues the previous references to the conflict presupposed by the promised conviction of an unbelieving world (16:8–11) and to the joy of the world at the departure of Jesus (16:20a–b). As such, I believe the "tribulation" includes not only the time between the departure and the return as its primary referent but also the scenario envisioned in the previous unit of discourse (15:18–16:4a) as its secondary referent.

93. The formulation of the call proper, which in itself parallels those of 14:1a and 14:27d in the first unit, is unique; the verb θαρσεῖν is not found outside the present unit. The formulation of the grounds for the call, the victory of Jesus over the world (conveyed by the verb νικᾶν, with a perfect of completed action), is also unique to the present unit. Its basic thrust, however, is also paralleled by the reference to Jesus' victorious encounter with the ruler of the world in 14:30–31c. Both units, therefore, conclude with a similar combination of elements: a promise of peace, a call to courage, and a reassuring explanation of the departure itself.

94. Cf. 16:8–11, esp. 16:10, where the ruler of the world is described as already condemned (see n. 21 above). As such, this anticipated victory of Jesus at the end matches the anticipated judgment of the ruler of the world at the beginning. This final shift in standpoint strongly reinforces the message of consolation and reassurance: the Jesus who speaks prior to the climactic events of "the hour" already speaks as if he has emerged victorious over the world.

The entire final section of the fourth unit of discourse, 16:25–33, represents a further exercise in the consolation and reassurance of the disciples in the face of the forthcoming departure, despite their misguided claims to belief and understanding and the subsequent prediction of their coming demise. Such consolation is evident within the beginning declaration itself (16:25–28). First, the time of the return is further described as a time of "open" revelation concerning the Father, thus implying an eventual full understanding of Jesus' mission and message. Second, the promise of a direct and fruitful relationship to the Father is reiterated and expanded: it is because of the Father's love for the disciples that he will grant whatever they request in Jesus' name. Finally, the departure itself is further explained in terms of the relationship between Jesus and the Father: Jesus reveals the Father because he has come from the Father and now returns to the Father. In other words, the forthcoming departure is set within the framework of Jesus' origins and destination, his status and role with regard to the Father.

This process of consolation and reassurance is reinforced in the concluding declarations of 16:31–33 (vv. 32b–33) as a direct response to both the misunderstanding of the disciples with regard to the beginning disclosures of Jesus (16:29–30) and the subsequent ironic prediction of their imminent scattering (16:31–32a). To begin with, the departure is further explained within the framework of Jesus' relationship to the Father, now presented in terms of his full status with regard to the Father (namely, the mutual presence of Jesus and the Father in one another). The Father, it is explained, does not leave Jesus alone but remains with him through the climactic moments of "the hour," so the departure itself functions as a further revelation of the Father by Jesus. Furthermore, the disciples are explicitly assured that in and through such a departure Jesus has triumphed over the world, thus giving way to a call for peace and courage in the midst of inevitable tribulation. As a result, the entire unit ends on a most positive tone—the departure means victory for Jesus, and its ultimate consequences are most beneficial to the disciples.

STRATEGIC CONCERNS AND AIMS

The fourth unit of discourse, 16:4b–33, can be seen not only as a coherent artistic whole but also as a strategic whole whose clear concerns and aims are realized through the use of the literary structure and development described earlier in this chapter. This unit concerns the final events of Jesus' mission and ministry, the climactic events of "the hour." It focuses on the correct interpretation of Jesus' forthcoming departure from the world from the point of view of both its fundamental meaning and its consequences for the disciples. Such concerns are guided and informed by a number of interdependent aims, yielding a variety of different strategic functions for the unit as a whole.

The supplementary strategic function with regard to the first unit is distinctive and can be described from a structural, thematic, and referential point of view. The supplementary function involves a prominent structural dimension: the fourth unit of discourse has been patterned largely after the literary structure and development of the first unit. Such patterning can be discerned, to begin with, in the overall structure of the unit. Like the first unit, this fourth unit has a threefold development with a beginning, a central, and a final major section. Furthermore, this threefold arrangement contains a similarly linear and progressive development with regard to the exposition of Jesus' departure (its meaning and consequences). Such patterning also can be discerned in the construction of all three major sections of the unit. Each section has a further threefold development in the form of an inclusion similar to that employed in 14:4–14: a beginning declaration of Jesus touches upon some aspect of the forthcoming departure; a reaction of the disciples reveals a failure to understand the full import of such a declaration; and a concluding declaration of Jesus expands upon the beginning declaration in the light of the intervening reaction and failure to understand. As such, the present unit, like the first, reveals a linear and progressive pattern of composition and development not only from major section to major section but also within each major section.

The supplementary function also involves an obvious thematic dimension. The unit clearly returns to the overarching themes of the first unit for further development. Such development, however, proceeds in a different direction altogether, going well beyond a simple restatement of these themes as presented in the first unit. The first section immediately introduces both the meaning and the consequences of the departure. It presents the meaning itself in terms of the Father as the destination of the departure, with very little further development of the relationship between Jesus and the Father. However, the consequences of the departure receive an extensive and sustained development. The second section does not pursue the meaning of the departure, but the consequences of the departure again receive an extensive and sustained development, though from a different perspective than that of the first section. Finally, the third section reintroduces the meaning of the departure and pursues it at greater length in terms of the relationship between Jesus and the Father. Further consequences of the departure are outlined from yet another perspective.

Finally, the supplementary function reveals an explicit referential dimension, which is most noticeable at the beginning of the unit. A first reference concerns the use of the demonstrative pronoun "these things"

(16:4b–5a and 16:5b–6), which recalls and reaffirms the earlier disclosures concerning the forthcoming departure. A second reference involves the first description of the disciples' reaction in 16:5b–c (their failure to pursue the question of the destination). This description goes directly against the first reaction of a disciple in the farewell (13:35) and signals a different development altogether of the themes from the first unit. A third reference concerns the second description of the disciples' reaction in 16:6 (the sorrow that has filled their hearts). This description, along with its corresponding call to courage of 16:33c, specifically recalls the exhortations to the disciples from the first unit to have neither fear nor consternation in their hearts.

In the end, the supplementary function can only be understood in the light of the unit's other strategic functions, as well as its own location within the speech itself. The basic reason for such a function will be clarified only by the synchronic analysis of chapter 6.

As in the first unit, consolation and teaching are the primary functions of the fourth unit. Now, however, the consolatory function is more prominent and pervasive than the didactic. The consolatory function is present in all three major sections and reveals a strong, effective cumulative development through the unit. A comparison with the first unit shows a different use and deployment of this function within the fourth unit. Gone is the first unit's distinctive series of mostly negative consequences in the introduction followed by a wide variety of brief positive consequences in the remainder of the unit. For example, although the beginning of the fourth unit immediately refers to certain negative consequences of the departure (16:5b–6), the statement is brief and followed by an extended exposition of the positive consequences of the departure. Similarly, although other negative consequences are mentioned in the remainder of the unit—within the first major section itself, as well as in the second and third major sections—they all follow the same pattern: they are brief and accompanied by an extended delineation of the positive consequences of the departure. Such a change in use and deployment considerably tones down the negative and troubling aspects of the departure and emphasizes its positive and reassuring dimensions.

The cumulative character of the consolatory function can be traced through all three major sections of the unit. In the first section the disciples are promised a successor to Jesus, the Spirit-Paraclete, with a twofold role. On the one hand, the presence of the Spirit-Paraclete among them will allow them to confront the fundamental values of an unbelieving and hostile world with the values of God and Jesus (which they represent and proclaim through their own mission and ministry to the world) and, in so doing, convict a world whose ruler is identified as the evil one. On the other hand, the presence of the Spirit-Paraclete among them will allow them to come to a full understanding of Jesus' revelation—both that revelation disclosed during the ministry as a whole and that revelation left undisclosed until the time of the return. As the Spirit of truth, the Paraclete will lead the disciples into the whole truth—a truth that the Paraclete receives from the Father through Jesus and then proclaims to the disciples. Such promises are interrelated; it is as the bearers of such truth to the world that the disciples will confront and convict the world.

In the second major section the disciples are promised that Jesus himself will return to them soon after the departure itself. The disciples are also promised that with this return, their inevitable sorrow will turn to a joy that is perfect and that no one will be able to wrest from them. The disciples are further promised that with this return, they will have no need to ask any further questions of Jesus. This implies that their failure to understand the import and thrust of Jesus' ongoing disclosures will end and that they will enjoy a direct relationship with the Father so that whatever they request in Jesus' name will be granted. In addition, the fact that the return is foreseen as following quickly upon the departure reinforces the power of such promises.

In the third major section a final promise is extended: with Jesus' return, an open revelation of the Father will take place. The previous promise of a direct relationship with the Father is reaffirmed and expanded for this time of open revelation, so the disciples are now further assured of the Father's own love for them. From beginning to end, therefore, a number of promises that are more expansive and developed than in the first unit are gradually unfolded. These promises increasingly assure the disciples that the coming departure of Jesus will be of direct benefit to them.

The didactic function also plays a primary role within the fourth unit, though it is limited to a few brief statements within the first and third major sections. This function involves, first of all, the figure of Jesus. A comparison with the first unit shows a different use and deployment of such teaching within the fourth unit. Instead of the extended and systematic exposition of the relationship between Jesus and the Father so carefully developed toward the first half of the first unit, both ends of the fourth unit contain a more limited exposition of this relationship. The beginning of the first section briefly identifies "the one who sent him" as the destination of the departure; this subtly introduces the question of Jesus' origins. In the course of the first section, this identification is repeated with an explicit mention of the Father as the destination. A brief development of the relationship between Jesus and the Father is included: the Father is the source of Jesus' revelation. The third section explores this relationship at greater length from the point of view of Jesus' role as revealer of the Father. First, it summarizes the relationship, providing thereby an excellent kernel of Johannine teaching on Jesus. Second, within this summary the question of Jesus' origins, mentioned only in passing within the first unit, becomes as important as that of his destination. In effect, along with the question of the destination, the question of origins, subtly introduced by way of preparation in the first major section, is now used to ground Jesus' role as revealer of the Father. It is because he has come from the Father and now returns to the Father that Jesus reveals the Father. Finally, the exposition of the relationship is brought to an end with an abbreviated reaffirmation of the climactic teaching of this relationship in the first unit—the mutual presence of the Father and Jesus in one another.

The didactic function also concerns the disciples themselves, and a comparison with the first unit again shows a different use and deployment of such teaching in the fourth unit. The emphasis of the first unit on belief in, and love for, Jesus as the essential condition for the reception of the farewell promises yields in the third section to a brief description of the disciples as those who love and believe in Jesus. One also finds a more highly programmatic and ironic use of the disciples' reactions throughout the fourth unit. The disciples' increasing failure to understand allows Jesus to proceed with further teaching about the meaning and consequences of the departure. However, such failure to understand—along with the disciples' predicted demise—is presented throughout as inevitable and temporary, and assurances of future understanding are repeatedly affirmed. Consequently, the privileged status and role of the disciples as disciples of Jesus are readily acknowledged and strongly reinforced in the unit.

As in the first unit, exhortation, warning, and polemics emerge as secondary functions of the fourth unit. The exhortative function can be discerned in the first and third sections of the unit. It is indirect in the first section. The disciples are told, in response to their initial reaction of sorrow and silence, that the announced and forthcoming departure of Jesus, given its many consequences, is actually to their benefit. The exhortative function is direct in the third section, where the disciples are urged to have peace and courage with regard to the forthcoming events in the light of the preceding disclosures. As in the first unit, such exhortations are based directly on the extensive consolation and teaching provided within the fourth unit itself.

The admonitory function can also be discerned within the first and third sections. In the former it is indirect: the role of convicting the world assigned to the disciples implies that the values of the world and the values of the disciples are at odds indeed and hence that conflict is inevitable. The admonitory function is direct in the third section: the disciples are warned of inevitable tribulation to come in and from the world. However, no concrete ramifications or manifestations of such tribulation are specified, so the warnings remain very general throughout.

Finally, the polemical function operates in all three major sections: the disciples are explicitly and repeatedly differentiated from the world at large. Whereas the claims of the world are directly called into question and attacked, the disciples' own claims are affirmed and reinforced. A comparison with the first unit again shows a different deployment of this function within the fourth unit. In the first unit, the differentiation from the world is briefly introduced at the beginning of the unit, systematically developed in the latter half of the main body by means of the radical denial to an unbelieving world of the promises extended to the disciples, and brought to a climax in the conclusion with the reference to the evil one as the ruler of the world. In the present unit, the contrast with the world appears prominently in all three major sections.

In the first section the differentiation begins with the specific role assigned to the disciples with regard to the world. Given the presence of the Spirit-Paraclete among them in the course of their own mission in and to the world, the disciples will confront and convict an unbelieving and hostile world whose very ruler is identified as Satan and whose fundamental values are diametrically opposed to those of God as revealed by Jesus and the Spirit-Paraclete. The second section ironically portrays the reaction of the world to the departure: although the departure will be greeted with joy, in the end it is the disciples who will possess a joy that is perfect and that no one will take from them. In the third section the process of differentiation ends with Jesus' triumphal declaration of victory over the world. As his disciples, therefore, such victory ultimately grounds and assures their own victory in and over the world. This process of differentiation is further sharpened by the clear parallelism between this concluding declaration of victory over the world and the first section's reference to the ruler of the world. As the disciples continue their mission in and to the world, therefore, they are assured that victory has in fact already been won and that the ruler of the world, the evil one, has already been condemned.

As a result, the disciples stand out as disciples of Jesus in the midst of an unbelieving and hostile world, a world that is under the direct and explicit dominion of the demonic powers. However, in this final unit the world is described in general terms, so the specific association with the Jews as its primary and preeminent representatives is not found at all. Despite all evidence to the contrary, therefore, the polemical function makes it clear that it is the disciples who represent the ways and values of God in the world.

The character of this unit as a strategic whole points to a twofold rhetorical situation, or view of the implied readers by the implied author, similar to that of the first unit. On the one hand, the disciples are viewed in a positive light: their status and role as disciples of Jesus (as those who believe in and love Jesus) are presupposed and affirmed; their repeated and progressive failure to understand, as well as their forthcoming abandonment of Jesus, is presented as temporary and as yielding in the end to a complete understanding; and their status and role in the world are sharply set off against an unbelieving, hostile, and demonic world. On the other hand, the disciples are viewed as being in great need of consolation and teaching. Although their status and role as disciples of Jesus are affirmed, the disciples are also clearly perceived to be under significant duress and hence in need of sustained and extensive reassurance. In the end, such a twofold rhetorical situation, with its perceived socioreligious exigencies, called forth the complex and effective response conveyed by this fourth unit of discourse.

6

A SYNCHRONIC AND
DIACHRONIC READING OF
THE FAREWELL DISCOURSE

THE CLOSE ANALYSIS OF THE farewell speech as a whole, as described in chapter 1, consists of two steps. The first step analyzes 13:31–16:33 as a self-contained and coherent artistic and strategic whole and hence explores the synchronic dimension of the farewell speech. The second step concerns the literary difficulties present in 13:31–16:33 and thus addresses the diachronic question regarding a possible process of accretion and expansion ultimately leading to the present form of the farewell speech. As chapter 1 explained, this analysis deliberately excludes the speech's climactic farewell prayer in John 17.[1]

THE FAREWELL DISCOURSE AS AN ARTISTIC AND
STRATEGIC WHOLE: A SYNCHRONIC PROPOSAL

The centrifugal forces of the previous four chapters must now become centripetal. The preceding close reading of the various units of discourse proposed within these chapters must now yield to a close examination of the relationship of these units of discourse to one another, given their present location and sequence within the farewell speech as a whole. This relationship has already been pursued to some extent in the preceding literary-rhetorical analysis of each unit; however, that examination dealt for the most part with specific points of terminology and style, grammar and syntax, themes and motifs, structure and development, and strategic concerns and aims. The examination in this chapter is concerned instead

1. The final chapter will use the expression "the speech as a whole," as has this entire study, with specific reference to John 13:31–16:33. This by no means implies that the prayer of John 17 does not form an essential part of this speech. In addition to the reasons already mentioned in chapter 1 for omission of John 17 in this study (its different genre as a farewell prayer, its extensive length, and its climactic role at the end of both speech and scene), I would also argue that John 13:31–16:33 functions as a self-contained and coherent prelude to the prayer.

with the broader and more fundamental dimensions of this relationship, with the units as artistic and strategic wholes in the light of their specific placement and function within the overall structure and development of the speech. As such, this first step will address the character of 13:31–16:33 as an artistic and strategic whole with a highly unified and coherent literary structure and development, unified and coherent strategic concerns and aims, and a distinctive rhetorical situation.

This first step involves five interrelated steps:

1. An overview of the thematic flow of the speech.
2. An overview of the strategic flow of the speech.
3. An overview of the rhetorical situation reflected in, and addressed by, the speech.
4. A comparative examination of the speech in terms of the farewell genre in antiquity.
5. An overview of the speech in the light of the farewell context of 13:1–30.

The Thematic Flow of the
Farewell Discourse

The farewell speech begins with an announcement of Jesus' glorification in 13:31–32. All that follows in chapters 13–17 is ultimately connected to this initial announcement. Indeed, the farewell prayer of John 17 clearly returns to this theme of Jesus' glorification. Furthermore, Jesus' final request of the Father in 17:24–26 provides a clear thematic clamp for the entire speech of 13:31–17:26 in terms of this glorification, so the speech as a whole is firmly demarcated and held together by this overall inclusion. All that follows 13:31–32, therefore, directly or indirectly constitutes a commentary on, or explication of, the beginning announcement of glorification. This extended explanation is developed in two interrelated directions: the fundamental meaning of Jesus' glorification and the immediate and extended consequences of this glorification for the community of disciples.

In the first unit of discourse, John 13:31–14:31, the connection to the announcement of 13:31–32 is immediate and direct, so the announcement's explanation becomes part of the structure of the unit itself. The fundamental meaning of the glorification is pursued in terms of Jesus' forthcoming departure from the disciples. A brief, undeveloped announcement of such a departure is followed by a long, detailed explanation concerning both the general and more concrete meanings of this departure in terms of the relationship between Jesus and God the Father. The departure's general meaning (its destination and reason) is extensively pursued in the first half of the unit, and its more concrete meaning (its mode) is briefly addressed at the end.

The consequences of the glorification are correspondingly pursued in terms of the consequences of this impending departure of Jesus for the disciples, who will be left behind in the world. A brief listing of negative consequences is followed by a long series of positive promises extended to the disciples and denied to the world for the time after the departure, thus bestowing upon the disciples a privileged status and role as disciples of Jesus in the world. These positive promises are both immediate and extended, are stated with little development, and are located in the latter half of the unit. The promises are grounded directly in the disciples' own belief in, and love for, Jesus; their own acceptance of, and obedience to, his commands or word(s), including the commands to believe in him and his claims (as delineated by way of summary within the unit itself); the command to love one another as he had loved them, the farewell legacy disclosed within the unit itself for the first time; and all other practical directives of Jesus disclosed in the course of the ministry. Such belief in Jesus and such love for Jesus ultimately allow, therefore, for the disciples' privileged status and role in the world, as well as for their sharp differentiation from an unbelieving and hostile world, a world characterized as being under the rule of Satan. Thus, at the beginning of the speech the overarching and controlling themes involve the fundamental meaning of the departure and its many immediate and extended consequences for the disciples.

After the first unit of discourse the connection to the beginning announcement of 13:31–32 becomes more indirect. In fact, the close structural development of this theme observed in the first unit is not resumed until the farewell prayer of chapter 17 (see 17:1–5).

The second unit of discourse, John 15:1–17, almost entirely bypasses the meaning of the forthcoming departure. It focuses on the extended consequences of the departure for the community of disciples. These consequences, moreover, almost exclusively involve the internal affairs of the community itself and are presented in a more sustained and guarded fashion than was the case in the first unit. What had remained largely implicit in the first unit is now brought explicitly to the fore.

The privileged status and role of the disciples, which were highlighted in the first unit, are explicitly reaffirmed: as those who have been cleansed by the word of Jesus, the disciples are like branches in the "true" vine of Jesus; as those who have been chosen and loved by Jesus, the disciples are also the friends or loved ones of Jesus. Therefore, a number of promises are again extended to the disciples as both branches and friends of Jesus. This further confirms their privileged status and role as disciples of Jesus.

In addition, the foundation for such a privileged status and role, previously outlined in terms of belief in, and love for, Jesus in the first unit, is highlighted in the second unit. As branches in the "true" vine of Jesus, the disciples must bear much and constant fruit and must abide in Jesus and his word in order to preserve and insure their privileged status and role as disciples of Jesus. As the friends of Jesus, the disciples must also bear much and constant fruit and must abide in his love by carrying out his commands—above all, the preeminent command to love one another as he himself had loved them, to the point of death if necessary (as it is now more explicitly stated)—in order to preserve and insure their status and role as disciples of Jesus. A failure to do so is openly portrayed as leading not only to a loss of their privileged status and role as disciples (that is, to a radical separation from the community of the chosen disciples) but also to ultimate desiccation and destruction. A proper response, in contrast, is described as preserving and insuring their privileged status and role, as the further promises extended clearly indicate.

With the second unit, therefore, the overarching controlling thematic concerns of the farewell speech shift to the more extended consequences of the departure for the disciples. These include the need for the community to be ever fruitful and to abide in Jesus (in his word and his love) if they are to remain disciples of Jesus (his branches and friends) in the time after the departure.[2]

The third unit of discourse, John 15:18–16:4a, again almost completely bypasses the fundamental meaning of Jesus' departure. However, although the focus remains on the extended rather than immediate consequences of the departure for the community of disciples, such consequences now primarily concern the external affairs of the community. They are presented in a more sustained and guarded fashion than was the case in the first unit. Once again, what had remained implicit in the first unit now comes to the fore (indeed, brutally so) in the third unit of discourse.

The relationship of the disciples to the world is presented in terms of severe and sustained opposition: in their continued witness to Jesus in and to the world, the disciples will meet with rejection and hatred, active persecution, radical social dislocation, and even loss of life. To be sure, some acceptance of their word is also foreseen, but the situation envisioned is largely portrayed as most trying and difficult. This relationship is also grounded explicitly in Jesus' own previous relationship to the world;

2. This shift can be further described as follows. First, the farewell legacy of 13:34–35, the preeminent and distinguishing command of the disciples' love for one another as Jesus had loved them, now comes fully to the fore. Second, the exhortations to belief of 14:1b–c, the essential condition of belief in Jesus and his claims of 14:11, and the essential condition of love for him of 14:15, 21a, 23b, and 24a come directly to the fore as well. Finally, a number of close bonds between the two units should be noted: (a) the reference to the "word" and "words" of Jesus (14:23, 24; 15:3, 7), (b) the theme of "abiding" (14:23; 15:4–7), (c) the promises of unlimited granting of petitions (14:13–14; 15:7–8, 16), (d) the theme of "carrying out or obeying" (14:13–14; 15:7–8, 16), and (e) the theme of "joy" (14:28; 15:11).

in the course of his own mission in and to the world he also encountered rejection and hatred, active persecution, social dislocation, and even death itself—as well as some acceptance. Thus, the envisioned situation of the disciples is presented as not surprising but inevitable, given their privileged status and role as disciples of Jesus in the world, as those who have been chosen by Jesus out of the world and who can no longer be considered of the world.

In the third unit, therefore, the overarching themes of the farewell speech continue to be the more extended consequences of Jesus' departure for the disciples, though the nature of such consequences changes. The disciples are still to be ever fruitful and abide in Jesus in order to preserve and insure their status and role as disciples of Jesus in the world, but they will also have to do so under the most severe circumstances, as they continue their witness to Jesus in and to the world. In other words, the bearing of much and constant fruit will be accompanied throughout by inescapable and unremitting hatred and persecution from the world, and it will be of the sort that Jesus himself had to endure. The disciples' failure to bear fruit will result, once again, in a loss of their status and role as disciples of Jesus, in a radical separation from the community of disciples.[3]

The fourth unit of discourse, John 16:4b–33, resumes the twofold explication of the beginning announcement of glorification in the first unit, though not from a directly structural point of view, as in the first unit. Thus, while the immediate and extended consequences of the impending departure for the disciples continue to be addressed in this unit, the fundamental meaning of the forthcoming departure again becomes a major focus of attention. In fact, the fourth unit ultimately functions as a direct supplement to the first unit.

On the one hand, the fundamental meaning of the forthcoming departure is pursued from the beginning in terms of the relationship between Jesus and the Father. A brief, straightforward explanation of such a departure at the beginning of the unit (a simple identification of God the Father as the destination of the departure) is developed at greater length toward the conclusion of the unit (the origins of the one about to depart and the

---

3. The shift can be further described as follows. With regard to the first unit, both the contrast between disciples and outsiders (13:33, 36; 14:17b–e, 18–20, 22, 27) and the contrast between Jesus and outsiders (14:30–31) come to the fore. Also, the theme of succession, the promise of the Spirit-Paraclete, is expanded in a new direction altogether—namely, that of witness in and to the world (14:16–17a, 25–26; 15:26–27). With regard to the second unit, the central theme of hatred from the outside provides a direct counterbalance to that of love inside the community. In addition, a number of close links should be noted: (a) the love of the world for its own as a direct contrast to the love of Jesus for his chosen ones (15:9, 12–13, 19), (b) the theme of the disciples as "chosen" (15:13, 19), (c) the use of the metaphorical contrast "slave"/"master" (15:14–15, 20), (d) the theme of "obeying or carrying out" (15:10, 20), and (e) the theme of Jesus' "word" (15:3, 20).

destination of the departure). This explanation, however, is by no means as extensive or as detailed as that of the first unit; it is brief and pointed. Indeed, if the explanation of the first unit can be regarded as an excellent compendium of Johannine teaching on the figure of Jesus as the Word of God, the explanation provided by this fourth unit should be characterized as a concise summary, a kernel, of such teaching.

On the other hand, the consequences of the forthcoming departure for the disciples are presented from the beginning as both negative and positive. The negative consequences are few, undeveloped, and widely scattered throughout the unit. The positive consequences, in contrast, are prominent, extensively developed, and used throughout the unit not only as a direct counterbalance to the negative consequences but also in a progressive fashion. As in the first unit, these positive promises (both immediate and extended) serve to differentiate sharply between the disciples and the world and thus to bestow on the disciples a privileged status and role as disciples of Jesus in the world. As in the first unit, moreover, these promises are grounded on the disciples' belief in Jesus and love for Jesus, though such a grounding is not as explicit or prominent here as in the first unit. Once again, therefore, such belief in, and love for, Jesus ultimately allow for the privileged status and role of the disciples in the world, as well as for the sharp differentiation between the disciples and an unbelieving and hostile world, a world now characterized as not only under the possession of the evil one but also as having been conquered by Jesus.

At the conclusion of the speech, therefore, the controlling and overarching themes again are the fundamental meaning of Jesus' departure and its consequences for the disciples.[4] However, the final unit places a much greater emphasis on the consequences than on the meaning of the departure.

In terms of its overall thematic flow, the farewell speech that leads up to the climactic prayer of John 17 can indeed be regarded as a self-contained artistic whole that is highly unified and carefully developed from beginning to end. Its overall structure reveals a chiastic arrangement following

---

4. This shift can be further described as follows. With regard to the first unit, the supplementary function of this unit as a whole is unmistakable, and the theme of succession, the coming of the Spirit-Paraclete, is expanded in the direction of the teaching of the disciples (14:16–17a, 25–26; 16:12–15). With regard to the preceding third unit, the theme of succession is again expanded in a new direction, that of convicting the world. This specifically addresses the relationship between the disciples and the world from a different perspective (15:26–27; 16:8–11). In addition, the following links and bonds can be detected: (a) the use of the recurring concluding formula of the discourse at the beginning (16:1, 4a, 6), (b) the theme of the "sin" of the world (15:22, 24; 16:8, 9), and (c) the further contrasts employed between the disciples and the world (15:20; 16:33).

an ABBA pattern. Its outer components (13:31–14:31; 16:4b–33) address the fundamental meaning of the departure itself and its immediate and extended consequences for the disciples, and the central components (15:1–17; 15:18–16:4a) deal with further extended consequences of this departure. Furthermore, whereas the consequences of the departure outlined in the outer components are primarily optimistic, the consequences anticipated in the central components are for the most part pessimistic. The overall development of this fourfold structure can be further described as follows.

The beginning of the first unit of discourse (13:31–14:31) includes a long, detailed, and systematic explanation of Jesus' departure in terms of the relationship between Jesus and the Father, of Jesus' status and role with regard to the Father. This explanation is briefly continued at the end of the first unit. The earlier, more extensive part of this explanation raises the issue of the destination of, and reason for, the departure, and the second part addresses the question of the mode of the departure. The beginning of the farewell speech, therefore, clarifies the fundamental meaning of the departure and thus provides an excellent compendium of Johannine teaching on Jesus. This sort of extended exposition subsequently disappears altogether from the remainder of the speech.

The first unit of discourse also extensively describes the consequences of the departure for the disciples. Aside from a few negative consequences, the status and role of the disciples in the world as disciples of Jesus are portrayed as distinctive and privileged indeed, though ultimately grounded in their own belief in, and love for, Jesus. Thus, the disciples are also sharply differentiated from an unbelieving world. Any direct opposition from, or conflict with, that world remains largely in the background, although it is strongly intimated. The beginning of the speech, therefore, clarifies the fundamental benefits of such a departure for the disciples.

The speech takes a very different turn in the two central units of discourse (15:1–17; and 15:18–16:4a). The attention focuses on the consequences of the departure for the disciples, but here the positive delineation of the disciples in the first unit becomes more problematic and guarded from both an internal and an external point of view.

The grounding of the disciples' privileged status and role in the first unit (their belief in, and love for, Jesus) now comes to the fore; the disciples are advised that their status and role as disciples of Jesus will be strongly tested in the time after the departure. Such testing will have both an internal and an external dimension. On the one hand, the disciples have to bear much and constant fruit in order to abide in Jesus; they must adhere to the word and the love of Jesus or lose their standing in the community. On the other hand, the disciples have to witness to Jesus in the world in the face of severe, unrelenting opposition or again lose their standing in the community. Thus, their privileged status and role as disciples of Jesus in the world are by no means final and irrevocable. Such a status and role have to be actively preserved and insured through continued belief in, and love of, Jesus (and one another), as well as through continued witness to Jesus in the world despite the inevitable consequences.

After the disturbing disclosures of the central components, in which the positive standing of the disciples as disciples of Jesus in the world of the first unit is balanced by a more guarded and problematic assessment of such a status and role, the speech again takes a different turn (16:4b–33). In the fourth unit of discourse, the speech returns full circle to the twofold thrust of the first unit. However, the consequences of the departure now play a more prominent role than the fundamental meaning of the departure.

The consequences of the departure for the disciples are once again positively described, along with a scattering of negative consequences. In comparison with the first unit of discourse, 16:4b–33 contains an even longer and more detailed description of such consequences, which extends from the beginning to the end of the unit. Consequently, the status and role of the disciples as disciples of Jesus in the world are again portrayed as distinctive and privileged indeed, though grounded once again in their belief in, and love for, Jesus. This again posits a sharp differentiation between the disciples and the world, though any direct opposition from, or conflict with, the world remains entirely in the background. The conclusion of the speech, therefore, strongly reaffirms and expands the fundamental benefits of the departure for the disciples, which is understandable in the light of the situation envisioned in the central components.

The fundamental meaning of the departure is also expanded in the fourth unit, though to a more limited extent. An initial introduction of the relationship between Jesus and the Father at the beginning of the unit is pursued in greater detail at the end. Furthermore, although the destination of the departure continues to be of paramount interest, the question of Jesus' provenance is now introduced as well. The speech thus closes with a concise summary of Johannine teaching on Jesus as the Word of God—it is from God that he came, and it is to God that he is about to return. The conclusion of the speech, therefore, again clarifies the fundamental meaning of the departure. The reduced prominence of this theme at this point is understandable, given the extended exposition of the relationship provided in the first unit and the primary stress on the promises in the central components. Nevertheless, its presence at the end of the speech is powerful as it recalls and reaffirms the beginning of the speech in a direct and concrete fashion.

In conclusion, an analysis of the thematic flow of the farewell speech shows a clear structure and careful development. The speech reveals a series of appropriate contrasting thrusts in its overall explication of the fundamental meaning and consequences of Jesus' departure. The speech moves from quite positive, to decidedly guarded and uncertain, to quite positive. It lays a secure foundation in its first unit, discloses the grave dangers threatening such a foundation in the central units, and then reaffirms and strengthens the foundation at the end. Therefore, the extended commentary on the beginning announcement of the glorification in 13:31–32 indeed emerges as a self-contained and coherent artistic whole.

The Strategic Flow of the Farewell Discourse

The farewell speech has been shown to be an extended commentary on, or explication of, the beginning announcement of Jesus' glorification in 13:31–32. It is clear, therefore, that its overall strategic concerns involve the final events of Jesus' ministry and mission as the Word of God in the world, the climactic events of his "hour." Given the two interdependent directions in which the explanation of this beginning announcement proceeds throughout the speech, a number of more specific and circumscribed strategic concerns, with corresponding strategic aims, can be detected.

As already discussed, the themes of the first unit of discourse (13:31–14:31) are the fundamental meaning of Jesus' forthcoming departure and the many consequences, both immediate and extended, of this departure for the disciples. Thus, the overall strategic concerns of this unit focus throughout on the climactic events of "the hour," on the correct interpretation of the forthcoming departure.

The unit is a sustained exercise in the teaching and consolation of the disciples. It has a linear or progressive construction involving three steps: a negative, disturbing introduction; immediately counterbalanced by a positive, reassuring main body; followed in turn by a similarly positive conclusion. The unit's primary functions, therefore, are didactic and consolatory. From a didactic point of view, the unit seeks to give the disciples a proper interpretation of the climactic events in terms of the relationship between Jesus and the Father, as well as to provide them with a parting legacy that is meant to serve as their preeminent and distinguishing principle of praxis in the world—love for one another as Jesus loved them. From a consolatory point of view, the unit seeks to offer solace to the disciples by describing at length their privileged position and role in the world as disciples of Jesus.

Three other functions play a subordinate role. First, in the light of such extended teaching and consolation, the disciples are called upon to have neither fear nor consternation, to believe in Jesus and the Father, and to love one another as Jesus had loved them—a clear exhortative function. Second, an admonitory function exists insofar as intimations of a more ominous side of discipleship are raised (the patterning of the disciples' love for one another on Jesus' own love for them, the further description of Jesus' peace as being not at all like that of the world, and the description of the mode of Jesus' departure as an encounter with the ruler of the world). Such a function, however, remains in the background within this unit. Third, a polemical function involving outsiders (in particular, the Jews) is to be acknowledged. The disciples are sharply differentiated from the world, a world that is repeatedly and radically denied all of their own privileges and is portrayed instead as being under the dominion of Satan. The claims of the disciples are greatly enhanced thereby, and the claims of the world are correspondingly attacked and questioned at a fundamental level. Furthermore, the implicit admonitory function can be associated with this more explicit polemical function: despite, and because of, their privileged status and role in the world, the disciples can also expect opposition from, and conflict with, the world and its ruler.

At the beginning of the farewell speech, therefore, open exhortation in the light of the forthcoming events is grounded on extensive teaching and consolation. At the same time, the external dimension of the consolation— the contrast with the world—introduces a sense of polemics with outsiders, and the subtle hints regarding conflict to come from the world keep an element of warning in the background.[5]

The overarching theme of the second unit of discourse (15:1–17) is the call to the disciples to abide in Jesus. This unit's strategic concerns thus shift to the internal situation of the community of disciples, to the proper relationship of the disciples to both Jesus and one another following the departure of Jesus. As the unit's structure (a successive use of a pattern of

5. In terms of Kennedy's rhetorical analysis (*Interpretation;* see chap. 1 of the present work), I would argue that this first unit of discourse represents an example of epideictic rhetoric. First, from a structural point of view, I see the threefold division of proem or exordium (13:31–38), main body devoted to an orderly sequence of amplified topics (14:1–27), and epilogue or peroration (14:28–31). I also see the unit as containing a proposition at the beginning of its main body (14:1–3). Second, from the point of view of development, I see a definite tendency in the unit toward amplification, with a fondness for description as well. In fact, I have argued for two material topics that are constantly restated throughout the unit. Third, from the point of view of strategy, I see the unit as an attempt to persuade an audience to hold and reaffirm a point of view in the present as the basis for a general policy of action, with a basic argument involving both a change of attitude and a deepening of values. The author clearly recalls for the disciples who they are and what they represent. However, I would not describe the unit as a "paramythetic," or speech of consolation, as such, though consolation represents one of its main aims. The unit has a number of other aims as well, in keeping with its farewell context and genre.

inclusion, with a direct appeal to the disciples at the center of each inclusion) indicates, one of the unit's primary functions is exhortation: a twofold call to the disciples to abide in the word of Jesus and the love of Jesus in order to preserve and insure their privileged status and role as disciples of Jesus. A second primary function is admonition. On the one hand, a failure to abide in Jesus, to respond to the calls, is portrayed as having the direst of consequences—separation, death, and destruction. On the other hand, it is now made more explicit that the love of the disciples for one another may well entail what is described as the highest form of love and as the form of love that Jesus himself embodied—the giving up of one's life for one's "friends." The first and open warning enormously enhances the power of the exhortations themselves by means of an either/or proposition. The second, more subtle warning presents such exhortations as being in keeping with the highest of human aspirations and ideals and, indeed, as being the way of the master himself.

These two primary functions are directly supported by a number of other functions. First, an important didactic function operates insofar as the privileged status and role of the disciples as disciples of Jesus are acknowledged and reaffirmed as a proper and solid foundation for the calls themselves. Second, a more limited consolatory function is present insofar as a proper response to the calls is depicted as having positive consequences, thus making the calls themselves most enticing despite the demands they may entail. Finally, a polemical function should be acknowledged as well. Insofar as the disciples are ultimately differentiated as those who belong to the "true" vine of Jesus and as the "chosen" friends of Jesus, such a polemic concerns outsiders (specifically, the Jews once again, though not in as direct a fashion as in the first unit). However, such a polemic involves above all insiders, insofar as the disciples themselves are sharply differentiated into the fruitful and the unfruitful, the abiding and the nonabiding. Whereas the claims of the abiding and fruitful disciples are reinforced, all other claims, whether of outsiders or insiders, are directly questioned and opposed. Once again, the admonitory function can be associated with this polemical function: the ultimate implications of a failure to abide in Jesus and to love one another as he had loved them can fit well into either the more implicit conflict with the world or the explicit conflict within the community.

In the second unit of discourse, therefore, exhortation and admonition in the light of the extended consequences of the departure emerge as primary, with a greater emphasis on exhortation. Teaching and consolation, though present, are not as prominent as in the first unit and are used here primarily as foundation and support. The element of teaching plays a more visible role than that of consolation. Finally, the polemical element remains prominent, though it is now expanded to include (and, indeed, to emphasize) insiders as well as outsiders.[6]

The controlling thematic concern of the third unit of discourse (15:18–16:4a) is the severe and inevitable hatred of the world for the disciples. The overall strategic concern of this unit, therefore, shifts from the internal to the external situation of the disciples, to the correct relationship of the disciples to the world at large following the departure of Jesus. The unit contains an overall inclusion in which the outer components describe in ascending fashion the opposition of the world to the disciples, and the central component grounds such opposition on the earlier opposition of the world to Jesus himself. This structure reveals a primary admonitory function: to warn the disciples in a concrete and explicit way of opposition and conflict from the world. A second primary function is exhortation: the disciples are urged to recall and keep in mind all these warnings and disclosures in the face of the opposition itself and thus to avoid stumbling and radical separation from the community of disciples. Such exhortations provide strong and much-needed encouragement in the light of the coming woes.

Several other functions directly support these primary functions. First, there is a prominent didactic function whereby the opposition of the world to the disciples is repeatedly grounded in the previous opposition of the world to Jesus himself and hence in the disciples' privileged status and role as disciples of Jesus—as those who have been chosen out of the world, who now bear Jesus' name, and who are therefore not of the world. Such teaching mollifies to some extent the tremendous impact of the warnings themselves; because of their status and role as disciples of Jesus, they cannot escape such opposition from the world and must face it head-on, regardless of consequences. Second, a more limited consolatory function exists, whereby the disciples are provided much-needed solace by way of specific promises in the midst of such opposition. This function attempts to mollify even further the impact of the warnings. Third, a polemical function is to be acknowledged as well: the disciples are sharply differentiated from outsiders and, in particular, from the Jews. Thus, the claims of the

---

6. I find it impossible to classify this second unit of discourse as primarily epideictic, although elements of epideictic rhetoric are certainly present. The unit represents, in my opinion, an example of deliberative rhetoric. For the following comments, see Kennedy, *Interpretation*, 19–25, 39–48. From the point of view of strategy, I see the unit as an attempt to persuade an audience to take some action in the future, with a basic argument involving self-interest and future benefits. From the point of view of structure, given the proposed successive patterns of inclusion, the issue is complex and deserves a more detailed treatment than can be provided here. Nevertheless, the following is a tentative suggestion: a proem (15:1–2, 9a–b), a proposition (15:3–4b, 9c), a proof (15:4c–7, 10–11), and an epilogue (15:8, 12–17). From the point of view of development, the twofold proof would consist of two material topics.

disciples are strongly reaffirmed, and those of the world are radically questioned. In this unit the admonitory function is explicitly related to the polemical function; the warnings detail the concrete channels for such opposition from the world.

With the third unit of discourse, exhortation and admonition in the light of the extended consequences of the departure continue as primary functions, though now there is greater emphasis on admonition. As in the second unit, teaching and consolation are present as well, though again more by way of foundation and support. Teaching plays a more prominent role than consolation. Finally, the polemical element becomes even more prominent, though again only with respect to outsiders, as in the first unit.[7]

The controlling and overarching thematic concerns of the fourth unit of discourse (16:4b–33) are the fundamental meaning of the departure and its many consequences, both immediate and extended, for the disciples. Because of these themes and the unit's supplementary role with regard to the first unit, the fourth unit's overall strategic concern returns to the climactic events of "the hour" as such—to the proper and correct interpretation of the forthcoming departure of Jesus.

The structure of the unit is characterized by a progressive development involving three basic steps that give positive disclosures of Jesus in ascending order. This structure points to both consolatory and didactic functions as primary. From a consolatory point of view, the unit seeks to offer solace to the disciples by setting forth at great length their privileged status and role as disciples of Jesus in the world. From a didactic point of view, the unit also seeks to provide the disciples with a correct interpretation of the climactic events in terms of the relationship between Jesus and the Father. This relationship is now presented with an even broader scope, as the text addresses the questions of Jesus' origins and initial journey into the world. In this fourth unit, however, the consolatory function plays a more extensive and prominent role than the didactic function.

Several other functions also play a supportive role. First, a limited exhortative function is present. At the beginning of the unit the disciples are told, in the midst of their sorrow, that the departure is in fact much to their advantage, and at the end they are urged to have peace and rejoice. Again,

---

7. I also find it impossible to classify this third unit of discourse as epideictic, though again elements of epideictic rhetoric are present. The unit represents, in my opinion, another example of deliberative rhetoric. From the point of view of strategy, I see the unit as an attempt to persuade an audience to take some action in the future, with a basic argument involving self-interest and future benefits. From the point of view of structure, the issue is again complex, given the overall pattern of inclusion employed; a much more detailed treatment is needed. The following is a tentative suggestion: a proem (15:18–21), a proof (15:22–24), and an epilogue (15:25–16:4a). From the point of view of development, I see the unit as treating several variations of the same material topic.

as in the first unit, extensive comforting and teaching provide the immediate foundation for such exhortations. Second, a limited admonitory function is discernible as well. To begin with, insofar as the disciples' conviction of the world is based on the opposition of its values concerning sin, righteousness, and judgment to those of God, an implicit warning is extended—the values of the world and of the disciples are in sharp opposition to one another. Then, insofar as the disciples are warned at the end of tribulation in the world, the implicit warning becomes explicit, though the specific ramifications or channels of such tribulation are not developed at all. Both the exhortative and admonitory functions, therefore, remain in the background in this unit. Finally, a more prominent polemical function must be acknowledged. The disciples are sharply differentiated throughout from outsiders, indeed to the point of acting as those who will convict an unbelieving, unrighteous, and sinful world (a world characterized again as being under the rule of Satan). Consequently, whereas the claims of the world are once more questioned and demolished, those of the disciples are explicitly affirmed and strongly reinforced. The admonitory function can and should be read from such a polemical perspective as well: as disciples of Jesus in the world, the disciples are to expect concrete opposition and conflict from the world.

In the fourth unit of discourse, consolation and teaching come back to the fore, with the former as the dominant element by far. Correspondingly, exhortation and admonition, though present, now play a much more minor role than they did in the first unit of discourse. The polemical element remains prominent, though less so than in the central units of the speech.[8]

The farewell speech leading up to the climactic prayer of John 17 can be described as a self-contained and coherent strategic whole that is highly unified and carefully developed from beginning to end. Following the chiastic literary structure posited in the previous section, the strategic aims of the speech can be described as follows. The framing components of the speech (13:31–14:31; 16:4b–33) involve for the most part the teaching and consolation of the disciples, and its central components (15:1–17 and

8. I would classify this fourth unit of discourse as an example of epideictic rhetoric. From the point of view of strategy, I see the unit as an attempt to persuade an audience to hold and reaffirm a point of view in the present as the basis for a general policy of action, with a basic argument involving both a change of attitude and a deepening of values. Once again, the author recalls for the disciples who they are and what they represent; in fact, the unit comes close to a "paramythetic," or speech of consolation. From the point of view of structure, the issue is complex. Whereas 14:6b–15 functions as a sort of proem and 16:25–33, as a sort of epilogue, 16:16–24 can be seen as an abbreviated main body. Finally, from the point of view of development, I see a tendency toward amplification, with a fondness for description. Again, I have argued for the presence of two material topics that are constantly restated throughout.

15:18–16:4a) deliver a strong message of exhortation and admonition. In addition, a polemical aim is present throughout. The overall development of this flow will be further described in the following paragraphs.

The farewell speech opens with a definite exhortation in the first outer component (13:31–14:31). After the introduction summarizes the forthcoming events, the first unit exhorts the disciples to have neither fear nor consternation, to believe in Jesus and God, and to love one another as Jesus had loved them. The grounds for such exhortations are immediately set forth: extensive teaching regarding the relationship between Jesus and God the Father is followed by extensive consolation involving many positive promises. A polemical aim is indicated as well by the sustained contrast with the Jews and the world and the direct association of the latter with the demonic powers. An element of admonition with regard to opposition and conflict from the world, although undeniably present, remains subtle throughout.

The central components (15:1–17 and 15:18–16:4a) change the aims of the speech. The formerly primary elements of teaching and consolation now become subordinate and auxiliary, whereas those of exhortation and admonition become primary and dominant.

In the second unit exhortation becomes prominent. The disciples are directly called upon to abide as disciples by bearing much and constant fruit. An element of admonition becomes explicit and important as well at this point. A failure to abide on the part of the disciples is said to entail a loss of their privileged status and role as disciples of Jesus, and it is also now made clear that the way of discipleship may lead to death itself. Whereas teaching is used to provide a solid foundation for the exhortations to abide, consolation is used as a strong incentive for such calls. In other words, the disciples are urged to remember who they are and what they represent, as well as to keep in mind what benefits they will enjoy. A polemical aim becomes even clearer, but now with insiders (fellow members of the community) rather than outsiders primarily in mind, though the latter are by no means bypassed.

In the third unit admonition comes directly to the fore. The disciples are increasingly warned of the concrete opposition and conflict to come from the world and, particularly, from the Jews. An element of exhortation also continues to be important as the disciples are urged not to stumble in the face of such opposition. Again, teaching provides a solid foundation for these warnings, and consolation supplies much-needed comfort; in other words, the disciples are asked to recall the fate of their master, who they are, what they represent, and what benefits they will enjoy. A polemical aim now becomes clearer than ever, once again with outsiders clearly in mind. The disciples have been chosen out of the world and are no longer of the world; consequently, nothing but severe and unrelenting opposition and conflict is to be expected from the world.

With the final outer component (16:4b–33) the speech again takes a distinctive turn. Exhortation and admonition yield once again to teaching and consolation as the dominant aims. Thus, the farewell speech comes to an end with even more extensive consolation of the disciples in the light of the preceding and very troubling disclosures regarding their forthcoming internal and external situations. Again, many positive promises are extended to them; in addition, further teaching regarding the relationship between Jesus and the Father is provided. Exhortation and admonition, though present, play a subordinate, auxiliary role at the end. Although the disciples are urged to be at peace and to rejoice, they are also warned of tribulation to come in and from the world. A polemical aim is again unmistakable in the sustained differentiation between the disciples and the world, the identification of the world with the demonic powers, and Jesus' final declaration of triumph over the world.

In conclusion, an analysis of the strategic flow of the speech shows a careful and effective arrangement and development. The speech reveals a series of varying strategic concerns: from the climactic events as such, to the future situation of the community, to the climactic events as such. The speech also reveals a series of corresponding strategic aims and functions: from extensive teaching and consolation, to strong and urgent exhortation and admonition, to extensive teaching and consolation. As such, the speech can again be said to provide a firm foundation at the beginning, setting forth the privileged status and role of the disciples as disciples of Jesus in the world; to address in the middle the severe and inevitable difficulties such a foundation will face in the future from both insiders and outsiders, showing how the disciples must actively adhere to such a privileged status and role or lose it altogether; and to reaffirm and strengthen such a foundation at the end, again setting forth the privileged status and role of the disciples as disciples of Jesus in the world.

In addition, the speech reveals a corresponding flow in the standpoint of Jesus as speaker. In the framing components (13:31–14:31; 16:4b–33), which pursue extensive teaching and consolation of the disciples, Jesus speaks as both a Jesus who is about to die (to undergo the climactic events of "the hour") and a Jesus who is risen and about to undertake the final events of "the hour" (the bestowal of the successor and the return to the Father). Moreover, whereas both points of view are strong in the first unit, the first is more prominent in the fourth unit. In the central components (15:1–17; 15:18-16:4a), where extensive exhortation and admonition of the disciples are found, Jesus speaks throughout as a risen Jesus. However, he speaks as a risen and fully glorified Jesus in the second unit and as a risen Jesus again

about to undertake the final events of "the hour" in the third unit. Therefore, it is a dying/risen (prior to final ascent) Jesus who provides the firm
foundation at the beginning; a risen (glorified/prior to final ascent) Jesus
who addresses the severe and inevitable difficulties to be faced by such a
foundation; and a dying/risen (prior to final ascent) Jesus who reaffirms and
strengthens such a foundation at the end, with a much stronger emphasis on
the dying Jesus in direct anticipation of the narrative of death and lasting
significance to come. As such, the extended commentary on the beginning
announcement of the glorification in 13:31–32 again emerges as a self-
contained and coherent strategic whole.[9]

The Rhetorical Situation of the Farewell Discourse

The farewell speech has been shown to be a self-contained and coherent
whole from both an artistic and a strategic point of view. The analysis of the
rhetorical situation reflected in, and addressed by, the speech as a whole
therefore becomes imperative. As indicated in chapter 1, this rhetorical
situation possesses a twofold dimension.

The first dimension involves the disciples as a character in the narrative itself, whether seen as a corporate character or as individuals, since
the latter ultimately function—with certain variations—as representatives or types of the larger group. From the point of view of the Gospel as
narrative, therefore, the rhetorical situation involves the characterization
of the disciples at this point in the developing plot. Its socioreligious
exigencies can be summarized as follows. First, an imminent departure
with ominous connotations is unexpectedly announced by Jesus, along
with a corresponding separation from the disciples. Second, the proper
meaning of the announced departure is explained at length, and the departure's many other consequences for the disciples, both immediate and
extended, are set forth in ample detail. Third, however, not only the
announcement of the departure and the coming separation but also the
explanation of such a departure and the further consequences disclosed
are given largely by way of anticipation. This is because the assembled
disciples, in keeping with their ongoing characterization throughout the

9. As a whole, therefore, I do not believe that the speech should be classified as primarily
epideictic. To do so is to favor the outer, or framing, units over the central units. I see the
central units as focal, however, with the outer units providing the necessary foundation and
support for the exhortations and admonitions of the central units. From the point of view of
strategy, therefore, I see the speech as a whole as an attempt to persuade an audience to take
some action in the future, with a basic argument involving self-interest and future benefits.
From the point of view of structure, I would argue for a proem (13:31–14:31), a proof (15:1–
17; 15:18–16:4b), and an epilogue (16:4b–33). From the point of view of development, I see
the proof as addressing two material topics, each of which possesses a number of variations.

narrative, fail to understand, and even misunderstand (to the point of a prophesied later abandonment of Jesus at the climax of "the hour," including a threefold denial by Peter) the content of these farewell disclosures. Fourth, at the same time, the proper status and role of the disciples in the world—their relationship with regard to Jesus and God, their relationship with regard to one another, and their relationship with regard to the world—for the time after the departure are also outlined at length. Both positive and negative consequences are explicitly listed side by side. Thus, the assembled disciples, who are about to be left behind in the world, are prepared in a direct and concrete way for the coming time of departure and separation (a time that is only partially narrated within the Gospel itself).

The second dimension of the speech's rhetorical situation involves the intended addressees of the Gospel. From the point of view of the Gospel as a communication from an author to a group of readers, this rhetorical situation concerns the view of these readers (the implied readers of the Gospel) held by the author, who in turn adopts, with specific concerns and aims in mind, a distinctive way of addressing and persuading such readers (the implied author of the Gospel) in the light of the perceived situation.

These two dimensions of the rhetorical situation are strongly interrelated. Indeed, it is through the first dimension, given the narrative medium employed, that the implied author attempts to reach the intended addressees with the message in question. The following discussion primarily concerns this second dimension of the rhetorical situation: the overall view of the community reflected in, and addressed by, the specific construction and deployment of this farewell speech as an artistic and strategic whole. This extended commentary on the beginning announcement of 13:31–32 reveals a distinct, unified, and coherent view of the addressed community, the implied readers, on the part of the implied author.

The rhetorical situation reflected in, and addressed by, the first unit of discourse (13:31–14:31) reveals a twofold dimension. On the one hand, the disciples are clearly viewed very positively. Their privileged status and role as disciples of Jesus in the world are strongly set forth and affirmed; in fact, their present failure to understand the message of farewell is taken specifically into account and portrayed as inevitable and temporary, to be definitively resolved with the coming of the promised successor, the Spirit-Paraclete. On the other hand, the disciples are also viewed as not at all beyond encouragement and reassurance. The reasons for such a perceived need include the fact of the departure itself and the ensuing separation (a sharp sense of being left behind or abandoned as "orphans" in the world), the mode of the departure (the manner of Jesus' death at the hands of the world and its ruler), and the consequences of the departure (a further, sharp sense of alienation and oppression from an unbelieving and hostile world thought to be under the full dominion of Satan, along with the possibility of death itself at the hands of this world).

Consequently, the disciples are urged to have neither fear nor consternation but rather to rejoice; to believe in Jesus and his claims with regard to God; and to love one another as Jesus had himself loved them, to the point of death if necessary. Such encouragement and exhortation is provided primarily by way of teaching and consolation, thereby recalling for the disciples who they are and what they represent as the "little children." This provides a correct interpretation of both the fact and the mode of the departure, as well as reaffirms their privileged status and role as disciples of Jesus in the world. Thus, despite all the difficulties that discipleship entails in the world, the way of discipleship is ultimately presented as the only way—in this world of evil powers—of joy; peace; love; and access to, and union with, God.

In conclusion, although the community is viewed as essentially united and firm, it is also viewed as in need of reassurance and encouragement, which is in turn provided by extensive instruction and consolation. The presence of opposition from the outside (above all, of Jewish provenance) is unmistakable, though its more specific ramifications, measures, and channels remain largely undeveloped. Furthermore, insofar as discipleship itself is ultimately grounded in belief in Jesus and love for Jesus, the possibility of a radical separation from the community is certainly present, though such a possibility remains in the background. Thus, whereas a sense of embattlement and oppression is palpable, a sense of holding on is clear as well, though accompanied by questions regarding self-definition in matters of belief and praxis.

The rhetorical situation reflected in, and addressed by, the second unit of discourse (15:1–17) can also be described in terms of a twofold dimension. On the one hand, the disciples are first viewed in a positive light. The privileged status and role of the disciples are explicitly acknowledged and reaffirmed—they are both the branches in the "true" vine of Jesus and the chosen friends of Jesus, the ones whom the word of Jesus has cleansed and whom Jesus has loved. On the other hand, the disciples are also viewed as in need of an urgent exhortation. The reasons for such a perceived need include a failure to bear fruit by abiding in the "true" vine of Jesus (by abiding in his word and claims) and a failure to bear fruit by abiding in the love of Jesus (by obedience to his commands, above all the preeminent command of love for one another as he had loved them, up to and including death, if need be).

Consequently, the disciples are urged to bear much and constant fruit: as branches in the "true" vine, they must abide in Jesus and his word; as the chosen friends of Jesus, they must abide in his love, obeying his commands and loving one another as he himself had loved them. A severe

warning accompanies such exhortations: unless they abide, the disciples
not only stand to lose their privileged status and role as disciples of Jesus
but will also meet with ultimate destruction. In other words, discipleship
is not to be interpreted as final or irrevocable but rather as in need of
constant exercise and validation. In conclusion, the community is no longer
viewed as essentially firm and united but instead as in serious danger of
abandoning its call and standing as disciples of Jesus, both by way of belief
and praxis.

Exhortation is therefore urgent and pointed: abide or else. On the one
hand, the presence of opposition from the outside is certainly in view, with
a Jewish provenance again specifically in mind. The disciples are, after all,
members of the true vine and the chosen friends of Jesus, and the possibility of death in their exercise of discipleship is mentioned more explicitly at
this point than before. It is possible, therefore, to see a failure to abide in
terms of such conflict, a surrender to the pressures of the world; however,
such external pressure is not as prominent here as in the first unit. On the
other hand, the presence of conflict from within now becomes primary.
Among the disciples themselves there are the fruitful and the unfruitful,
and discipleship itself is now seen as a fragile possession. Thus, the grounds
for differentiating the disciples from the world in the first unit have now
become problematic in and of themselves. As a result, it is possible to see a
failure to abide in terms of serious disagreements regarding belief and
praxis within the community itself, though the possibility of death would
then take on much more of a metaphorical than a physical or literal meaning (for example, a failure to show total service or self-giving among the
chosen friends of Jesus). To be sure, the precise nature of such disagreements involving belief and praxis does not come to the fore.

A sense of embattlement and oppression continues, therefore, but its
source seems to have shifted, with the community itself as the main source
of controversy now. At the same time, the sense of holding on is less secure
and less uncertain. Problems of self-understanding in the areas of belief
and praxis seemingly afflict the community at a fundamental level.

A twofold dimension is again present in the rhetorical situation reflected
in, and addressed by, the third unit of discourse (15:18–16:4a). On the one
hand, the community is viewed as in need of a sharp admonition because of
the overwhelming presence of severe and unrelenting pressure from the
outside (again with a clear Jewish provenance), so rejection, hatred, persecution, social dislocation, and death are seen as marking the way of discipleship at every turn. On the other hand, the community is also viewed as
essentially firm and united, despite the attendant circumstances in question. Although the possibility of stumbling in the face of such woes is raised
and used as the very purpose for the unit, such a situation is not pursued

with the same intensity that it was in the second unit. In the third unit it is mentioned but not developed, so it does not appear to be a common occurrence at this point. In other words, the community is still viewed as holding on to their privileged status and role as disciples of Jesus—as those who have been chosen out of the world, who bear his name, and who are no longer of the world.

As a result, the disciples are repeatedly warned that the concrete sufferings they experience in the course of their continued witness to Jesus in and to the world should be seen as an essential and inevitable part of discipleship itself and therefore as not unexpected—as the world reacted to Jesus, so it reacts to his disciples. The disciples are urged to remember these disclosures at all times so that they can proceed with their witness in and to the world and avoid a possible stumbling. The disciples are further reminded that they will be directly assisted and informed in this task by Jesus' successor in the world, the Spirit-Paraclete; that they will indeed meet with some acceptance in the world, howsoever limited; and that the opposition, despite all their claims to the contrary, is guilty of hatred without cause, hatred of God, and inexcusable sin. In conclusion, although viewed as being under tremendous pressure from the outside, the community is also viewed as still firm in the exercise of their witness to Jesus in and to the world. Admonition is therefore urgent and pointed: such brutal opposition from the world is inevitable and ultimately testifies in a most ironic way to their privileged status and role as disciples of Jesus in the world.

At this point, the sense of embattlement and oppression becomes painfully clear. The source of controversy again shifts as the world replaces the community as the main problem. The disciples are portrayed as holding on, although questions regarding self-definition in the area of belief continue at a fundamental level.

The rhetorical situation reflected in, and addressed by, the fourth unit of discourse (16:4b–33) also reveals a twofold dimension not unlike that of the first unit (as one would expect, given the supplementary character of the fourth unit) but with definite variations as well.

On the one hand, the disciples are viewed in a positive light: their privileged status and role as disciples of Jesus in the world are described and affirmed at length. Once again, not only their failure to understand the message of farewell but also their anticipated abandonment of Jesus at the crucial time of his "hour" are taken directly into account and explained as inevitable and temporary, to be definitively resolved only with the coming of the announced successor, the Spirit-Paraclete. On the other hand, the disciples are also viewed as being in great need of encouragement and reassurance. The reasons for such a perceived need include the very fact of the departure (a sharp sense of sorrow and separation) and the consequences of such a departure (a further, sharp sense of alienation and oppression from an unbelieving and hostile world—a world that rejoices greatly over Jesus' own death, a world whose fundamental values are completely contrary to the values the disciples themselves represent, a world that is a constant source of tribulation for them, and a world that is regarded as being under the complete control of the demonic powers).

As a result, the disciples receive extensive consolation and further teaching to help them recall who they are and what they represent as disciples of Jesus. They are shown how the departure is to their immediate benefit and are given a proper interpretation of it. This strengthens the privileged status and role of the disciples as disciples of Jesus: despite the tribulations that discipleship implies in the world, it is presented thereby as the only way (in this world of demonic powers) of joy; peace; access to, and union with, God; and assured victory. In conclusion, although the community is viewed as essentially firm and united, it is also viewed as being in need of great solace and further teaching. The presence of opposition from the outside is clear, though again its specific ramifications, measures, and channels remain undisclosed. Moreover, insofar as discipleship itself is grounded in belief in Jesus and love for Jesus, the possibility of a radical separation from the community is still present. However, this unit does not highlight such a grounding as much as the first unit did, so such a possibility recedes further into the background. Thus, a sense of embattlement and oppression is undeniable, but it is joined by a sense of holding on, amidst questions regarding self-definition in the area of belief.

In terms of the rhetorical situation reflected in, and addressed by, these chapters, the farewell speech preceding the climactic prayer of John 17 points to a distinct, unified, and coherent view of the addressed community (the implied readers) on the part of the implied author. Again, following the chiastic structure and development of these chapters, the proposed rhetorical situation can be described as follows. The outer units of the speech (13:31–14:31; 16:4b–33) depict a community that is essentially firm and united but also in need of encouragement and reassurance through extensive teaching and consolation. The inner units (15:1–17; 15:18–16:4a) portray a community that is regarded as being in danger of rupture and dissolution and hence as being in need of urgent exhortation and admonition. The overall development of this fourfold rhetorical situation is described in the following paragraphs.

The farewell speech begins with a positive view of the disciples in the first unit (13:31–14:31). However, in the light of obvious pressure from the outside (an unbelieving and hostile world under the dominion of Satan) and of ongoing questioning from the inside with regard to the fact and mode of the departure and its consequences for the community left behind, the first unit also presents a view of the disciples as being in need of teaching and consolation. This teaching and consolation, in turn, provide the basis for the given exhortations: be not afraid or troubled, believe, and love one another as I have loved you.

This positive view of the disciples continues through the middle of the speech. However, in the central components (15:1–17 and 15:18–16:4a) the positive view is balanced by a straightforward account of the grave dangers awaiting the disciples in the world, both from within and without. As a result, a more guarded or uncertain view of the disciples emerges at the center of the speech. Their fate will depend on how they carry out their proper role as disciples of Jesus in the world.

The second unit (15:1–17) focuses, to begin with, on the dangers from within. The disciples, though still viewed in a positive light indeed as disciples of Jesus, are now also viewed as in serious danger of losing their discipleship. A failure to abide in Jesus and his word, along with a failure to abide in the love of Jesus and in love for one another, now appear as real possibilities. Consequently, the disciples are exhorted to abide in Jesus (in his word and in his love) if they wish to remain his disciples. Otherwise, they are warned, separation is immediate and radical.

The third unit (15:18–16:4a) then focuses on the dangers from without. Although the disciples continue to be viewed in a positive light as disciples of Jesus, they are now also viewed as undergoing severe and unrelenting pressure from the outside and thus as being in danger of caving in to an unbelieving and hostile world that hates God and is guilty of inexcusable sin. Consequently, the disciples are warned of the various channels in which such an opposition is to take place, as well as of the inevitability of such opposition. The disciples are also exhorted to keep such warnings in mind in the course of their continued witness in and to the world in order to avoid an immediate and radical separation from the community.

The relationship of these two units to one another, with their respective dangers awaiting the disciples, is complex. In part, the second unit should be read in the light of the third unit: it is because of such severe and unrelenting pressure from the outside, from an unbelieving and hostile world, that a failure to abide in Jesus has become a distinct possibility in the community. In the face of such opposition, it is not difficult to see why an unspecified number of disciples have either ceased to abide or are on the verge of ceasing to abide in Jesus (in his word and in a love that demands death itself if necessary). At the same time, given the salient lack of any direct reference to pressure from the outside within the second unit itself, it should not be read exclusively in the light of the third unit. In other words, the failure of an unspecified number of disciples to abide in Jesus should be seen as pointing to opposition and conflict from the inside as well (from within the community itself), a conflict that involves not only profound disagreements with regard to the figure of Jesus but also with regard to community praxis. However, the specific nature of the disagreements, which give rise to a distinction between the fruitful and the unfruitful, remains undeveloped.

The serious possibility of rupture and dissolution raised and addressed in the central section of the speech, therefore, has both external and internal causes. The external causes are delineated in the third unit, but the internal causes are not explicitly addressed anywhere within the farewell speech. In fact, only John 21 and the Johannine Letters point in the same general direction.

The farewell speech ends, in 16:4b–33, with a return to the positive view of the disciples presented in the first unit. As in the first unit, moreover, this positive view is accompanied by a further view of the disciples as being in need of encouragement and reassurance. In the light of obvious pressure from the outside (from an unbelieving and hostile world under the dominion of Satan) and ongoing questioning from the inside regarding the fact of the departure itself and its consequences for the community, the final unit also presents the disciples as being in need of consolation and teaching, which again provide the grounding for a concluding exhortation: rejoice and be at peace.

In conclusion, an analysis of the rhetorical situation reflected in, and addressed by, the farewell speech shows a careful and effective arrangement and development: from a positive view of the disciples as disciples of Jesus, with extensive encouragement and reassurance by way of teaching and consolation; to a view of the disciples as being in grave danger of rupture and disintegration and therefore in need of urgent exhortation and admonition, though with an underlying positive view of the disciples as disciples of Jesus; to a positive view of the disciples as disciples of Jesus, with extensive encouragement and reassurance by way of consolation and teaching.

At this point, a fundamental decision has to be faced: one may choose to emphasize either the framing components or the central components of the chiastic-like structure. If the first alternative is chosen, the disciples emerge as a basically united and firm community in need of further teaching and consolation. If the second alternative is followed instead, the disciples emerge as a community under extreme pressure, both from within and without, and in clear danger of rupture and disintegration. In either case, the role of the other components must be given a satisfactory explanation within the chosen alternative.

Given the focal position of the central components in the structure and the sustained polemical aim of the speech as a whole, from the first to the final unit, I favor the second position: the disciples as a community that is deeply embattled and oppressed, in serious danger of rupture and dissolution and thus facing the radical loss of their privileged call and identity as disciples of Jesus in the world, and hence in need of urgent exhortation and admonition. The farewell prayer for unity of chapter 17 follows effectively upon such a farewell speech: the disciples must be one as Jesus and the Father are one. Within such a proposal, the framing components provide the necessary foundation and support for the central exhortations and admonitions: recall who you are and what you represent, and recall what benefits and privileges are yours if you endure and abide; do not stumble, therefore, but abide and endure. Once again, therefore, the speech can be said to lay a firm foundation at the beginning, to call for adherence to such a foundation in the middle, and then to reaffirm this foundation at the end.

The extended commentary on the beginning announcement of the glorification in 13:31–32, therefore, further reveals a highly unified and coherent view of the implied readers—of the socioreligious exigencies seen as facing the implied readers—by the implied author. First, the fact, the mode, and certain consequences of the departure have given rise to fundamental questions of self-identity involving belief and praxis in the community. Such questions have become especially acute because of a definite feeling of embattlement and oppression. On the one hand, the outside world (primarily the Jews) reacts with unbelief and hostility to their witness to Jesus. The disciples experience hatred, persecution, social dislocation, and even death as a result of their belief in Jesus and their praxis within the community—to the extent that such a world is seen as being under the full dominion of the evil one. On the other hand, the community itself is in turmoil. The disciples profoundly disagree about both belief in Jesus and praxis within the community—so much so that those responsible for such turmoil are seen as meeting with removal and ultimate destruction. Not only are the disciples an embattled and oppressed community in a demonic world, therefore, but also certain unabiding and unfruitful sectors from within the community itself have sharply intensified this sense of embattlement and oppression.

Second, such a reading leads to a message of teaching and consolation. Despite, and because of, their situation of oppression and embattlement in the world, the disciples are reminded throughout of who they are. A proper interpretation of the mode and causes of Jesus' departure is provided; the disciples' privileged relationship to Jesus and God the Father is explained; a correct interpretation of the corresponding position of the world with regard to Jesus and God the Father is set forth; and a proper assessment of the corresponding position of the unfruitful and unabiding disciples with regard to Jesus and the Father is further outlined. The disciples are also reminded throughout of what they possess and enjoy as disciples of Jesus: a wide number of benefits that establishes beyond doubt their privileged status and role in the world as disciples of Jesus, including above all the possession of another Paraclete from the Father, the holy Spirit of truth. Teaching and consolation, therefore, become direct instruments of affirmation and confirmation.

Third, such a reading also extends a message of exhortation and admonition. Despite their oppression and embattlement in the world, the disciples are urged to carry out their proper and expected role as disciples of Jesus regardless of consequences. They must bear much and constant fruit; they must believe and abide in the word of Jesus; they must love one another as he loved them, giving up their lives for one another if need be; they must not stumble in the face of such pressure from the outside or follow the example of those insiders who bear fruit no more; they must have neither fear nor consternation, but rejoice and be at peace. Otherwise, they are directly warned, separation is immediate and radical.

In conclusion, despite all appearances to the contrary, the disciples are asked to consider themselves as the "little children" and the "chosen friends" of Jesus and the Father. Not only do they constitute the only "abiding place" of Jesus and the Father while in the world, but also it is "the house" of the Father that ultimately awaits them, along with an eternal reunion with Jesus in the world above, in the world of glory. As in the case of Jesus, therefore, the disciples' given fate in the world—from rejection and hatred to betrayal and death—is ultimately and ironically one of glory and glorification.

John 13:31–16:33 as a Farewell Speech

A comparative analysis of 13:31–16:33 in relation to the farewell genre in antiquity sheds further light not only on the character of this speech as a farewell but also on the unique nature of this Johannine farewell.

Constitutive Farewell Motifs

As discussed in chapter 1, a maximalist approach is preferred to a minimalist approach in the analysis of constitutive motifs. Such an approach, furthermore, should avoid too extensive or disjointed a listing of motifs and follow instead a more controlled arrangement of such motifs. Michel has advanced the best proposal in this regard.[10] It outlines thirteen groupings or categories, of which nine involve the farewell speech as such. Of these nine groupings, six appear prominently in John 13:31–16:33, and three do

10. Michel, *Abschiedsrede*, 17–38.

not. As chapter 1 indicated, a proper listing of farewell motifs should draw on the farewell tradition in both the Greco-Roman and Jewish literature because of the wide similarities between the two traditions. Michel's proposal can be modified accordingly by incorporating within his relevant categories the missing farewell motifs that Stauffer mentions.[11]

The groupings that do not appear in John 13:31–16:33 involve a prayer, instructions concerning burial, and promises and vows requested of the gathering in order to secure the observance of the preceding exhortations and commands. A farewell prayer is indeed present in the Johannine farewell, though not within 13:31–16:33. In fact, such a prayer has been significantly expanded—encompassing a whole chapter of the Gospel—and placed at the end of the speech, as a climax to it (John 17). In effect, therefore, only two of these groupings do not appear at all in the Johannine farewell. One of these, the instructions concerning burial, would be out of place, given the later portrayal of Jesus' burial in the narrative (19:38–42). The other, the demand for promises and vows on the part of the assembled gathering, would also be out of place, given the prominent, sustained portrayal of the disciples' failure to understand the message of farewell prior to the completion of "the hour" and the bestowal of the Spirit-Paraclete (20:19–23). On the one hand, it is outsiders—secret disciples who have not identified themselves openly with the group of assembled disciples—who actually bury the body of Jesus. On the other hand, both the portrayal of individual disciples in the first unit and of the disciples as a group in the final unit show their failure to come to terms with the notion of the forthcoming departure itself, let alone its fundamental meaning and consequences. All farewell motifs need not be present in each example of the genre, but the omission of these two motifs in the Johannine farewell can be readily explained.

The six groupings that do appear include the announcement of approaching death, parenetic sayings or exhortations, prophecies or predictions, retrospective accounts of the individual's life, determination of a successor, and final instructions. The motif of announcing the forthcoming death—a death that in itself is not revealed to Jesus, since he already has full knowledge of it and of its proximity (13:1–4)—is very important in the Johannine farewell speech; however, it is presented in largely metaphorical terms throughout (for example, glorification and departure). The first announcement, at the beginning of the speech, is by far the most important (13:31–32), since the remainder of the speech functions as an extended commentary on it. Implicit and indirect references to the forthcoming death are numerous in the speech. Explicit references are also common throughout, above all in the first unit, 13:31–14:31 (for

11. Stauffer, "Abschiedsreden," 29–32; *Theology*, 344–47.

example, 13:33a–b; 14:2–3a, 19a, 25, 30), and the final unit, 16:4b–33 (for example, 16:4b–5a, 7a–b, 16–20, 28).[12]

The motif of parenetic sayings or exhortations plays a most prominent role in the Johannine farewell. It involves the following three elements: moral exhortations and calls to obedience, words of encouragement and consolation, and promises for those who obey with woes for those who do not. Neither theological overviews of history nor the use of figures from the past are used as models or examples.

The moral exhortations and calls to obedience are found for the most part in the two central units, though the two outer units provide the foundation for such calls and exhortations (the privileged status and role of the disciples is grounded in their own belief in, and love for, Jesus). In the central units, therefore, the disciples are called upon to abide in such belief and love: to abide in the word and love of Jesus (15:1–17) and not to stumble in the way of discipleship in the face of external opposition (15:18–16:4b). In the outer units such calls and exhortations appear as well but receive a more general formulation. The disciples are urged to have neither fear nor consternation but to rejoice, to believe in Jesus and God, and to love one another as Jesus had loved them (13:31–14:31), as well as to rejoice and have peace (16:4b–33).

Words of encouragement and consolation are common throughout the speech. In fact, both immediate and extended promises are found in all four units, though most are contained in the two outer units (13:31–14:31; 16:4b–33). The two central units emphasize either the promise of hearing and granting the requests of the disciples (15:1–17)—an important promise in the farewell speech, affirmed in three of the four units[13]— or the promise of a successor to Jesus (15:18–16:4a). All these promises reinforce the privileged status and role of the disciples as disciples of Jesus in the world and, by being denied to the world, intensify the encouragement and consolation of the disciples.

The combination of promises and woes—addressed to those who obey and disobey, respectively—is found above all in the second unit, 15:1–17. Whereas those who fail to heed the calls to abide are threatened with

12. One of the farewell motifs proposed by Stauffer that Michel does not incorporate into his groupings is that of death as better for those left behind (see chap. 1, n. 21). Though such thinking actually underlies the whole of the Johannine farewell speech, the motif itself is to be found explicitly only in the final unit (16:4b–33, v. 7).

13. Another farewell motif proposed by Stauffer and not incorporated by Michel is that of intercession (see chap. 1, n. 21). This motif appears in the Johannine farewell both with regard to this promise regarding the future needs and requests of the disciples and the promise of a successor. In every case but one (15:7) where the promise of hearing and granting the requests of the disciples is extended, one finds an explicit reference to the intercessory role of Jesus in this regard (14:13–14; 15:16; 16:23–24, 26–27).

removal or separation from the community, death, and destruction, those who do respond are extended, as indicated in the previous paragraph, the common promise of a hearing and granting of their petitions, as well as the further promise of a continued abiding of Jesus in their midst. The third unit, 15:18–16:4a, also mentions the threat of separation or removal, although such a threat does not receive as sharp a formulation, with stumbling envisioned as a possibility on account of the opposition forthcoming from the world. At the same time, the promise of a successor is also extended to the disciples, to those who endure, in the midst of such opposition.

The motif of prophecies or predictions is also common in the Johannine farewell. These predictions are clearly noneschatological, even though they involve both immediate and extended events. (At the same time, eschatological connotations cannot be ruled out altogether in a couple of instances, for example, 14:3 and 15:6.) To be sure, many of the promises extended to the disciples in the farewell would qualify as prophecies or predictions. However, as shown in the preceding section, such promises are more properly listed under the category of parenetic sayings and exhortations. Most of these are of a pessimistic sort.

Predictions of an immediate sort appear in both the first and final units. The threefold denial of Jesus by Peter is prophesied at the beginning of the speech (13:31–14:31), and both the scattering of the disciples and their abandonment of Jesus at the time of his arrest and death are anticipated at the end of the speech (16:4b–33).[14] Extended predictions are found above all in the third unit (15:18–16:4b). On the one hand, limited success on the part of the disciples in the world is assured. On the other hand, the concrete measures to be employed by the world in its opposition to the disciples are disclosed at length to the disciples (hatred, persecution, social dislocation, and death itself). The fourth unit confirms such predictions or prophecies in a general way: in the world the disciples will find tribulation (16:4b–33).

In the Johannine farewell the motif of a retrospective account of the individual's life is as prominent as that of parenetic sayings and exhortations. Indeed, this category could contain all the teaching related to both Jesus and his disciples in the Johannine farewell.[15] In the case of Jesus, the

14. The explicit and public failures of the disciples provide a very effective encompassing arch in the speech as a whole: from the failure of an individual disciple, Peter, to the failure of the group as a whole. Such public and explicit failures, moreover, reflect in a very concrete way their more general failure to understand not only the very message of farewell but also its location within or relationship to the whole of Jesus' ministry and mission, teaching and revelation.

15. Another farewell motif mentioned by Stauffer and omitted by Michel is that of didactic speech (see chap. 1, nn. 6, 7, 30); indeed, this is Michel's most salient and important

retrospective account deals with an extended justification or vindication
of the individual in the light of his status and role. In the case of the
disciples, such an account outlines their privileged role and status as disciples of Jesus in the world.

Teaching regarding Jesus is found in all four units. The first unit explains the death of Jesus at length in terms of the overall relationship between Jesus and the Father, thus ultimately explaining the nature of Jesus'
own love for the disciples as well (13:31–14:31). The second unit further
develops the nature of this love in terms of Jesus' disclosure to the disciples
of all that the Father had revealed to him and above all of his own death on
their behalf (15:1–17). The third unit details the opposition of the world
to Jesus himself during his ministry in the world: hatred, persecution,
social dislocation, and death itself (15:18–16:4a). The fourth unit pursues
the death of Jesus, though to a much more limited extent, in terms of the
relationship between Jesus and the Father, a relationship that is now expanded to include the origins of Jesus with the Father (16:4b–33).

Teaching regarding the disciples—aside from the positive promises extended—is conveyed for the most part in the two central units. Whereas
the disciples are affirmed as the branches of the true vine of Jesus and
as the chosen friends of Jesus in the second unit (15:1–17), their fate in
and at the hands of the world as the chosen ones of Jesus is patterned
directly on that of Jesus himself in the third unit (15:18–16:4a). Moreover, the theme of the disciples as "chosen" in and out of the world greatly
intensifies the impact of such teaching.

The motif of succession appears in all but one of the four units of discourse: at the beginning (13:31–14:31), in the middle (15:18–16:4a), and
at the end (16:4b–33). To be sure, there is a sense in which all the disciples
function as Jesus' successors in the world, with further distinctions made
within the body of disciples itself in this regard (for example, John 21).
However, the farewell also presents a definite successor to Jesus, who in
turn allows the disciples, by virtue of this successor's own appointed mission and role among them, to function as Jesus' successors in the world.

This successor—whose actual determination takes place by means of an
actual naming or appointment, with a formal installation to follow later in
the narrative (20:19–23)—is the figure of the promised Spirit-Paraclete.
Its origins and role greatly resemble those of Jesus, and it is directly subordinated to Jesus, as Jesus himself was to the Father.[16] Like Jesus, the

---

omission. I place such didactic speech within this category because it concerns not only the
status and role of Jesus as disclosed through the narrative but also the status and role of those
who have accepted Jesus' claims and disclosures in the narrative.

16. Once again, the farewell motif of intercession is to be found in the Johannine farewell
in connection with the promise of the Spirit-Paraclete as Jesus' successor among the disciples

Spirit-Paraclete also comes from the world of God the Father into the created world. Also like Jesus, the Spirit-Paraclete plays a multidimensional role among the disciples themselves. This role is similar to Jesus' role and is effectively developed in the speech: from teaching the disciples all things and recalling for them all that Jesus said and revealed in the course of his mission (13:31–14:31), to guiding and informing their own continued witness to Jesus in and to the world (15:18–16:4a), to allowing them to convict the world and leading them into the whole truth (16:4b–33). Finally, the Spirit-Paraclete remains as tied to Jesus as Jesus was to the Father. The Spirit recalls all that Jesus said and revealed; witnesses to Jesus at all times; and reveals both what Jesus has left unsaid and the things to come, all of which it ultimately receives from Jesus himself.[17] In the end, moreover, it is the presence of Jesus' successor in and among the disciples themselves that allows the latter to serve as the one and true "dwelling" or "abode" of Jesus and God the Father in the world.

The motif of final instructions is not common in the Johannine farewell, but it is important and prominent nonetheless. Aside from the teaching, exhortations, warnings, and prophecies—all of which have been placed in other groupings—there is only one final instruction given to the disciples in this farewell speech: the "new" command to love one another as Jesus had loved them (13:34–35). At the end of the ministry, therefore, this "new" command, presented as the preeminent and distinguishing command of Jesus, is issued to the disciples as the basic principle of community praxis in the time after the departure. The command itself is briefly introduced at the beginning of the speech and presented as the one legacy left behind by the departing Jesus (13:31–14:31). The command is then further explained in the second unit of discourse as the mode of behavior proper to the chosen friends of Jesus, to the members of the chain of love (15:1–17).

In conclusion, the Johannine farewell makes ample use of most of the constitutive motifs of the farewell speech in antiquity. It draws upon farewell motifs from all three categories of frequency mentioned by Michel—the most common, the quite common, and the common. Only a few of these recurrent motifs are omitted altogether. In terms of content, therefore, the Johannine farewell emerges as an excellent and complete example of the genre in antiquity. At the same time, the Johannine farewell brings together all these farewell motifs in a unique way. Michel proposes as

---

(see n. 13 above). In every case where such a promise is extended, the intercessory role of Jesus is clear (14:16–17a, 26; 15:26–27; 16:7).

17. As in the case of the explicit and public failures of the disciples, therefore, the figure of the successor also provides an effective encompassing arch in its role as the Spirit of truth: from the recalling of the truth that was revealed, to an ongoing witness to such truth, to a disclosure of the truth that was left unrevealed because of the disciples' inability to comprehend it.

a basic overall sequence an announcement of coming death at the beginning; parenetic sayings, prophetic sayings, and accounts of the individual's life in the middle; and determination of a successor and final instructions at the end. In the Johannine farewell, however, most of the farewell motifs appear in all four units. Consequently, their arrangement within the speech itself is directly governed by the speech's own literary structure and development, overall strategy, and underlying rhetorical situation.

The distribution of these farewell motifs in the speech can be summarized as follows. At the beginning, within the first unit of discourse (13:31–14:31), the key announcement of the forthcoming death is made. Next come the following:

1. Further explicit references to the coming death.
2. A few moral exhortations and calls to obedience, but extensive words of encouragement and consolation.
3. A prophecy of failure.
4. An extensive retrospective account of Jesus.
5. Two brief promises of a coming successor.
6. A final instruction.

In the middle, within the two central units of discourse (15:1–17 and 15:18–16:4a), are the following:

1. Some implicit references to the coming death.
2. Extensive moral exhortations and calls to obedience, limited words of encouragement and consolation, and a sharp combination of promises and woes.
3. Extensive prophecies of dangers.
4. A limited retrospective account of both the disciples and Jesus.
5. A brief promise of a successor.
6. Further development of the final instruction.

At the end, in the final unit of discourse (16:4b–33), one finds the following:

1. Several explicit references to the coming death.
2. A few moral exhortations and calls to obedience, but extensive words of encouragement and consolation.
3. A prophecy of failure.
4. A more limited retrospective account of Jesus.
5. A long, twofold promise of a successor.

The most significant distribution of such motifs in the speech, either in terms of unique appearance or actual emphasis, can be summarized as follows. At the beginning and end of the speech are announcements of the coming death, words of encouragement and consolation, prophecies of failure, and retrospective accounts of Jesus. In the middle of the speech are moral exhortations and calls to obedience, a combination of promises and woes, prophecies of dangers, and a retrospective account of the disciples.

Functions of Farewell Motifs

Chapter 1 indicated that the question of the function of farewell motifs is as important as the question of the motifs themselves and that the two should be correlated as much as possible, as both Cortès and Kurz have done in their own ways.[18] The present study has analyzed the farewell speech from the point of view of five basic strategic aims: didactic, consolatory, admonitory, exhortative, and polemical (with a sixth supplementary function in the case of the final unit of discourse). This section will correlate the different farewell motifs of the speech with the function or functions they serve within it.

The motif of announcing the forthcoming death itself represents a warning: the presence of Jesus among the disciples is rapidly drawing to a close. At the same time, this motif is ultimately at the service of all other aims: consolatory, insofar as such a death opens up a wide number of heretofore unattainable possibilities for the disciples; didactic, insofar as such a death forms a key component of the mission entrusted to Jesus by the Father; exhortative, insofar as this death on behalf of the disciples provides a basic exemplar for them to follow; and polemical, insofar as such a death will be brought about by this world and its ruler.

The motif of parenetic sayings or exhortations is also at the service of various aims, depending on the subgroup in question: exhortative, on account of the moral exhortations and calls to obedience (the calls to abide, as well as the more general calls to courage, belief, love, joy, and peace); consolatory, on account of the words of encouragement and consolation (the many promises extended); and admonitory, on account of the promises and woes (the explicit threats of removal or separation). All of these subgroups also reveal, to one extent or another, a subordinate polemical aim.

The motif of prophecies or predictions is used with a distinct admonitory aim in mind, whether with regard to the explicit and public failures of the disciples or the opposition to come from the world. Again, a subordinate polemical aim is unmistakable as well.

The motif of a retrospective account of the individual's life, both with regard to Jesus himself and to the disciples as disciples of Jesus, has a didactic aim. At the same time, it is at the service of other aims as well:

18. Cortès, *Discursos* 62–70; Kurz, "Luke 22," 262–67.

consolatory (such teaching is meant to provide solace to the disciples) and polemical (such teaching sharply distinguishes the disciples from the world).

The motif of succession, the promise of the Spirit-Paraclete, reveals a distinct consolatory aim. A further polemical aim also is undeniable, given not only the Spirit's restricted presence to the group of disciples but also its assigned role among them with regard to the world at large.

The motif of final instructions, the giving of the "new" command of love for one another, is at the service of various aims. These are primarily didactic (this is new and final teaching), exhortative (the disciples are urged to adopt this command as their one preeminent principle of praxis within the community), and polemical (this principle of action will serve to distinguish the disciples from the world and its own praxis).

In conclusion, the farewell motifs employed by the Johannine farewell are all at the service of various strategic functions. One such function usually predominates while others are clearly in the background as well. In terms of function, therefore, the Johannine farewell emerges as a very complex and multidimensional example of the genre in antiquity.

The specific use of these motifs is again directly governed by the literary structure and development, the overall strategy, and the underlying rhetorical situation of the Johannine farewell as such. In terms of the overall distribution of these motifs in the speech outlined above, the following primary functions can be discerned throughout its major components. The beginning, the first unit of discourse (13:31–14:31), uses teaching and consolation, with some exhortations and warnings. In the middle, in the second and third units of discourse (15:1–17; 15:18–16:4a), are found exhortation and warning, with some teaching and consolation. The end, the last unit of discourse (16:4b–33), employs consolation and teaching, with some exhortations and warnings. In addition, a polemical dimension is present throughout.

This comparative analysis of the Johannine farewell speech confirms what the literary-rhetorical analysis has already demonstrated: from the point of view of both content and function, the speech emerges as a highly unified and coherent whole. It is a complete and complex example of the farewell genre.

John 13:31–16:33 and the Farewell Context of 13:1–30

The two beginning narrative units, 13:1–20 and 13:21–30, set and describe the farewell context for the speech that follows, as chapter 1 discussed. Thus, these units contain several farewell motifs that can be immediately associated with two of the four groupings advanced by Michel with regard to the farewell context proper: (1) the summoning of the circle of confidants, which is carried out here by means of a gathering of the disciples in an unspecified location in Jerusalem, and (2) the use of farewell gestures in the course of such a gathering—namely, the specific setting of a last meal involving Jesus and his disciples, as well as the presence of conversation or dialogue between Jesus and the disciples in the course of this last meal. In fact, as has already been suggested, perhaps even a third such grouping is present, if the foot washing itself is regarded as a variation of the farewell blessing.

Chapter 1 also pointed out that the motif of conversation or dialogue introduces a number of other farewell motifs, which receive further expansion and development in the farewell speech proper. The preceding comparative analysis of John 13:31–16:33 shows how the farewell context of 13:1–30 directly prepares the way for the farewell speech that follows and how the farewell speech itself is closely linked to its immediate farewell context. Indeed, the farewell speech continues and incorporates within itself the motif of conversation or dialogue between Jesus and the disciples, which plays a limited, though important, role both at the beginning and the end (13:31–14:31; 16:4b–33).

The first motif involves parenetic sayings or exhortations. Within the farewell context are moral exhortations and calls to obedience (the call to the disciples to wash one another's feet), as well as the juxtaposition of promises and woes (the disciples as having no part of Jesus if they refuse to receive the foot washing; the disciples as blessed if they comply with the washing and so act with regard to one another). Aside from this latter promise, however, no further words of encouragement and consolation appear in the farewell context. In the farewell speech, then, moral exhortations and calls to obedience, as well as the juxtaposition of promises and woes, are not only continued but multiplied and widened, ultimately playing a central role within the speech itself, especially within its middle section (15:1–17; 15:18–16:4a). At the same time, words of encouragement and consolation are common throughout, above all in the framing units (13:31–14:31; 16:4b–33).

The second motif concerns the use of prophecies and predictions. In the farewell context these involve only the forthcoming betrayal of Jesus by Judas Iscariot. In all, there are two allusions and two explicit disclosures concerning such a betrayal and its perpetrator in the two scenes of the farewell context. In the farewell speech, the scope of such prophecies is considerably widened to encompass not only further explicit and public failures of the disciples during "the hour" but also the concrete channels of opposition the disciples will encounter in their continued witness to Jesus in and to the world.

The third motif involves the retrospective account of the individual's life and hence, as argued above, final and definitive teaching. In the farewell context such teaching applies in a highly interrelated way not only to Jesus himself but also to the disciples. Such teaching focuses on foot washing and on the relationship of this act to the status and role of both Jesus and the disciples: with regard to Jesus, the foot washing as proper praxis for the "master" and as a model or example to be imitated by his disciples or "slaves"; with regard to the disciples, both the reception of the foot washing by Jesus and the foot washing itself as proper praxis with regard to one another as essential to their full purification and union with Jesus.

Once again, the farewell speech widens and expands such teaching. Teaching concerning Jesus himself and his relationship to the Father abounds in all four units, whereas teaching concerning the disciples (aside from the promises themselves) is found above all in the central units (15:1–17; 15:18–16:4a). Most important is the theme of love, a theme that provides the overall orientation for the farewell context as a whole and hence for the foot washing itself (13:1): the foot washing as an example and symbol of Jesus' continued love for the disciples to the end.

In the farewell speech the love of Jesus for the disciples during the ministry is explained in terms of his disclosure to them of all that the Father had revealed to him and of his own death for them in keeping with the highest of human ideals. In addition, such love on Jesus' part is then used as both grounding and exemplar in the "new" command of the disciples' love for one another, the preeminent and distinguishing command that is to serve as their fundamental principle of praxis as disciples of Jesus in the world. In the light of the preceding farewell context and the symbolic character of the foot washing, therefore, such love takes on a distinctive dimension, which is not actually pursued within the speech itself. Insofar as the foot washing represents a way of praxis unbecoming to a "lord or master," not only does such a symbolic washing bestow on Jesus' love for the disciples a unique and quintessential tone of total service and self-giving—best exemplified by his death on the cross—but it also bestows on the disciples' own love for one another a similar tone of supreme service and self-giving, possibly involving the loss of life itself for the sake of one another. The speech as such could be said to focus on the climax of such praxis and such love, on the possibility of death itself, on the final and logical outcome of such self-giving and service.

The fourth motif—pursued not only within the conversation itself but also by the narration—concerns the determination of a successor. In the farewell context the question of the succession reveals a twofold dimension: a disclosure that not all the disciples are proper and faithful disciples

of Jesus and the introduction of rank among the faithful disciples themselves. The farewell speech further develops both these dimensions. On
the one hand, although it is clear that the disciples will function as the
successors of Jesus in and to the world (13:31–14:31; 16:4b–33), the calls
to abide and not to stumble show that such a privileged position is neither
final nor irrevocable but can be totally and radically compromised or
betrayed, as in the case of Judas (15:1–17; 15:18–16:4a). On the other
hand, the distinction in rank introduced by the figure of "the disciple
whom Jesus loved" is not only bypassed but considerably tempered in two
specific ways: the introduction of the Spirit-Paraclete as Jesus' announced
successor to and among the disciples and the concluding prophecy regarding the abandonment of Jesus by the disciples—without exception, in one
way or another—at the crucial time of "the hour." Thus, separation and
betrayal continue as distinct possibilities for the disciples in the time after
the departure, and the question of rank is considerably tempered insofar
as the Spirit-Paraclete is assigned the same role with regard to the group as
a whole and insofar as the group as a whole does fail in one way or another.

A last motif is that of final instructions. In the farewell context this
motif again involves the foot washing and, more specifically, the need for
the disciples to wash one another's feet as Jesus himself washed theirs,
with all the symbolism that such a washing implies. The farewell speech
continues such final instructions while limiting them to the one "new"
command of love for one another. This command, as was argued above
with regard to the motif of teaching, is closely related to this final instruction of the farewell context.

In conclusion, the farewell speech is closely and directly connected to its
preceding farewell context. In fact, all the farewell categories found in the
speech are introduced in that context, except the announcement of the
forthcoming death, which is not explicitly announced but certainly implied
throughout, and even disclosed by the narrator to the reader (13:1–4). In
addition, the speech proper develops and expands all such farewell motifs
so the farewell context indeed paves the way directly and concretely for the
farewell speech that follows. It thereby contributes to the self-contained
and coherent character of this narrative scene as a whole.

THE FAREWELL DISCOURSE AS A
COMPOSITE SPEECH:
A DIACHRONIC PROPOSAL

The centripetal forces of the previous section must now become centrifugal once again, not only from the point of view of the various units of
discourse with the farewell speech, as in the first stage of this work, but

also from the point of view of a possible process of accretion and expansion with regard to these units of discourse. Despite the fact that the farewell speech can indeed be seen as an artistic and strategic whole, as well as a complete, complex example of the farewell genre, it is necessary to return to the questions of disproportionate length and compositional difficulties set forth in chapter 1. The present farewell can also be explained as being the result of a three-stage process of accretion and expansion. This final section will advance an overall redactional proposal in the light of the preceding literary-rhetorical analysis. This proposal, like the rest of the study, deals with the various self-contained and coherent units as wholes and forgoes the possibility of a literary prehistory for each individual unit—with one salient example.

The question of authorship is without resolution, and ultimately not that important, although I no longer see the need to argue for a plurality of authors. All the units of discourse, could well have come from one individual who responded to a variety of different rhetorical situations with different strategies. The farewell itself provides an important ideological and theological justification for such a series of responses, especially with regard to the figure of the successor, the Spirit-Paraclete. The different stages can be seen as a further leading of the disciples into the whole truth on the part of someone who claimed responsibility in this regard, again in keeping with the distinction of rank introduced within the farewell scene itself.

As the literary-rhetorical analysis has shown, such responses have not been simply added to the farewell scene without regard for the integrity and development of the context as a whole. In fact, as shown by the overall thematic and strategic flows, as well as the links and bonds between and among units, these responses have been well integrated with one another as constitutive parts of an ongoing, developing whole. One finds, therefore, not simply a collection of successive individual units but a literary and artistic whole, though again not without compositional difficulties of its own. It is because of these difficulties that the following proposal is offered.

First Stage of Composition:
John 13:31–14:31

The first unit of discourse, John 13:31–14:31, also represents the first stage in the proposed process of accretion and expansion. This unit of discourse is brought to a definite, proper, and effective close with the two-fold command of 14:31d, "Arise! Let us depart from here!" This command follows the concluding exhortation for belief at the time of the departure itself, the reference to the departure as a forthcoming encounter with the ruler of the world, and the explanation of such an encounter in terms of the relationship between Jesus and the Father. It not only concludes the message of farewell but leads immediately into the final narrative of death that encompasses the whole of John 18–21 and begins with the scene of Jesus' arrest in 18:1–12 (the betrayal of Judas; the definitive separation of Jesus from the group of disciples and his seizure by the ruling authorities of Jerusalem, both Jewish and Gentile; and the beginning of the actual encounter with the ruler of the world, in and through his own children). The issue of disproportionate length would not even arise at this stage; such a farewell speech would have been well in keeping with other similar speeches of Jesus in the Gospel.

This farewell speech is marked by extensive teaching concerning the fundamental meaning of the departure in terms of the relationship between Jesus and the Father and by extensive consolation in terms of the many positive consequences of such a departure for the disciples. Such teaching and consolation further reflect and address a twofold view of the community: the disciples as essentially firm and united but also in need of much exhortation and encouragement. Although no sign of rupture within the community is evident at this point, aside from the forthcoming betrayal of Judas Iscariot, the disciples are seen as deeply embattled and oppressed in the midst of an unbelieving and hostile world, a world under the dominion of Satan himself and identified above all with the Jews. Such teaching and consolation therefore affirm and reinforce the privileged status and role of the disciples as disciples of Jesus—"the little children"—set apart in and from the world, given their belief in, and love for, Jesus (that is, their acceptance of his teaching and revelation concerning his own status and role with regard to the Father and their obedience to his commands, above all the command of love for one another). As such, the disciples are urged to have neither fear nor consternation but to rejoice, to believe in Jesus and God, and to love one another as Jesus himself loved them.

This final instruction of Jesus—the "new" command of love for one another—is important, given its explicit and salient presentation at this point as the distinguishing command of Jesus to his disciples in the world. It has been argued at times that such a command is altogether out of place in its present position within 13:31–38; that it was added, along with 15:1–17, at a later time; and that such an addition changes the essential thrust of the original speech. Among the arguments advanced in this regard, the following are the most substantial: (1) the break in sequence of thought between Jesus' declaration of 13:33 and Peter's response of 13:36 (that is, the complete omission of the theme of departure in 13:34–35), (2) the lack of any other mention of the love of the disciples for one another either prior to this unit or in the remainder of the unit itself, and (3) the introduction of praxis in a context having to do only with faith.[19] Although I formerly held this position, I would now argue that as a final farewell instruction, this "new" command should be seen as an integral component (from both a literary and a theological point of view) of this first unit of discourse and not as a later addition to an essentially alien context.

First, as argued in chapter 2, all of 13:33c–36 can be seen as a distinctive inclusion whose purpose it is to outline, by way of introduction, the negative consequences of the forthcoming departure announced in 13:33a–b. These consequences include a seemingly definitive separation of Jesus and the disciples, with the latter unable to follow Jesus (13:33c–e); a seemingly unique legacy of farewell for the coming time of radical separation (13:34–35); and a concluding prophecy of forthcoming and repeated denial on the part of Simon Peter, the common spokesperson for the group (13:36–38). In fact, only the subtle, though radical, revision of the separation envisioned in 13:36 provides a distinct glimmer of hope at this point. In other words, from a structural point of view, the "new" command can be seen as fitting very well into its context. In fact, the giving of the "new" command at this point sharpens and reinforces the radical nature of the forthcoming separation previously announced, as if no other legacy of farewell were contemplated.

Second, the observed break in the sequence of thought forms part of an ironic type of development found within the introduction itself. Peter bypasses the "new" command of love of 13:34–35 in his first question of 13:36a–b; Jesus bypasses Peter's question about the destination of the departure in his response of 13:36c–e; and Peter bypasses Jesus' radical revision of the envisioned separation in his second question of 13:37. The entire dialogue is marked by statements and responses that fail to address one another. Once again, therefore, the giving of the "new" command at this point, totally bypassed as it is by Peter, can be seen as fitting well into its present context.

Third, the inclusion of final instructions is not uncommon in farewell speeches of antiquity. Therefore, it can be argued that this command is given at this point and characterized as "new" not only because it was not disclosed to the disciples during the course of the ministry itself but also because it has been reserved as the final, definitive instruction of farewell on the part of Jesus to the disciples, as the command that is meant to serve

---

19. See, e.g., Heitmüller, "Johannes," 823; E. Hirsch, *Studien zum vierten Evangelium*, Beiträge zur historischen Theologie 11 (Tübingen: Mohr-Siebeck, 1936) 103; Becker, 220; Schnackenburg, 3:59–61. This is a position that I adopted in an earlier study of this first unit ("The Structure, *Tendenz*, and *Sitz im Leben* of John 13:31–14:31," *JBL* [1985] 471–93); see also F. Segovia, *Love Relationships in the Johannine Tradition: Agapē/Agapan in I John and the Fourth Gospel*, SBLDS 58 (Atlanta: Scholars Press, 1982) 121–25.

as the fundamental principle of praxis within the community (which praxis in turn will serve as the distinguishing feature of the disciples within and before the world as disciples of Jesus).

Finally, although the love of the disciples for one another is not mentioned as such in the remainder of the unit, such love is evident in the development of the main body of the unit (14:4–27). In 14:15–27 love for Jesus on the part of the disciples, the basic condition for the farewell promises to follow, is specifically defined in terms of carrying out or obeying the commands or word(s) of Jesus. Thus, love for Jesus encompasses not only belief in him, as set forth in 14:4–14, but also the "new" command of love for one another, as well as all other practical directives of Jesus.

In conclusion, the "new" command of 13:34–35 is an integral component of this first unit of discourse. The unit itself advances a view of discipleship that entails not only belief in Jesus but also a distinct way of praxis—a love for one another that ultimately signifies love for Jesus as well. In this first unit, therefore, the profound alienation of the disciples as disciples of Jesus in and from the world (an alienation deeply rooted within the unit itself in Jesus' own final encounter with the prince of the world) is directly counterbalanced by a specific and distinctive way of praxis: as disciples of Jesus, the disciples are to love one another as Jesus loved them (that is, with a love that is marked by total service and self-giving, to the point of death, if necessary). As a final farewell instruction, this "new" command of love proves to be a powerful instrument of persuasion. In the "abiding place" of Jesus and the Father in the world, in the community itself, love grounded in belief must be the norm. This is, in fact, what distinguishes the community so sharply from the surrounding world of Satan and what can only sustain them in "the way" of Jesus.

Second Stage of Composition:
John 15:18–16:4a and John 16:4b–33

The second stage in the process of accretion and expansion involves two units of discourse, the third unit (15:18–16:4a) and the fourth unit (16:4b–33), which I see as having been added in unison and in tandem. The second stage, therefore, extensively develops and expands the original farewell speech. This expansion, furthermore, is carried out in terms of an overall pattern of inclusion, in which 13:31–14:31 and 16:4b–33 form the outer components, and 15:18–16:4a functions as the central component. Consequently, what was originally a farewell speech of proportionate length in the Gospel now becomes a speech of singularly disproportionate length.

Moreover, the twofold command of 14:31d, which served originally as a distinctive concluding marker, is now bypassed altogether and replaced by another concluding marker at the end of the expansion, at the conclusion of chapter 16. In effect, the addition of the second stage ends the farewell speech with the definite, proper, and effective triumphal cry of 16:33, "I have conquered the world!" Following upon the prediction of the forthcoming abandonment of Jesus by the disciples and the exhortation to the disciples to have peace and rejoice despite the inevitable tribulation to come in and from the world, this triumphal cry again not only ends the now extended message of farewell but also leads directly into the narrative of death. Despite all appearances to the contrary, all that is to follow, beginning with the scene of the arrest itself, represents a definitive victory of Jesus over the world, its rulers, and the ruler of these rulers—the devil.

Such an expansion also gives rise to other difficulties: repetition of material from the first unit in the expansion, especially in 16:4b–33; a reproach of the disciples in 16:4b–33 for failing to pursue a question that Simon Peter raised at the beginning of the first unit; and a prediction within 16:4b–33 concerning a forthcoming abandonment of Jesus by the disciples that is not entirely in accord with the sequence of events as portrayed in the scene of the arrest itself. However, the reason for the expansion can provide a satisfactory answer for the presence of all such compositional difficulties.

The first and focal part of the expansion, the central component of 15:18–16:4, reveals the basic reason for the expansion. This unit is characterized by a series of warnings concerning the forthcoming opposition to the disciples from the world and the concrete measures such an opposition will take: hatred, persecution, social dislocation involving expulsions from synagogues, and death itself—all in the name of God. The unit is further characterized by a strong concluding exhortation to the disciples to recall all of these warnings in the midst of the opposition itself and thereby avoid stumbling.

Such warnings and exhortations reflect and address a different twofold view of the community. The disciples are still essentially firm and united, and such stumbling is not an everyday reality. At the same time, however, the disciples are now under severe, unrelenting opposition from the world, and stumbling is a real possibility, given the circumstances; hence they are in need of sharp, direct admonition and exhortation. Thus, while the community still shows no definite signs of rupture, the sense of embattlement in the world is now portrayed in the strongest possible terms; the unbelieving world, again characterized above all in terms of the Jewish synagogue, is displaying almost overwhelming hostility and oppression. Consequently, the disciples are urged to recall and endure in their continued witness to Jesus in and to the world, since it is their inescapable lot as disciples of Jesus in the world to suffer the consequences of an unjust and sinful opposition. This is because of not only their privileged status and role as those chosen by Jesus out of the world and set apart in the world but also because of the earlier, similar opposition of the world to Jesus himself.

The second part of the expansion, the concluding component of 16:4b–33, deliberately returns to the first unit in the light of the expanded message of farewell conveyed in 15:18–16:4a. In so doing, the expansion supplements the positive thrust of the first unit and thus counteracts the negative thrust of the intervening unit. Despite such tribulation in the world, there is much cause for peace and rejoicing among the disciples of Jesus.

This unit is marked, therefore, by further, though more limited, teaching concerning the fundamental meaning of the departure in terms of Jesus' relationship to the Father and by more extensive consolation in terms of the positive consequences of such a departure for the disciples. This teaching and consolation reflect and address a twofold view of the community: the disciples as essentially firm and united but also in need of encouragement and consolation. No sign of substantial rupture is evident, aside from the envisioned temporary abandonment of the disciples themselves, but the disciples are again presented as deeply embattled and oppressed in the midst of an unbelieving and hostile world that is described again as being under the dominion of Satan himself. Such consolation and teaching further reinforce, especially in the light of the intervening disclosures, the privileged status and role of the disciples as the disciples of Jesus set apart in and from the world, given once again their belief in, and love for, Jesus. The disciples are urged to have no sorrow but to rejoice and be at peace, especially because of not only the triumph of Jesus over the world but also their own assigned role of convicting the world on the basis of its fundamental values.

After the harsh warnings of 15:18–16:4a, therefore, 16:4b–33 immediately provides extensive encouragement and reassurance, thereby significantly expanding the message of farewell of the first unit, especially by way of consolation. Consequently, although 16:4b–33 repeats material from the first unit of discourse (including the sustained use of its overarching and controlling themes), such repetition is not only understandable and appropriate but also forms part of a different line of development. Similarly, the beginning reproach of the disciples in 16:4b–33 for failing to pursue a question already pursued at the beginning of the first unit itself can be seen as deliberately pointing to, and beginning, this different line of development. Finally, the concluding anticipation of the forthcoming failure of the disciples in 16:4b–33 can be seen as keeping fully in view (in a concrete, direct way, given the thrust of the expansion itself) the possibility of stumbling in and because of the world. However, although such stumbling is fully incorporated into the developing portrayal of the disciples in the narrative and is presented as inevitable and temporary, it is also now envisioned as a distinct possibility for the community that entails the loss of discipleship itself.

Third Stage of Composition:
John 15:1–17

The second unit of discourse, 15:1–17, represents the third and final stage in the proposed process of accretion and expansion. With this third stage the farewell speech is further developed and expanded. Moreover, by placing this unit within the expanded farewell speech of the second stage, a chiastic structure is adopted. John 13:31–14:31 and 16:4b–33 continue to function as the framing components, but there now are two central components, 15:1–17 and 15:18–16:4a. Such a placement also allows the concluding marker of the second stage in 16:4b–33 to continue to function as the concluding marker for the farewell speech as a whole. With this third stage of expansion, therefore, the farewell speech becomes even more disproportionate in length within the Gospel narrative.

This final unit is characterized by exhortation and admonition. The disciples are urged to abide as disciples of Jesus by bearing much and constant fruit: to abide in Jesus, the true vine, by abiding in his word, in the whole of his teaching and revelation; to abide in the love of Jesus, in the chain of love, by carrying out his commands, above all the command to love one another as he had loved them. The disciples also are warned that a failure to abide and bear fruit as disciples of Jesus has immediate and severe consequences: not only a radical separation from the community and loss of discipleship but also ultimate death and destruction.

Such exhortations and admonitions reflect and address a very different view of the community. The disciples are still acknowledged as disciples of Jesus, as branches in the true vine of Jesus and as friends or beloved ones of Jesus; however, the disciples now are also perceived as being in grave danger of losing their discipleship. Such danger, moreover, reveals a twofold dimension. On the one hand, the disciples are still seen as deeply embattled and oppressed in the midst of an unbelieving and hostile world, a world primarily identified once again with the Jews; in part, therefore, the danger in question is still related to the severe, unrelenting opposition behind the second stage of the expansion. In other words, stumbling—in the sense of caving in to such an opposition—has clearly become by now an everyday reality and not just a real but still distant possibility. On the other hand, the disciples now are also seen as being embroiled in internal conflicts over questions of belief and praxis (though neither the source— aside from the inevitable impact of the external struggle—nor the character of such controversies is disclosed). In fact, the perceived danger from within far outweighs the continued danger from without in this unit. As a result, in this final unit signs of rupture within the community become evident; the "little children" are regarded as being in serious disarray. Such signs of rupture, however, by no means match the situation observed in the Johannine Letters. Nevertheless, with this final unit the road to the breakdown of the Letters has begun.

These exhortations and admonitions therefore remind the disciples of their privileged status as disciples of Jesus—as branches in the true vine of Jesus and as the chosen friends of Jesus—set apart in and from the world. The exhortations and admonitions also remind them of their privileged role as disciples of Jesus in the world—to bear much and constant fruit. Only by abiding in the word of Jesus that cleansed them and carrying out the commands of Jesus can the disciples insure their privileged status and role as disciples of Jesus.

The placement of this final expansion is by no means haphazard. As a part of the expanded central section, the unit amplifies the focal admonitions and exhortations of 15:18–16:4a. In so doing, the unit also provides the other problematic side of discipleship in the world; whereas 15:18–16:4a focuses on the external dangers, 15:1–17 concentrates on the internal dangers. Despite the many great promises extended in the outlying components, therefore, the central units specify that the way of discipleship is by no means to be conceived as final and definitive or as devoid of fundamental difficulties; in fact, the possibility of stumbling will always exist. Furthermore, in following immediately upon 13:31–14:31, this unit explicitly addresses what is presupposed in the first unit: belief in Jesus and love for Jesus, especially with regard to the final instruction regarding the "new" command, are not to be looked upon as things already achieved but rather as a foundation that needs to be constantly reaffirmed and reinforced in the course of discipleship. Further, because this unit immediately precedes 15:18–16:4a, it explicitly calls for such a reaffirmation and reinforcement of the foundations in the midst of severe and unrelenting opposition from the outside on account of that same foundation. Finally, the now much-extended description of the dangers awaiting discipleship in the middle section of the speech is still directly counteracted by the final component of 16:4b–33: despite such inevitable tribulation in the world, the disciples are ultimately reminded that Jesus has already conquered the world.

The farewell speech can be seen, from a diachronic point of view, as a repository for ongoing and developing messages to the community. As a farewell the speech readily lends itself to such an expansion and role. Such addresses become part of the farewell message for the community for the time after the departure and the time of separation; as the perceived situation of the community changes, so do the messages. Again, such a repository by no means emerges as diffuse or unplanned; it shows clear signs of careful and deliberate integration throughout. Indeed, 13:31–16:33 does constitute, from both a diachronic and a synchronic point of view, a call to an embattled Christian community to abide and endure in an oppressive world. This is a world whose preeminent representatives become the leaders of the Jews, but also in the end it is a world that encompasses all those who reject and oppose the Word of God, including those members of the community who do not bear fruit as they should and thus betray their call and status as disciples of Jesus.

A FINAL WORD

The conclusion of chapter 1 remarked that the reading of the Johannine farewell speech offered in this study was but one reading and by no means the only and proper way to interpret this text. I lay no claims to an objective and scientific reading or interpretation of the speech; in fact, I would argue strongly against any such claims on behalf of any reading. All readings are intrinsically, inescapably, and thankfully perspectival. What I have proposed here, therefore, is but one way of seeing the material in question as a unified and coherent artistic and strategic whole.

Such a reading is unfinished. I have deliberately left out of consideration the climax of the farewell speech, the farewell prayer of the departing Word of God. As indicated in chapter 1, a future project will analyze John 17 not only as a unified and coherent literary and strategic whole in and of itself but also as an integral part of the much larger literary and strategic whole comprised by John 13:31–17:26. Suffice it to say at this point that the climactic prayer of John 17 sharpens the call to abide and endure in a world of oppression, with the unity of the community perceived to be in grave danger.

Such a reading also remains unfinished in another way. I have deliberately left out of consideration my own perspective as a reader. This perspective could be described in a number of different ways. It is sufficient to say in this context that this reader was born and raised in the Third World (in Latin America to be exact) and now lives in the First World (in North America). The reader thus stands within a distinct and peculiar setting, that of the Hispanic-American, and as such belongs to a group that is bicultural and faced at all times and at a fundamental level with socioeconomic deprivation, sociopolitical and socioreligious exclusion, and sociocultural disdain and assimilation. For this reader, therefore, the call to abide and endure in a world of oppression represents much more than an ancient option; it continues to be a living dilemma with profound cultural and religious dimensions. For this reader, the similar call of the Fourth Gospel—its reach, strategy, and applicability—is open to complete analysis and evaluation in terms of the context and praxis of his group, to a reading of and for liberation. However, such an analysis must remain outside the scope of the present volume. This study represents but a first and basic step toward such a reading. The next step must be what I call an exercise in intercultural dialogue from the perspective of liberation and with the aim of liberation, which is after all a fundamental goal of the Fourth Gospel itself (8:32).

BIBLIOGRAPHY

REFERENCE WORKS

Aland, K., M. Black, C. M. Martini, et al., eds. *The Greek New Testament*. 3d ed., rev. New York: United Bible Societies, 1975.

Bauer, W. *A Greek-English Lexicon of the New Testament and Other Early Christian Literature*. Edited by W. F. Arndt and F. W. Gingrich. 2d ed., rev. and enl. Edited by F. W. Gingrich and F. W. Danker. Chicago: University of Chicago Press, 1979.

Blass, F., and A. Debrunner. *A Greek Grammar of the New Testament and Other Early Christian Literature*. Edited by R. W. Funk. Chicago: University of Chicago Press, 1961.

Dana, H. and J. Mantey, *A Manual Grammar of the Greek New Testament*. New York: Macmillan, 1962.

Liddell, H. G., R. G. Scott, and H. S. Jones. *A Greek-English Lexicon*. 9th ed. Oxford: Clarendon, 1978.

Metzger, B. M. *A Textual Commentary on the Greek New Testament*. London: United Bible Societies, 1971.

Smyth, H. W. *Greek Grammar*. Revised by G. M. Messing. Cambridge, Mass.: Harvard University Press, 1956.

FAREWELL STUDIES

Berger, K. "Hellenistische Gattungen im Neuen Testament." In *ANRW* 25:2, edited by W. Haase, 1034–52. Berlin and New York: Walter de Gruyter, 1984.

Beutler, J. "Literarische Gattungen im Johannesevangelium: Ein Forschungsbericht 1919–1980." In *ANRW* 25:3, edited by W. Haase, 2508–68. Berlin and New York: Walter de Gruyter, 1984.

Cortès, Enric. *Los discursos de adiós de Gn 49 a Jn 13–17: Pistas para la historia de un género literario en la antigua literatura judía*. Colectánea San Paciano 23. Barcelona: Herder, 1976.

Kennedy, G. A. *New Testament Interpretation through Rhetorical Criticism*. Chapel Hill: University of North Carolina Press, 1984.

Kurz, William S. "Luke 22:14–38 and Greco-Roman and Biblical Farewell Addresses." *JBL* 104 (1985) 251–68.

Michel, H.-J. *Die Abschiedsrede des Paulus an die Kirche Apg. 20.17–38: Motivgeschichte und theologische Bedeutung*. SANT 35. Munich: Kösel, 1973.

Munck, Johannes. "Discours d'adieu dans le Nouveau Testament et dans la littérature biblique." In *Aux sources de la tradition chrétienne: Mélanges offerts à M. Maurice Goguel,* 155–70. Bibliothèque théologique. Neuchâtel and Paris: Delachaux & Niestlé, 1950.

Nordheim, E. von. *Die Lehre der Alten: 1. Das Testament als Literaturgattung im Judentum der Hellenistisch-Römischen Zeit.* ALGHJ 13. Leiden: E. J. Brill, 1980.

Randall, J. *The Theme of Unity in John 17:20–23.* Louvain: Louvain University Press, 1962.

———. "The Theme of Unity in John 17:20–23." *EThL* 41 (1965) 373–94.

Schmidt, W. *De ultimis morientium verbis.* Marburg: Chr. Schaaf, 1914.

Schnackenburg, Rudolf. "Abschiedsreden." *LThK* 1 (1957) 68–69.

Stauffer, E. "Abschiedsreden." *RAC* 1 (1950) 29–35.

———. *Die Theologie des Neuen Testaments.* 4th ed. Stuttgart: W. Kohlhammer, 1948. Translated by J. Marsh, under the title *New Testament Theology.* New York: Macmillan, 1955.

STUDIES ON THE JOHANNINE FAREWELL

Beutler, J. *Habt Keine Angst: Die erste johanneische Abschiedsrede (Joh 14).* Stuttgart: Verlag Katholisches Bibelwerk GmbH, 1984.

Bover, J. M. *Comentario al Sermón de la Cena.* 2d ed. BAC 68. Madrid: La Editorial Católica, 1955.

Carson, D. A. *The Farewell Discourse and Final Prayer of Jesus.* (Grand Rapids: Baker, 1980).

Corssen, P. "Die Abschiedsreden Jesu in dem vierten Evangelium." *ZNW* 8 (1907) 125–42.

Durand, A. "Le discours de la Cène (Saint Jean xiii, 31–xvii,26)." *RSR* 1 (1910) 97–131, 513–39; *RSR* 2 (1911) 321–49, 521–45.

Gächter, P. "Der formale Aufbau der Abschiedsreden Jesu." *ZNW* 58 (1934) 155–207.

Hauret, C. *Les adieux du Seigneur: S. Jean XIII–XVII.* Paris: J. Gabalda, 1951.

Huby, J. *Le discours de Jésus après la Cène.* 2d ed., rev. VS. Paris: Beauchesne et ses Fils, 1942.

Kaefer, J. Ph. "Les discours d'adieu en Jn 13:31–17:26. Rédaction et Théologie." *NovT* 26 (1984) 253–82.

Keppler, P. W. von. *Unseres Herrn Trost.* 3d. ed. Freiburg: Herder, 1914.

Könn, J. *Sein Letztes Wort: Bibellesungen über die Abschiedsreden des Herrn.* Einsiedeln-Köln: Benzinger, 1955.

Painter, J. "The Farewell Discourses and the History of Johannine Christianity." *NTS* 27 (1981) 525–43.

Reese, J. M. "Literary Structure of Jn. 13:31–14:31; 16:5–6, 16–33." *CBQ* 34 (1972) 321–31.

Schnackenburg, R. "Das Anliegen der Abschiedsrede in Joh 14." In *Wort Gottes in der Zeit: Festschrift Karl Hermann Schelkle zum 65. Geburtstag,* edited by H. Feld and J. Nolte, 95–110. Düsseldorf: Patmos, 1973.

Schneider, J. "Die Abschiedsreden Jesu: Ein Beitrag zur Frage der Komposition von Johannes 13,31–17,26." In *Gott und die Götter: Festschrift für E. Fascher,* 103–12. Berlin: Evangelische Verlaganstalt, 1958.

Segovia, F. F. "John 15:18–16:4a: A First Addition to the Original Farewell Discourse?" *CBQ* 45 (1983) 210–30.

——. "The Structure, *Tendenz*, and *Sitz im Leben* of John 13:31–14:31." *JBL* 104 (1985) 471–93.

——. "The Theology and Provenance of John 15:1–17." *JBL* 101 (1982) 115–28.

Simoens, Y. *La gloire d'aimer: Structures stylistiques et intérpretatives dans le Discours de la Cène (Jn 13–17).* AB 90. Rome: Biblical Institute Press, 1981.

Swete, H. B. *The Last Discourse and Prayer of Our Lord: A Study of St. John* xiv–xvii. London: Macmillan & Co., 1913.

van den Bussche, H. *Le discours d'adieu de Jésus: Commentaire des chapitres 13 à 17 de l'évangile selon Saint Jean.* Translated by C. Charlier and P. Goidts. *BVC.* Tournai: Éditions Castermann, 1959.

Woll, D. B. "The Departure of 'the Way': The First Farewell Discourse in the Gospel of John." *JBL* 99 (1980) 225–39.

——. *Johannine Christianity in Conflict: Authority, Rank, and Succession in the First Farewell Discourse.* SBLDS 60. Atlanta: Scholars Press, 1981.

Zimmermann, H. "Struktur und Aussageabsicht der johanneischen Abschiedsreden (Jo 13–17)." *BibLeb* 8 (1967) 279–90.

COMMENTARIES

Barrett, C. K. *The Gospel According to St. John.* 2d ed., rev. Philadelphia: Westminster, 1978.

Becker, J. *Das Evangelium nach Johannes.* 2 vols. Ökumenischer Taschenbuchkommentar zum Neuen Testament 4. Gütersloh: Gütersloher Verlaghaus Mohn; Würzburg: Echter, 1979–81.

Bernard, J. H. *A Critical and Exegetical Commentary on the Gospel According to St. John.* 2 vols. ICC. Edinburgh: T. & T. Clark, 1928.

Bouyer, L. *The Fourth Gospel.* Translated by P. Byrne. Westminster, Md.: Newman, 1964.

Bultmann, R. *The Gospel of John: A Commentary.* Translated by G. R. Beasley-Murray et al. Philadelphia: Westminster, 1971.

Corluy, J. *Comentarius in Evangelium S. Joannis in Usum Prealectionum.* 3d ed. Gandavi: C. Poelman, 1889.

Durand, A. *Évangile selon Saint Jean.* 2d ed., rev. Edited by J. Huby. VS 4. Paris: Gabriel Beauchesne, 1938.

Godet, F. *Commentaire sur l'Évangile de Saint Jean.* 3d ed., rev. and enl. Bibliothèque théologique. 3 vols. Neuchâtel: J. Attinger, 1885.

Haenchen, Ernst. *John: A Commentary on the Gospel of John.* 2 vols. Edited by U. Busse. Translated by R. W. Funk. Hermeneia. Philadelphia: Fortress, 1984.

Hoskyns, E. C. *The Fourth Gospel.* 2d ed., rev. and enl. Edited by F. N. Davey. London: Faber & Faber, 1956. (1st pub., 1940.)

Knabenbauer, J. *Comentarius in Quatuor S. Evangelia Domini Nostri Iesu Christu. Pars IV: Evangelium secundum Ioannem.* Paris: P. Lethielleux, 1898.

Lagrange, M.-J. *Évangile selon Saint Jean.* 3d ed., rev. Paris: J. Gabalda, 1927.

Lightfoot, R. H. *St. John's Gospel: A Commentary.* Edited by C. F. Evans. Oxford: Oxford University Press, 1960. (1st pub., 1956.)

Lindars, Barnabas. *The Gospel of John.* NCBC. Grand Rapids: Eerdmans, 1972.

Loisy, A. *Le quatrième évangile.* Paris: A. Picard et fils, 1903.

————. *Le quatrième évangile: Les épîtres dites de Jean.* 2d ed., rev. Paris: Émile Nourry, 1921.

Macgregor, G. H. C. *The Gospel of John.* MNTC. New York: Harper & Brothers, 1928.

Marsh, J. *The Gospel of Saint John.* PNTC. Baltimore: Penguin, 1968.

Mollat, D. *L'évangile et les épîtres de Saint Jean.* La Sainte Bible traduite en français. Paris: Les Éditions du Cerf, 1953.

Morris, L. *The Gospel According to John.* NICNT. Grand Rapids: Eerdmans, 1971.

Sanders, J. N. *A Commentary on the Gospel According to St. John.* Edited by B. A. Mastin. HNTC. New York: Harper & Row, 1968.

Schnackenburg, R. *The Gospel According to St. John.* 3 vols. Translated by K. Smyth et al. New York: Crossroad Publishing, 1982.

Schulz, S. *Das Evangelium nach Johannes.* NTD 4. Göttingen: Vandenhoeck & Ruprecht, 1972.

Spitta, F. *Das Johannesevangelium als Quelle der Geschichte Jesu.* Göttingen: Vandenhoeck & Ruprecht, 1910.

Strathmann, H. *Das Evangelium nach Johannes.* NTD 4. Göttingen: Vandenhoeck & Ruprecht, 1951.

Tillmann, F. *Das Johannesevangelium.* 4th ed. Die heilige Schrift des Neuen Testaments 3. Bonn: Hanstein, 1931.

Wellhausen, J. *Das Evangelium Johannis.* Berlin: G. Reimer, 1908.

Wendt, H. H. *Das Johannesevangelium.* Göttingen: Vandenhoeck & Ruprecht, 1900.

Westcott, B. F. *The Gospel According to St. John.* London: John Murray, 1903. (1st pub., 1880.)

Wikenhauser, A. *Das Evangelium nach Johannes.* 2d ed. RNT 4. Regensburg: Friedrich Pustet, 1957.

Zahn, Th. *Das Evangelium des Johannes.* 5th and 6th eds., rev. and enl. Kommentar zum Neuen Testament 4. Leipzig: A. Deichert, 1908.

MONOGRAPHS AND ARTICLES

Alter, R. *The Art of Biblical Narrative.* New York: Basic Books, 1981.

Bacon, B. W. "The Displacement of John 14." *JBL* 13 (1894) 64–76.

————. *The Fourth Gospel in Research and Debate.* New Haven: Yale University Press, 1918.

Balzer, K. *Das Bundesformular.* WMANT 4. 2d ed. Neukirchen: Neukirchener, 1964.

Becker, H. *Die Reden des Johannesevangelium und der Stil der gnostischen Offenbarungsrede.* FRLANT 68. Göttingen: Vandenhoeck & Ruprecht, 1956.

Boismard, M.-E. "L'évolution du thème eschatologique dans les traditions johanniques." *RB* 68 (1961) 507–24.

Borig, R. *Der wahre Weinstock: Untersuchungen zu Jo 15, 1–10.* STANT 16. Munich: Kösel, 1967.

Boyd, W. J. P. "The Ascension According to St. John: Chapters 14–17 Not Pre-Passion but Post-Resurrection." *Theology* 70 (1967) 207–11.

Brinkmann, B. "Qualis fuerit ordo originarius in quarto Evangelium." *Gregorianum* 20 (1939) 563–69.

———. "Zur Frage der ursprünglich Ordnung im Johannesevangelium." *Gregorianum* 20 (1939) 55–82.

Burge, G. *The Anointed Community: The Holy Spirit in the Johannine Tradition.* Grand Rapids: Eerdmans, 1987.

Caird, G. B. "The Glory of God in the Fourth Gospel: An Exercise in Biblical Semantics." *NTS* 15 (1968–69) 265–77.

———. *The Language and Imagery of the Bible.* Philadelphia: Westminster, 1980.

Carson, D. A. "The Function of the Paraclete in John 16:7–11." *JBL* 98 (1979) 547–60.

Clemen, C. *Die Entstehung des Johannesevangelium.* Halle: M. Niemeyer, 1912.

Clogg, F. B. *An Introduction to the New Testament.* London: University of London Press, 1937.

Deeks, D. "The Structure of the Fourth Gospel." *NTS* 15 (1968–69) 107–29.

Dewey, J. *Markan Public Debate: Literary Technique, Concentric Structure, and Theology in Mark 2:1–3:6.* SBLDS 48. Atlanta: Scholars Press, 1980.

Dewey, K. "*Paroimiai* in the Gospel of John." *Semeia* 17 (1980) 81–99.

Dibelius, M. "Joh 15:13: Eine Studie zum Traditionsprobleme des Johannesevangelium." In *Festgabe für Adolf Deissman zum 60. Geburtstag,* 168–86. Tübingen: Mohr-Siebeck, 1927. Reprinted in *Botschaft und Geschichte I,* edited by G. Bornkamm, 204–20. Tübingen: Mohr-Siebeck, 1953.

Dodd, C. H. *The Interpretation of the Fourth Gospel.* Cambridge: Cambridge University Press, 1970.

Fauré, A. "Die alttestamentliche Zitate im 4. Evangelium und die Quellenscheidungshypothese." *ZNW* 21 (1922) 99–121.

Franck, E. *Revelation Taught: The Paraclete in the Gospel of John.* ConBNT 14. Uppsala: C. W. K. Gleerup, 1985.

Freed, E. D. *Old Testament Quotations in the Gospel of John.* NovTSup 11. Leiden: E. J. Brill, 1965.

George, A. "'L'heure' de Jean xvii." *RB* 61 (1954) 392–97.

Grundmann, W. *Zeugnis und Gestalt des Johannes-Evangelium: Eine Studie zur denkerischen und gestalterischen Leistung des vierten Evangelisten.* Arbeiten zur Theologie 7. Stuttgart: Calwer, 1961.

Guiraud, P. *Essais de stylistique.* Initiation à la linguistique B:1. Paris: Klincksieck, 1969.

Hauck, F. "*Paroimia.*" *TDNT* 5 (1967) 854–56.

Hawkes, T. *Metaphor.* The Critical Idiom 25. London: Methuen, 1972.

Heise, J. *Bleiben: Menein in den johanneischen Schriften.* HUT. Tübingen: J. C. B. Mohr, 1967.

Hermaniuk, M. *La parabole évangelique.* Louvain: Louvain University Press, 1947.

Horbury, W. "The Benediction of the *Minim* and Early Jewish-Christian Controversy." *JTS* 33 (1982) 19–61.

Howard, W. F. *The Fourth Gospel in Recent Criticism and Interpretation.* 4th ed., rev. Edited by C. K. Barrett. London: Epworth, 1955.

Jaubert, A. "L'image de la vigne (Jean 15)." In *Oikonomia: Heilsgeschichte als Thema der Theologie. Oscar Cullmann zum 65. Geburtstag gewidmet,* edited by F. Christ, 93–99. Hamburg: B. Reich, 1967.

Kawin, B. F. *Telling It Again and Again: Repetition in Film and Literature.* Ithaca: Cornell University Press, 1972.

Kimelman, R. *"Birkat Ha-Minim* and the Lack of Evidence for an Anti-Christian Jewish Prayer in Late Antiquity." In *Jewish and Christian Self-Definition,* 3 vols., edited by E. P. Sanders, 2:226–44. Philadelphia: Fortress, 1981.

Langbrandtner, W. *Weltferner Gott oder Gott der Liebe. Der Ketzerstreit in der johanneischen Kirche. Eine exegetisch-religionsgeschichtliche Untersuchung mit Berücksichtigung der koptisch-gnostischen Texte aus Nag-Hammadi.* BET 6. Bern: Lang, 1976.

Lattke, M. *Einheit im Wort: Die spezifische Bedeutung von "agapē/agapan" und "philein" im Johannesevangelium.* SANT 41. Munich: Kösel, 1975.

Lepin, M. *La valeur historique du quatrième évangile.* 2 vols. Paris: Letouzey et Ané, 1910.

Lewis, F. W. *Disarrangements in the Fourth Gospel.* Cambridge: Cambridge University Press, 1910.

L'Hour, J. *La morale de l'alliance.* Cahiers de la Revue Biblique 5. Paris: J. Gabalda, 1966.

Lindars, B. "The Persecution of Christians in John 15:18–16:4a." In *Suffering and Martyrdom in the New Testament: Studies Presented to G. N. Styler by the Cambridge New Testament Seminar,* edited by W. Horbury and B. McNeil, 48–69. Cambridge: Cambridge University Press, 1981.

Lohmeyer, E. "Über Aufbau und Gliederung des viertens Evangeliums." *ZNW* 27 (1928) 225–63.

Martyn, J. L. *History and Theology in the Fourth Gospel.* 2d ed., rev. and enl. Nashville: Abingdon, 1979.

Mlakuzhyil, G. *The Christocentric Literary Structure of the Fourth Gospel.* AB 117. Rome: Pontifical Biblical Institute Press, 1987.

Moffatt, J. *The Historical New Testament.* 2d ed. Edinburgh: T. & T. Clark, 1928.

Potterie, I. de la. *La verité dans Saint Jean.* 2 vols. AB 73–74. Rome: Pontifical Biblical Institute Press, 1977.

Richter, G. "Die Deutung des Kreuzestodes Jesu in der Leidensgeschichte des Johannesevangelium (Jo 13–19)." *BibLeb* 9 (1968) 21–36. Reprinted in G. Richter. *Studien zum Johannesevangelium,* 42–57. Regensburg: Pustet, 1977.

———. "Die Fusswaschung Joh 13:1–20." *MTZ* 16 (1965) 13–26. Reprinted in G. Richter. *Studien zum Johannesevangelium,* edited by J. Hainz, 58–73. Regensburg: Pustet, 1977.

Riffaterre, M. *Essais de stylistique structurale.* Nouvelle bibliothèque scientifique. Paris: Flammarion, 1971.

Scholes, R., and R. Kellogg. *The Nature of Narrative.* Oxford: Oxford University Press, 1966.

Schulz, S. *Untersuchungen zur Menschensohnchristologie im Johannesevangelium.* Göttingen: Vandenhoeck & Ruprecht, 1957.

Schweizer, E. *Ego Eimi: Die religionsgeschichtliche Herkunft und theologische Bedeutung der johanneischen Bildreden, zugleich ein Beitrag zur Quellenfrage des vierten Evangeliums.* FRLANT 38. Göttingen: Vandenhoeck & Ruprecht, 1965.

Segovia, F. F. "John 13:1–20, The Footwashing in the Johannine Tradition." *ZNW* 73 (1982) 31–51.

———. *Love Relationships in the Johannine Tradition: Agapē/Agapan in I John and the Fourth Gospel.* SBLDS 58. Missoula: Scholars Press, 1982.

Smith, D. M. *The Composition and Order of the Fourth Gospel: Bultmann's Literary Theory.* New Haven: Yale University Press, 1967.

Stählin, G. *"Phileō." TDNT* 9 (1974) 151–54.

Strathmann, H. *"Latreuō, latreia." TDNT* 4 (1967) 58–65.

Streeter, B. H. *The Four Gospels: A Study of Origins.* London: Macmillan & Co., 1924.

Talbert, C. H. *Literary Patterns, Theological Themes, and the Genre of Luke-Acts.* SBLMS 20. Missoula: Scholars Press, 1974.

Thyen, H. "Entwicklungen innerhalb der johanneischen Theologie und Kirche im Spiegel von Joh 21 und der Lieblingsjüngertexte des Evangeliums." In *L'Évangile de Jean: Sources, rédaction, théologie,* edited by M. de Jonge, 259–99. BETL 44. Gembloux: Duculot, 1977.

———. "Joh. 13 und die 'kirchliche Redaktion' des vierten Evangeliums." In *Tradition und Glaube: Das frühe Christentum in seiner Umwelt: Festgabe für K. G. Kuhn,* edited by G. Jeremias, H.-W. Kuhn, and H. Stegemann, 343–56. Göttingen: Vandenhoeck & Ruprecht, 1971.

Vanhoye, A. "La composition de Jn 5.19–30." In *Mélanges bibliques en hommage au R. P. Béda Rigaux,* edited by A. Descamps and A. de Halleux, 259–74. Gembloux: Duculot, 1970.

———. *La structure littéraire de l'Épître aux Hébreux.* 2d ed. SN 1. Paris: Desclée de Brouwer, 1976.

Wead, D. *The Literary Devices in John's Gospel.* Theologischen Dissertationen 4. Basel: Friedrich Reinhardt Kommissionsverlag, 1970.

Wellhausen, J. *Erweiterungen und Änderungen im vierten Evangelium.* Berlin: G. Reimer, 1907.

Wheelwright, P. *Metaphor and Reality.* Bloomington: Indiana University Press, 1968.

Wilkens, W. *Die Entstehungsgeschichte des vierten Evangeliums.* Biel: Evangelischer Verlag A.G., Zollikon, 1958.

INDEX